Digital
Computer Simulation

Fred Maryanski

HAYDEN BOOK COMPANY, INC.
Rochelle Park, New Jersey

To
KAREN
KRISTA
DAVID
PETER

Library of Congress Cataloging in Publication Data

Maryanski, Fred.
  Digital computer simulation.

  Includes bibliographical references and index.
  1. Digital computer simulation.   I. Title.
QA76.9.C65M37   001.4'24   80–10675
ISBN 0–8104–5118–2

Printed in the United States of America

1	2	3	4	5	6	7	8	9	PRINTING
80	81	82	83	84	85	86	87	88	YEAR

Preface

One of the most widespread scientific applications of computers is the modeling of systems.

Programs are developed to simulate space flights, manufacturing processes, war games, biological structures, the potential effects of economic policy, and a myriad of other situations. Decisions based upon these computer models have a major impact upon our everyday lives. This book provides an introduction to the subject of simulation.

The emphasis is upon supplying the reader with sufficient background to perform a complete simulation experiment. All aspects of a simulation study are treated including specification, design, coding, debugging, analysis, validation, and interpretation. Four simulation programming languages, GPSS, SIMSCRIPT, CSMP, and DYNAMO, are presented with detailed examples and exercises. A presentation of the basic notions of probability and statistics is included to aid the reader in the analysis and understanding of simulation results. In the final chapter, the applications and limitations of simulation are discussed so that the reader can properly evaluate the impact of a simulation study.

The book is structured so that a complete simulation experiment can be carried out by a reader whose only prior experience is programming in a high-level language. Each simulation programming language chapter contains a single example which grows as new features of the language are introduced. Sample listings and output from actual runs are provided with each example. Tested exercises are provided after each chapter.

The book can serve as a text for a first course in simulation at the junior, senior, or first year graduate level in a computer science, industrial engineering, electrical engineering, or business administration department. Prior high-level language programming language and a limited amount of mathematical sophistication is assumed. People in industry with the need to design, develop, manage, or commission a simulation study will find the material helpful.

The text begins with a discussion of the basic concepts of system modeling and simulation in Chapter 1. Attention is then focused on the modeling of discrete systems for the next three chapters. In Chapter 2, the basic problems of discrete system simulation are presented along with some elementary queuing concepts. Chapter 3 is devoted to the GPSS simulation programming language, while SIMSCRIPT is the subject of Chapter 4. The next two chapters are the most mathematically oriented. Chapter 5 presents basic concepts of probability and statistics useful to the modeler. The sixth chapter focuses upon the design and analysis of simulation experiments, discussing common errors and validation techniques. In Chapter 7 the emphasis switches to continuous systems with the presentation of the CSMP programming language. The following chapter details the DYNAMO language and the Systems Dynamics approach to simulation. The concluding chapter discusses the value of simulation so that the reader may form a perspective on the applicability of simulation to a particular discipline.

I would like to thank Dianne Littwin for her encouragement and support in the development of this book. The helpful comments and insights of Michael Marcotty of General Motors Research Institute are appreciated. Madi McArthur is to be thanked for her heroic efforts in transcribing my unusual script into a readable manuscript. My final thanks go to the students in CS710 at Kansas State University from 1975 to 1978 who served as a test population and provided many helpful suggestions.

Fred Maryanski

Contents

1 System Modeling and Simulation   **1**

  1.1 System Models   1
  1.2 System Modeling   3
  1.3 System Simulation   6
  1.4 Simulation Studies   7
  1.5 Conducting a Simulation Study   8
  1.6 Conclusion   10

2 Discrete System Simulation   **11**

  2.1 Introduction   11
  2.2 Discrete Event Simulation   11
  2.3 Representation of Time   11
  2.4 Generation of Event Distributions   14
  2.5 Scheduling of Events   17
  2.6 Approaches to Discrete Simulation   18
  2.7 Queuing Models   20
  2.8 Multiqueue and Multiserver Models   24
  2.9 Queuing Statistics   28
  2.10 Bias in Queuing Statistics   31
  2.11 Conclusion   32

3 The General-Purpose Simulation System (GPSS)   **35**

  3.1 Organization of GPSS   35
  3.2 Creation and Destruction of Entities   36

3.3	Timing	37
3.4	Facilities	38
3.5	Interpretation of GPSS Output	39
3.6	Control Cards	42
3.7	Storages	43
3.8	Queues	52
3.9	Standard Numerical Attributes	53
3.10	Variables	56
3.11	Random Distributions	58
3.12	Decisions	70
3.13	Priorities	80
3.14	Parameters	84
3.15	Indirect Addressing	96
3.16	Looping	101
3.17	Savevalues	109
3.18	Facility Preemption	111
3.19	Tables	121
3.20	Debugging Statements	123
3.21	Conclusion	142

4	**Simscript**	**146**
4.1	Organization of Simscript	146
4.2	Events	147
4.3	Representation of Time	150
4.4	Variables	150
4.5	Computations	151
4.6	Temporary Entities	152
4.7	Sets	153
4.8	Transfer Statements	156
4.9	Conditional Statements	156
4.10	Input/Output	159
4.11	Statistics	161
4.12	Permanent Entities	165
4.13	Loops	168
4.14	Selectivity	173
4.15	Searching	177
4.16	User-Defined Distributions	181
4.17	External Events	189
4.18	Subprograms	193
4.19	Conclusion	202

5   **Probability and Statistics in Simulation**   **207**

5.1   Introduction   207
5.2   Probability Functions   207
5.3   Conditional and Joint Probability Functions   212
5.4   Statistical Independence   214
5.5   Correlation   216
5.6   Independence and Correlation   222
5.7   Random Numbers   224
5.8   Congruence Method of Random Number Generation   226
5.9   Generation of Discrete Stochastic Distributions   227
5.10 Generation of Continuous Stochastic Distributions   230
5.11 Uniformity and Independence of Random Numbers   232
5.12 Chi-Square Test   233
5.13 Generation of Exponentially Distributed Random
      Numbers   237
5.14 Normally Distributed Random Numbers   243
5.15 Conclusion   244

6   **Design and Analysis of Simulation Experiments**   **250**

6.1   Introduction   250
6.2   Estimation of System Parameters   250
6.3   Maximum Likelihood Parameter Estimation   251
6.4   Goodness of Fit of Estimated Distributions   254
6.5   Selection of Intervals for the Chi-Square Test   255
6.6   Potential Errors in Simulation Studies   257
6.7   Simulation Output Analysis   261
6.8   Effect of Initial Conditions on Simulation Results   262
6.9   Effect of Final Conditions on Simulation Results   262
6.10 Determination of Sample Size   262
6.11 Variance Reduction   263
6.12 Validation   267
6.13 Conclusion   271

7   **The Continuous Simulation Modeling Program
          (CSMP)**   **274**

7.1   Continuous Simulation   274
7.2   Analog Computers   275
7.3   Organization of CSMP   276

7.4   Structural Statements   277
7.5   Organization of Structural Model   280
7.6   Data Statements   282
7.7   Termination Control Statements   284
7.8   Output Control Statements   285
7.9   Execution Control Statement   286
7.10 Comments and Continuations   286
7.11 Conclusion   295

8   Dynamo   298

8.1   Introduction   298
8.2   System Dynamics Models   298
8.3   Feedback   300
8.4   The Dynamo Language   302
8.5   Dynamo Equations   302
8.6   Auxiliary Variables   304
8.7   Supplementary Variables   305
8.8   Output Control Statements   307
8.9   Execution Control Statements   308
8.10 Execution of Dynamo Programs   309
8.11 Conclusion   313

9   The Value of Simulation   320

9.1   Introduction   320
9.2   Deductive and Inductive Information   320
9.3   Degrees of Deductivity   321
9.4   Application of Simulation Models   322
9.5   Conclusion   323

Index   325

1
System
Modeling and Simulation

1.1 SYSTEM MODELS

The purpose of this text is to present methods for using digital computers to perform system simulation studies. The word *system* is perhaps redundant since every simulation by definition characterizes the behavior of some type of system. System here means any orderly collection of objects. The simulation studies are specialized to describe computer systems, biological systems, economic systems, and so forth. Rather than concentrate on any one area, this section emphasizes general properties of systems that are significant in digital computer simulations.

The initial step in a simulation study is the development of a system model. A system is composed of objects, called *entities*, that have properties or attributes. One of the key operations in developing the system model is *abstraction*. Abstraction entails eliminating all but the significant attributes from the entities in the system. For example, consider a simulation study made by a bank to determine the best organization for its teller stations. Table 1.1 shows the entities and a list of possible attributes of this system. If the goal of our simulation study is to configure the teller waiting lines in a manner that minimizes customer waiting time and maximizes the service time of tellers, then many of the attributes of Table 1.1 can be removed from the model. In fact, a useful model of this system can be derived with only one attribute per entity (i.e., Transaction Processing Rate for the Teller and Number of Transactions for the Customer).

Simulation models describe changes in a system. Processes that cause system changes are called *activities*. The *state* of a system is a description of all entities, attributes, and activities at any given time. The concept of system state is somewhat abstract. Most systems have a very large number of possible states. It is the purpose of simulation models to describe changes in the system state. If a system reaches a state from which no change is possible, it is said to be in a *steady* state. States that are not steady are known as *transient* states.

In our bank teller model, the activities include a customer entering the

1

bank, a customer selecting a line, a teller processing the customer's transactions, and a customer leaving the bank. The state of the bank could be described by the number of active tellers, the number of customers in each waiting line, the amount of time spent waiting by each customer, the number of transactions per customer, and the percentage of idle time by each teller. It is likely that the bank will reach a steady state only if the simulation continues until the end of the banking day. Then the state with all lines empty and all tellers idle is a steady state. All of the intermediate states passed through from the beginning of the simulation until the close of banking are transient states.

Each system resides in an environment. For purposes of a simulation, the interaction between the system and its environment must be clearly defined. Activities whose effects remain wholly within the system are termed *endogenous*. *Exogenous* activities are those in the environment that affect the system. Systems can be classified by the type of activities that they contain. Systems with exogenous activity are considered to be *open*. A system with strictly endogenous activity is *closed*.

For example, a simulation model of the growth of a cell is a closed system. However, the bank model previously described is an open system since the activities of customer arrival and departure affect the bank's immediate environment as well as the bank.

A means of classifying system behavior that has a substantial bearing on the type of simulation model for the system is based on the certainty of reaching a given state from the current state. If for a given initial state the sequence of inputs uniquely determines the sequence of states that the system attains, the system is said to be *deterministic*. If for a given initial state and input sequence the behavior of the system varies randomly, the system is *stochastic*.

An example of a deterministic model can be found in a simulation of electronic circuits—that is, digital computer components. Provided that the cir-

Table 1.1 Entities and Attributes

Entity	Teller	Customer
A	Height	Account No.
t	Weight	Age
t	Hair Color	Eye Color
r	Name	Number of Transactions
i	Social Security No.	Marital Status
b	Transaction Processing Rate	Education
u	Years of Service	Number of Accounts
t	Salary	Net Worth
e	Unused Vacation Time	Political Party
s	Favorite Color	Sign of Zodiac

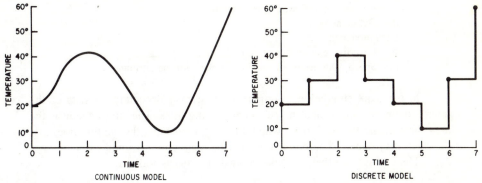

Figure 1.1

cuit has no faults, for a particular set of input signals a unique set of output signals will result.

This model becomes stochastic if we associate a failure probability with each component in the system. In this situation the output signals will have a random distribution due to the possibility of hardware failures.

Virtually all the simulation techniques presented in this text are for stochastic system models. The reason for conducting a simulation study is to gain information about a system that cannot be obtained through observation or analysis. Systems with random behavior or driven by random inputs are particularly difficult to analyze. Consequently, stochastic simulation methods are an important tool for studying many systems.

There are two basic techniques for modeling stochastic systems. A *discrete* system model allows changes at fixed time intervals. A discrete model in essence provides a series of snapshots of the system state. The alternative approach is *continuous* system modeling, in which system behavior is described as a continuous function from the beginning to the termination of the simulation. In general, the output of a discrete system simulation is a set of points, while a continuous simulation will produce a smooth curve. Figure 1.1 illustrates the basic difference between discrete and continuous functions.

1.2 SYSTEM MODELING

The previous section established the terminology of system models. In this section the important aspects of creating system models for digital simulations are presented. System modeling can be considered as a two-step process.

Steps in System Model Synthesis

1. Structural modeling
    a. Define boundaries between system and environment
    b. Identify entities

      c.   Abstract critical attributes of entities
      d.   Define activities
2.   Data modeling
      a.   Describe relationship of activities and attributes
      b.   Specify the means of obtaining values for the attributes

In the bank simulation example, the system under study consists of the tellers, their customers, and the customer waiting lines. The environment is the area surrounding the bank from which the customers enter the waiting lines and to which they depart. The boundaries are the bank entrances and exits.

The entities and their associated attributes are as follows:

1.   Customers—number of transactions, arrival rate
2.   Tellers—number of tellers, transaction processing rate
3.   Waiting Lines—average length, average time per customer

The single activity of the system is processing of a transaction by a customer. This activity depends upon attributes of the customers and tellers and affects the attributes of the customer waiting line.

In order to develop the model further, several pieces of data are necessary. Methods for obtaining and verifying data are discussed in later chapters.

The process of constructing a simulation model is quite similar to the development of computer programs and digital hardware. In all cases, a systematic approach is used to implement an algorithm. Therefore, many of the principles of structured programming and hardware design are applicable to simulation modeling. The commonality among these three tasks is that all require a high-level system description and a well-defined procedure for the implementation of the model.

Principles of System Modeling

1.   Modularity—divide system into logical subsystems each of which is conceptually simple
2.   System diagramming—use a high-level diagram (i.e., flowchart) to relate subsystems
3.   Relevance—include only pertinent information in the model
4.   Understandability—model should be as straightforward as possible; terminology should be standard
5.   Verification—check the structural and computational accuracy of the model

The most common question asked in reference to modularity is "How big should a module be?" There is no standard numerical answer. A rule of thumb is

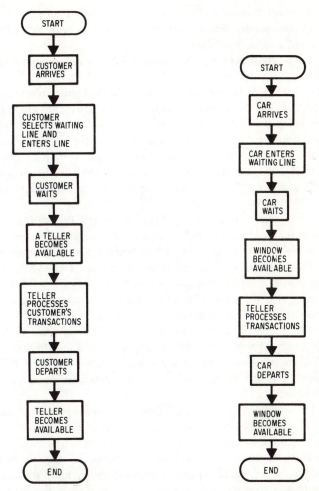

Figure 1.2   High-level Diagram
for Teller Subsystem

Figure 1.3   High-level Diagram for
Drive-in Window Subsystem

that a module should describe one distinct portion of the system. Most such subsystems can be described with a one- or two-page diagram.

EXAMPLE 1.1

Let us consider the application of these modeling principles to a bank simulation. Since we have not discussed any implementation languages, our modeling will be carried out at a very high level. Initially, the modeling process must begin from a problem statement.

Problem Statement: Determine the optimum number of tellers and the optimum waiting line organization for a bank with up to five inside tellers and a drive-in window.

Let us construct a high-level model of the bank system using the five principles as guidelines.

1. *Modularity.* The system can be divided into two subsystems: the inside tellers and the drive-in windows. These subsystems are in fact completely independent. Each of the subsystems could be further subdivided if necessary to describe the arrival of a customer, the selection of a waiting line, and the processing of the transactions. Since we do not require a great amount of detail, two modules—inside tellers and drive-in windows—will be sufficient. As will be shown in Chapter 3, the level of detail is adequate for a GPSS model.

2. *System Diagramming.* Figures 1.2 and 1.3 are high-level diagrams of the inside teller and drive-in window modules, respectively.

3. *Relevance.* As discussed in Section 1.1, only those attributes critical to the purpose of the simulation should be included for each entity. Of the possible attributes listed in Table 1.1, only the teller transaction processing rate and the number of transactions per customer are crucial in the evaluation of the bank model.

4. *Understandability.* In an effort to be consistent with the terminology throughout the model, it may be desirable to replace the term "car" with "customer" in the subsystem diagram of Figure 1.3. Strictly speaking, it is the customers and not the cars that engage in banking transactions.

5. *Verification.* A model should be thoroughly checked at each phase of its development. Statistical verification methods that can be applied once the model has been implemented are discussed in Chapter 6. In the early stages of the development of the model, the structure can be checked to ensure that the model describes the behavior of the real system. A step-by-step manual simulation using the subsystem diagrams is a very useful verification technique.

1.3 SYSTEM SIMULATION

System simulation is the technique of using a dynamic model to describe the behavior of a system with respect to time. It is important to note that the above definition does not explicitly state that computer programming is required in a simulation. However, a system simulation does involve the study of dynamic, not static, models. For example, a program that solves a set of equations indicating the energy requirements of a large building for a given set of environmental parameters is not considered a simulation. However, if the program were expanded to allow for the projection of energy requirements for an arbitrary time span with varying environmental requirements, it would become a simulation of the energy system of the building.

1.4 SIMULATION STUDIES

A *simulation study* is an attempt to answer a well-defined set of questions by means of system simulation. In the case of the bank teller model used in this chapter, the goal of the simulation study is to determine an optimum number of open teller stations.

The definition of simulation study should be interpreted very liberally. The "well-defined set of questions" does not restrict the person carrying out the study to a rigid, preset group of topics to be explored. A simulation study must have a purpose even if it is somewhat vague, such as "determine the internal structure of the system." Many simulation studies can be quite flexible, evolving as the study progresses. This is characteristic of research environments. In most production or planning situations the concept of an invariant statement of simulation purpose is carefully followed.

The other portion of the simulation study definition that requires careful interpretation is the phrase "attempt to answer." A simulation model mimics a real-life system. It is not identical to the system. Results from simulations are projections of the expected behavior of the system being modeled. The accuracy of this projection is heavily dependent upon the nature of the simulation. Karplus [1.1] has characterized the reliability of simulation results by the "hardness" or "softness" of the underlying discipline. Simulation studies in the electrical and physical sciences can produce accurate numerical results. However, in the humanities and social sciences, simulations are intended to identify trends and critical areas rather than to quantify social or behavioral phenomena. See Chapter 9 for an expanded discussion of the value of simulation in various disciplines. For example, a general rule of thumb proposed by Paul Roth for simulation studies of computer systems is that numerical results obtained from such studies be considered accurate within 20% [1.2].

Simulation studies are performed for a wide variety of motives. For purposes of discussion, the reasons for simulation studies can be grouped into the following four categories:

1. *Performance Evaluation.* Project the behavior of an existing or proposed system under a wide range of environmental conditions. In cases where it is impractical or too expensive to observe system behavior in a real environment, simulation is a useful alternative. Instances of simulation studies in this category are battlefield simulations, aerodynamic studies, and computer network modeling. If a large company determined that it required additional computing resources, two alternative solutions are adding a large computer to a central loca-

tion or adding several small computers in remote locations. A simulation study can be used to project the performance effects of each alternative.

2. *Design Aid*. A simulation model of a system under development is often used in making design decisions and determining the probable effects of alternate design schemes. Simulation can be a very cost-effective mechanism for choosing directions and determining the critical points in the development of a system. Automated design systems are common in the electronics industry. These systems permit engineers to specify the components and connections of a circuit and then simulate the circuit to indicate its behavior under all possible conditions. Based upon the simulation results, the engineer modifies or accepts the design.

3. *Structural Investigation*. In many scientific fields, a study concentrates upon a system whose external behavior is observable but whose internal structure is unknown. Under these circumstances, the investigator develops a hypothetical system model and exercises the model by simulation in a number of environments. The validity of the model is determined by comparisons with observed system behavior. Simulations of this type are frequently carried out by biological and life scientists in the investigation of cellular microorganisms. Simulations have proved an invaluable aid in determining the structure of many submicroscopic organisms. Laboratory tests measure the organism's behavior in carefully selected environments. The researcher applies his/her knowledge of similar systems to create a simulation model of the organism in these environments. The simulation models indicate which hypothesized structures for the organism correctly describe its behavior in those environments.

4. *Project Planning*. A large number of system models are developed for the sake of projecting the future behavior of the system. Many socioeconomic systems are simulated in order to estimate the long-term effects of policy decisions. This area of simulation requires the utmost care in the interpretation of the projections obtained as output. An example of this type of simulation study is a project in the state of Oregon that modeled the economic and environmental effects of administrative policy decisions [1.3].

1.5 CONDUCTING A SIMULATION STUDY

Although the emphasis in many simulation courses is on the programming aspect of simulation, programming the model is but one step in a complete simulation study. The stages of a simulation study that are listed here occur in simulations conducted in both classroom projects and practical applications. The main difference in the two situations is that in a classroom project the emphasis is on model development, whereas in the practical environment the emphasis is on model application. Once a model is developed and successfully executed in a class assignment, it is generally abandoned. In industrial applications or academic research a model is repeatedly executed with varying inputs to obtain as much information as possible concerning the behavior of the system.

The steps involved in conducting a simulation study are as follows:

1. *Statement of Purpose*. The system to be modeled must be defined precisely and the goals of the project stated as clearly as possible. This does not imply that a simulation study may not change directions as additional information is obtained. In such cases, however, it is necessary that the original objectives of the project still be satisfied.

2. *Scheduling*. The effort involved in completing the simulation must be estimated. A work schedule is then determined from this estimate with consideration given to available personnel and machine resources and external time constraints.

3. *Modeling*. Those aspects of system behavior that are pertinent to the study must be identified for inclusion in the model. It is important to hold the amount of detail in the model to a manageable level. Once the structure of the model is defined, data can be collected to parameterize the model. Here again, the determination of the appropriate amount of data to be collected is a subjective process. There must be sufficient data to provide a good estimate of the parameters. However, the cost of the resources expended to gather the parameterization data must remain in proper proportion to the expected return from the simulation study.

4. *Programming*. Once the model has been formalized, it can be implemented on a computer. The selection of the type of computer and language to be used is dependent upon the nature of the system and the resources available to the programmer. If the problem and model have been properly specified, the computer implementation should entail exercising a well-defined coding procedure.

5. *Experimental Design*. An execution of a simulation program is equivalent to performing a laboratory experiment. A complete simulation experiment requires several executions with different input data when appropriate. Here again, accuracy and economy are the factors that affect the decision as to the number of executions necessary.

6. *Validation*. This is the most critical aspect of the study. However, methods of validation may vary widely depending upon the system being simulated. Validation requires an answer to the age-old question "Is the program correct?" Simulation program validation methods range from carefully checking a program to logically proving its correctness, and from deciding whether the results are reasonable to statistically verifying the outcome of the simulation. The validation techniques employed in a particular study are determined principally by the amount of information available on the actual behavior of the system.

7. *Analysis*. In a well-planned study, the simulation runs should answer a predefined set of questions. The result of the simulation runs must be carefully analyzed to understand their meaning. In stochastic simulations the effects of

randomness must be carefully weighed. The analyst must bear in mind that the runs are simulations and not actual observations. Therefore, the results must not be treated as precise measures.

1.6 CONCLUSION

In this chapter the basic concepts and definitions of simulation of systems are presented. The emphasis here is upon development of system models and the organization of simulation studies. Later chapters will concentrate upon computer implementation of simulation models in both discrete and continuous programming languages.

EXERCISE

1.1   For each of the systems listed below, develop a high-level system diagram. List the activities, the entities, and the attributes. Indicate the system parameters and the experimental parameters. Describe the system environment and classify the system as either open or closed.

  a.   A supermarket with both regular and express checkouts. The purpose of the simulation is to determine optimum number of checkouts.

  b.   The elevators in a large office building where both people and freight share the same elevators, in order to determine the need for a freight elevator.

  c.   The traffic pattern in a parking lot with multiple exits onto busy streets so that the best exit during the evening rush hour can be determined.

  d.   A computer system that accepts both batch and interactive jobs. The purpose of the simulation is to determine possible processing bottlenecks.

REFERENCES

[1.1]   Karplus, W. J., "The Spectrum of Mathematical Modeling and Systems Simulation," in *Simulation of Systems* (L. Dekker, ed.). Amsterdam: North-Holland, August 1976, pp. 5–13.

[1.2]   Roth, P., "Simulation of Computers: A Tutorial Introduction," *ACM Simuletter,* vol. 6, no. 4, July 1975, pp. 51–53.

[1.3]   Calligan, C. C., et al., "The Oregon State Simulation Model: A Laboratory for Policy Makers," in *Simulation of Systems* (L. Dekker, ed.). Amsterdam: North-Holland, August 1976, pp. 673–682.

2   Discrete System Simulation

2.1 INTRODUCTION

This chapter concentrates on the mechanisms for the development of programs that simulate discrete systems. Two points of view are considered. Methods used in special-purpose languages tailored for the simulation of discrete systems are discussed. In addition, the problems faced by a programmer simulating a discrete system using a general-purpose language are presented along with possible solutions. The particular features of the discrete simulation languages GPSS and Simscript II.5 will be discussed in later chapters.

2.2 DISCRETE EVENT SIMULATION

As mentioned in Chapter 1, a discrete system is one in which changes may occur at regular intervals. Simulations of discrete systems take the snapshot approach; that is, time is halted periodically and all activities that may have occurred in the last time interval are carried out.

The concept of an *event* is central to discrete simulation. An *event* is an occurrence of a change at a point in time. This may entail a change in the value of an attribute of an entity, the creation or destruction of an entity, or the initiation or termination of an activity. A discrete simulation can be viewed as a description of the events that occur at each time interval. For example, in the bank teller model discussed in Chapter 1, the events are the arrival of a customer, the processing of a customer by a teller, and the departure of the customer from the bank.

2.3 REPRESENTATION OF TIME

A system simulation projects the behavior of a system over a period of time. Consequently, the representation of time and the method of modeling the passage of time in the simulation program are basic design decisions. Consideration of methods for advancing the simulated time leads to two practical alternatives.

Perhaps the most straightforward approach is to advance time in uniform increments. This approach can be implemented in the simulation program by using a loop with the structure shown in Figure 2.1. As shown in that figure, a time variable is initialized prior to the execution of the loop body. After testing to determine whether the termination condition exists, a pass is made through the loop body. On each pass through the loop body, each event is tested to determine whether it should be activated in this particular time period. Those events scheduled for a particular time are then simulated. Upon completion of an iteration through the loop body, the time variable is incremented. This process is repeated until the termination condition is satisfied. Scheduling events entails maintaining a list of activation times for each event. The flowchart in Figure 2.2 illustrates the uniform time incrementing approach applied to our bank teller model.

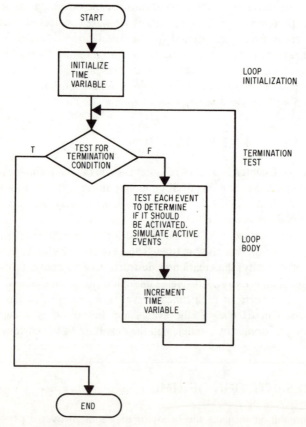

Figure 2.1 Basic Structure of Uniform Time Increment Loop

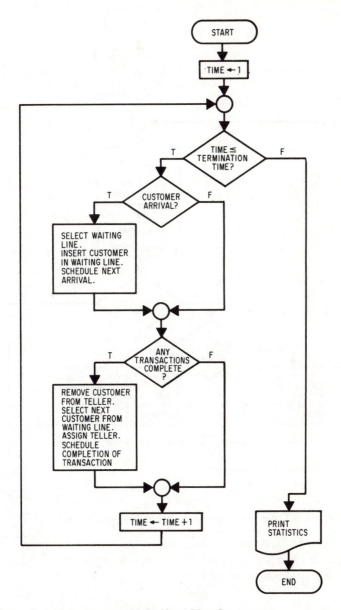

Figure 2.2 Bank Teller Model with Uniform Time Increment

The other method of simulating the passage of time is to maintain a list of future events sorted by activation time. The time variable is set to the time of the first event on the future event list and that event is simulated. Scheduling an event requires placing the event in the proper position in the future events list.

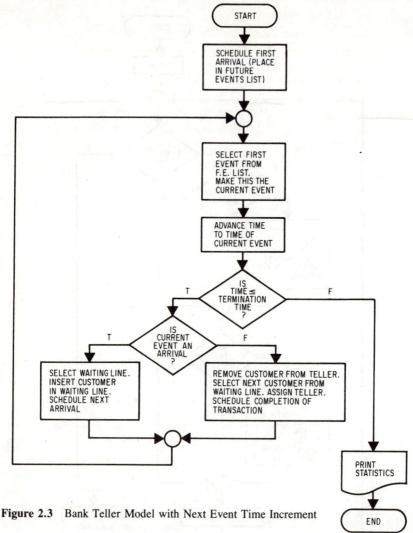

Figure 2.3 Bank Teller Model with Next Event Time Increment

When an event is simulated, the next event is selected from the future events list and the process is repeated. Figure 2.3 depicts the application of the next time-incrementing approach to the bank model.

2.4 GENERATION OF EVENT DISTRIBUTIONS

In the course of a stochastic simulation, the occurrence of events varies randomly over time. In order to describe the occurrence of events, some function that produces the time of the next event is required. In the simplest case, this function could yield constant values. For example, in the bank teller model, customer arrivals should occur at random intervals. If a constant is used to describe the interarrival time, a very unrealistic model will result. The function that describes customer arrivals must produce random values that correspond to the interarrival times in the real system. A function which describes random interevent times is known as an *event distribution.*

Event distributions can be described by some common statistical function such as a uniform or normal distribution (see Chapter 5) or by a set of (X,Y) coordinates. The X values are the inputs to the distribution function that produce the corresponding Y values as output. The Y values represent the next event time. The X values are often probability measures that cause the generation of random event times.

For example, Figure 2.4 pictures a customer arrival distribution. According to the graph, 20% of the arrivals occur within 1 minute of the previous arrival, whereas 50% occur within 2 minutes. For this sample event distribution, the X values and the probabilities are the first arrival times, and the corresponding Y coordinates are the next arrival times. If a probability value

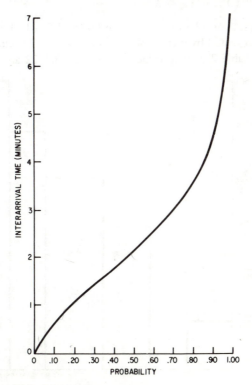

Figure 2.4   Arrival Time Distribution

of .70 were generated by the simulation program as an input to the distribution, the next arrival would occur in 3 minutes.

The use of random distributions in simulations is not limited to interevent times. Any stochastic activity or attribute may be described by a random distribution.

When a distribution is represented by a finite set of coordinates and an infinite number of X values may occur, where X represents a probability value, a mechanism is required for computing a Y value when the program generates an X that was not specified explicitly.

If the distribution is discrete, it can be represented by a staircase function, as shown in Figure 2.5. The rule for selecting a Y value for a given X coordinate is as follows:

1. Assume that points (X_1,Y_1), (X_2,Y_2), . . ., (X_k,Y_k) are given.
2. For a given X,

$$Y = \begin{cases} Y_i, \text{ if } X_{i-1} < X \leq X_i & 2 \leq i \leq k \\ Y_1, \text{ if } X \leq X_1 \\ Y_k, \text{ if } X_k \leq X \end{cases}$$

For example, consider the function in Figure 2.5, which indicates the type of transaction presented by a customer to a bank teller. The function values are summarized in Table 2.1. If X values of .51, .12, and .22 are generated by the

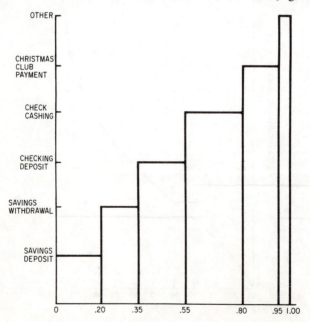

Figure 2.5 Transaction-type Distribution

Table 2.1 Summary of Transaction-type Distribution

X (Probability)	Y (Transaction Type)
.20	Savings Deposit
.35	Savings Withdrawal
.55	Checking Deposit
.80	Check Cashing
.95	Christmas Club Payment
1.00	Other

simulation program as inputs to the transaction distribution for the first three customers, the customers would be assigned the transactions of Checking Deposit, Savings Deposit, and Savings Withdrawal, respectively.

If a continuous distribution is to be represented by a finite number of points, the behavior of the distribution between the specified points must be approximated by some curve, as in Figure 2.4. For a given function, the value of $Y = f(X)$, where $X = X_i$, $1 \leq i \leq K$, can easily be determined. However, if only a set of points of the distribution is given, it is not possible to compute the unspecified coordinates exactly. The process of estimating the unspecified values from the given coordinates is known as *interpolation.* The simplest type of approximation is *linear interpolation,* which involves the construction of a straight line between each pair of points. There are other interpolation methods involving the use of higher-order curves for approximation. These techniques are more exact and more complex than linear interpolation. Interpolation is discussed in detail in Chapter 5.

2.5 SCHEDULING OF EVENTS

The scheduling of events in a stochastic simulation study may be implemented by employing either a prescheduling policy or a dynamic scheduling technique. Both mechanisms assume the existence of a distribution describing the frequency of events and the ability to generate event occurrences randomly from that distribution. For purposes of discussion we shall assume that the events under consideration are arrivals (or the creation of entities).

In the prescheduling method, all arrivals are scheduled prior to the beginning of the simulation. To implement a prescheduling policy a list of arrivals must be constructed. The number of arrivals to be scheduled can be determined from the termination conditions of the simulation. Generally termination is based upon the number of entities processed or a time constraint. In some situations it may not be possible to schedule the precise number of arrivals required for the simulation. Under such conditions an estimate of the number of arrivals required could be made. The estimated number of arrivals could then be scheduled, with provisions made for additional scheduling if necessary.

A dynamic scheduling strategy requires that an arrival be scheduled only after the occurrence of the previous arrival. This scheme does not require the maintenance of a future-arrival list. Using a dynamic scheduling approach, at most one unprocessed arrival will be scheduled.

A comparison between the two approaches to scheduling indicates that the dynamic technique requires less memory and probably fewer computations than the prescheduling method. The difference in memory requirements is due to the fact that the prescheduling approach requires the maintenance of a future-arrival list, whereas dynamic scheduling requires only the time of the next arrival to be retained. If the termination of the simulation is not dependent upon the number of arrivals, then the potential for extraneous scheduling exists. Under similar circumstances the dynamic scheduling approach would schedule only those arrivals that are processed* and thus would not expend any unnecessary computations.

The dynamic scheduling approach is better suited for events whose occurrence depends upon the actions of the simulation model. For example, in the bank model the time of a customer departure depends upon the arrival, waiting, and processing times. If the waiting time and processing time are described by random distributions, then the departure must be scheduled dynamically.

2.6 APPROACHES TO DISCRETE SIMULATION

Several approaches can be employed in discrete event simulation. These methods are used by the major discrete simulation languages as well as being strategies that a programmer writing in a general-purpose language may employ. Since the computer implementation of a simulation model requires a substantial amount of internal statistical and bookkeeping operations, several special-purpose simulation languages have been developed to relieve the user of the burden of the internal manipulations and allow concentration upon the task of modeling. Two of the most common discrete system simulation languages, GPSS (General-Purpose Simulation System) and Simscript, are discussed in this text. The three major approaches to the implementation of a discrete simulation model are described in the following paragraphs.

1. *Process Interaction Approach.* This approach concentrates upon the progress of an entity as it passes through the model. The program flow describes the processes that operate on the entity as it moves from creation to termination.

---

*The dynamic scheduling approach may schedule one additional arrival if the next arrival has been scheduled prior to termination.

A process interaction model can be pictured by a diagram in which the blocks represent the processes and their interconnections represent paths over which entities may move between processes. Figure 2.6 illustrates the application of the process interaction approach to the bank teller model.

Internally, the process interaction approach requires that for each entity a record be maintained indicating the current status of the entity. A portion of this status information consists of the conditions that must be satisfied in order for the entity to move to the next process in the flow of the model. These conditions may merely be the passage of simulated time, or they may be a set of event results involving other entities. GPSS uses the process interaction approach. A detailed presentation of GPSS is given in Chapter 3.

A programmer implementing a simulation model in a general-purpose language using the process interaction approach would develop a set of routines to describe the processes of the model. Lists must be maintained to sequence properly the movement of entities among the processes.

2. *Event Scheduling Approach*. In the event scheduling approach a detailed description of the actions performed is provided whenever an event occurs.

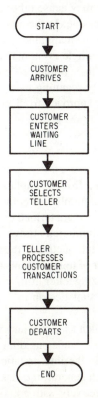

Figure 2.6 Bank Teller Model Using the Process Interaction Approach

Simscript is a discrete simulation language which takes the event scheduling approach. In Simscript, the programmer writes routines which describe the effect of each event on the system. A list of scheduled events is maintained and ordered by time of activation. The event routines may operate upon the attributes of entities and schedule or cancel events. Time is advanced in Simscript to the next scheduled event. All events that may occur in that instant of time are simulated by execution of the appropriate event routines. Simscript provides mechanisms for determining the order of execution of event routines when more than one event is scheduled for a given time period. More information on Simscript is provided in Chapter 4. Figure 2.3 is an example of an event scheduling model.

For a programmer working in a general-purpose language, the use of the event scheduling approach requires the maintenance of a list of scheduled events and the development of event routines.

3. *Activity Scanning Approach.* When the activity scanning approach is used, the status of all activities in the model are scanned to determine which can be activated whenever time is advanced. If the conditions for the initiation of an activity are satisfied, it is scheduled for execution in that time period. The execution of an activity routine may cause other activities to be executed during the same time period or at a later one. In the activity scanning approach the time of the next scheduled event must be maintained, along with a set of conditions for the initiation of each activity. A single event may be simulated by several activity routines, which are executed if their initiation conditions are satisfied. No major simulation languages use activity scanning methods. The diagram in Figure 2.2 illustrates the activity scanning approach to discrete simulation.

2.7 QUEUING MODELS

Much of the information obtained from a simulation indicates the amount of time an entity waits for service or the number of entities waiting for a particular type of service. Waiting lines for service are termed queues. Modeling of queues is an essential part of almost every simulation study. In our bank model the primary emphasis is on the behavior of the queues at the teller stations. The goal of the study is to determine the number of teller stations that minimize queue length and time in the queue while maximizing teller utilization. Therefore, the modeling of the queue and the gathering of statistics on its behavior are critical steps in the simulation.

In simulation languages such as GPSS and Simscript, queues are managed automatically by the system. An understanding of the mechanisms of queue management aids the modeler in the interpretation of the results obtained from the special-purpose languages. In general, the task of analyzing simulation statistics can be performed more effectively with a knowledge of the procedures used to compute the statistics. If the programmer is implementing a simulation model in a general-purpose language, he/she must encode routines to manage the queues and calculate queuing statistics.

There are two basic operations of queues in simulation—the arrival and departure of entities. The exact form of a queuing model depends upon the number of servers and the number of queues holding entities waiting for service. The most basic model is the single-queue, single-server situation. All of the essential problems of queue management occur in that model. The more complex situations can be described by enhancing the basic single-queue, single-server model.

Figures 2.7 and 2.8 illustrate arrival and departure operations for a queue with a single server. As can be seen from these figures, the queue operations are reasonably straightforward. However, the lack of complexity should not be interpreted as a lack of significance in system simulations.

In the departure block diagram there is an entry labeled "Select an Entity for Service." The manner in which an entity is added to and selected from a queue is known as the queuing discipline. It should be noted that "queue" is used here to mean a waiting line and not in the classical data structures sense [2.1]. Thus a queuing discipline is a rule for adding entities to and removing

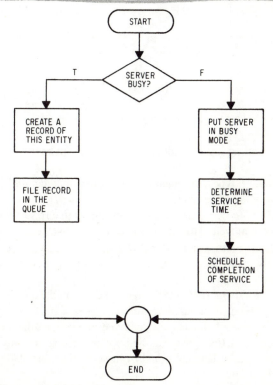

Figure 2.7 Arrival for Single-server Queue

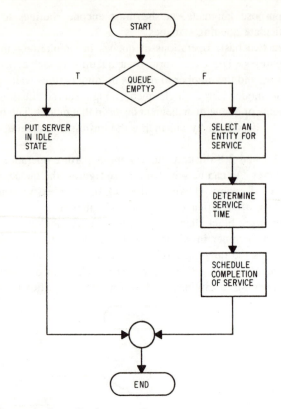

Figure 2.8 Departure for a Single-server Queue

entities from a waiting line. The queuing discipline can be used to categorize the type of queue.

The different types of queuing disciplines that could be applied in a system simulation are listed here.

1. *First In First Out (FIFO)*. The oldest entity in terms of time in the queue is the first to be removed. This discipline describes a standard waiting line such as a line of customers in a bank. A FIFO queue can be implemented either as a singly linked list or as an array with pointers to the oldest and newest entries [2.1].

2. *Last In First Out (LIFO)*. The newest entity in the queue is the first to be removed. This type of queue is often referred to as a stack. Cargo carried by a truck or plane is generally loaded and removed in a manner that can be described by a LIFO queue. A LIFO queue can be implemented as an array with a pointer to the last entry. Many languages and even some machines have built-in stack manipulation features.

3. *Service Time*. The entity with the maximum (or minimum) expected service time is removed from the queue. Unlike the two previous disciplines, the

time of arrival has no bearing upon the time of departure, except perhaps as a tie-breaking mechanism. A service-time-based queuing discipline could be used to model an environment such as computer system or job shop scheduling. In order to implement a service time queuing discipline, the queue must be maintained in sorted order.

4. *Priority*. Each entity is assigned a priority number either randomly or based upon its attributes. The expected service time discipline is actually a special case of the priority discipline. Implementation considerations are the same for both disciplines.

5. *Random*. Entities are removed from the queue in a completely random order. The discipline would only be applicable to the modeling of physical processes since most human systems exhibit some ordering in their queuing. A random discipline requires that the queue be maintained as an indexed list. A random index is generated, and the corresponding entity is removed from the

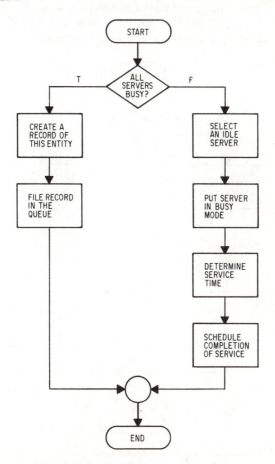

Figure 2.9   Single-queue, Multiserver Arrival

queue. A random queuing discipline requires the utilization of memory management techniques (see Knuth [2.1]) to ensure that the queue does not contain empty locations.

2.8 MULTIQUEUE AND MULTISERVER MODELS

The basic single server, single-queue model can be extended to include various combinations of queues and servers. Figures 2.9 and 2.10 illustrate the arrival and departure operations for a single-queue, multiserver environment. The most important consideration in these operations is the requirement for an algorithm that selects one of a set of idle servers to be activated. This selection algorithm is very similar to a queuing discipline in that approximately the same set of choices are available. The server can be selected based upon a least (or most) recently used scheme, using some priority ordering or at random.

If in the bank example that has been discussed thus far a ''jet-teller'' concept were installed, a single-queue, multiserver model could describe cus-

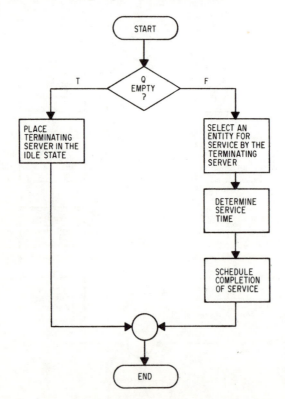

Figure 2.10   Single-queue, Multiserver Departure

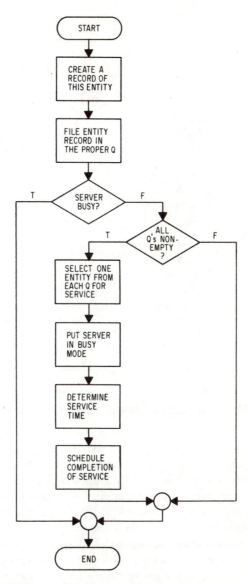

Figure 2.11   Arrival for Multiqueue, Single-server Model

tomer flow. In a jet-teller arrangement, a single waiting line is made available to the customers. When the bank is busy, the customer at the head of the line proceeds to the teller that has finished processing the last customer. Only in the case of no waiting line or if several tellers simultaneously complete service is a selection algorithm necessary.

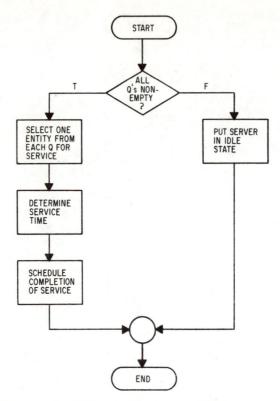

Figure 2.12   Departure for Multiqueue, Single-server Model

A multiqueue, single-server model describes an environment in which the server requires several entities (or resources) before service can be initiated. An environment in which this model is applicable is a manufacturing environment in which the manufacture of an item must wait until all the component parts are available. In Figures 2.11 and 2.12 it is assumed that service cannot be initiated until an entity from every queue is available.

The consummate queuing model consists of multiple queues and multiple servers. This situation is a combination of the two previous cases. The two most important rules of such queuing models are as follows:

1. When several servers are available, a server selection algorithm is necessary.
2. Service cannot be initiated until all resources are available. In terms of the models presented here, all queues must be nonempty in order to begin service.

Figures 2.13 and 2.14 describe the arrival and departure operations for a multiqueue, multiserver model. If in the manufacturing environment mentioned previously several units were assembling the items simultaneously, a multiqueue, multiserver model would be appropriate.

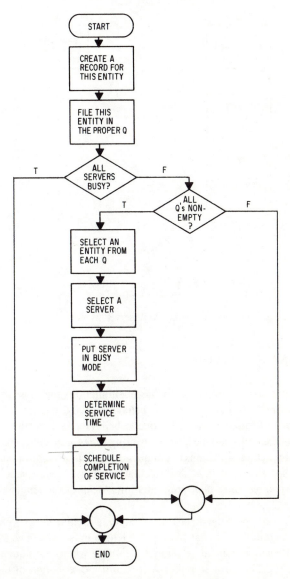

Figure 2.13 Arrival for Multiqueue, Multiserver Model

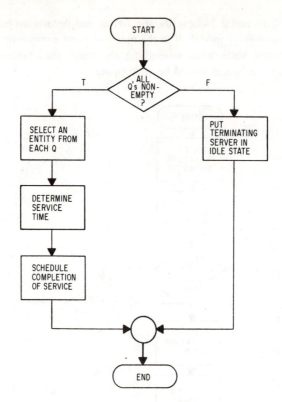

Figure 2.14   Departure for Multiqueue, Multiserver Model

2.9 QUEUING STATISTICS

As indicated previously, in many stochastic simulations the most important information obtained is statistics on the behavior of the queues. The types of statistics commonly used to describe queue behavior include the average and maximum queue lengths and the average waiting time for an entity in the queue.

The computation of the maximum queue length is straightforward and need not be discussed in any detail. The calculation of the mean queue length and waiting time requires an in-depth presentation. Mean queue length will be considered first.

In order to compute the mean queue length, a monitoring process that notes the time and magnitude of a change in queue length must exist. The monitor may be activated at each increment of simulated time or whenever a queue arrival or departure occurs. The queue monitor will record a distribution of queue length with respect to time.

Let t_k be the amount of time that the queue had a length of k.
Let T be the total simulation time.
Then

$$T = \sum_{k=0}^{\infty} t_k \tag{2.1}$$

The mean queue length, $\bar{Q}$, is the weighted average of the monitored queue lengths with respect to time; that is,

Mean Q length

$$\bar{Q} = \frac{1}{T}\sum_{k=0}^{\infty} k * t_k \tag{2.2}$$

2 tellers

EXAMPLE 2.1

Let us assume that the bank we have been discussing is simulated using a jet-teller arrangement and that there are two tellers. The queue monitor checks the queue length whenever a customer enters or departs the queue. In 20 minutes the queue behavior shown in Table 2.2 was observed.

From Table 2.2, the following values for t_k can be obtained by calculating the amount of time the queue had a length of k, for $k = 0, 1, 2, 3$.

k = 0, 1, 2, 3

$$t_0 = 4 \qquad t_1 = 7 \qquad t_2 = 6 \qquad t_3 = 3$$

The mean queue length for this simulation is

$$
\begin{aligned}
\bar{Q} &= \frac{1}{20}\sum_{k=0}^{\infty} k * t_k \\
&= \frac{0*4 + 1*7 + 2*6 + 3*3}{20} = \frac{28}{20} = 1.4
\end{aligned}
$$

The mean queue length is computed with respect to time. However, the mean waiting time is determined per entity. Therefore, the number of entities that have passed through the queue must be known in order to compute the mean waiting time.

Let N be the number of entities departing the queue.
Let W_t be the total waiting time for all jobs.
W_t can be computed as

$$W_t = \sum_{k=1}^{\infty} k * t_k \qquad (2.3)$$

The mean waiting time is then

$$\bar{W} = \frac{W_t}{N} \qquad (2.4)$$

Table 2.2 First Sample Queue Behavior

Time	Number of Arrivals in Time Period	Queue Length	Number of Busy Tellers
0	0	0	0
1	1	0	1
2	1	0	2
4	1	1	2
5	1	2	2
8	0	1	2
12	2	3	2
15	0	2	2
18	0	1	2
20	0	0	2

EXAMPLE 2.2

For the bank model described in Example 2.1,

$$N = 6$$

$$W_t = \sum_{k=1}^{\infty} k * t_k$$

$$= 1 * 7 + 2 * 6 + 3 * 3 = 28$$

$$\bar{W} = \frac{W_t}{N} \quad \frac{28}{6} = 4.67$$

2.10 BIAS IN QUEUING STATISTICS

In situations in which the initial and final queue lengths are 0, Eqs. (2.3) and (2.4) for computing the mean waiting time are valid. However, problems arise if entities remain in the queue upon termination of the simulation or if entities are already in the queue at the beginning of the simulation. The first situation is illustrated in Example 2.3.

EXAMPLE 2.3

Assume that the bank teller line is to be simulated for the first 20 minutes of the bank's business day. Table 2.3 indicates the behavior of the jet-teller queue. Note that the only difference between Tables 2.2 and 2.3 is that a customer entered the line at time 16 and remained in the line at the termination of the simulation.

The mean queue length is

$$\bar{Q} = \frac{1}{20} \sum_{k=0}^{3} k * t_k$$

$$= \frac{0*4 + 1*5 + 2*6 + 3*5}{20} = \frac{32}{20} = 1.6$$

Using Eqs. (2.3) and (2.4) to compute the mean waiting time yields

$$W_t = \sum_{k=1}^{3} k*t_k = 32$$

$$\bar{W} = \frac{W_t}{6} = 5.33$$

Our computation in Example 2.2 yielded a mean waiting time of 4.67. Since the behavior of the customers that left the queue in both examples is identical, the mean waiting times should be the same. However, the introduction of the customer who did not begin service before termination has biased the mean waiting time. The reason for the bias is that the mean waiting time is computed using N, the number of customers departing the queue, whereas W_t, the total waiting time, includes all customers entering the queue.

The influence of the unserviced entities can be eliminated by including only those entities leaving the queue in the composition of W_t. In order to accomplish this effect, the waiting time for each entity must be individually determined. W_t is then calculated by

$$\bar{W}_t = \sum_{i=1}^{N} W_i \tag{2.5}$$

where W_i is the waiting time of the ith entity, $1 \leqslant i \leqslant N$. The value of $\bar{W}$ can then be computed using Eq. (2.4).

Table 2.3 Second Sample Queue Behavior

Time	Number of Arrivals in Time Period	Queue Length	Number of Busy Tellers
0	0	0	0
1	1	0	1
2	1	0	2
4	1	1	2
5	1	2	2
8	0	1	2
12	2	3	2
15	0	2	2
16	1	3	2
18	0	2	2
20	0	1	2

In order to apply Eq. (2.5) to Example 2.3, a set of customer waiting times must be obtained. The following W_i values can be derived from Table 2.4:

$$W_1 = 0 - 0 = 0 \qquad W_2 = 1 - 1 = 0 \qquad W_3 = 8 - 4 = 4$$
$$W_4 = 15 - 5 = 10 \qquad W_5 = 18 - 12 = 6 \qquad W_6 = 20 - 12 = 8$$

$$W_t = \sum_{i=1}^{4} W_i = 28$$
$$\bar{W} = \frac{W_t}{N} = 4.67$$

This result now corresponds to the mean waiting time computed in Example 2.2. It should be noted that the computation of mean queue length and mean waiting time is now completely disjoint and requires the maintenance of two sets of counters.

2.11 CONCLUSION

The material in this chapter provides a basis for the development of discrete system simulation programs. A moderately experienced programmer should be capable of applying the techniques of this chapter to the modeling and simulation of a wide variety of systems. In attempting such simulations in a general-purpose language, the programmer will discover that a large amount of effort must be devoted to queue management and statistics. The design and implementation of these bookkeeping functions may overshadow the system modeling processes. It is for this reason that special purpose simulation languages have emerged. The next two chapters present the two most popular discrete system simulation languages, GPSS and Simscript.

EXERCISES

2.1 The number of children per family requiring housing in a simulation of a city's economic structure is specified by the distribution shown in the following table:

Probability	Number of Children
.10	0
.30	1
.60	2
.85	3
.95	4
1.00	5

If the simulation program generates the five random probability values shown below for five families, how many children will be assigned to each of the families? Generated probability values: .39, .21, .96, .78, .05.

2.2 For a supermarket model with several regular checkouts and one express checkout, give high-level diagrams for the model using the process interaction, event scheduling, and activity scanning methods.

2.3 Develop diagrams for arrival and departure operations for queues in the following systems. Indicate the queuing discipline for each queue.
   a. Treatment of patients in a hospital emergency room served by multiple doctors. Patients are selected for treatment by the severity of illness and then by waiting time.
   b. Treatment of patients in an outpatient clinic staffed by a single doctor with no appointments permitted.
   c. The passage of ships through a lock of a canal, where each ship must be guided through by a tugboat.
   d. The airlift of a motorized military unit. Each aircraft contains vehicles, fuel, and personnel. The vehicles are stored in a staging area with a single entrance. The fuel containers are piled on pallets. Personnel arrive from various bases but are assigned to particular vehicles. The depot is served by three runways.

2.4 Compute the mean queue length and mean waiting time for the FIFO queues whose behavior is described by the following tables:

a.

Time	Number of Arrivals in Time Period	Number of Departures in Time Period
0	0	0
8	5	0
21	3	0
37	0	1
54	0	4
79	1	0
82	0	2
106	2	1
107	0	1
131	0	2
149	4	0
200	0	4

b.

Time	Number of Arrivals in Time Period	Number of Departures in Time Period
0	4	0
14	0	3
25	1	1
31	1	0
39	0	1
86	0	1
94	2	0
121	3	0
122	0	2
123	0	2
172	2	0
184	0	1
199	3	2
200	0	2

REFERENCE

[2.1] Knuth, D. E., *The Art of Computer Programming,* 2nd ed., vol. 1. Reading, Mass.: Addison-Wesley, 1973.

3 The General-Purpose Simulation System (GPSS)

3.1 ORGANIZATION OF GPSS

The General-Purpose Simulation System (GPSS) is a discrete stochastic simulation language that evolved from a block-diagram-oriented approach to simulation. Because of this origin, GPSS has a terminology oriented toward describing a block diagram system model. GPSS statements are called *Blocks;* they represent the activities of the model. The entities of a GPSS program are termed *Transactions* in the GPSS manuals. However, to maintain consistency with the other chapters, the use of *Entity* is retained. The sequence of events in a GPSS model is indicated by the movement of entities between statement blocks. Several entities may exist simultaneously in the system. At any given time each entity is positioned at a particular statement block. A single statement block can hold more than one entity at a time. When an entity moves between statement blocks, the transfer occurs instantaneously without any simulated time elapsing.

Internally, GPSS operates using the process interaction approach. Two main lists of entities are maintained. The current events list holds all entities that are active at the present clock time. This includes entities entering a statement block in this time period and entities that may be conditionally activated during this time period. Entities that have been scheduled for activation at a later time are held in the future events list. The future events list is sorted by the time of activation.

A GPSS program is processed in two phases—*assembly* (translation) and *execution*. In the assembly phase a source program is mapped into an internal GPSS representation, which is operated upon in the execution phase. During the assembly of the program each statement is assigned a unique number for reference by other statements. The statement numbers are assigned sequentially and are displayed in one of the outputs produced by GPSS to indicate the flow of entities through the model.

Statements may be given symbolic labels to facilitate their reference. Labels must be from three to five characters in length, with the first three characters being letters. For example, the following identifiers are valid GPSS labels:

VALID, BLCK1, EXPON, VAR11, BUY

However, the identifiers listed below are not acceptable as labels in a GPSS program:

B1, GO, AR142, BLOCK1, X

A GPSS statement may have several arguments, all of which need not be present each time a statement occurs. If an argument is not explicitly given a value, a default value is assumed. The order of arguments is significant in GPSS. All arguments are separated by commas, with embedded blanks not permitted. Two successive commas indicate the omission of an argument. No commas are necessary after the last argument used.

Some sample GPSS statements include

GENERATE 4,3,2,5

GENERATE 4

GENERATE ,,,5

The meaning of these statements is explained in the next section.

A comment line is indicated by an asterisk (*) at the beginning of the line. Comments may be appended to GPSS statements following a blank after the final argument.

3.2 CREATION AND DESTRUCTION OF ENTITIES

The GENERATE and TERMINATE statements are used to create and destroy entities in a GPSS program. Every GPSS program must contain at least one of each of these blocks. The GENERATE block has the following general form:

GENERATE A,B,C,D,E,F,G,H,I

where

A is the mean time of next generation

B is the generation time modifier

C is the offset start time of generation

D is the total number of entities to be generated

E is the initial priority of transaction (see Section 3.13)

F through I specify the number of parameters (see Section 3.14)

The following examples illustrate the meaning of the first four GENER-ATE arguments and the use of default argument values.

GENERATE 4

An entity is generated every 4 time units. Since no B argument is present, generation will occur at precisely 4 time unit intervals. The lack of a C argument implies that this generation process will begin at time 0. Since no D argument is present, this statement will continue generating entities until the simulation is concluded.

GENERATE 4,3

Entities are generated every 4 ± 3 time units, starting at time 0 for the duration of the simulation. When the B argument is anything other than a function (Section 3.11), a uniform distribution is assumed. Thus, for the above statement the generation times will be distributed uniformly from 1 to 7 time units.

GENERATE 4,3,2

Entities are generated at intervals of 1 to 7 time units, uniformly distributed, beginning at time 2 for the duration of the simulation.

GENERATE 4,3,2,5

A total of five entities are generated at intervals of 1 to 7 time units, uniformly distributed, beginning at time 2.

GENERATE ,,2,5

Five entities are generated at time 2.

GENERATE ,,,5

Five entities are generated at the start of the simulation.

The TERMINATE statement serves to remove entities from the model. In addition, the terminate statement is a part of the mechanism for determining the end of a simulation experiment. The TERMINATE statement has the following format:

TERMINATE A

where

A is the termination count; default is 0

Whenever an entity reaches a TERMINATE statement, it is removed from the simulation. The termination count value is then subtracted from the start count which was established at the initiation of the simulation using the START control card (see Section 3.6). The simulation ceases when the start count becomes equal to or less than 0. Consider the following examples:

TERMINATE 1

An entity is removed from the model and the start count is decremented by 1.

TERMINATE 0

An entity is removed from the model, but the start count is not decremented.

3.3 TIMING

Time is represented in GPSS as an internal integer counter, which is accessible to the user program (see Section 3.9). The value of the counter is in abstract time units, which the programmer must mentally relate to a real measure of time. The programmer is responsible for all conversions. Thus if the programmer selects 1 second as the basic time unit of the system, the value of 120 represents 2 minutes of simulated time. The unit time must be taken to represent the smallest time interval in the model since the clock is represented internally as an integer.

In a GPSS program, the clock is advanced whenever the current event list contains no entities that can be processed. The clock is then advanced to the time of the first entity on the future events list.

In order to simulate the passage of time while an entity is in a given state, the ADVANCE block is utilized. ADVANCE has the following format:

> ADVANCE A,B

where

> A is the mean time
> B is the modifier of the mean

The arguments of ADVANCE have the same interpretation as the first two arguments of GENERATE as shown by the examples below.

> ADVANCE 4

The entity is held in the ADVANCE statement block for 4 time units. An entry is made in the future events list indicating that the entity will attempt to enter the next statement block in 4 time units.

> ADVANCE 4,3

The entity remains in the ADVANCE statement block for 1 to 7 time units, uniformly distributed. The departure of the entity from the ADVANCE statement block is scheduled in the future events list.

3.4 FACILITIES

In GPSS a facility is an activity that can be engaged by a single entity at a given time. A facility is used in the modeling of a single-server environment such as a bank teller, a central processor of a computer, a car wash, a single traffic lane, and the like. A facility is not explicitly defined in GPSS but rather is implicitly defined by the use of statements causing entities to engage or disengage the facility.

The SEIZE block permits the entering entity to obtain a facility. An entity yields the facility upon entering a RELEASE block. The formats of these blocks are as follows:

> SEIZE A
> RELEASE A

where

> A is the facility name

A facility may be referenced by either a number or a symbolic name. This mode of reference holds for all types of GPSS system entities. For example, the following two GPSS statements cause a facility named TELER, representing a bank teller, to become busy, then idle:

> SEIZE TELER
> RELEASE TELER

One of the key pieces of information that can be obtained from a GPSS simulation is the average utilization of the facilities. This statistic is computed automatically by GPSS and included in the standard output.

We have now covered a sufficient variety of GPSS statements to implement a simple model.

EXAMPLE 3.1

Let us model the drive-in window at a bank. We will assume the following set of parameters:

1. Customer arrival rate—from 1 to 5 minutes, uniformly distributed
2. Time required to drive from entrance to drive-in window—1 minute
3. Teller processing rate—from 1 to 3 minutes per customer, uniformly distributed
4. Length of simulation—250 customers

Based upon these parameters, we can equate one GPSS time unit with one minute of simulated time. The GPSS program shown simulates the drive-in window model.

```
BLOCK                                                            STATEMENT
NUMBER  *LOC   OPERATION  A,B,C,D,E,F,G,H,I        COMMENTS       NUMBER
        ****************************************************************   1
        *   PROGRAM TO SIMULATE A DRIVE-IN WINDOW AT A BANK            2
        *                                                              3
        *   PARAMETERS                                                 4
        *                                                              5
        *      ARRIVALS - 1 TO 5 MINUTES , UNIFORMLY DISTRIBUTED       6
        *      PROCESSING - 1 TO 3 MINUTES , UNIFORMLY DISTRIBUTED     7
        *      TERMINATION CONDITION - 250 CUSTOMERS PROCESSED         8
        *                                                              9
        ****************************************************************  10
        *                                                             11
               SIMULATE                                               12
   1           GENERATE   3,2           CUSTOMERS ARRIVE              13
   2           ADVANCE    1             CUSTOMERS DRIVE TO WINDOW     14
   3           SEIZE      WINCO         CUSTOMER REACHES WINDOW       15
   4           ADVANCE    2,1           TRANSACTION IS PROCESSED      16
   5           RELEASE    WINDO         CUSTOMER DEPARTS              17
   6           TERMINATE  1                                           18
        *                                                             19
               START      250           PROCESS 250 CUSTOMERS         20
               ENC                                                    21
```

3.5 INTERPRETATION OF GPSS OUTPUT

There are two types of output produced by a GPSS program: assembly output and execution output. The assembly output consists of the source listing of the program as submitted, the cross-reference list, and the assembled program listing. In Example 3.1 only the source listing of the drive-in window model was presented. The remaining portions of the listing for that program are included in this section.

The cross-reference list relates symbolic names to their numerical values and indicates the statements at which the names are referenced. The assembly listing has numerical values in place of symbolic names and all comments stripped off the statements. The assembly listing represents the form the program takes for execution. Both the cross-reference list and assembly listing are useful in program debugging. The cross-reference list and assembly listing for Example 3.1 are shown here.

```
                            CROSS-REFERENCE
                            FACILITIES


SYMBOL            NUMBER          REFERENCES

WINDO               1              15     17


                        **** ASSEMBLY TIME = .01 MINUTES ****



*****************************************************************
*    PROGRAM TO SIMULATE A DRIVE-IN WINDOW AT A BANK
*
*      PARAMETERS
*
*        ARRIVALS - 1 TO 5 MINUTES , UNIFORMLY DISTRIBUTED
*        PROCESSING - 1 TO 3 MINUTES , UNIFORMLY DISTRIBUTED
*        TERMINATION CONDITION - 250 CUSTOMERS PROCESSED
*
*****************************************************************
*
         SIMULATE
1        GENERATE    3,2
2        ADVANCE     1
3        SEIZE       1
4        ADVANCE     2,1
5        RELEASE     1
6        TERMINATE   1
*
         START       250
```

The execution output of a GPSS program is determined by the types of statements used. For each of several statement types, GPSS provides a statistical breakdown of the status of these statements at completion of the simulation. Upon successful termination of the simulation, the relative and absolute clock times are printed. The difference between these values is explained in the next section. Then GPSS lists all statements by number, with the total number of entities entering the statement block and the current number of entities remaining in the statement block at termination. As indicated below, all statements except the first two processed 250 entities and had no entities remaining at termination.

```
RELATIVE CLOCK          762   ABSOLUTE CLOCK          762
BLOCK COUNTS
BLOCK CURRENT  TOTAL   BLOCK CURRENT  TOTAL   BLOCK CURRENT  TOTAL   BLOCK CURRENT  TOTAL   BLOCK CURRENT  TOTAL
  1      0      251
  2      1      251
  3      0      250
  4      0      250
  5      0      250
  6      0      250
```

```
**************************************
*                                    *
*            FACILITIES              *
*                                    *
**************************************
```

```
                             -AVERAGE   UTILIZATION DURING-
         NUMBER   AVERAGE    TOTAL     AVAIL.   UNAVAIL.   CURRENT   PERCENT        TRANSACTION NUMBER
FACILITY ENTRIES  TIME/TRAN  TIME      TIME     TIME       STATUS    AVAILABILITY   SEIZING  PREEMPTING
WINDO     250      1.980     .649                                    100.0
END
```

```
***** TOTAL RUN TIME (INCLUDING ASSEMBLY) = .02 MINUTES *****
```

The example indicates that the second statement is processing its 251st entity at termination time. In terms of the model, the 251st customer arrived and was driving to the window when the 250th customer completed the transaction at the window. The block count is useful in determining the flow of entities in the model and in locating bottlenecks.

The only system entity used in Example 3.1 that produces statistical output is the facility WINDO. The most informative statistic on the facility for this simulation is the percentage utilization, which indicates that the drive-in window remained busy 64.9% of the time. In many models the average time spent by an entity in a facility is significant. However, in Example 3.1, that statistic merely illustrates the randomness of the customer processing time.

As other GPSS features that produce output are introduced in later sections, the type of statistics generated and their interpretation are discussed. Examples illustrating the statistical output are provided. In all subsequent examples the cross-reference list and assembly listing will not be shown.

3.6 CONTROL CARDS

To execute even a minimal GPSS program, such as Example 3.1, several control cards are necessary. Three control cards—SIMULATE, START, and END—appeared in the listing of Example 3.1. In addition, the CLEAR, RESET, and JOB statements are frequently utilized and are explained in this section.

The SIMULATE statement must appear if a GPSS model is to be executed. If SIMULATE is not used, the program is translated and checked for syntax errors and then immediately terminated.

The START statement has two basic functions. A START statement signifies the end of a model description and then initiates the execution of the model, if a SIMULATE statement is present. The START statement also indicates by means of its A argument the termination condition for the simulation. The A argument of START sets a counter, which is decremented by each TERMINATE statement executed in the program until it reaches 0.

START has three additional arguments, only one of which is discussed here. The B argument can be optionally used to suppress the statistical output of the program. This option is useful in conjunction with the RESET statement in removing statistical bias due to initial conditions from a model. See Section 6.8 for an explanation of this problem. For information on the C and D arguments of START, see Reference [3.1]. Some sample START statements are shown here.

> START 250

The model as described by the preceding GPSS statements is simulated until the start count, which is initially set to 250, reaches 0.

> START 10,NP

The model is simulated until the start count reaches 0 from an initial value of 10. No statistics are printed. The END statement marks the conclusion of the program input.

In many situations, it is desirable to execute a simulation program and then make a minor change to the program and execute the program again. GPSS provides two control statements for repeating program execution. RESET is used to restart the execution of a model while retaining all entities in queues, facilities, and storages. CLEAR reinitiates simulation but removes all entities from the model. Both RESET and CLEAR restart the computation of all statistics, and neither statement causes the internal random number generator seeds to be reset to their default values. RESET causes the relative clock to be set to zero, whereas CLEAR sets both the absolute and relative clocks to zero. The following example portrays a usage of the RESET statement.

EXAMPLE 3.2

Suppose that the teller in the drive-in of Example 3.1 works for 4 hours and then is replaced by a slower teller who requires 1 to 5 minutes, uniformly distributed, to process a transaction. The second teller also works for 4 hours. In order to illustrate the use of RESET, it is assumed that after 4 hours the drive-in window is closed while the tellers change. Any customers waiting for the window at this time remain in line and are serviced by the second teller.

Note that the simulation termination criterion is time, not number of customers as in Example 3.1. In order to accomplish this, a separate timing section is required to produce an entity at exactly 4 hours into the simulation. This entity, which is immediately terminated, is the only entity to decrement the start count.

The multiple-definition warning obtained by the redefinition of TELER does not affect the program since it occurs after the RESET statement. Later in this chapter, a mechanism for redefining the ADVANCE time that does not result in this warning is presented.

The output of the simulation model indicates that the second teller does require more time than the first. Although the second teller had fewer customers due to the randomness of the arrivals, that teller was busy 85.4% of the time, compared to 69.5% for the first teller.

3.7 STORAGES

As indicated in Section 3.4, a facility is used to model an activity that involves at most one entity at a time. In order to describe an activity involving multiple entities, a storage is used. A storage is defined to have a fixed size for a single execution of a GPSS model. The size of a storage—that is, the number of storage units—may be varied using a RESET or CLEAR card.

Unlike facilities, storages must be explicitly defined. A STORAGE statement serves this purpose. The form is as follows:

LABEL STORAGE A

where

LABEL is the name of the storage

A is the size of the storage

```
BLOCK                                                                    STATEMENT
NUMBER  *LOC    OPERATION  A,B,C,D,E,F,G,H,I        COMMENTS              NUMBER
        ***************************************************************     1
        * PROGRAM TO SIMULATE A DRIVE-IN WINDOW AT A BANK                   2
        *   WITH A SLOW TELLER REPLACING A FAST TELLER AFTER                3
        *   4 HOURS                                                         4
        *                                                                   5
        * PARAMETERS                                                        6
        *                                                                   7
        *       ARRIVALS - 1 TO 5 MINUTES , UNIFORMLY DISTRIBUTED           8
        *       PROCESSING(FAST TELLER) - 1 TO 3 MINUTES , UNIFORMLY        9
        *                                DISTRIBUTED                       10
        *       PROCESSING(SLOW TELLER) - 1 TO 5 MINUTES , UNIFORMLY       11
        *                                DISTRIBUTED                       12
        *       TERMINAL CONDITIONS - 4 HOURS EACH TELLER                  13
        *                             WINDOW CLOSES WHILE TELLERS CHANGE   14
        ***************************************************************    15
                SIMULATE                                                   16
1               GENERATE   3,2      CUSTOMERS ARRIVE          3+2          17
2               ADVANCE    1        CUSTOMERS DRIVE TO WINDOW              18
3               SEIZE      WINDO    CUSTOMER REACHES WINDOW                19
4       TELER   ADVANCE    2,1      TRANSACTION IS PROCESSED               20
5               RELEASE    WINDO    CUSTOMER DEPARTS                       21
6               TERMINATE  0                                               22
        *                                                                  23
        *****************************************************               24
        * TIMING SECTION                                                   25
        *****************************************************               26
        *                                                                  27
7               GENERATE   240      SIMULATE FOR 4 HOURS                   28
8               TERMINATE  1                                               29
        *                                                                  30
                START      1        SIMULATE FAST TELLER                   31
        *                                                                  32
        ***********************************                                33
        * CHANGE MODEL FOR SLOW TELLER                                     34
        ***********************************                                35
        *                                                                  36
                RESET                                                      37
4       TELER   ADVANCE    3,2      PROCESSING RATE OF SLOW TELLER        38
MULTIPLE DEFINITION OF SYMBOL IN ABOVE STATEMENT
        *                                                                  39
                START      1        SIMULATE SLOW TELLER                   40
                END                                                        41
```

```
        RELATIVE CLOCK        240  ABSOLUTE CLOCK            240
        BLOCK COUNTS
        BLOCK CURRENT    TOTAL    BLOCK CURRENT   TOTAL   BLOCK CURRENT   TOTAL
          1       0       85
          2       2       85
          3       0       83
          4       1       83
          5       0       82
          6       0       82
          7       0        1
          8       0        1
```

```
*********************
*                   *
*                   *   FACILITIES
*                   *
*********************

                                              -AVERAGE UTILIZATION DURING-
FACILITY    NUMBER    AVERAGE    TOTAL    AVAIL.    UNAVAIL.    CURRENT                 TRANSACTION NUMBER
            ENTRIES   TIME/TRAN  TIME     TIME      TIME        STATUS     AVAILABILITY SEIZING  PREEMPTING
  WINDO       83       2.012     .695                                                   PERCENT
                                                                                        100.0      3

*****************************
* CHANGE MODEL FOR SLOW TELLER
*****************************
*
      RESET
  4   ADVANCE    3,2
*
      START    1

RELATIVE CLOCK    240   ABSOLUTE CLOCK    480
BLOCK COUNTS
BLOCK CURRENT    TOTAL    BLOCK CURRENT    TOTAL    BLOCK CURRENT    TOTAL
  1      0        77
  2      4        77
  3      0        75
  4      1        75
  5      0        75
  6      0        75
  7      0         1
  8      0         1

*********************
*                   *
*                   *   FACILITIES
*                   *
*********************

                                              -AVERAGE UTILIZATION DURING-
FACILITY    NUMBER    AVERAGE    TOTAL    AVAIL.    UNAVAIL.    CURRENT                 TRANSACTION NUMBER
            ENTRIES   TIME/TRAN  TIME     TIME      TIME        STATUS     AVAILABILITY SEIZING  PREEMPTING
  WINDO       76       3.000     .950                                                   PERCENT
  END                                                                                   100.0      3

***** TOTAL RUN TIME (INCLUDING ASSEMBLY) = .02 MINUTES *****
```

The statements permitting entities to enter and leave storages are ENTER and LEAVE, respectively. Their formats are as follows:

ENTER A,B

LEAVE A,B

where

A is the storage name

B is the number of units of storage to be occupied or released; default value is 1

When an entity attempts to enter a storage, it requests the number of storage units specified in the B argument of the ENTER statement. If insufficient units of storage are available, the entity is blocked until a sufficient number of units are free. When an entity leaves a storage, the number of units indicated by the B argument of the LEAVE statement are freed.

The sample statements listed below illustrate the functions of STORAGE, ENTER, and LEAVE.

SEATS STORAGE 100

A storage named SEATS of size 100 is defined.

ENTER SEATS

If there is an available storage unit in SEATS, an entity occupies 1 unit in the storage.

LEAVE SEATS

An entity leaves the storage SEATS, freeing 1 unit.

ENTER SEATS,10

If at least 10 storage units in SEATS are available, an entity enters the storage and occupies 10 units.

LEAVE SEATS,8

An entity leaves the storage SEATS and frees 8 units.

The example below shows the use of a storage in a simple model.

EXAMPLE 3.3

Let us move inside the bank and model the activity at the teller windows. Assume that the bank has adopted a "jet-teller" organization in which all customers wait in a single line for a free teller rather than in individual lines for each teller. The following set of parameters are used in the first execution of the model:

1. Number of tellers—4
2. Customer arrival rate—from 1 to 3 minutes, uniformly distributed
3. Teller processing rate—1 to 5 minutes, uniformly distributed
4. Time required for customer to enter line—1 minute
5. Termination condition—8 hours

The model is simulated a second time with 3 tellers to determine the effect on service.

The GPSS program shown simulates the teller activity.

The simulation model indicates that, on the average, slightly less than 1.5 tellers are busy at any given time. From the point of view of personnel utilization, 3 tellers appear to be as effective as 4. The MAXIMUM CONTENTS field does indicate that at some time all 4 tellers were busy. In order to make a personnel decision, customer waiting time must be included in the statistics printed by the model. The next section describes the methods for obtaining queuing statistics.

In Example 3.3 each entity occupies a single location in storage. As shown in the sample statement, an entity may occupy an arbitrary number of storage locations. In GPSS there is a generalized mechanism for selecting an entity to enter a storage. All entities blocked from entering a storage are maintained in a list ordered by arrival time. When locations are available in the storage, GPSS selects the first entity in the list whose storage requirement is less than or equal to the amount of available storage units. Note that under this algorithm an entity with a large storage requirement may be prevented from entering the storage, while later arriving entities with smaller requirements may be permitted to enter the storage. The selection of entities to enter storage is the focus of the following abstract example.

EXAMPLE 3.4

Assume a storage of capacity 50 containing the following entities:

Entity	Number of Units	Departure Time
E1	10	14
E2	12	17
E3	21	19
E4	5	23

Initially, there are 2 free units in the storage. Let there be a waiting line as shown below:

Entity	Number of Units	Arrival Time
E5	14	10
E6	9	11
E7	28	12
E8	3	13

```
BLOCK
NUMBER    *LOC  OPERATION  A,B,C,D,E,F,G,H,I        COMMENTS          STATEMENT
                                                                     NUMBER
          ****************************************************          1
          * SIMULATION OF THE TELLER ACTIVITY IN A                     2
          *BANK.  A SINGLE WAITING LINE IS ASSUMED.                    3
          *                                                            4
          * TWO RUNS ARE MADE - FIRST WITH 4 TELLERS,                  5
          * THEN WITH 3 TELLERS.                                       6
          *                                                            7
          * PARAMETERS                                                 8
          *                                                            9
          * CUSTOMER ARRIVALS - 1 TO 3 MINUTES , UNIFORMLY DISTRIBUTED 10
          * PROCESSING RATES - 1 TO 5 MINUTES , UNIFORMLY DISTRIBUTED  11
          * TIME REQUIRED TO ENTER LINE - 1 MINUTE                     12
          * TERMINATION CONDITION - 8 HOURS                            13
          *                                                            14
          ****************************************************          15
          *                                                            16
                SIMULATE                                               17
      1         GENERATE    2,1         CUSTOMERS ARRIVE               18
      2         ADVANCE     1           CUSTOMER WALKS TO LINE         19
      3         ENTER       TELRS       CUSTOMER GETS A TELLER         20
      4         ADVANCE     3,2         CUSTOMER'S TRANSACTION IS PROCESSED 21
      5         LEAVE       TELRS       CUSTOMER LEAVES TELLER         22
      6         TERMINATE   0                                          23
          *                                                            24
          ***************************************************           25
          * TIMING SECTION                                             26
          ***************************************************           27
          *                                                            28
      7         GENERATE    480         SIMULATE FOR 8 HOURS           29
      8         TERMINATE   1                                          30
          *                                                            31
          ********************************************                  32
          * DEFINE STORAGE                                             33
          ********************************************                  34
          *                                                            35
          TELRS STORAGE     4                                          36
          *                                                            37
```

```
********************************************
* CONTROL SECTION
********************************************
*
        START     1          SIMULATE WITH 4 TELLERS
        CLEAR
TELRS  STORAGE    3          REDEFINE STORAGE TO MODEL 3 TELLERS
        START     1          SIMULATE WITH 3 TELLERS
        END
```

RELATIVE CLOCK   480   ABSOLUTE CLOCK   480

BLOCK COUNTS

BLOCK	CURRENT	TOTAL	BLOCK	CURRENT	TOTAL	BLOCK	CURRENT	TOTAL
1	0	239						
2	0	239						
3	0	239						
4	2	239						
5	0	237						
6	0	237						
7	0	1						
8	0	1						

```
                           ****************************
                           *                          *
                           *        STORAGES          *
                           *                          *
                           ****************************

                                             -AVERAGE  UTILIZATION DURING-
STORAGE  CAPACITY  AVERAGE   ENTRIES  AVERAGE   TOTAL   AVAIL.  UNAVAIL.  CURRENT    PERCENT    CURRENT   MAXIMUM
                   CONTENTS           TIME/UNIT  TIME    TIME     TIME    STATUS   AVAILABILITY CONTENTS  CONTENTS
TELRS       4       1.490      239     2.992     .372                              100.0           2         4
     CLEAR
1    STORAGE   3
     START     1


RELATIVE CLOCK        480    ABSOLUTE CLOCK      480
BLOCK COUNTS
BLOCK CURRENT   TOTAL    BLOCK CURRENT   TOTAL    BLOCK CURRENT    TOTAL
   1    0        235
   2    1        235
   3    0        234
   4    1        234
   5    0        233
   6    0        233
   7    1          1
   8    0          1


                           ********************************
                           *                              *
                           *          STORAGES            *
                           *                              *
                           ********************************

                                             -AVERAGE  UTILIZATION DURING-
STORAGE  CAPACITY  AVERAGE   ENTRIES  AVERAGE   TOTAL   AVAIL.  UNAVAIL.  CURRENT    PERCENT    CURRENT   MAXIMUM
                   CONTENTS           TIME/UNIT  TIME    TIME     TIME    STATUS   AVAILABILITY CONTENTS  CONTENTS
TELRS       3       1.446      234     2.966     .481                              100.0           1         3
     END

          ***** TOTAL RUN TIME (INCLUDING ASSEMBLY) = .03 MINUTES *****
```

To complete the example, further assume that at time 18, entity E9 arrives with a requirement for 1 unit.

Let us follow the actions taken from times 14 to 18 in order to understand the internal mechanism used by GPSS to manage storages. The proper usage of storages requires an understanding of the internal management by the programmer. At time 14, E1 leaves the storage, thus making a total of 12 storage units available. Since E5 requires 14 units, it cannot enter the storage. Therefore, E6 is permitted to enter the storage, leaving 3 units available. E8 is also permitted to enter the storage since it requires only 3 units. After the actions at time 14, the storage and the queue hold the entities listed below.

For storage,

Entity	Number of Units	Departure Time
E1	12	17
E3	21	19
E4	5	23
E6	9	24
E8	3	25

For queue,

Entity	Number of Units	Arrival Time
E5	14	10
E7	28	12

At this point, the storage is 100% full.

At time 17, E2 departs the storage and frees 12 units. Since both entities in the queue require more than the number of available units, no new entries are made in the storage.

At time 18, entity E9 arrives and immediately enters the storage since its storage requirement is less than the number of available units. All of the entities already in the queue are blocked since their storage requirements exceed the number of free units.

At time 19, the storage and queue have the contents listed below.

For storage,

Entity	Number of Units	Departure Time
E3	21	19
E4	5	23
E6	9	24
E8	3	25
E9	1	31

For queue,

Entity	Number of Units	Arrival Time
E5	14	10
E7	28	12

The reader should keep in mind that all of the operations described in Example 3.4 are internal to GPSS and result from the use of ENTER and LEAVE statements. If the programmer does not wish the storage to select entities according to the default method, a special code must be included in the program. Methods for altering the discipline of entering storages are discussed in Sections 3.12 and 3.13.

3.8 QUEUES

Chapter 2 emphasized the importance of queuing statistics in discrete stochastic simulations. The sample programs presented thus far have been devoid of statistics on queue behavior. GPSS contains features that provide extensive queuing statistics. The use of queues in GPSS resembles the mechanism for using facilities in that queues are declared implicitly in the program, not explicitly by a definition statement.

The bookkeeping mechanism for a queue is activated whenever an entity executes a QUEUE statement. The departure of an entity from a queue is indicated by the execution of DEPART. Entities are never blocked from executing either a QUEUE or DEPART statement.

QUEUE and DEPART have identical formats:

> QUEUE A,B
> DEPART A,B

where

> A is the queue name
> B is the number of entries entering (or departing) the queue

Whenever a queue for some type of service is modeled in a GPSS program, the QUEUE and DEPART blocks should be adjacent to the block that determines if the service is to be granted. For example, if queuing statistics for the facility WINDO are desired, then the following sequence should appear in the program:

> QUEUE WINDO
> SEIZE WINDO
> DEPART WINDO

In this example, the queue and the facility have identical names. GPSS permits the duplication of names, provided two entities of the same type do not have identical names. In the case of queues, any erroneous duplicate names are treated as references to the same queue.

The statistics that GPSS automatically provides for a queue are maximum contents, average contents, total entries, number of entries that spent zero time in the queue, percentage of 0 time entries, average time in queue per entry, average time in queue for entries that remained in the queue for more than 0 time units, and contents at the termination of the simulation. These statistics are provided for each queue in the model.

EXAMPLE 3.5

The GPSS program shown here is an expanded version of Example 3.1, which collects queuing statistics for the drive-in window.

The queuing statistics indicate only occasional customer waiting, although at least once the length of the line reached 3. Almost two-thirds of the customers (66.5%) were processed without any waiting. On the average, a customer waited .713 minute, although those that had to wait were in line for an average time of 2.130 minutes.

3.9 STANDARD NUMERICAL ATTRIBUTES

Thus far the arguments of the GPSS statements in the sample programs have been very limited in scope. Constants have been used in almost all cases. Fortunately, this is not a limitation of GPSS but rather a result of the sequence of the presentation of the material in this chapter. GPSS provides the programmer with access to a large variety of system attributes termed Standard Numerical Attributes (SNAs). Each SNA is identified by a one- or two-letter code followed by a dollar sign and then a qualifying name or number. Table 3.1 lists the GPSS Standard Numerical Attributes relating to the GPSS features discussed in this chapter. For a complete list, see Reference [3.1].

SNAs can be used as arguments for most GPSS statements. In the samples presented thus far, any constant arguments could be replaced by an appropriate SNA. Some sample statements using SNAs are given for illustrative purposes.

GENERATE 4,,,R$SEATS

Every 4 time units, a group of entities is generated with the number of entities in the group equal to the number of available locations in the storage, SEATS, at the time of generation.

ADVANCE S$MEMRY

An entity is held in the ADVANCE statement for a time equal to the current contents of the storage MEMRY. A change in the contents of the storage during the time that the entity is held in the ADVANCE statement block does not affect the amount of time that the entity remains in the statement block.

```
BLOCK
NUMBER    *LOC    OPERATION  A,B,C,D,E,F,G,H,I          COMMENTS
          ****************************************************************
          *    PROGRAM TC SIMULATE A CRIVE-IN WINDOW AT A BANK
          *
          *    PARAMETERS
          *
          *    ARRIVALS - 1 TO 5 MINUTES , UNIFORMLY DISTRIBUTED
          *    PROCESSING - 1 TO 3 MINUTES , UNIFORMLY DISTRIBUTED
          *    TERMINATION CONDITION - 250 CUSTOMERS PROCESSED
          *
          ****************************************************************
          *
                 SIMULATE
    1            GENERATE   3,2           CUSTOMERS ARRIVE
    2            ADVANCE    1             CUSTOMERS DRIVE TO WINDOW
    3            QUEUE      WINDO         CUSTOMER WAITS FOR WINDOW
    4            SEIZE      WINDO         CUSTOMER REACHES WINDOW
    5            DEPART     WINDO         REMOVE CUSTOMER FROM QUEUE
    6            ADVANCE    2,1           TRANSACTION IS PROCESSED
    7            RELEASE    WINDO         CUSTOMER DEPARTS
    8            TERMINATE  1
          *
                 START      250           PROCESS 250 CUSTOMERS
                 END
```

```
STATEMENT
NUMBER
   1
   2
   3
   4
   5
   6
   7
   8
   9
  10
  11
  12
  13
  14
  15
  16
  17
  18
  19
  20
  21
  22
  23
```

```
RELATIVE CLOCK           762   ABSOLUTE CLOCK          762
BLOCK COUNTS
BLOCK CURRENT    TCTAL    BLCCK CURRENT    TOTAL    BLOCK CURRENT    TOTAL
  1      0        251
  2      0        251
  3      1        251
  4      0        250
  5      0        250
  6      0        250
  7      0        250
  8      0        250
```

```
***********************************
*                                 *
*          FACILITIES             *
*                                 *
***********************************
```

FACILITY	NUMBER ENTRIES	AVERAGE TIME/TRAN	-AVERAGE UTILIZATION DURING- TOTAL TIME	AVAIL. TIME	UNAVAIL. TIME	CURRENT STATUS	PERCENT AVAILABILITY	TRANSACTION NUMBER SEIZING	NUMBER PREEMPTING
WINDO	250	1.980	.649				100.0		

```
***********************************
*                                 *
*            QUEUES               *
*                                 *
***********************************
```

QUEUE	MAXIMUM CONTENTS	AVERAGE CONTENTS	TOTAL ENTRIES	ZERO ENTRIES	PERCENT ZEROS	AVERAGE TIME/TRANS	$AVERAGE TIME/TRANS	TABLE NUMBER	CURRENT CONTENTS
WINDO	3	.234	251	167	66.5	.713	2.130		1

$AVERAGE TIME/TRANS = AVERAGE TIME/TRANS EXCLUDING ZERO ENTRIES

END

***** TOTAL RUN TIME (INCLUDING ASSEMBLY) = .02 MINUTES *****

Table 3.1   Standard Numerical Attributes

Standard Numerical Attribute	Code
Function	FN
Queue Length	Q
Fullword Savevalue	XF
Halfword Savevalue	XH
Byte Savevalue	XB
Floating Point Savevalue	XL
Storage Contents	S
Remaining Free Storage Units	R
Random Number	RN
Fullword Parameter	PF
Halfword Parameter	PH
Byte Parameter	PB
Floating-Point Parameter	PL
Transit Time	MI
Priority	PR
Variable	V

As additional GPSS features are introduced, the associated SNA will be used in sample statements and example programs.

3.10 VARIABLES

The utilization of SNAs increases the flexibility of GPSS models by making system attributes available to the programmer. The VARIABLE statement provides significant power to a GPSS program by allowing computations to be performed in the program. VARIABLE statements act as arithmetic expressions which are defined at translation time and then executed whenever referenced as arguments.

The VARIABLE statement defines an arithmetic expression according to the following format:

> label   VARIABLE   expression

where the expression is formed from the operators

> + (addition)
> − (subtraction)
> * (multiplication)
> / (division)
> @ (modulo division)

The operands are any SNAs, including constants and variables. Precedence rules follow the convention that addition and subtraction have lower precedence than the other three operators, and operators of equal priority are evaluated in a left-to-right order. Up to five levels of parentheses are permitted to clarify or modify the order of operator evaluation.

An important factor in the use of VARIABLEs is that, by default, all GPSS variable expressions return integer variables with truncation occurring *after the evaluation of each operator*. The programmer can avoid the intermediate truncations by using the FVARIABLE statement to define an expression. However, an expression defined using FVARIABLE still truncates the final result.

Variable expressions are referenced at run time by the use of an SNA V$label as an argument in any statement. Whenever a reference occurs, the expression is evaluated using the current values of all operands and the result is then utilized as the argument value.

The two sets of sample statements provide examples of variable usage:

       FREE VARIABLE R$SEATS/2
       ENTER SEATS, V$FREE

This ENTER statement results in the entity occupying one-half of the available locations in the storage SEATS.

       SCHED VARIABLE 3*Q$CPU+200
       ADVANCE V$SCHED

An entity remains in the advance statement block for 3 times the length of the queue CPU plus 200 time units.

Variables provide a clean mechanism for changing simulation parameters for multiple executions of the same model. In this mode, the variable expressions may be constants. This may appear to be an extraneous use of a VARIABLE statement. However, if this parameter is referenced in several statements in the program, the change of the parameter following a CLEAR or RESET card can be accomplished by simply redefining the variable. The sequence of sample statements below shows this application of the VARIABLE statement.

       WASH VARIABLE 14
       ADVANCE   V$WASH
       CLEAR
       WASH VARIABLE 21

The GPSS program containing the statements shown above would first execute the model with the value of WASH equal to 14 and then with a WASH value of 21.

The following example provides a demonstration of VARIABLE expressions.

EXAMPLE 3.6

In Example 3.2 the drive-in window at a bank was simulated with the original teller replaced by a slow teller after 4 hours. The method used to redefine the teller processing rate produced a multiple definition warning. A VARIABLE statement can be used to redefine the teller rate without a warning message. The program illustrated produces results that are identical to the program of Example 3.2.

```
BLOCK                                                                            STATEM
NUMBER  *LOC   OPERATION  A,B,C,D,E,F,G,H,I          COMMENTS                     NUMBE
        *******************************************************************        1
        * PROGRAM TC SIMULATE A CRIVE-IN WINDOW AT A BANK                          2
        *    WITH A SLCW TELLER REPLACING A FAST TELLER AFTER                      3
        *    4 HOURS                                                               4
        *                                                                          5
        * PARAMETERS                                                               6
        *                                                                          7
        *      ARRIVALS - 1 TO 5 MINUTES , UNIFORMLY DISTRIBUTED                   8
        *      PROCESSING(FAST TELLER) - 1 TO 3 MINUTES , UNIFORMLY                9
        *                                 DISTRIBUTED                             10
        *      PROCESSING(SLOW TELLER) - 1 TO 5 MINUTES , UNIFORMLY               11
        *                                 DISTRIBUTED                             12
        *      TERMINAL CCNDITIONS - 4 HOURS EACH TELLER                          13
        *******************************************************************       14
        *                                                                         15
        *******************************************************************       16
        * VARIABLES                                                               17
        *******************************************************************       18
        *                                                                         19
        MEAN   VARIABLE   2              MEAN TRANSACTION PROCESSING TIME          20
        MOD    VARIABLE   V$MEAN-1       TRANSACTION PROCESSING MODIFIER           21
        *                                                                         22
               SIMULATE                                                           23
1              GENERATE   3,2            CUSTOMERS ARRIVE                          24
2              ADVANCE    1              CUSTOMERS DRIVE TO WINDOW                 25
3              QUEUE      WINCO          CUSTOMER WAITS FOR WINDOW                 26
4              SEIZE      WINCO          CUSTOMER REACHES WINDOW                   27
5              DEPART     WINDO          REMOVE CUSTOMER FROM QUEUE                28
6       TELER  ADVANCE    V$MEAN,V$MOD   TRANSACTION IS PROCESSED                 29
7              RELEASE    WINCO          CUSTOMER DEPARTS                          30
8              TERMINATE  0                                                        31
        *                                                                         32
        *******************************************************                   33
        * TIMING SECTICN                                                          34
        *******************************************************                   35
        *                                                                         36
9              GENERATE   240            SIMULATE FOR 4 HOURS                     37
10             TERMINATE  1                                                        38
        *                                                                         39
               START      1              SIMULATE FAST TELLER                     40
        *                                                                         41
        *****************************                                             42
        * CHANGE MODEL FOR SLOW TELLER                                            43
        *****************************                                             44
        *                                                                         45
               RESET                                                              46
        MEAN   VARIABLE   3              MEAN TRANS. PROCESS. RATE OF SLOW TELLER  47
        *                                                                         48
               START      1              SIMULATE SLOW TELLER                     49
               ENC                                                                50
```

3.11 RANDOM DISTRIBUTIONS

As indicated in Chapter 2, stochastic simulation models have the need to generate events according to various random distributions. GPSS provides this capability to the user in three ways. On certain statements, such as ADVANCE and GEN-ERATE, a random event time can be produced from a uniform distribution by providing the endpoints of the interval as arguments.

GPSS also contains a built-in random number generator, which provides uniform integer random numbers over the interval from 0 to 999. The random numbers can be referenced as SNAs by using RN_i, $1 \leq i \leq 8$, in a program. The eight random number generators operate independently. It is advisable to use distinct random number generators wherever possible to prevent undesirable dependencies between events that are unrelated in the real system. GPSS uses RN1 to generate random numbers for its internal usage, such as selection of a value from a uniform distribution.

All GPSS random number generators work on the congruence method (see Chapter 5) by producing the $(i + 1)$th random number from the ith random number. The initial random number is produced from a seed value. For a given seed value, a random number generator will produce a fixed sequence of random numbers. This fact has two implications in terms of simulation techniques. If it is necessary to reproduce exactly a set of random events, then the same random number seed should be utilized for all runs. The default seed value for all random number generators is 37, which has been determined to be a seed value that maximizes randomness for the generation methods used. In many situations there is a need to repeat a simulation experiment using different random number sequences in order to establish a basis for the statistical verification of the model. GPSS provides the RMULT statement for establishing random number generator seeds. RMULT has the following format:

$$\text{RMULT } A_1, A_2, A_3, A_4, A_5, A_6, A_7, A_8$$

where A_i, $1 \leq i \leq 8$, is the seed value for the ith random number generator; if the ith argument is not specified, it defaults to 37.

The sample statement below depicts the application of RMULT.

RMULT 31,743,6352,,31

Random number generation seeds 1 and 5 are set to 31, while random number generator 2 is set to 743 and random number generator 3 is initialized to 6352; random number generators 4, 6, 7, and 8 have their seed values set to the default value of 37. The values 37, 31, 743, and 6352 are suggested in Reference [3.1] as good seed values for the random number generators.

RMULT is often used with RESET or CLEAR to reset the random number generators after a modification to the model. If the model is to be preserved while changing only the random number seed, the CLEAR, RMULT combination should be used. In this case, if the A_i argument of RMULT is not present, the ith random number generator is not reset. Example 3.7 presents the reinitialization of a random number generator after a change to the model. In Example 3.7, successive executions of a model are performed using different random number seeds.

EXAMPLE 3.7

In Example 3.5 the activity at the drive-in window of a bank was simulated using the default seed values of the random number generators. Let us repeat the experiment three times using different random number seeds. Since the only use of random numbers was done implicitly by the system in the GENERATE and ADVANCE statements, only random number generator 1 need be reinitialized.

The use of different random number generator seeds has produced minor changes in the statistics obtained from this model. Such changes are expected because of the stochastic nature of the system. The average value of a statistic over the three runs is the value to be interpreted as the result of the simulation experiment. For example, the average busy time of the teller is .671. The analysis of statistics from replicated simulation runs is discussed in Chapter 6.

The third mechanism in GPSS for the utilization of stochastic variables is the FUNCTION statement, which permits the definition of stochastic distribution. User-defined functions are referenced by the SNA, FN_i.

The user specifies the behavior of a stochastic variable by providing the following information in a FUNCTION statement and its associated specification statements:

1. The type of stochastic variable (i.e., continuous or discrete)
2. The number of points used to specify the function
3. Data statements containing the function points as (X,Y) pairs
4. The SNA that will be used as the function argument to provide dynamically the X value for which a corresponding Y will be computed

The formats of a FUNCTION statement and its associated data statements are as follows:

> Label FUNCTION A,B

where

> A is any valid SNA
>
> B is the function type—C for continuous, D for discrete—and the number of points provided in the data statements

The data points are given as $X_1, Y_1 / X_2, Y_2 / \ldots / X_k, Y_k$, where X_i and Y_i, $1 \le i \le k$, are integer or decimal constants.

GPSS supports several function types [3.1]. However, only continuous and discrete functions, which are the most commonly used, are discussed here.

Whenever FN_i appears as an argument of a statement, the value of the SNA designated as the argument of the ith function is compared against the X values of the data points for that function. If a match is found, the Y portion of the (X,Y) data point is used as the value of FN_i. If an exact match between the argument SNA and an X value is not found, the behavior of the function varies

BLOCK
NUMBER

	*LOC	OPERATION	A,B,C,D,E,F,G,H,I	COMMENTS	STATEMENT NUMBER
	***				1
	*	PROGRAM TC SIMULATE A CRIVE-IN WINDOW AT A BANK			2
	*				3
	*	PARAMETERS			4
	*				5
	*	ARRIVALS - 1 TO 5 MINUTES , UNIFORMLY DISTRIBUTED			6
	*	PROCESSING - 1 TO 3 MINUTES , UNIFORMLY DISTRIBUTED			7
	*	TERMINATION CONDITION - 250 CUSTOMERS PROCESSED			8
	*				9
	***				10
	*				11
		SIMULATE			12
1		GENERATE	3,2	CUSTOMERS ARRIVE	13
2		ADVANCE	1	CUSTOMERS DRIVE TO WINDOW	14
3		QUEUE	WINDO	CUSTOMER WAITS FOR WINDOW	15
4		SEIZE	WINCO	CUSTOMER REACHES WINDOW	16
5		DEPART	WINDO	REMOVE CUSTOMER FROM QUEUE	17
6		ADVANCE	2,1	TRANSACTION IS PROCESSED	18
7		RELEASE	WINCO	CUSTOMER DEPARTS	19
8		TERMINATE	1		20
	*				21
		START	250	PROCESS 250 CUSTOMERS	22
		CLEAR			23
		RMULT	31	RESET RANDOM NUMBER GENERATOR	24
		START	250	SIMULATE FOR 250 CUSTOMERS	25
		CLEAR			26
		RMULT	743	RESET RANDOM NUMBER GENERATOR	27
		START	250	SIMULATE FOR 250 CUSTOMERS	28
		ENC			29

RELATIVE CLOCK   762   ABSOLUTE CLOCK   762*

BLOCK COUNTS						
BLOCK	CURRENT	TOTAL	BLOCK	CURRENT	BLOCK	CURRENT	TOTAL
1	0	251					
2	0	251					
3	1	251					
4	0	250					
5	0	250					
6	0	250					
7	0	250					
8	0	250					

TOTAL

```
 *****************************************
 *                                       *
 *               FACILITIES              *
 *                                       *
 *****************************************
```

FACILITY	NUMBER ENTRIES	AVERAGE TIME/TRAN	-AVERAGE TOTAL TIME	UTILIZATION DURING- AVAIL. TIME	UNAVAIL. TIME	CURRENT STATUS	PERCENT AVAILABILITY	TRANSACTION NUMBER SEIZING PREEMPTING
WINDO	25C	1.980	.649				100.0	

```
 *****************************************
 *                                       *
 *                 QUEUES                *
 *                                       *
 *****************************************
```

QUEUE	MAXIMUM CONTENTS	AVERAGE CONTENTS	TOTAL ENTRIES	ZERO ENTRIES	PERCENT ZEROS	AVERAGE TIME/TRANS	$AVERAGE TIME/TRANS	TABLE NUMBER	CURRENT CONTENTS
WINDO	3	.234	251	167	66.5	.713	2.130		1

$AVERAGE TIME/TRANS = AVERAGE TIME/TRANS EXCLUDING ZERO ENTRIES

```
          CLEAR    31
          RMULT   250
          START
```

738 ABSOLUTE CLOCK   738

RELATIVE CLOCK   738

BLOCK COUNTS

BLOCK	CURRENT	TOTAL	BLOCK	CURRENT	TOTAL	BLOCK	CURRENT	TOTAL
1	0	252						
2	0	252						
3	2	252						
4	0	250						
5	0	250						
6	0	250						
7	0	250						
8	0	250						

```
*********************************
*                               *
*          FACILITIES           *
*                               *
*********************************

                                                    -AVERAGE   UTILIZATION DURING-
FACILITY    NUMBER   AVERAGE      TOTAL    AVAIL.   UNAVAIL.                PERCENT        TRANSACTION NUMBER
            ENTRIES  TIME/TRAN    TIME     TIME     TIME     CURRENT        AVAILABILITY   SEIZING   PREEMPTING
WINDO       250      2.028        .686                       STATUS         100.0          2


*********************************
*                               *
*            QUEUES             *
*                               *
*********************************

QUEUE       MAXIMUM   AVERAGE    TOTAL     ZERO      PERCENT   AVERAGE      $AVERAGE     TABLE     CURRENT
            CONTENTS  CONTENTS   ENTRIES   ENTRIES   ZEROS     TIME/TRANS   TIME/TRANS   NUMBER    CONTENTS
WINDO       3         .208       252       171       67.8      .611         1.901                  2
$AVERAGE TIME/TRANS = AVERAGE TIME/TRANS EXCLUDING ZERO ENTRIES
       CLEAR          743
       RMULT          250
       START          250

RELATIVE CLOCK      753   ABSOLUTE CLOCK      753
BLOCK COUNTS
BLOCK CURRENT  TOTAL       BLOCK CURRENT  TOTAL    BLOCK CURRENT  TOTAL    BLOCK CURRENT  TOTAL
1      0       250
2      0       250
3      0       250
4      0       250
5      0       250
6      0       250
7      0       250
8      0       250
```

```
****************************
*                          *
*       FACILITIES         *
*                          *
****************************

                                         -AVERAGE UTILIZATION DURING-
FACILITY   NUMBER    AVERAGE      TOTAL   AVAIL.  UNAVAIL.  CURRENT    PERCENT       TRANSACTION NUMBER
           ENTRIES   TIME/TRAN    TIME    TIME    TIME      STATUS     AVAILABILITY  SEIZING  PREEMPTING
WINDO      25C       2.044        .678                                            100.0


****************************
*                          *
*        QUEUES            *
*                          *
****************************

QUEUE    MAXIMUM   AVERAGE    TOTAL    ZERO     PERCENT   AVERAGE     $AVERAGE    TABLE    CURRENT
         CONTENTS  CCNTENTS   ENTRIES  ENTRIES  ZEROS     TIME/TRANS  TIME/TRANS  NUMBER   CONTENTS
WINDO    2         .237       250      161      64.3      .715        2.011
$AVERAGE TIME/TRANS = AVERAGE TIME/TRANS EXCLUDING ZERO ENTRIES
 END

            ***** TOTAL RUN TIME (INCLUDING ASSEMBLY) = .04 MINUTES *****
```

depending upon its type. Under these circumstances, a discrete function is treated as a stairstep function while values for a continuous function are selected using linear interpolation. Section 2.4 discusses the techniques used to determine function values using these methods. Note that if a random number is used as a function argument, its value is in the range 0–.999, not 0–999.

The following simple statements illustrate the definition and use of functions.

EXPONENTIAL DISTRIBUTION

EXPO FUNCTION RN2,C24

.0000,.000/.1000,.104/.2000,.222/.3000,.355/.4000,.509/.5000,.690/.6000,.915/
.7000,1.20/.7500,1.38/.8000,1.60/.8400,1.83/.8800,2.12/.9000,2.30/.9200,2.52/
.9400,2.81/.9500,2.99/.9600,3.20/.9700,3.50/.9800,3.90/.9900,4.60/.9950,5.30/
.9980,6.20/.9990,7.00/.9997,8.00/

GENERATE 3,FN$EXPO

When the GENERATE statement is executed, the reference to FN$EXPO will cause random number generator 2 to produce a number between 0 and 1 for use as the X argument to the function EXPO. The X coordinates of the function points specified on the data cards are then searched for an exact match, in which case the associated Y coordinate is returned as the function value. If no exact match exists for the random number, the scan stops at the first X value greater than the X argument. Since EXPO is defined to be continuous, linear interpolation is employed to determine the function value. The value of FN$EXPO is then multiplied by 3 and truncated to produce the time of the next transaction generation.

TTYPE FUNCTION RN3,D6

.20,1/.35,2/.55,3/.80,4/.95,5/1.0,6/

TTIME FUNCTION FN$TTYPE,D6

1,3/2,3/3,4/4,6/5,2/6,9/

ADVANCE FN$TTIME

When a transaction reaches the ADVANCE block, the system must compute a value for FN$TTIME. Since FN$TTYPE is the argument of TTIME, the function TTYPE must be evaluated first. Random number generator 3 is referenced to provide the argument for TTYPE that yields a value of 1 through 6 depending on the value of the random number. Since TTYPE is discrete, its value is the Y coordinate less than or equal to the random number. The value of TTYPE then acts as the input to TTIME whose value is selected in the same manner as was that of the TTYPE function. This sample illustrates the use of a function as an argument to another function and also the use of an SNA other than a random number as the input. The particular configuration illustrated here would be practical only if different TTYPE functions were to be used in repeated executions of the model. Otherwise, TTYPE and TTIME could be incorporated into a single function.

In Example 3.8 the model of Example 3.7 is modified to utilize exponentially distributed stochastic variables in place of uniform distributions.

```
BLOCK
NUMBER
       *LOC   OPERATION  A,B,C,D,E,F,G,H,I      COMMENTS
       ***************************************************************
       *  PROGRAM TO SIMULATE A DRIVE-IN WINDOW AT A BANK
       *  USING 3 RANDOM NUMBER SEEDS
       *  PARAMETERS
       *
       *    ARRIVALS - 3 MINUTES , EXPONENTIALLY DISTRIBUTED
       *    PROCESSING - 2 MINUTES , EXPONENTIALLY DISTRIBUTED
       *    TERMINATION CONDITION - 250 CUSTOMERS PROCESSED
       *
       ***************************************************************
       *
       *  EXPONENTIAL FUNCTION
       *
       EXPO  FUNCTION   RN2,C24
       .0000,.000/.1000,.104/.2000,.222/.3000,.355/.4000,.509/.5000,.690/
       .6000,.915/.7000,1.20/.7500,1.38/.8000,1.60/.8400,1.83/.8800,2.12/
       .9000,2.30/.9200,2.52/.9400,2.81/.9500,2.99/.9600,3.20/.9700,3.50/
       .9800,3.90/.9900,4.60/.9950,5.30/.9980,6.20/.9990,7.00/.9997,8.00/
       *
       ***************************************************************
             SIMULATE
1            GENERATE   3,FN$EXPO     CUSTOMERS ARRIVE
2            ADVANCE    1             CUSTOMERS DRIVE TO WINDOW
3            QUEUE      WINDO         CUSTOMER WAITS FOR WINDOW
4            SEIZE      WINDO         CUSTOMER REACHES WINDOW
5            DEPART     WINCO         REMOVE CUSTOMER FROM QUEUE
6            ADVANCE    2,FN$EXPO     TRANSACTION IS PROCESSED
7            RELEASE    WINDO         CUSTOMER DEPARTS
8            TERMINATE  1
       *
             START      250           PROCESS 250 CUSTOMERS
             CLEAR
             RMULT      31            RESET RANDOM NUMBER GENERATOR
             START      250           SIMULATE FOR 250 CUSTOMERS
             CLEAR
             RMULT      743           RESET RANDOM NUMBER GENERATOR
             START      250           SIMULATE FOR 250 CUSTOMERS
             END
```

STATEMENT
NUMBER
1
2
3
4
5
6
7
8
9
10
11
12
13
14
15
16
17
18
19
20
21
22
23
24
25
26
27
28
29
30
31
32
33
34
35
36
37
38
39
40

BLOCK COUNTS
BLOCK CURRENT	TOTAL	BLOCK CURRENT	TOTAL	BLOCK CURRENT	TOTAL
1 0	251				
2 1	251				
3 0	250				
4 0	250				
5 0	250				
6 0	250				
7 0	250				
8 0	250				

```
****************************
*                          *
*        FACILITIES        *
*                          *
****************************
```

FACILITY	NUMBER ENTRIES	AVERAGE TIME/TRAN	—AVERAGE UTILIZATION DURING— TOTAL TIME	AVAIL. TIME	UNAVAIL. TIME	CURRENT STATUS	PERCENT AVAILABILITY	TRANSACTION NUMBER SEIZING PREEMPTING
WINDO	250	1.432	.620				100.0	

```
************************************
*                                  *
*             QUEUES               *
*                                  *
************************************
```

QUEUE	MAXIMUM CONTENTS	AVERAGE CONTENTS	TOTAL ENTRIES	ZERO ENTRIES	PERCENT ZEROS	AVERAGE TIME/TRANS	$AVERAGE TIME/TRANS	TABLE NUMBER	CURRENT CONTENTS
WINDO	9	1.284	250	105	41.9	2.963	5.110		

$AVERAGE TIME/TRANS = AVERAGE TIME/TRANS EXCLUDING ZERO ENTRIES

```
CLEAR
RMULT    31
START    25C
```

RELATIVE CLOCK   645   ABSOLUTE CLOCK   645

BLOCK COUNTS
BLOCK CURRENT	TOTAL	BLOCK CURRENT	TOTAL	BLOCK CURRENT	TOTAL
1 0	252				
2 1	252				
3 1	251				
4 0	250				
5 0	250				
6 0	250				
7 0	250				
8 0	250				

```
                              *************************
                              *                       *
                              *       FACILITIES       *
                              *                       *
                              *************************

                                              -AVERAGE  UTILIZATION  DURING-
FACILITY   NUMBER   AVERAGE   TOTAL    AVAIL.  UNAVAIL.  CURRENT   PERCENT       TRANSACTION NUMBER
           ENTRIES  TIME/TRAN  TIME     TIME    TIME      STATUS    AVAILABILITY  SEIZING  PREEMPTING
WINDO      250      1.540      .596                                 100.0


                              *************************
                              *                       *
                              *        QUEUES          *
                              *                       *
                              *************************

QUEUE    MAXIMUM   AVERAGE   TOTAL    ZERO      PERCENT   AVERAGE     $AVERAGE     TABLE    CURRENT
         CONTENTS  CONTENTS  ENTRIES  ENTRIES   ZEROS     TIME/TRANS  TIME/TRANS   NUMBER   CONTENTS
WINDO    11        1.243     251      95        37.8      3.195       5.141                 1
$AVERAGE TIME/TRANS = AVERAGE TIME/TRANS EXCLUDING ZERO ENTRIES
         CLEAR
         RMULT     743
         START     250


                   581 ABSOLUTE CLOCK          581
RELATIVE CLOCK
BLOCK COUNTS
BLOCK CURRENT   TOTAL   BLOCK CURRENT   TOTAL   BLOCK CURRENT   TOTAL
   1      0      250
   2      0      250
   3      0      250
   4      0      250
   5      0      250
   6      0      250
   7      0      250
   8      0      250
```

```
*********************
*                   *
*    FACILITIES     *
*                   *
*********************

                                          -AVERAGE UTILIZATION DURING-
          NUMBER    AVERAGE      TOTAL     AVAIL.    INAVAIL.    CURRENT      PERCENT        TRANSACTION NUMBER
FACILITY  ENTRIES   TIME/TRAN    TIME      TIME      TIME        STATUS       AVAILABILITY   SEIZING   PREEMPTING
WINDO     25C       1.424        .612                                                       100.0


*********************************
*                               *
*           QUEUES              *
*                               *
*********************************

          MAXIMUM   AVERAGE      TOTAL     ZERO      PERCENT     AVERAGE      $AVERAGE       TABLE     CURRENT
QUEUE     CONTENTS  CONTENTS     ENTRIES   ENTRIES   ZEROS       TIME/TRANS   TIME/TRANS     NUMBER    CONTENTS
WINDO     10        1.444        250       116       46.3        3.355        6.261
$AVERAGE TIME/TRANS = AVERAGE TIME/TRANS EXCLUDING ZERO ENTRIES
   END

                        ***** TOTAL RUN TIME (INCLUDING ASSEMBLY) = .05 MINUTES *****
```

EXAMPLE 3.8

Although the distributions used for customer arrivals and processing in this and the previous example have the same means, they result in different behavior by the models. Using the exponential distribution, the customers arrive more rapidly and required less processing time. In Example 3.7 an average of 751 minutes was required to process 250 customers, each of whom used an average of 2.017 minutes of the teller's time. In the current model with the exponential distribution, the corresponding average values are 601 minutes for all customers and 1.465 minutes per customer at the window. The effect of the faster arrivals is not completely balanced by the faster processing, and longer queue length is observed. The increase is from an average of .226 customer with the uniform distributions to 1.324 using the exponential arrival and processing rates.

The differences in the results of Examples 3.7 and 3.8 point out the importance of using the random distribution that most closely describes the physical system being modeled. This subject is discussed in detail in Chapters 5 and 6.

3.12 DECISIONS

The processor units of computers are capable of three types of operations—computations, decisions, and transfer of control. Thus far, only computational GPSS statements have been discussed. In this section the decision and transfer control operations are presented. The reason for grouping these operations together is that in GPSS the result of a decision is either to execute the next sequential statement or to transfer to another portion of the program. Decisions may be made randomly, logically, or arithmetically. Each of the three types of branching utilizes a different GPSS construct.

The random decision feature is one of the options available on the TRANSFER statement. The TRANSFER statement has the following general format:

TRANSFER A,B,C

where

A is the optional mode. There are several options available (see Reference [3.1]). Only the random mode is considered here. In this case, A would be a three-digit number between 0 and 1. If A is not present, an unconditional transfer takes place.

B is a statement label indicating the primary transfer location. The probability of a branch to B is $1-A$.

C is a statement label indicating the secondary transfer location. The probability of transfer to C is A.

The unconditional and random conditional transfer modes are illustrated in the following samples.

TRANSFER .250,LOC1,LOC2

GPSS will generate a random number between 0 and 1 using RN1. If the number is less than .750, the program will transfer to LOC1. If the number is greater than or equal to .750, the program will transfer to LOC2.

TRANSFER ,LOC1

The program transfers to LOC1.

EXAMPLE 3.9

Let us model a bank with two tellers each having their own waiting lines. Assume that customers select the teller based upon personal preference only, with 55% choosing the first teller.

Selection of the tellers by personal preference produces a considerable imbalance in waiting lines, as shown by the queuing statistics. The first teller must work harder, who is busy 95.4% of the time compared to 75.8% for the second teller.

Logical branching is accomplished in GPSS using the GATE statement, which permits the testing of conditions. The GATE statement provides a mechanism for testing the status of facilities and storages as well as user-specified conditions. The status of user-defined conditions is maintained by a set of binary variables, known as logic switches, that are operated upon by LOGIC statements.

Since GATE statements may utilize logic switches, the LOGIC statement is explained first. The LOGIC statement specifies the logic switch to be operated upon and the type of operation to be performed. The format of LOGIC is as follows:

LOGIC X A

where

X is the operation; either S for set to 1, R for reset to 0, or I for invert; that is, change value from 0 to 1 or vice versa

A is the logic switch identifier

Strictly speaking, the X field is not an argument but rather a qualifier of the LOGIC statement. Note that X and A are separated by blanks rather than commas as with the case of arguments. The GATE statement also makes use of a qualifier. Some sample LOGIC statements follow.

LOGIC S EMPTY

The logic switch labeled EMPTY is set to 1.

LOGIC R EMPTY

The logic switch labeled EMPTY is set to 0.

LOGIC I EMPTY

The value of the logic switch labeled EMPTY is inverted.

```
BLOCK                                                                                          STATEMENT
NUMBER                                                                                          NUMBER

        *LOC   OPERATION  A,B,C,D,E,F,G,H,I        COMMENTS                                        1
        ***************************************************************                           2
        *     PROGRAM TO SIMULATE A BANK WITH TWO TELLERS                                          3
        *     WITH SEPARATE WAITING LINES.  55% OF THE                                             4
        *     CUSTOMERS SELECT FIRST TELLER                                                        5
        *                                                                                          6
        *     PARAMETERS                                                                           7
        *                                                                                          8
        *        CUSTOMER ARRIVALS - 2 MINUTES, EXPONENTIALLY DISTRIBUTED                          9
        *        PROCESSING RATES - 3 MINUTES , EXPONENTIALLY DISTRIBUTED                         10
        *        TERMINATION CONDITION - 8 HOURS                                                  11
        *                                                                                         12
        *                                                                                         13
        ***************************************************************                          14
        *                                                                                         15
        *                                                                                         16
        *     EXPONENTIAL FUNCTION                                                                17
        *                                                                                         18
        EXPO  FUNCTION  RN2,C24                                                                   19
        .0000,.000/.1000,.104/.2000,.222/.3000,.355/.4000,.509/.5000,.690/                       20
        .6000,.915/.7000,1.20/.7500,1.38/.8000,1.60/.8400,1.83/.8800,2.12/                       21
        .9000,2.30/.9200,2.52/.9400,2.81/.9500,3.20/.9700,3.50/                                  22
        .9800,3.90/.9900,4.60/.9950,5.30/.9980,6.20/.9990,7.00/.9997,8.00/                       23
        *                                                                                         24
        ***************************************************************                          25
              SIMULATE                                                                           26
    1         GENERATE   2,FN$EXPO           CUSTOMER ARRIVES                                     27
    2         TRANSFER   .450,FIRST,SECON    CUSTOMER SELECTS A TELLER                           28
    3   FIRST QUEUE      TELR1               CUSTOMER WAITS FOR FIRST TELLER                     29
    4         SEIZE      TELR1               CUSTOMER REACHES FIRST TELLER                       30
    5         DEPART     TELR1               REMOVE CUSTOMER FROM WAITING LINE1                  31
    6         ADVANCE    3,FN$EXPO           TRANSACTION IS PROCESSED                            32
    7         RELEASE    TELR1               CUSTOMER LEAVES TELLER                              33
    8         TERMINATE  0                                                                       34
    9   SECON QUEUE      TELR2               CUSTOMER WAITS FOR SECOND TELLER                    35
    10        SEIZE      TELR2               CUSTOMER REACHES SECOND TELLER                      36
    11        DEPART     TELR2               REMOVE CUSTOMER FROM WAITING LINE2                  37
    12        ADVANCE    3,FN$EXPO           TRANSACTION IS PROCESSED                            38
    13        RELEASE    TELR2               CUSTOMER LEAVES SECOND TELLER                       39
    14        TERMINATE  0
```

```
         *
         *****************************
         * TIMING SECTION
         *
   15          GENERATE   480
   16          TERMINATE  1
         *
         *****************************
         *
               START   1
               END
```

40
41
42
43
44
45
46
47
48
49
50

					BLOCK CURRENT	TOTAL

RELATIVE CLOCK
BLOCK COUNTS

BLOCK	CURRENT	TOTAL		480 ABSOLUTE CLOCK			480
				BLOCK	CURRENT	TOTAL	
1	0	336		11	0	150	
2	0	336		12	1	150	
3	21	185		13	0	149	
4	0	164		14	0	149	
5	1	164		15	0	1	
6	1	163		16	0	1	
7	0	163					
8	0	151					
9	1	151					
10	0	150					

```
*****************************
*                           *
*        FACILITIES         *
*                           *
*****************************

                                      -AVERAGE  UTILIZATION DURING-
              NUMBER   AVERAGE   TOTAL   AVAIL.  UNAVAIL.  CURRENT   PERCENT      TRANSACTION NUMBER
FACILITY      ENTRIES  TIME/TRAN  TIME    TIME     TIME    STATUS   AVAILABILITY  SEIZING  PREEMPTING
  TELR1        164      2.793    .954                                   100.0       13
  TELR2        15C      2.427    .758                                   100.0       14


*****************************
*                           *
*          QUEUES           *
*                           *
*****************************

           MAXIMUM   AVERAGE   TOTAL    ZERO    PERCENT   AVERAGE     $AVERAGE    TABLE   CURRENT
QUEUE      CONTENTS  CONTENTS  ENTRIES  ENTRIES  ZEROS   TIME/TRANS  TIME/TRANS  NUMBER  CONTENTS
  TELR1       28     13.643     185      11      5.9      35.399      37.637              21
  TELR2       14      2.370     151      35     23.1       7.536       9.810               1
$AVERAGE TIME/TRANS = AVERAGE TIME/TRANS EXCLUDING ZERO ENTRIES
  END

            ***** TOTAL RUN TIME (INCLUDING ASSEMBLY) = .03 MINUTES *****
```

If these three sample statements were executed in sequence, the value of EMPTY after the last statement would be 1. In GPSS, the system initializes all logic switches to 0.

The GATE statement tests a condition and then optionally may cause a branch to a new program location if the test has failed. If the optional branch is not included, entities are held at the GATE statement until the condition is satisfied. The format for GATE is given by the following:

GATE X A,B

where

X is a qualifier indicating the type of the condition

A is an argument indicating the specific entity being tested

B is an optional argument indicating the statement to which control is transferred if the condition is not satisfied

The GPSS conditions and their corresponding mnemonics are listed in Table 3.2. The sample statements given below illustrate the application of the GATE statement.

GATE LS EMPTY

An entity executing this statement will immediately pass to the next statement if the logic switch EMPTY has a value of 1. If EMPTY is 0, the entity will remain at this statement.

GATE LR EMPTY,ALTER

An entity executing this statement will immediately pass to the next statement if the logic switch EMPTY has a value of 0. If EMPTY is 1, the entity will be passed to the statement labeled ALTER.

Table 3.2 Qualifiers for GATE Statement _

Qualifier	Meaning
LS	Logic Switch Set
LR	Logic Switch Reset
U	Facility in Use
NU	Facility Not in Use
SF	Storage Full
SNF	Storage Not Full
SE	Storage Empty
SNE	Storage Not Empty

EXAMPLE 3.10

Let us assume that the drive-in window teller in Example 3.8 has been granted coffee break and lunch privileges. Two hours after opening and after lunch, the teller closes the window for 10 minutes. After 4 hours, the teller takes 30 minutes for lunch. During the time the window is closed, the cars in line must continue to wait. The teller finishes processing the current customer before closing the window. In the program shown, a logic switch is used to indicate whether the window is open or closed, and the status of the window is tested using a gate. In this model the drive-in window is open for 8 hours, including breaks.

The use of logic switches produces a listing of those switches set at completion of the program. The queuing statistics show an average waiting line of 2.582 customers. However, the maximum line length was 15, which was most likely achieved at lunch hour.

The final type of GPSS branching, arithmetic, is implemented using the TEST statement that permits comparisons between the values of two SNAs. The branching features of TEST are identical to those of GATE.

The format of TEST is

    TEST X A,B,C

where

X is a qualifier indicating the comparison operation (see Table 3.3)

A and B are SNAs whose values are compared using the operator indicated by X

C is an optional label indicating the location to which the entity will transfer if the result of the comparison is false; if the comparison fails and C is not present, the entity remains at the TEST statement

Table 3.3 Qualifiers for TEST Statement

Qualifier	Meaning
G	$A > B$
GE	$A \geq B$
L	$A < B$
LE	$A \leq B$
E	$A = B$
NE	$A \neq B$

The sample TEST statements illustrate the various forms of operations possible using TEST.

    TEST G V$PEOPL,S$ROOM

If the value of the variable PEOPL is greater than the number of entries in the storage ROOM, the entity moves to the next statement. Otherwise the entity will remain at the TEST statement until the value of PEOPL is greater than the number of entries in ROOM.

    TEST GE FN$ITEMS,10,EXPRS

If the value of the function ITEMS is greater than or equal to 10, the entity passes to the next statement. If the value of ITEMS is less than 10, the entity transfers to the statement labeled EXPRS.

The next example illustrates the use of the TEST statement.

BLOCK
NUMBER

STATEMENT
NUMBER

```
*LOC   OPERATION  A,B,C,D,E,F,G,H,I          COMMENTS                              1
********************************************************************               2
*    PROGRAM TO SIMULATE A DRIVE-IN WINDOW AT A BANK                               3
*    AFTER 4 HOURS , TELLER CLOSES WINDOW FOR A 30 MINUTE LUNCH                    4
*    TWO HOURS AFTER THE START OF WORK AND LUNCH , THE                             5
*    TELLER TAKES A 10 MINUTE COFFEE BREAK.                                        6
*    DURING BREAKS , CARS REMAIN IN THE WAITING LINE                               7
*                                                                                  8
*    PARAMETERS                                                                    9
*                                                                                 10
*    ARRIVALS - 3 MINUTES , EXPONENTIALLY DISTRIBUTED                             11
*    PROCESSING - 2 MINUTES , EXPONENTIALLY DISTRIBUTED                           12
*    TERMINATION CONDITION - 8 HOURS                                              13
*                                                                                 14
********************************************************************              15
********************************************************************              16
*                                                                                 17
*    EXPONENTIAL FUNCTION                                                         18
*                                                                                 19
EXPO  FUNCTION  RN2,C24                                                           20
.0000,.000/.1000,.104/.2000,.222/.3000,.355/.4000,.509/.5000,.690/               21
.6000,.915/.7000,1.2/.7500,1.38/.8000,1.60/.8400,1.83/.8800,2.12/                22
.9000,2.30/.9200,2.52/.9400,2.81/.9500,2.99/.9600,3.20/.9700,3.50/               23
.9800,3.90/.9900,4.60/.9950,5.30/.9980,6.20/.9990,7.00/.9997,8.00/               24
*                                                                                 25
********************************************************************              26
*                                                                                 27
SIMULATE                                                                          28
      GENERATE    3,FN$EXPO      CUSTOMERS ARRIVE                                  29
      ADVANCE     1             CUSTOMERS DRIVE TO WINDOW                          30
      QUEUE       WINDO         CUSTOMER WAITS FOR WINDOW                          31
      GATE LS     WINDO         CHECK IF WINDOW IS OPEN                            32
      SEIZE       WINDO         CUSTOMER REACHES WINDOW                            33
      DEPART      WINDO         REMOVE CUSTOMER FROM QUEUE                         34
      ADVANCE     2,FN$EXPO     TRANSACTION IS PROCESSED                          35
      RELEASE     WINDO         CUSTOMER DEPARTS                                   36
      TERMINATE   0
```

1
2
3
4
5
6
7
8
9

```
*****************************************************************
*
* TIMING SECTION
*
*****************************************************************

10  GENERATE   ,,,1       CREATE A TELLER TRANSACTION
11  LOGICS     WINDO      OPEN WINDOW
12  ADVANCE    120        WORK FOR 2 HOURS
13  LOGICR     WINDO      CLOSE WINDOW
14  ADVANCE    10         TAKE A 10 MINUTE BREAK
15  LOGICS     WINDO      OPEN WINDOW
16  ADVANCE    110        WORK UNTIL LUNCH
17  LOGICR     WINDO      CLOSE WINDOW
18  ADVANCE    30         TAKE 30 MINUTES FOR LUNCH
19  LOGICS     WINDO      OPEN WINDOW
20  ADVANCE    120        WORK FOR 2 HOURS
21  LOGICR     WINDO      CLOSE WINDOW
22  ADVANCE    10         10 MINUTE BREAK
23  LOGICS     WINDO      OPEN WINDOW
24  ADVANCE    80         WORK FOR REMAINDER OF THE DAY
25  TERMINATE  1          GO HOME

*****************************************************************
*
* CONTROL SECTION
*
*****************************************************************

    START   1                    SIMULATE FOR 8 HOURS
    END
```

RELATIVE CLOCK 481   ABSOLUTE CLOCK 481
BLOCK COUNTS

BLOCK	CURRENT	TOTAL	BLOCK	CURRENT	TOTAL	BLOCK	CURRENT	TOTAL
1	0	194	11	0	1	21	0	1
2	2	194	12	0	1	22	0	1
3	0	192	13	0	1	23	0	1
4	0	192	14	0	1	24	0	1
5	0	192	15	0	1	25	0	1
6	0	192	16	0	1			
7	1	192	17	0	1			
8	0	191	18	0	1			
9	0	191	19	0	1			
10	0	1	20	0	1			

```
                              ******************
                              *                *
                              *   FACILITIES   *
                              *                *
                              ******************

                          -AVERAGE UTILIZATION DURING-
          NUMBER   AVERAGE    TOTAL  AVAIL.  UNAVAIL.  CURRENT   PERCENT      TRANSACTION NUMBER
FACILITY  ENTRIES  TIME/TRAN  TIME   TIME    TIME      STATUS    AVAILABILITY  SEIZING PREEMPTING
WINCO     192      1.469      .586                               100.0        18


                              ******************
                              *                *
                              *     QUEUES     *
                              *                *
                              ******************

       MAXIMUM   AVERAGE   TOTAL    ZERO     PERCENT  AVERAGE    $AVERAGE    TABLE   CURRENT
QUEUE  CONTENTS  CONTENTS  ENTRIES  ENTRIES  ZEROS    TIME/TRANS TIME/TRANS  NUMBER  CONTENTS
WINDO  15        2.582     192      61       31.7     6.468      9.480
$AVERAGE TIME/TRANS = AVERAGE TIME/TRANS EXCLUDING ZERO ENTRIES


                              ********************
                              *                  *
                              *   LOGIC SWITCHES  *
                              *                  *
                              ********************

LOGIC SWITCH - SET (CN) STATUS
NUMBER  NUMBER  NUMBER  NUMBER  NUMBER  NUMBER  NUMBER  NUMBER  NUMBER  NUMBER  NUMBER  NUMBER
WINDO   END

***** TOTAL RUN TIME (INCLUDING ASSEMBLY) = .03 MINUTES *****
```

EXAMPLE 3.11

In Example 3.9 the tellers were selected using a 55-45 preference ratio. In that example the line for the preferred teller grew much more rapidly than the line for the second teller. In a more realistic model, the customers would select the teller with the shorter waiting line. In case of lines of equal length, the customers in our model will choose the teller who is closest to the door.

When the customers select tellers based upon waiting-line length instead of personal preference, the waiting line for the first teller is reduced dramatically. The lines for the second teller show very little change. Overall, the model exhibits a more reasonable behavior than that of Example 3.9. The stochastic nature of the model is brought to light by the change in the number of customers arriving, from 336 in Example 3.9 to 315 in the present model. Since the function EXPO is referenced for transaction processing as well as customer arrivals, the sequence of values used for interarrival time is different for the two models. The amount of the discrepancies between the two arrival values can be reduced by several repetitions of the simulation experiment employing different random number needs.

3.13 PRIORITIES

As described in Section 3.2, the function of the E argument of the GENERATE statement is to set the initial priority of the entity. Every GPSS entity has a priority field associated with it. The value of the priority field is in the range of 0 to 127 and can be set and modified by the program. The priority field is used in the selection of entities to enter a storage or facility. GPSS selects the entity with the highest priority for entrance into a facility. In case of equal priorities, the entity waiting the longest is selected. In the case of storages, GPSS selects the highest-priority entity that will fit into the storage.

Priorities are set using the PRIORITY statement, which has the following format:

PRIORITY A

where A is an SNA indicating the value to be assigned to the priority field of the entity.

The sample statement shown below illustrates the use of the PRIORITY statement.

PRIORITY FN$PRIOR

When an entity executes this statement, a value is obtained from the function PRIOR and stored in the entity's priority field.

The next example illustrates the use of the PRIORITY statement.

```
BLOCK                                                                              STATEMENT
NUMBER  *LOC   OPERATION A,B,C,D,E,F,G,H,I         COMMENTS                         NUMBER
        **************************************************************************    1
        *    PROGRAM TO SIMULATE A BANK WITH TWO TELLERS                              2
        *    WITH SEPARATE WAITING LINES.  CUSTOMERS SELECT SHORTEST LINE.            3
        *    IN CASE OF A TIE , CUSTOMERS SELECT FIRST TELLER                         4
        *                                                                             5
        *    PARAMETERS                                                               6
        *                                                                             7
        *    CUSTOMER ARRIVALS - 2 MINUTES, EXPONENTIALLY DISTRIBUTED                 8
        *    PROCESSING RATES - 3 MINUTES , EXPONENTIALLY DISTRIBUTED                 9
        *    TERMINATION CONDITION - 8 HOURS                                         10
        *                                                                            11
        **************************************************************************   12
        *                                                                            13
        **************************************************************************   14
        *                                                                            15
        *    EXPONENTIAL FUNCTION                                                    16
        *                                                                            17
EXPO    FUNCTION  RN2,C24                                                            18
.0000,.000/.1000,.104/.2000,.222/.3000,.355/.4000,.509/.5000,.690/                  19
.6000,.915/.7000,1.20/.7500,1.38/.8000,1.60/.83/.8800,2.12/                         20
.9000,2.30/.9200,2.52/.9400,2.81/.9500,2.99/.9600,3.20/.9700,3.50/                  21
.9800,3.90/.5900,4.60/.9950,5.30/.9980,6.20/.9990,7.00/.9997,8.00/                  22
*                                                                                   23
        **************************************************************************   24
        SIMULATE                                                                    25
   1    GENERATE  2,FN$EXPO            CUSTOMER ARRIVES                              26
   2    TEST LE   Q$TELR1,Q$TELR2,SECON   CUSTOMER SELECTS A TELLER                 27
   3 FIRST QUEUE    TELR1              CUSTOMER WAITS FOR 1ST TELLER                28
   4      SEIZE     TELR1              CUSTOMER REACHES FIRST TELLER                29
   5      DEPART    TELR1              REMOVE CUSTOMER FROM 1ST LINE                30
   6      ADVANCE   3,FN$EXPO          TRANSACTION IS PROCESSED                    31
   7      RELEASE   TELR1              CUSTOMER LEAVES TELLER                      32
   8      TERMINATE 0                                                             33
   9 SECON QUEUE    TELR2              CUSTOMER WAITS FOR 2ND TELLER              34
  10      SEIZE     TELR2              CUSTOMER REACHES SECOND TELLER             35
  11      DEPART    TELR2              REMOVE CUSTOMER FROM 2ND LINE              36
  12      ADVANCE   3,FN$EXPO          TRANSACTION IS PROCESSED                  37
  13      RELEASE   TELR2              CUSTOMER LEAVES SECOND TELLER             38
  14      TERMINATE 0                                                           39
```

```
     *
     *****************************
     * TIMING SECTION
     *
     *****************************
     *
15       GENERATE    480
16       TERMINATE   1
         START       1
         END
```

480 ABSOLUTE CLOCK   480

RELATIVE CLOCK
BLOCK COUNTS

BLOCK	CURRENT	TOTAL	BLOCK	CURRENT	TOTAL	BLOCK	CURRENT	TOTAL	BLOCK	CURRENT	TOTAL
1	0	315	11	0	136						
2	2	315	12	1	136						
3	2	178	13	0	135						
4	0	176	14	0	135						
5	1	176	15	0	1						
6	1	176	16	0	1						
7	0	175									
8	0	175									
9	1	137									
10	0	136									

```
********************
*                  *
*   FACILITIES     *
*                  *
********************

                                   -AVERAGE UTILIZATION DURING-
FACILITY   NUMBER    AVERAGE      TOTAL   AVAIL.  UNAVAIL.  CURRENT   PERCENT        TRANSACTION NUMBER
           ENTRIES   TIME/TRAN    TIME    TIME    TIME      STATUS    AVAILABILITY   SEIZING  PREEMPTING
  TELR1     176      2.511        .920                                100.0            20
  TELR2     136      2.728        .772                                100.0            12


********************
*                  *
*    QUEUES        *
*                  *
********************

QUEUE    MAXIMUM   AVERAGE    TOTAL    ZERO     PERCENT   AVERAGE     $AVERAGE    TABLE    CURRENT
         CONTENTS  CONTENTS   ENTRIES  ENTRIES  ZEROS     TIME/TRANS  TIME/TRANS  NUMBER   CONTENTS
  TELR1    11      2.758       178      31       17.4      7.438        9.006                 2
  TELR2    11      2.506       137      30       21.8      8.781       11.242                 1
$AVERAGE TIME/TRANS = AVERAGE TIME/TRANS EXCLUDING ZERO ENTRIES
  END

          **** TOTAL RUN TIME (INCLUDING ASSEMBLY) = .03 MINUTES ****
```

EXAMPLE 3.12

During the course of a banking day, a bank officer occasionally may have the need to perform a banking transaction with a teller. We will expand the model of Example 3.11 to include this event. In the program, every 45 to 75 minutes a bank officer moves to the front of the first teller's line. To point out the effect of the PRIORITY statement, a special queue is maintained so that statistics on the officer's waiting time can be contrasted with those of the customers.

The introduction of the officer section into the program illustrates a very important GPSS feature, parallel execution of distinct sections of code. Customer activities are modeled by statements 2 through 14, whereas the behavior of the officer is simulated in statements 15 through 24. Entities pass through their respective sections of code in the same simulated time. GPSS can simulate any number of parallel processes in the same program.

Since the officer requires service infrequently, there is not a substantial impact on the teller activity. The only noticeable increase is in the average length of the first teller's waiting line, which increased from 2.758 in Example 3.11 to 3.237. This is due partially to the presence of the officer in this line.

3.14 PARAMETERS

In many models it is desirable to associate some information with each entity, such as time, weight, storage requirements, and so on. GPSS permits this capability by allowing an entity to have parameters. Each parameter is a signed integer, which may be assigned values by the program and whose contents may be referenced as a standard numerical attribute.

Parameters may be designated as full word, half word, byte, or floating point. An entity may have up to 255 parameters of each type. The number of parameters is set in the GENERATE statement. The ASSIGN statement is used to set parameter values. The standard numerical attributes PF, PH, PB, PL are used for full-word, half-word, byte, and floating-point parameters. The attributes PF, PH, and PB indicate integer parameters of various sizes. For example, on a 32-bit computer, a full word is 32 bits, a half word 16 bits, and a byte 8 bits. A floating-point parameter is a real number.

Arguments F through I of the GENERATE statement indicate the number of full-word, half-word, byte, and floating-point parameters. These arguments are optional and may occur in any order. The default is 12 half-word parameters. The maximum value is 255 parameters of each type. The form of the argument is the number of parameters followed by the appropriate SNA. Consider the following samples.

```
BLOCK                                                                                    STATEMENT
NUMBER                                                                                    NUMBER

       *LOC  OPERATION  A,B,C,D,E,F,G,H,I      COMMENTS                                      1
       ****************************************************************                      2
       *     PRCGRAM TC SIMULATE A BANK WITH TWO TELLERS                                     3
       *  WITH SEPARATE WAITING LINES.  CUSTOMERS SELECT THE SHORTEST LINE.                  4
       *  CUSTOMERS SELECT FIRST TELLER IN CASE OF A TIE.                                    5
       *     A BANK CFFICER ARRIVES WITH A TRANSACTION AND MOVES TO THE FRONT                6
       *  OF THE FIRST TELLER'S LINE.                                                        7
       *                                                                                     8
       *     PARAMETERS                                                                      9
       *                                                                                    10
       *     CUSTCMER ARRIVALS - 2 MINUTES, EXPONENTIALLY DISTRIBUTED                        11
       *     OFFICER ARRIVALS - 45 TO 75 MINUTES , UNIFORMLY DISTRIBUTED                     12
       *     PROCESSING RATES - 3 MINUTES , EXPONENTIALLY DISTRIBUTED                        13
       *     TERMINATION CCNDITION - 8 HOURS                                                 14
       ****************************************************************                      15
       *                                                                                    16
       *     EXPONENTIAL FUNCTION                                                            17
       *                                                                                    18
       EXPO  FUNCTICN   RN2,C24                                                              19
       .0000,.000/.1000,.104/.2000,.222/.3000,.355/.4000,.509/.500C,.690/                   20
       .6000,.915/.7000,1.20/.7500,1.38/.8000,1.60/.8400,1.83/.8800,2.12/                   21
       .9000,2.30/.9200,2.52/.9400,2.81/.9500,2.99/.9600,3.20/.9700,3.50/                   22
       .9800,3.90/.9900,4.60/.9950,5.30/.9980,6.20/.9990,7.00/.9997,8.00/                    23
       *                                                                                    24
       ****************************************************************                      25
       *                                                                                    26
       *     CUSTOMER SECTION                                                                27
       *                                                                                    28
       ****************************************************************                      29
                                                                                            30
             SIMULATE                                                                        31
             GENERATE    2,FN$EXPO              CUSTOMER ARRIVES                             32
             TEST LE     QSTELR1,QSTELR2,SECON  CUSTOMER SELECTS A TELLER                    33
       FIRST QUEUE       TELR1                  CUSTOMER WAITS FOR 1ST TELLER               34
             SEIZE       TELR1                  CUSTOMER REACHES FIRST TELLER               35
             DEPART      TELR1                  REMOVE CUSTOMER FROM 1ST LINE               36
             ADVANCE     3,FN$EXPO              TRANSACTION IS PROCESSED                    37
             RELEASE     TELR1                  CUSTOMER LEAVES TELLER                      38
             TERMINATE   0                                                                   39
       SECON QUEUE       TELR2                  CUSTOMER WAITS FOR 2ND TELLER               40
             SEIZE       TELR2                  CUSTOMER REACHES 2ND TELLER                 41
             DEPART      TELR2                  REMOVE CUSTOMER FRCM 2ND LINE               42
             ADVANCE     3,FN$EXPO              TRANSACTION IS PROCESSED                    43
             RELEASE     TELR2                  CUSTOMER LEAVES SECOND TELLER               44
             TERMINATE   0                                                                   45
                                                                                            46
```

```
BLOCK
NUMBER
  1
  2
  3
  4
  5
  6
  7
  8
  9
 10
 11
 12
 13
 14
```

```
*
******************************
*
*      OFFICER SECTION
*
******************************
*
15        GENERATE    60,15       OFFICER ARRIVES
16        PRIORITY    1           ASSIGN OFFICER PRIORITY
17        QUEUE       OFICR       ENTER SPECIAL OFFICER QUEUE
18        QUEUE       TELR1       OFFICER WAITS FOR FIRST TELLER
19        SEIZE       TELR1       OFFICER REACHES FIRST TELLER
20        DEPART      TELR1       REMOVE OFFICER FROM LINE
21        DEPART      OFICR       LEAVE SPECIAL OFFICER QUEUE
22        ADVANCE     3,FN$EXPO   TRANSACTION IS PROCESSED
23        RELEASE     TELR1       OFFICER LEAVES FIRST TELLER
24        TERMINATE   0
*
*********************************
*
* TIMING SECTION
*
*********************************
*
25        GENERATE    480
26        TERMINATE   1
          START       1
          END
```

RELATIVE CLOCK   480   ABSOLUTE CLOCK   480
BLOCK COUNTS

BLOCK	CURRENT	TOTAL	BLOCK	CURRENT	TOTAL	BLOCK	CURRENT	TOTAL
1	0	340	11	0	160	21	0	8
2	0	340	12	1	160	22	1	8
3	7	175	13	0	159	23	0	7
4	0	168	14	0	159	24	0	7
5	0	168	15	0	8	25	0	1
6	0	168	16	0	8	26	0	1
7	0	168	17	0	8			
8	0	168	18	0	8			
9	5	165	19	0	8			
10	0	160	20	0	8			

```
*******************************
*                             *
*         FACILITIES          *
*                             *
*******************************
```

			-AVERAGE	UTILIZATION DURING-			TRANSACTION NUMBER	
	NUMBER	AVERAGE	TOTAL	AVAIL.	UNAVAIL.	CURRENT	PERCENT	
FACILITY	ENTRIES	TIME/TRAN	TIME	TIME	TIME	STATUS	AVAILABILITY	SEIZING	PREEMPTING
TELR1	176	2.562	.939				100.0	16	18
TELR2	160	2.431	.810				100.0	18	

```
*******************************
*                             *
*           QUEUES            *
*                             *
*******************************
```

QUEUE	MAXIMUM CONTENTS	AVERAGE CONTENTS	TOTAL ENTRIES	ZERO ENTRIES	PERCENT ZEROS	AVERAGE TIME/TRANS	$AVERAGE TIME/TRANS	TABLE NUMBER	CURRENT CONTENTS
TELR1	12	3.237	183	27	14.7	8.491	9.961		7
TELR2	11	2.681	165	39	23.6	7.799	10.214		5
OFICR	1	.074	8	3	37.5	4.500	7.199		

$AVERAGE TIME/TRANS = AVERAGE TIME/TRANS EXCLUDING ZERO ENTRIES
END

***** TOTAL RUN TIME (INCLUDING ASSEMBLY) = .04 MINUTES *****

GENERATE 5

An entity is generated every 5 time units with 12 half-word parameters.

GENERATE 5,,,,,6PF

An entity is generated every 5 time units with 6 full-word parameters and 12 half-word parameters.

GENERATE 5,,,,,3PH,9PF

An entity is generated every 5 time units with 3 half-word and 9 floating-point parameters.

GENERATE 5,,,,,1PF,2PH,3PB,4PL

An entity is generated every 5 time units with 1 full-word, 2 half-word, 3 byte, and 4 floating-point parameters.

The ASSIGN statement actually has two formats, depending on whether a function is utilized to compute the value of the parameter. If no function is present, then the first format, as shown below, is applicable:

ASSIGN A,B,C

where

A is the number of the parameter to receive a value

B is an SNA indicating the value to be assigned to the parameter designated in argument A

C is either PF, PH, PB, or PL for a full-word, half-word, byte, or floating-point parameter, respectively

For example, in the statement ASSIGN 4,V$SIZE,PF the variable SIZE is evaluated, and its value is stored in full-word parameter 4 of the entity entering the block.

EXAMPLE 3.13

In order to illustrate the use of parameters, the bank teller model of the previous example is enhanced to allow each customer to have from 1 to 5 banking transactions per customer. The number of transactions is stored in a parameter field. The time required by the teller to process a customer is thus a function of the number of banking transactions.

When a function is used, the following ASSIGN format is appropriate:

ASSIGN A,B,C,D

where

A is the parameter number as before

B is the mean of the function

C is the *function number*, not a reference to the function but the actual number of the function

D is the parameter type as before

The first sample shown below indicates the proper usage of ASSIGN with a function. The second sample is *not equivalent* to the first.

ASSIGN 4,12,1,PL

```
BLOCK
NUMBER

*LOC  OPERATION  A,B,C,D,E,F,G,H,I      COMMENTS                              STATEMENT
*****************************************************************              NUMBER
*      PROGRAM TO SIMULATE A BANK WITH TWO TELLERS                            1
*      WITH SEPARATE WAITING LINES.  CUSTOMERS SELECT THE SHORTEST LINE.      2
*      CUSTOMERS SELECT FIRST TELLER IN CASE OF A TIE.                        3
*      A BANK OFFICER ARRIVES WITH A TRANSACTION AND MOVES TO THE FRONT       4
*      OF THE FIRST TELLER'S LINE.                                            5
*                                                                            6
*      PARAMETERS                                                            7
*                                                                            8
*                                                                            9
*      NUMBER OF TRANSACTIONS - 1 TO 5 PER CUSTOMER , AS SPECIFIED BY        10
*              TRANS FUNCTION.  1 TRANSACTION PER OFFICER.                   11
*      CUSTOMER ARRIVALS - 2 MINUTES, EXPONENTIALLY DISTRIBUTED              12
*      OFFICER ARRIVALS - 45 TO 75 MINUTES , UNIFORMLY DISTRIBUTED           13
*      PROCESSING RATE -  1.2 MINUTES PER TRANSACTION                        14
*      TERMINATION CONDITION - 8 HOURS                                       15
*                                                                            16
*****************************************************************            17
*                                                                            18
*      EXPONENTIAL FUNCTION                                                  19
*                                                                            20
EXPO   FUNCTION   RN2,C24                                                    21
.0000,.000/.1000,.104/.2000,.222/.3000,.355/.4000,.509/.5000,.690/          22
.6000,.915/.7000,1.20/.7500,1.38/.8000,1.60/.8400,1.83/.8800,2.12/          23
.9000,2.30/.9200,2.52/.9400,2.81/.9500,2.99/.9600,3.20/.9700,3.50/          24
.9800,3.90/.9900,4.60/.9950,5.30/.9980,6.20/.9990,7.00/.9997,8.00/          25
*                                                                            26
*      TRANSACTION FUNCTION                                                  27
*                                                                            28
TRANS  FUNCTION   RN3,D5                                                     29
.20,1/.45,2/.75,3/.90,4/1.0,5                                                30
*                                                                            31
*      PROCESSING TIME VARIABLE                                             32
*                                                                            33
PROCS  FVARIABLE   1.2*PH1                                                   34
*                                                                            35
*****************************************************************            36
*                                                                            37
*      CUSTOMER SECTION                                                      38
*                                                                            39
*****************************************************************            40
*                                                                            41
       SIMULATE                                                              42
1      GENERATE   2,FN$EXPO              CUSTOMER ARRIVES                     43
2      ASSIGN     1,FN$TRANS,PH          SET NUMBER OF TRANSACTIONS           44
                                                                             45
```

```
 3              TEST LE    QSTELR1,QSTELR2,SECON   CUSTOMER SELECTS A TELLER
 4        FIRST QUEUE      TELR1                   CUSTOMER WAITS FOR 1ST TELLER
 5              SEIZE      TELR1                   CUSTOMER REACHES 1ST TELLER
 6              DEPART     TELR1                   REMOVE CUSTOMER FROM 1ST LINE
 7              ADVANCE    V$PROCS                 TRANSACTIONS ARE PROCESSED
 8              RELEASE    TELR1                   CUSTOMER LEAVES TELLER
 9              TERMINATE  0
10        SECON QUEUE      TELR2                   CUSTOMER WAITS FOR 2ND TELLER
11              SEIZE      TELR2                   CUSTOMER REACHES 2ND TELLER
12              DEPART     TELR2                   REMOVE CUSTOMER FROM 2ND LINE
13              ADVANCE    V$PROCS                 TRANSACTIONS ARE PROCESSED
14              RELEASE    TELR2                   CUSTOMER LEAVES 2ND TELLER
15              TERMINATE  0
          *
          *******************************
          *
          *     OFFICER SECTION
          *
          *******************************
          *
16              GENERATE   60,15                   OFFICER ARRIVES
17              PRIORITY   1                        ASSIGN OFFICER PRIORITY
18              ASSIGN     1,1,PH                   OFFICER HAS 1 TRANSACTION
19              QUEUE      OFICR                    ENTER SPECIAL OFFICER QUEUE
20              QUEUE      TELR1                    OFFICER WAITS FOR FIRST TELLER
21              SEIZE      TELR1                    OFFICER REACHES FIRST TELLER
22              DEPART     TELR1                    REMOVE OFFICER FROM LINE
23              DEPART     OFICR                    LEAVE SPECIAL OFFICER QUEUE
24              ADVANCE    3,FN$EXPO                TRANSACTION IS PROCESSED
25              RELEASE    TELR1                    OFFICER LEAVES FIRST TELLER
26              TERMINATE  0
          *
          ****************************************
          *
          *     TIMING SECTION
          *
          ****************************************
          *
27              GENERATE   480
28              TERMINATE  1
                START      1
                END
```

46
47
48
49
50
51
52
53
54
55
56
57
58
59
60
61
62
63
64
65
66
67
68
69
70
71
72
73
74
75
76
77
78
79
80
81
82
83
84
85
86
87

RELATIVE CLOCK   480   ABSOLUTE CLOCK   480

BLOCK COUNTS

BLOCK	CURRENT	TOTAL	BLOCK	CURRENT	TOTAL	BLOCK	CURRENT	TOTAL
1	0	315	11	0	137	21	0	8
2	0	315	12	0	137	22	0	8
3	0	315	13	1	137	23	0	8
4	8	171	14	0	136	24	1	8
5	0	163	15	0	136	25	0	7
6	0	163	16	0	8	26	0	7
7	0	163	17	0	8	27	0	1
8	0	163	18	0	8	28	0	1
9	0	163	19	0	8			
10	7	144	20	0	8			

```
****************************************
*                                      *
*              FACILITIES              *
*                                      *
****************************************
```

FACILITY	NUMBER ENTRIES	AVERAGE TIME/TRAN	—AVERAGE TOTAL TIME	UTILIZATION DURING— AVAIL. TIME	UNAVAIL. TIME	CURRENT STATUS	PERCENT AVAILABILITY	TRANSACTION NUMBER SEIZING	PREEMPTING
TELR1	171	2.550	.908				100.0	6	
TELR2	137	2.737	.781				100.0	16	

```
****************************************
*                                      *
*                QUEUES                *
*                                      *
****************************************
```

QUEUE	MAXIMUM CONTENTS	AVERAGE CONTENTS	TOTAL ENTRIES	ZERO ENTRIES	PERCENT ZEROS	AVERAGE TIME/TRANS	$AVERAGE TIME/TRANS	TABLE NUMBER	CURRENT CONTENTS
TELR1	8	2.018	179	28	15.6	5.413	6.417		8
TELR2	8	1.658	144	21	14.5	5.527	6.471		7
OFICR	1	.012	8	4	50.0	.750	1.500		

$AVERAGE TIME/TRANS = AVERAGE TIME/TRANS EXCLUDING ZERO ENTRIES
END

***** TOTAL RUN TIME (INCLUDING ASSEMBLY) = .04 MINUTES *****

The entity reaching this statement receives a new value in its fourth floating-point parameter. This value is determined by evaluating FN1, the first user-defined function, and multiplying the result by 12.

The following sample is *not equivalent* even if EXPO is the first user-defined function.

ASSIGN 4,12,FN$EXPO,PL

As in the previous sample, the fourth floating-point parameter of the entity is to receive a new value. However, in this case the function EXPO is evaluated and the result is used as the function number to be evaluated and then multiplied by 12 to obtain the parameter value. Note the extra function evaluation in this sample statement. It is likely that this statement would give an execution time error since the EXPO function may yield a value that does not correspond to the number of a user-defined function.

It is important to be aware of the difference between the first sample, which is correct, and the second sample, which is not, because the correct use of functions with ASSIGN differs from their correct usage in other statements.

In addition to simply assigning a new value to a parameter, the ASSIGN statement can also be utilized to perform an addition or subtraction on the current contents of the parameter. The result of the operation is assigned as the new value of the parameter. The use of this parameter modification feature is indicated by a + or − sign concatenated to the A argument of the ASSIGN statement as shown in the following samples.

ASSIGN 1+,2,PH

Here the half-word parameter 1 is incremented by 2.

ASSIGN 3−,PB5,PB

In this case byte parameter 5 is subtracted from byte parameter 3, and the result is stored in byte parameter 3.

The internal mechanism used by GPSS to select the next entity for entry into a storage is presented in Section 3.7. It was mentioned that the default mechanism can be modified by the programmer. The introduction of parameters makes possible an example showing the standard mechanism and a modification.

EXAMPLE 3.14

A simulation model of a computer system provides a good vehicle for illustrating different approaches to storage manipulation. The first model uses the standard GPSS mechanism: selection of the highest priority entity that will fit. In this example, all entities have equal priorities.

EXAMPLE 3.15

The computer system model of the previous example can be modified to include a different discipline for selecting jobs for entrance into mem-

```
BLOCK
NUMBER                                                                                    STATEMENT
                                                                                          NUMBER
        *LOC   OPERATION  A,B,C,D,E,F,G,H,I          COMMENTS                                 1
        ****************************************************************************         2
        *                                                                                    3
        *               COMPUTER SYSTEM SIMULATION                                           4
        *                                                                                    5
        *                                                                                    6
        *        PARAMETERS                                                                  7
        *                                                                                    8
        *        MEMORY SIZE - 256K (K = 1024 UNITS)                                         9
        *        TIME SLICE - 500 MILLISECS                                                 10
        *        ( THE TIME SLICE IS THE MAXIMUM AMOUNT OF TIME A JOB                       11
        *          HAS CONTROL OF THE CENTRAL PROCESSOR UNIT                                12
        *          BEFORE YIELDING CONTROL TO ANOTHER JOB )                                 13
        *        JOB ARRIVAL RATE - 27 SECS , EXPONENTIALLY DISTRIBUTED                     14
        *        EXECUTION TIME - 30 SECS , EXPONENTIALLY DISTRIBUTED                       15
        *        JOB SIZE - 16K-64K , UNIFORMLY DISTRIBUTED                                 16
        *        OPERATING SYSTEM BEHAVIOR - WHEN JOBS ARRIVE , THEY ARE                    17
        *          LOADED INTO MEMORY USING A SCHEDULING ALGORITHM.  JOBS ARE               18
        *          EXECUTED IN A ROUND-ROBIN MANNER , I.E. GIVEN ONE TIME SLICE             19
        *          AT A TIME UNTIL EXECUTION IS COMPLETE. IF A JOB COMPLETES                20
        *          EXECUTION , A NEW JOB IS LOADED INTO MEMORY.                             21
        *        SCHEDULING POLICY - FIRST FIT                                              22
        *        TERMINATION CONDITION - 1 HOUR                                             23
        *                                                                                   24
        ****************************************************************************        25
        *                                                                                   26
        *               EXPONENTIAL FUNCTION                                                27
        *                                                                                   28
        EXPO   FUNCTION   RN2,C24                                                           29
        .0000,.000/.1000,.104/.2000,.222/.3000,.355/.4000,.509/.5000,.690/                 30
        .6000,.915/.7000,1.20/.7500,1.38/.8000,1.60/.84C0,1.83/.8800,2.12/                 31
        .9000,2.30/.9200,2.52/.9400,2.81/.9500,2.99/.9600,3.20/.9700,3.50/                 32
        .9800,3.90/.9900,4.60/.9950,5.30/.9980,6.20/.9990,7.00/.9997,8.00/                 33
        *                                                                                   34
        *               UNIFORM DISTRIBUTION                                                35
        *                                                                                   36
        UNI    VARIABLE   16+48*RN4/1000                                                    37
        *                                                                                   38
        ****************************************************************************        39
        *                                                                                   40
        *               STORAGE                                                             41
        *                                                                                   42
        MEMOR  STORAGE    256          MEMORY IS 256K                                       43
        *                                                                                   44
```

```
****************************************************************
*
*     COMPUTER SYSTEM MODEL
*
****************************************************************
*
        SIMULATE
1       GENERATE    270,FN$EXPO       JOB ARRIVES
2       ASSIGN      1,300,1,PH        SET EXECUTION TIME OF JOB
3       ASSIGN      2,V$UNI,PH        SET MEMORY SIZE OF JOB
4       QUEUE       MEMOR             JOB WAITS TC BE LOADED INTO MEMORY
5       ENTER       MEMOR,PH2         JOB IS LOADED INTO MEMORY
6       DEPART      MEMOR             LEAVE MEMORY QUEUE
7 EXEC  QUEUE       CPU               JOB WAITS FOR CPU
8       SEIZE       CPU               JOB GETS CPU
9       DEPART      CPU               LEAVE CPU QUEUE
10      TEST G      PH1,5,LAST        CHECK IF LAST TIME SLICE FOR JOB
11      ADVANCE     5                 JOB EXECUTES FOR 1 TIME SLICE
12      RELEASE     CPU               JOB YIELDS CPU
13      ASSIGN      1-,5,PH           COMPUTE EXECUTICN TIME LEFT
14      TRANSFER    ,EXEC
15 LAST ADVANCE     PH1               JOB EXECUTES FOR REMAINING TIME
16      RELEASE     CPU               JOB YIELDS CPU
17      LEAVE       MEMOR,PH2         JOB LEAVES MEMORY
18      TERMINATE   0
****************************************************************
*
*     TIMING SECTION
*
****************************************************************
*
19      GENERATE    36000             SIMULATE FOR 1 HOUR
20      TERMINATE   1
        START       1
        END

RELATIVE CLOCK  36000   ABSOLUTE CLOCK    36000
BLOCK COUNTS
```

BLOCK	CURRENT	TOTAL	BLOCK	CURRENT	TOTAL
1	0	136	11	1	6788
2	0	136	12	0	6787
3	0	136	13	0	6787
4	10	136	14	0	6787
5	0	126	15	0	118
6	0	126	16	0	118
7	7	6913	17	0	118
8	0	6906	18	0	118
9	0	6906	19	0	1

```
******************
*                *
*   FACILITIES   *
*                *
******************

                            -AVERAGE UTILIZATION DURING-
         NUMBER   AVERAGE     TOTAL   AVAIL.  UNAVAIL.  CURRENT    PERCENT      TRANSACTION NUMBER
FACILITY ENTRIES  TIME/TRAN   TIME    TIME    TIME      STATUS   AVAILABILITY   SEIZING PREEMPTING
CPU      6906     4.963       .952                                  100.0           17


****************
*              *
*   STORAGES   *
*              *
****************

                                        -AVERAGE UTILIZATION DURING-
                           AVERAGE            TOTAL   AVAIL.  UNAVAIL.  CURRENT    PERCENT
STORAGE  CAPACITY  ENTRIES  AVERAGE  AVERAGE  TIME    TIME    TIME      STATUS   AVAILABILITY   CURRENT    MAXIMUM
                            CONTENTS TIME/UNIT                                                 CONTENTS   CONTENTS
MEMOR    256       4765     191.129  1443.997  .746                                 100.0         245        256


**************
*            *
*   QUEUES   *
*            *
**************

        MAXIMUM  AVERAGE   TOTAL    ZERO     PERCENT  AVERAGE     $AVERAGE    TABLE   CURRENT
QUEUE   CONTENTS CONTENTS  ENTRIES  ENTRIES  ZEROS    TIME/TRANS  TIME/TRANS  NUMBER  CONTENTS
MEMOR   17       5.770     136      52       38.2     1527.602    2473.261            10
CPU     9        4.651     6913     6799     98.3     24.224      1468.973            7
$AVERAGE TIME/TRANS = AVERAGE TIME/TRANS EXCLUDING ZERC ENTRIES
END

***** TCTAL RUN TIME (INCLUDING ASSEMBLY) = .21 MINUTES *****
```

ory. Instead of the first-fit policy, which is the default in GPSS, this new model employs a strictly first-come–first-served policy.

A comparison of the results of the two computer system models points out the difference between the two approaches to placing entities in the storage, MEMOR. While the number of jobs and the CPU utilization are the same in both cases, the first model, using the first-fit approach, has better utilization of storage, 74.6% to 70.5%, and a shorter average memory queue, 5.770 to 7.025. Thus, the default, first-fit storage entry mechanism puts more entities into the storage than the first-come–first-served approach.

In terms of the computer system simulation, the difference in jobs processed is not significant, 118 to 115. The reason is that since the first-fit strategy places more jobs in memory, it results in longer average CPU waiting times, 24.224 to 19.386. Consequently, part of the advantage obtained upon entering memory is lost.

3.15 INDIRECT ADDRESSING

Standard numerical attributes are referenced by supplying a prefix that indicates the type of the SNA and a number that specifies the particular SNA of the given type. The number of the SNA is generally coded directly by the programmer or substituted in place of an identifier by the GPSS translator. For example,

RN3 is the third built-in random number generator, and

FN$EXPO is the user-defined function labeled as EXPO.

Whenever the SNA number is specified using either of the above methods, it is invariant for the execution of the program. There are situations in which it is desirable to vary the number of an SNA during program execution. GPSS provides a mechanism, called indirect addressing,[1] which permits an SNA number to be determined by the value of a parameter. The use of indirect addressing for an SNA is denoted by replacing the name, or number, of the SNA with * followed by the SNA for the parameter holding the value. Consider the following sample.

TEST G Q*PF3,10,SHORT

The queue length to be used in the evaluation of this TEST statement depends upon the value of the third full-word parameter of the entity entering the block. If the value of PF3 were 4, then the SNA Q4 indicating the length of the fourth queue would be compared against 10; if the queue length were greater than 10, the entity passes to the next statement. Otherwise, control transfers to SHORT.

---

[1]Those readers versed in assembly language programming should not attempt to form an exact correspondence between the indirect addressing feature of GPSS and indirect addressing as found in many assembly languages.

BLOCK
NUMBER

STATEMENT
NUMBER

```
*LOC  OPERATION  A,B,C,D,E,F,G,H,I        COMMENTS                    1
********************************************************************   2
*                                                                     3
*            COMPUTER SYSTEM SIMULATION                               4
*                                                                     5
*       PARAMETERS                                                    6
*                                                                     7
*  MEMORY SIZE - 256K (K = 1024 UNITS )                               8
*  TIME SLICE - 500 MILLISECCNDS                                      9
*  ( THE TIME SLICE IS THE MAXIMUM AMOUNT OF TIME A JOB              10
*    HAS CONTROL OF THE CENTRAL PROCESSOR UNIT                       11
*    BEFCRE YIELCING CONTRCL TO ANOTHER JOB )                        12
*  JOB ARRIVAL RATE - 27 SECS , EXPONENTIALLY DISTRIBUTED           13
*  EXECUTICN TIME - 30 SECS , EXPONENTIALLY DISTRIBUTED             14
*  JOB SIZE - 16K-64K, UNIFORMLY DISTRIBUTED                         15
*  OPERATING SYSTEM BEHAVIOR - WHEN JOBS ARRIVE , THEY ARE          16
*    LOADEC INTO MEMORY USING A SCHEDULING ALGORITHM.  JOBS ARE     17
*    EXECUTEC IN A ROUND-ROBIN MANNER , I.E. GIVEN ONE TIME SLICE   18
*    AT A TIME UNTIL EXECUTICN IS COMPLETE. IF A JOB COMPLETES      19
*    EXECUTION , A NEW JOB IS LOADED INTC MEMCRY.                   20
*  SCHECULING POLICY - FIRST-COME-FIRST-SERVE                        21
*  TERMINATICN CONDITICN - 1 HOUR                                    22
*                                                                    23
********************************************************************  24
*                                                                    25
*            EXPCNENTIAL FUNCTION                                     26
*                                                                    27
EXPO   FUNCTION   RN2,C24                                             28
.0000,.000/.1000,.104/.2000,.222/.3000,.355/.40C0,.509/.500C,.690/   29
.6000,.915/.7000,1.20/.7500,1.38/.8000,1.60/.8400,1.83/.8800,2.12/   30
.9000,2.3C/.92C0,2.52/.9400,2.81/.9500,2.99/.9600,3.20/.9700,3.50/   31
.9800,3.90/.9900,4.60/.9950,5.30/.9980,6.20/.9990,7.00/.9997,8.00/   32
*                                                                    33
*            UNIFORM DISTRIBUTION                                     34
*                                                                    35
UNI    VARIAELE  16+48*RN4/1000                                       36
*                                                                    37
********************************************************************  38
*                                                                    39
*            STORAGE                                                  40
*                                                                    41
********************************************************************  42
MEMOR  STORAGE    256              MEMORY IS 256K                     43
*                                                                    44
```

```
*****************************************************
*
*   COMPUTER SYSTEM MODEL
*
*****************************************************
*
        SIMULATE
    1   GENERATE    270,FN$EXPO           JOB ARRIVES
    2   ASSIGN      1,300,1,PH            SET EXECUTION TIME OF JOB
    3   ASSIGN      2,V$UNI,PH            SET MEMORY SIZE OF JOB
    4   QUEUE       MEMCR                 JOB WAITS TO BE LOADED INTO MEMORY
    5   GATE LR     FIRST                 ENFORCE FCFS POLICY
    6   LOGICS      FIRST                 DO NOT LET ANOTHER JOB INTO MEMORY
    7   ENTER       MEMCR,PH2             JOB IS LOADED INTO MEMORY
    8   LOGICR      FIRST                 LET NEXT JOB INTO MEMORY
    9   DEPART      MEMOR                 LEAVE MEMORY QUEUE
   10 EXEC QUEUE    CPU                   JOB WAITS FOR CPU
   11   SEIZE       CPU                   JOB GETS CPU
   12   DEPART      CPU                   LEAVE CPU QUEUE
   13   TEST G      PH1,5,LAST            CHECK IF LAST TIME SLICE FOR JOB
   14   ADVANCE     5                     JOB EXECUTES FOR 1 TIME SLICE
   15   RELEASE     CPU                   JOB YIELDS CPU
   16   ASSIGN      1-,5,PH               COMPUTE EXECUTION TIME LEFT
   17   TRANSFER    ,EXEC
   18 LAST ADVANCE  PH1                   JOB EXECUTES FOR REMAINING TIME
   19   RELEASE     CPU                   JOB YIELDS CPU
   20   LEAVE       MEMCR,PH2             JOB LEAVES MEMORY
   21   TERMINATE   0
*
*****************************************************
*
*   TIMING SECTION
*
*****************************************************
*
   22   GENERATE    360000                SIMULATE FOR 1 HOUR
   23   TERMINATE   1
        START       1
        END
```

45
46
47
48
49
50
51
52
53
54
55
56
57
58
59
60
61
62
63
64
65
66
67
68
69
70
71
72
73
74
75
76
77
78
79
80
81
82
83

RELATIVE CLOCK   36000 ABSOLUTE CLOCK   36000
BLOCK COUNTS

BLOCK	CURRENT	TOTAL	BLOCK	CURRENT	TOTAL	BLOCK	CURRENT	TOTAL
1	0	136	11	0	6902	21	0	115
2	0	136	12	0	6902	22	0	1
3	0	136	13	0	6902	23	0	1
4	13	136	14	1	6787			
5	0	123	15	0	6786			
6	1	123	16	0	6786			
7	0	122	17	0	6786			
8	0	122	18	0	115			
9	0	122	19	0	115			
10	6	6508	20	0	115			

```
**************************************
*                                    *
*           FACILITIES               *
*                                    *
**************************************
```

FACILITY	NUMBER ENTRIES	AVERAGE TIME/TRAN	—AVERAGE UTILIZATION DURING— TOTAL TIME	AVAIL. TIME	UNAVAIL. TIME	CURRENT STATUS	PERCENT AVAILABILITY	TRANSACTION NUMBER SEIZING	PREEMPTING
CPU	6902	4.966	.952				100.0	6	

```
**************************************
*                                    *
*            STORAGES                *
*                                    *
**************************************
```

STORAGE	CAPACITY	AVERAGE CONTENTS	AVERAGE TIME/UNIT	ENTRIES	—AVERAGE UTILIZATION DURING— TOTAL TIME	AVAIL. TIME	UNAVAIL. TIME	CURRENT STATUS	PERCENT AVAILABILITY	CURRENT CONTENTS	MAXIMUM CONTENTS
MEMOR	256	180.723	1365.951	4763	.705				100.0	239	256

```
                                      ***************************************
                                      *                                     *
                                      *               QUEUES                *
                                      *                                     *
                                      ***************************************

QUEUE     MAXIMUM    AVERAGE    TOTAL    ZERO    PERCENT    AVERAGE     $AVERAGE      TABLE    CURRENT
          CONTENTS   CONTENTS   ENTRIES  ENTRIES  ZEROS    TIME/TRANS   TIME/TRANS   NUMBER   CONTENTS
MEMOR        21       7.025      136       50      36.7     1859.764     2941.023               14
CPU           8       3.719     6908     6793      98.3       19.386     1164.521                6
$AVERAGE TIME/TRANS = AVERAGE TIME/TRANS EXCLUDING ZERO ENTRIES


                              ***********************************************
                              *                                             *
                              *               LOGIC SWITCHES                *
                              *                                             *
                              ***********************************************

LOGIC SWITCH - SET (ON) STATUS
NUMBER  NUMBER  NUMBER  NUMBER  NUMBER  NUMBER  NUMBER  NUMBER  NUMBER  NUMBER  NUMBER
 FIRST    END

                   ***** TOTAL RUN TIME (INCLUDING ASSEMBLY) = .19 MINUTES *****
```

It is the responsibility of the programmer to ensure that the value placed in the parameter to be used in indirect addressing is within the proper range. Failure to control this value can lead to run-time errors. For example, if the value in PF3 were less than 1 or greater than the number of queues in the model, an error message would be produced and the program terminated.

EXAMPLE 3.16

Let us return to the bank teller model and modify the program of Example 3.13 to include information on the type of transaction presented to the teller by the customer. The following distribution of transaction types is assumed:

Savings Deposit	20%
Savings Withdrawal	15%
Checking Deposit	20%
Check Cashing	25%
Christmas Club Payment	15%
Other	5%

We will also assume that each transaction takes the amount of time, in minutes, shown below:

Savings Deposit	0.8
Savings Withdrawal	1.2
Checking Deposit	1.6
Check Cashing	2.0
Christmas Club Payment	2.2
Other	2.3

The customer may have from 1 to 5 transactions. For purposes of this example, all transactions of a single customer are assumed to be of the same type.

The introduction of the variable processing time and transaction type has dramatically increased the demand on the tellers. The waiting lines have increased by approximately a factor of 10.

3.16 LOOPING

An important feature of any programming language is the ability to perform a group of statements iteratively. GPSS provides this ability with the LOOP statement. In most programming languages a group of iterated statements, or a loop, has the structure shown below:

Loop Initiation Statement
    Body of Loop (statements to be executed iteratively)
Loop Termination Statement

```
BLOCK                                                                    STATEMENT
NUMBER  *LOC   OPERATICN  A,B,C,C,E,F,G,H,I        COMMENTS                 NUMBER
        ****************************************************************       1
        *     PROGRAM TO SIMULATE A BANK WITH TWC TELLERS                      2
        *  WITH SEPARATE WAITING LINES.  CUSTOMERS SELECT THE SHORTEST LINE.   3
        *  CUSTOMERS SELECT FIRST TELLER IN CASE OF A TIE.                     4
        *     A BANK OFFICER ARRIVES WITH A TRANSACTICN AND MCVES TO THE FRONT 5
        *  OF THE FIRST TELLER'S LINE.                                         6
        *                                                                      7
        *     PARAMETERS                                                       8
        *                                                                      9
        *     NUMBER OF TRANSACTIONS - 1 TO 5 PER CUSTOMER , AS SPECIFIED BY   10
        *         TRANS FUNCTICN.  1 TRANSACTION PER CFFICER.                  11
        *     CUSTOMER ARRIVALS - 2 MINUTES, EXPCNENTIALLY DISTRIBUTED         12
        *     OFFICER ARRIVALS - 45 TO 75 MINUTES , UNIFORMLY DISTRIBUTED      13
        *     PROCESSING RATE -  1.2 MINUTES PER TRANSACTION                   14
        *     TERMINATION CONDITION - 8 HOURS                                  15
        *                                                                      16
        ****************************************************************       17
        *                                                                      18
        *    EXPONENTIAL FUNCTION                                              19
        *                                                                      20
        EXPO   FUNCTICN   RN2,C24                                              21
        .0000,.000/.1C00,.104/.2000,.222/.3000,.355/.4000,.509/.5000,.690/    22
        .6000,.915/.7CCO,1.20/.7500,1.38/.8000,1.60/.8400,1.83/.8800,2.12/    23
        .9000,2.30/.9200,2.52/.9400,2.81/.9500,2.99/.96C0,3.20/.9700,3.50/    24
        .9800,3.90/.9900,4.60/.9950,5.30/.9980,6.20/.9990,7.00/.9997,8.00/    25
        *                                                                      26
        *    TRANSACTION FUNCTION                                              27
        *                                                                      28
        TRANS  FUNCTICN   RN3,D5                                               29
        .20,1/.45,2/.75,3/.90,4/1.0,5                                          30
        *                                                                      31
        *     TRANSACTICN TYPE FUNCTION                                        32
        *                                                                      33
        TYPE   FUNCTION   RN4,D6                                               34
        .20,1/.35,2/.55,3/.80,4/.95,5/1.0,6                                    35
        *                                                                      36
        *    PROCESSING TIME VARIABLES                                         37
        *                                                                      38
        PROC1  FVARIABLE   0.8*PH1                                             39
        PROC2  FVARIABLE   1.2*PH1                                             40
        PROC3  FVARIABLE   1.6*PH1                                             41
        PROC4  FVARIABLE   2.0*PH1                                             42
        PROC5  FVARIABLE   2.2*PH1                                             43
        PROC6  FVARIABLE   2.3*PH1                                             44
        *                                                                      45
        ****************************************************************       46
        *                                                                      47
        *    CUSTOMER SECTION                                                  48
        *                                                                      49
        ****************************************************************       50
               SIMULATE                                                        51
    1          GENERATE   2,FN$EXPO          CUSTOMER ARRIVES                  52
    2          ASSIGN     1,FN$TRANS,PH      SET NUMBER OF TRANSACTIONS        53
    3          ASSIGN     2,FN$TYPE,PH       SET TRANSACTION TYPE              54
    4          TEST LE    Q$TELR1,Q$TELR2,SECON  CUSTOMER SELECTS A TELLER     55
    5    FIRST QUEUE      TELR1              CUSTOMER WAITS FOR 1ST TELLER      56
    6          SEIZE      TELR1              CUSTOMER REACHES 1ST TELLER        57
    7          DEPART     TELR1              REMCVE CUSTCMER FROM 1ST LINE      58
    8          ADVANCE    V*PH2              TRANSACTIONS ARE PROCESSED         59
    9          RELEASE    TELR1              CUSTOMER LEAVES TELLER             60
    10         TERMINATE  0                                                     61
    11   SECON QUEUE      TELR2              CUSTOMER WAITS FOR 2ND TELLER      62
    12         SEIZE      TELR2              CUSTOMER REACHES 2ND TELLER        63
    13         DEPART     TELR2              REMCVE CUSTOMER FROM 2ND LINE      64
    14         ADVANCE    V*PH2              TRANSACTIONS ARE PROCESSED         65
    15         RELEASE    TELR2              CUSTOMER LEAVES 2ND TELLER         66
    16         TERMINATE  0                                                     67
        *                                                                      68
```

```
************************ **                                                      69
*                                                                               70
*    OFFICER SECTION                                                            71
*                                                                               72
************************* *                                                      73
*                                                                               74
        GENERATE    60,15           OFFICER ARRIVES WITH TRANSACTI              75
        PRIORITY    1               ASSIGN OFFICER PRIORITY                     76
        ASSIGN      1,1,PH          OFFICER HAS 1 TRANSACTION                   77
        ASSIGN      2,FN$TYPE,PH    SET TRANSACTION TYPE                        78
        QUEUE       OFICR           ENTER SPECIAL OFFICER QUEUE                 79
        QUEUE       TELR1           OFFICER WAITS FOR 1ST TELLER                80
        SEIZE       TELR1           OFFICER REACHES 1ST TELLER                  81
        DEPART      TELR1           REMOVE OFFICER FROM 1ST LINE                82
        DEPART      OFICR           LEAVE SPECIAL OFFICER QUEUE                 83
        ADVANCE     V*PH2           OFFICER'S TRANSACTION IS PROCE              84
        RELEASE     TELR1           OFFICER LEAVES FIRST TELLER                 85
        TERMINATE   0                                                          86
*                                                                               87
***************************** ****                                             88
*                                                                               89
* TIMING SECTION                                                                90
*                                                                               91
***************************** ****                                             92
*                                                                               93
        GENERATE    480                                                        94
        TERMINATE   1                                                          95
        START       1                                                          96
        END                                                                    97
```

```
RELATIVE CLOCK          480  ABSOLUTE CLOCK          480
BLOCK COUNTS
BLOCK CURRENT    TOTAL    BLOCK CURRENT    TOTAL    BLOCK CURRENT    TOTAL
  1      0       297       11     31       150       21     0        8
  2      0       297       12     C        119       22     0        8
  3      0       297       13     0        119       23     0        8
  4      0       297       14     1        119       24     0        8
  5      31      147       15     0        118       25     0        8
  6      0       116       16     C        118       26     0        8
  7      0       116       17     0          8       27     0        8
  8      1       116       18     0          8       28     0        8
  9      0       115       19     0          8       29     0        1
 10      0       115       20     C          8       30     0        1
```

```
                         ********************************
                         *       *       *
                         *       *       *
                         *     FACILITIES *
                         *       *       *
                         *       *       *
                         ********************************
```

| | | | -AVERAGE | UTILIZATION DURING- | | | | TRANSACTION NUMBER | |
FACILITY	NUMBER ENTRIES	AVERAGE TIME/TRAN	TOTAL TIME	AVAIL. TIME	UNAVAIL. TIME	CURRENT STATUS	PERCENT AVAILABILITY	SEIZING	PREEMPTING
TELR1	124	3.815	.985				100.0	41	
TELR2	119	3.992	.989				100.0	56	

```
                         ********************************
                         *       *       *
                         *       *       *
                         *       QUEUES  *
                         *       *       *
                         *       *       *
                         ********************************
```

QUEUE	MAXIMUM CONTENTS	AVERAGE CONTENTS	TOTAL ENTRIES	ZERO ENTRIES	PERCENT ZEROS	AVERAGE TIME/TRANS	$AVERAGE TIME/TRANS	TABLE NUMBER	CURRENT CONTENTS
TELR1	34	18.485	155	6	3.8	57.245	59.550		31
TELR2	33	17.966	150	1	.6	57.493	57.879		31
CFICR	1	.043	8	1	12.5	2.625	3.000		

$AVERAGE TIME/TRANS = AVERAGE TIME/TRANS EXCLUDING ZERO ENTRIES
END

***** TOTAL RUN TIME (INCLUDING ASSEMBLY) = .05 MINUTES *****

In GPSS the LOOP statement serves as the Loop Termination Statement. Any labeled GPSS statement may act as the Loop Initiation Statement. The Body of the Loop can be formed from any executable GPSS statements.

The LOOP statement has the following form:

    LOOP A,B

where

> A is the parameter that is decremented by one each time the statement is executed. The form of argument A is number followed by SNA code rather than SNA code followed by number. For example, 2PH is used instead of PH2.
>
> B is the label of the statement to which control is transferred if the value of the parameter specified in argument A is not 0 *after* it has been decremented. If the parameter is equal to 0, the entity passes sequentially to the next statement in the program.

For example, the statement

    LOOP 3PF,LINIT

causes full-word parameter 3 of the entity entering this statement to be decreased by 1. If the value of the parameter becomes 0, the entity passes to the next sequential statement. If the parameter does not reach 0 after being decremented, the entity is passed to the statement labeled LINIT. Note that if the value of the parameter indicated by the A argument is less than or equal to 0 the first time through the loop, then the LOOP statement will always pass control to B. Thus an "infinite" loop will occur.

EXAMPLE 3.17

> In the previous example the customer waiting lines grew quite large—up to 34 people. One approach to reducing the length of the waiting lines is to add more tellers. In terms of the GPSS model, additional facilities must be added, since each teller is modeled as a facility with its own queue. If the number of tellers is to be varied in order to determine the number providing the best service, the test for the shortest line cannot be coded as in Example 3.16. However, using parameters, indirect addressing, and a LOOP statement, the shortest-line test can be easily implemented for a variable number of teller lines.
>
> A model with four tellers is given in the listing. A change for the previous mode of operation is that in case of equal line lengths, the fourth teller is selected.
>
> By expanding the number of tellers to four, the waiting time of the customers is drastically reduced. All of the waiting lines have an average length of less than one. The average waiting time per customer drops from approximately 57 minutes with two tellers to roughly 2.5 minutes using four tellers. Surprisingly, the first two tellers are busy less than half the time in this model.

```
 LOCK                                                                        STATEMENT
 UMBER  *LCC     OPERATION  A,B,C,D,E,F,G,H,I            COMMENTS             NUMBER
        **************************************************************          1
        *      PROGRAM TO SIMULATE A BANK WITH A VARIABLE NUMBER OF TELLERS     2
        *  WITH SEPARATE WAITING LINES.  CUSTOMERS SELECT THE SHORTEST LINE.    3
        *  CUSTOMERS SELECT LAST TELLER IN CASE OF A TIE.                       4
        *      A BANK OFFICER ARRIVES WITH A TRANSACTION AND MOVES TO THE FRONT 5
        *  OF THE FIRST TELLER'S LINE.                                          6
        *                                                                       7
        *    PARAMETERS                                                         8
        *                                                                       9
        *    NUMBER OF TRANSACTIONS - 1 TO 5 PER CUSTOMER , AS SPECIFIED BY    10
        *         TRANS FUNCTION.  1 TRANSACTION PER OFFICER.                   11
        *    CUSTOMER ARRIVALS - 2 MINUTES, EXPONENTIALLY DISTRIBUTED          12
        *    OFFICER ARRIVALS - 45 TO 75 MINUTES , UNIFORMLY DISTRIBUTED       13
        *    PROCESSING RATE -  SPECIFIED BY TYPE FUNCTION AND PROC VARIALBES  14
        *    TERMINATION CONDITION - 8 HOURS                                   15
        *                                                                      16
        ************************************************************************ 17
        *                                                                      18
        *   EXPONENTIAL FUNCTION                                               19
        *                                                                      20
         EXPO   FUNCTION   RN2,C24                                             21
        .0000,.000/.1000,.104/.2000,.222/.3000,.355/.4000,.509/.5000,.690/    22
        .6000,.915/.7CCC,1.20/.7500,1.38/.8000,1.60/.84CC,1.83/.8800,2.12/    23
        .9000,2.30/.9200,2.52/.9400,2.81/.9500,2.99/.96CC,3.20/.97CC,3.50/    24
        .9800,3.9C/.9900,4.60/.9950,5.30/.9980,6.20/.9990,7.00/.9997,8.00/    25
        *                                                                      26
        *   TRANSACTION FUNCTION                                               27
        *                                                                      28
         TRANS FUNCTION    RN3,D5                                              29
        .20,1/.45,2/.75,3/.90,4/1.0,5                                          30
        *                                                                      31
        *    TRANSACTION TYPE FUNCTION                                         32
        *                                                                      33
         TYPE  FUNCTION   RN4,D6                                               34
        .20,1/.35,2/.55,3/.80,4/.95,5/1.0,6                                    35
        *                                                                      36
        *   PROCESSING TIME VARIABLES                                          37
        *                                                                      38
         PROC1 FVARIABLE   0.8*PH1                                             39
         PROC2 FVARIABLE   1.2*PH1                                             40
         PROC3 FVARIABLE   1.6*PH1                                             41
         PROC4 FVARIABLE   2.0*PH1                                             42
         PROC5 FVARIABLE   2.2*PH1                                             43
         PROC6 FVARIABLE   2.3*PH1                                             44
        *                                                                      45
        *   NUMBER CF TELLERS                                                  46
        *                                                                      47
         TELRS VARIABLE    4               NUMBER CF TELLERS                   48
         TELR1 VARIABLE    V$TELRS-1                                           49
        *                                                                      50
        ************************************************************************ 51
        *                                                                      52
        *   CUSTOMER SECTION                                                   53
        *                                                                      54
        ************************************************************************ 55
```

```
      *                                                                          56
            SIMULATE                                                             57
            GENERATE    2,FN$EXPC       CUSTOMER ARRIVES                         58
            ASSIGN      1,FN$TRANS,PH   SET NUMBER OF TRANSACTIONS               59
            ASSIGN      2,FN$TYPE,PH    SET TRANSACTION TYPE                     60
            ASSIGN      3,V$TELRS,PH    SET LAST TELLER'S LINE AS SHORTEST       61
            ASSIGN      4,V$TELR1,PH    P4 HAS CANDIDATE SHORTEST LINE           62
      SHORT TEST L      Q*PH4,Q*PH3,NLOOP  TEST IF NEW SHORTEST LINE IS FOUND    63
            ASSIGN      3,PH4,PH        SET NEW SHORTEST LINE IN PH3             64
      NLOOP LOOP        4PH,SHORT       REPEAT FOR ALL LINES                     65
            QUEUE       PH3             CUSTOMER WAITS IN SHORTEST LINE          66
            SEIZE       PH3             CUSTOMER REACHES TELLER                   67
            DEPART      PH3             REMOVE CUSTOMER FROM WAITING LINE        68
            ADVANCE     V*PH2           TRANSACTIONS ARE PROCESSED               69
            RELEASE     PH3             CUSTOMER LEAVES TELLER                    70
            TERMINATE   0                                                        71
      *                                                                          72
      ****************************                                               73
      *                                                                          74
      *     OFFICER SECTION                                                      75
      *                                                                          76
      ****************************                                               77
      *                                                                          78
            GENERATE    60,15           OFFICER ARRIVES WITH TRANSACTION         79
            PRIORITY    1               ASSIGN OFFICER PRIORITY                  80
            ASSIGN      1,1,PH          OFFICER HAS 1 TRANSACTION                81
            ASSIGN      2,FN$TYPE,PH    SET TRANSACTION TYPE                     82
            QUEUE       10              ENTER SPECIAL OFFICER QUEUE              83
            QUEUE       1               OFFICER WAITS FOR FIRST TELLER           84
            SEIZE       1               OFFICER REACHES FIRST TELLER             85
            DEPART      1               REMOVE OFFICER FROM WAITING LINE         86
            DEPART      10              LEAVE SPECIAL OFFICER QUEUE              87
            ADVANCE     V*PH2           OFFICER'S TRANSACTION IS PROCESSED       88
            RELEASE     1               OFFICER LEAVES FIRST TELLER              89
            TERMINATE   0                                                        90
      *                                                                          91
      ****************************                                               92
      *                                                                          93
      * TIMING SECTION                                                           94
      *                                                                          95
      ****************************                                               96
      *                                                                          97
            GENERATE    480                                                      98
            TERMINATE   1                                                        99
            START       1                                                       100
            END                                                                 101
```

```
            RELATIVE CLOCK            480   ABSOLUTE CLOCK           480
            BLOCK COUNTS
            BLOCK CURRENT     TOTAL     BLOCK CURRENT    TOTAL    BLOCK CURRENT    TOTAL
               1        0      297        11       0      294       21       0        8
               2        0      297        12       3      294       22       0        8
               3        0      297        13       0      291       23       0        8
               4        0      297        14       0      291       24       0        8
               5        0      297        15       0        8       25       0        8
               6        0      891        16       0        8       26       0        8
               7        0      187        17       0        8       27       0        1
               8        0      891        18       0        8       28       0        1
               9        3      297        19       0        8
              10        0      294        20       0        8
```

```
**********************************
*                                *
*          FACILITIES            *
*                                *
**********************************
```

FACILITY	NUMBER ENTRIES	AVERAGE TIME/TRAN	-AVERAGE TOTAL TIME	UTILIZATION DURING- AVAIL. TIME	UNAVAIL. TIME	CURRENT STATUS	PERCENT AVAILABILITY	TRANSACTION NUMBER SEIZING	PREEMPTING
1	40	2.950	.245				100.0	15	
2	63	3.587	.470				100.0	12	
3	87	4.080	.739				100.0	16	
4	112	3.937	.918				100.0		

```
**********************************
*                                *
*            QUEUES              *
*                                *
**********************************
```

QUEUE	MAXIMUM CONTENTS	AVERAGE CONTENTS	TOTAL ENTRIES	ZERO ENTRIES	PERCENT ZEROS	AVERAGE TIME/TRANS	$AVERAGE TIME/TRANS	TABLE NUMBER	CURRENT CONTENTS
1	2	.102	40	26	64.9	1.224	3.500		1
2	2	.243	64	30	46.8	1.828	3.441		1
3	3	.474	88	34	38.6	2.590	4.222		1
4	3	.754	113	31	27.4	3.203	4.414		
10	1	.000	8	8	100.0	.000	.000		

$AVERAGE TIME/TRANS = AVERAGE TIME/TRANS EXCLUDING ZERO ENTRIES
END

***** TOTAL RUN TIME (INCLUDING ASSEMBLY) = .05 MINUTES *****

3.17 SAVEVALUES

In GPSS, the value of parameters describes the status of each entity and the value of SNAs indicates the state of the system attributes. In many models, however, it is necessary to maintain numerical values that describe a part of the overall system state but are not provided as SNAs. Values that fall in this class are counters, temporary variables, or previous SNA values that will be referenced at a later time. Such values can be represented in GPSS as *savevalues*.

A savevalue is an SNA that is associated with the system rather than a particular entity. Savevalues can be accessed by all entities in the model. The number of savevalue locations available is dependent upon the particular GPSS implementation, but is generally in the range of 100. Values are assigned to savevalue locations using the SAVEVALUE statement. The SAVEVALUE statement has the following format:

> SAVEVALUE A,B,C

where

> A is the number of the savevalue location to be assigned a value; A may specify a range of savevalues. Also, as with the ASSIGN statement, a + or − may be appended to the A argument to indicate an addition or subtraction operation.
>
> B is an SNA whose value will be stored in (or added to or subtracted from) the savevalue location (or locations) designated in A.
>
> C is an optional indicator of the savevalue type. Either XF, XH, XB, or XL may be used to indicate full-word, half-word, byte, or floating-point savevalues, respectively. If C is omitted, a full-word savevalue is utilized.

The following sample statements illustrate the use of savevalues.

> SAVEVALUE 1,V$MONEY,XH

This statement causes the variable MONEY to be evaluated with the result stored in half-word savevalue 1.

> SAVEVALUE PF5,FN$CREDT,XL

When an entity enters this statement block, the function CREDT is evaluated and the result is stored in the floating-point savevalue indicated by full-word parameter 5 of the entity. For example, if full-word parameter 5 contained the value 2, then the result of CREDT would be stored in floating-point savevalue 2.

> SAVEVALUE 11+,1,XB

The contents of byte savevalue 11 are incremented by 1.

> SAVEVALUE 2−,Q$WAIT,XH

The length of the queue WAIT is subtracted from the value of half-word savevalue 2 and the result is stored in half-word savevalue 2.

> SAVEVALUE 3−9,0,XB

The byte savevalues 3 through 9 are set to 0.

> SAVEVALUE 1−3−,2,XH

The half-word savevalues 1 through 3 are decremented by 2.

    SAVEVALUE 4,PH7

The value of the seventh half-word parameter of the entity entering this statement block is stored in full-word savevalue 4. This statement could also be written as

    SAVEVALUE 4,PH7,XF

The contents of savevalue locations can be accessed by means of the SNA codes XF, XH, XB, or XL, which reference full-word, half-word, byte, or floating-point savevalue. The prefix X may optionally be used in place of XF. The statements below provide some instances of savevalue references.

    SAVEVALUE 1,V$MONEY,XH

This statement causes the variable MONEY to be evaluated, with the result stored in half-word savevalue 1.

    SAVEVALUE PF5,FN$CREDT,XL

When an entity enters this statement block, the function CREDT is evaluated and the result is stored in the floating-point savevalue indicated by full-word parameter 5 of the entity. For example, if full-word parameter 5 contained the value 2, then the result of CREDT would be stored in floating-point savevalue 2.

    SAVEVALUE 11+,1,XB

The contents of byte savevalue 11 are incremented by 1.

    SAVEVALUE 2−,Q$WAIT,XH

The length of the queue WAIT is subtracted from the value of half-word savevalue 2 and the result is stored in half-word savevalue 2.

    SAVEVALUE 3−9,0,XB

The byte savevalues 3 through 9 are set to 0.

    SAVEVALUE 1−3−,2,XH

The half-word savevalues 1 through 3 are decremented by 2.

    SAVEVALUE 4,PH7

The value of the seventh half-word parameter of the entity entering this statement block is stored in full-word savevalue 4. This statement could also be written as

    SAVEVALUE 4,PH7,XF

The contents of savevalue locations can be accessed by means of the SNA codes XF, XH, XB, or XL, which respectively reference full-word, half-word, byte, or floating-point savevalue. The prefix X may optionally be used in place of XF. The statements below provide some instances of savevalue references.

    ASSIGN 7,XF4,PF

The contents of full-word savevalue 4 are assigned to full-word parameter 7 of the entity entering the statement block.

    LOAD VARIABLE 5*FN$EXPON−2*(XH1−PH3)

The contents of half-word savevalue 1 are used in the evaluation of the expression specified for the variable LOAD.

GPSS automatically initializes all savevalue locations to 0. The final values of any savevalue locations that have been altered during the execution of a program are printed upon program termination. The output generated by the use of savevalues is shown in the next example.

EXAMPLE 3.18

A very important aspect of a bank's business is the flow of cash through the teller stations. Let us expand the model of Example 3.17 to include information on the amount of cash on hand for each teller and for a head teller. Savevalue locations retain the amount of cash each teller and the head teller have on hand.

The printout of the savevalue locations shows the range of the teller cash on hand at closing time, 1186 to 3894. The block counts indicate that statements 22 through 24 were never executed. Thus, no teller ever required additional cash from the head teller.

3.18 FACILITY PREEMPTION

The normal mode of operation by a facility, as presented in Section 3.4, is for an entity to seize the facility, hold the facility for an amount of time determined by one or more ADVANCE blocks, and then release the facility. An entity requiring access to the facility must wait until the facility is released before attempting to gain control of the facility in the normal operational mode. However, the normal sequence of facility operations can be altered by use of the facility preemption feature of GPSS. By means of the PREEMPT statement, an entity can gain control of a facility that is engaged by another transaction.

There are two methods of preemption in GPSS, priority and nonpriority. The simpler of the two modes is nonpriority, in which any entity may preempt any facility from any other entity. The preempting entity holds the facility until its operations with the facility are complete, at which time the facility returns to the preempted entity. In the nonpriority mode, a preempting facility may not be preempted.

Under the priority preemption mode, an entity may preempt a facility if its priority is greater than the priority of the entity currently holding the facility. This rule does imply that a preempting entity may be preempted by a higher priority entity. When a facility is freed by a preempting entity, control of the facility is granted to the highest priority preempted entity under the priority mode. In either preemption mode an entity may preempt an empty facility. In this case the

```
BLOCK                                                              STATEMENT
NUMBER  *LOC    OPERATION  A,B,C,D,E,F,G,H,I         COMMENTS         NUMBER
        ****************************************************************   1
        *      PROGRAM TO SIMULATE A BANK WITH A VARIABLE NUMBER OF TELLERS  2
        *   WITH SEPARATE WAITING LINES.  CUSTOMERS SELECT THE SHORTEST LINE.  3
        *   CUSTOMERS SELECT LAST TELLER IN CASE OF A TIE.                  4
        *      A BANK OFFICER ARRIVES WITH A TRANSACTION AND MOVES TO THE FRONT  5
        *   OF THE FIRST TELLER'S LINE.                                     6
        *      THE AMOUNT OF CASH ON HAND AT EACH TELLER STATION            7
        *   AND HELD BY THE HEAD TELLER IS MAINTAINED IN SAVEVALUES.        8
        *      THE TOTAL AMOUNT OF CASH AT THE END OF THE DAY IS PRINTED AS THE  9
        *   CONTENTS OF SAVEVALUE LOCATION 11.                             10
        *                                                                  11
        *      PARAMETERS                                                  12
        *                                                                  13
        *      NUMBER OF TRANSACTIONS - 1 TO 5 PER CUSTOMER , AS SPECIFIED BY  14
        *         TRANS FUNCTION.  1 TRANSACTION PER OFFICER.              15
        *      CUSTOMER ARRIVALS - 2 MINUTES, EXPONENTIALLY DISTRIBUTED    16
        *      OFFICER ARRIVALS - 45 TO 75 MINUTES , UNIFORMLY DISTRIBUTED  17
        *      PROCESSING RATE -  SPECIFIED BY TYPE FUNCTION AND PROC VARIABLES  18
        *      TERMINATION CONDITION - 8 HOURS                            19
        *   CASH WITHDRAWN PER CUSTOMER - FROM -499 TO 500 , UNIFORM DIST.  20
        *                                                                  21
        ****************************************************************   22
        *                                                                  23
        *   EXPONENTIAL FUNCTION                                          24
        *                                                                  25
        EXPO  FUNCTION    RN2,C24                                         26
        .0000,.000/.1000,.104/.2000,.222/.3000,.355/.4000,.509/.5000,.690/  27
        .6000,.915/.7000,1.20/.7500,1.38/.8000,1.60/.8400,1.83/.8800,2.12/  28
        .9000,2.30/.9200,2.52/.9400,2.81/.9500,2.99/.9600,3.20/.9700,3.50/  29
        .9800,3.90/.9900,4.60/.9950,5.30/.9980,6.20/.9990,7.00/.9997,8.00/  30
        *                                                                  31
        *   TRANSACTION FUNCTION                                          32
        *                                                                  33
        TRANS FUNCTION    RN3,D5                                          34
        .20,1/.45,2/.75,3/.90,4/1.0,5                                     35
        *                                                                  36
        *   TRANSACTION TYPE FUNCTION                                     37
        *                                                                  38
        TYPE  FUNCTION    RN4,D6                                          39
        .20,1/.35,2/.55,3/.80,4/.95,5/1.0,6                               40
        *                                                                  41
        *   PROCESSING TIME VARIABLES                                     42
        *                                                                  43
        PROC1 FVARIABLE   0.8*PH1                                         44
        PROC2 FVARIABLE   1.2*PH1                                         45
        PROC3 FVARIABLE   1.6*PH1                                         46
        PROC4 FVARIABLE   2.0*PH1                                         47
        PROC5 FVARIABLE   2.2*PH1                                         48
        PROC6 FVARIABLE   2.3*PH1                                         49
        *                                                                  50
        *   CASH WITHDRAWAL VARIABLE                                      51
        *                                                                  52
        CASH  VARIABLE    RN5-500                                         53
        *                                                                  54
        *   NUMBER OF TELLERS                                             55
```

```
*                                                                        56
  TELRS VARIABLE    4                    NUMBER OF TELLERS               57
  TELR1 VARIABLE    V$TELRS-1                                            58
*                                                                        59
*    INITIAL AMOUNT OF CASH PER TELLER                                   60
*                                                                        61
  AMNT VARIABLE     2000                                                 62
*                                                                        63
*************************************************************************  64
*                                                                        65
*    TELLER START UP SECTION                                             66
*                                                                        67
*************************************************************************  68
*                                                                        69
        SIMULATE                                                         70
        GENERATE    ,,,1                 GENERATE A DUMMY ENTITY         71
        ASSIGN      6,V$TELRS,PH         PARM. 6 IS A LOOP INDEX         72
        SAVEVALUE   10,100000,XF         LOC. 10 IS HEAD TELLER'S CASH   73
  INIT  SAVEVALUE   PH6,V$AMNT,XF        EACH TELLER STARTS WITH V$AMNT  74
        SAVEVALUE   10-,V$AMNT,XF        SUBTRACT FROM HEAD TELLER'S CASH 75
        LOOP        6PH,INIT             PROCESS ALL TELLERS             76
        TERMINATE   0                    REMOVE DUMMY ENTITY             77
*                                                                        78
*************************************************************************  79
*                                                                        80
*    CUSTOMER SECTION                                                    81
*                                                                        82
*************************************************************************  83
*                                                                        84
        GENERATE    2,FN$EXPO            CUSTOMER ARRIVES                85
        ASSIGN      1,FN$TRANS,PH        SET NUMBER OF TRANSACTIONS      86
        ASSIGN      2,FN$TYPE,PH         SET TRANSACTION TYPE            87
        ASSIGN      5,V$CASH,PH          SET NET AMOUNT OF CASH TO BE WITHD 88
        ASSIGN      3,V$TELRS,PH         SET LAST TELLER'S LINE AS SHORTEST 89
        ASSIGN      4,V$TELR1,PH         P4 HAS CANDIDATE SHORTEST LINE  90
  SHORT TEST L      Q*PH4,Q*PH3,NLOOP    TEST IF NEW SHORTEST LINE IS FOUND 91
        ASSIGN      3,PH4,PH             SET NEW SHORTEST LINE IN PH3    92
  NLOOP LOOP        4PH,SHORT            REPEAT FOR ALL LINES            93
        QUEUE       PH3                  CUSTOMER WAITS IN SHORTEST LINE 94
        SEIZE       PH3                  CUSTOMER REACHES TELLER         95
        DEPART      PH3                  REMOVE CUSTOMER FROM WAITING LINE 96
        ADVANCE     V*PH2                TRANSACTIONS ARE PROCESSED      97
        TEST L      X*PH3,PH5,CUST       TEST IF TELLER HAS ADEQUATE FUNDS 98
        SAVEVALUE   PH3+,V$AMNT,XF       GIVE CASH TO TELLER             99
        SAVEVALUE   10-,V$AMNT,XF        ADJUST HEAD TELLER'S CASH       100
        ADVANCE     2                    2 MINUTES ARE NEEDED TO GET CASH 101
  CUST  SAVEVALUE   PH3-,PH5             ADJUST TELLER'S CASH            102
        RELEASE     PH3                  CUSTOMER LEAVES TELLER          103
        TERMINATE   0                                                   104
*                                                                        105
******************************                                           106
*                                                                        107
*    OFFICER SECTION                                                     108
*                                                                        109
******************************                                           110
*                                                                        111
        GENERATE    60,15                OFFICER ARRIVES WITH TRANSACTION 112
```

```
29        PRIORITY    1,1,PH            ASSIGN OFFICER PRIORITY
30        ASSIGN      1,1,PH            OFFICER HAS 1 TRANSACTION
31        ASSIGN      2,FN$TYPE,PH      SET TRANSACTION TYPE
32        QUEUE       10                ENTER SPECIAL OFFICER QUEUE
33        QUEUE       1                 OFFICER WAITS FOR FIRST TELLER
34        SEIZE       1                 OFFICER REACHES FIRST TELLER
35        DEPART      1                 REMOVE OFFICER FROM WAITING LINE
36        DEPART      10                LEAVE SPECIAL OFFICER QUEUE
37        ADVANCE     V*PH2             OFFICER'S TRANSACTION IS PROCESSED
38        RELEASE     1                 OFFICER LEAVES FIRST TELLER
39        TERMINATE   0
     *
     *  *********************************
     *  TERMINATION SECTION
     *  *********************************
     *
40        GENERATE    480               PARM. 6 IS LOOP INDEX
41        ASSIGN      6,V$TELRS,PH
42 TOTAL  SAVEVALUE   11+,XF*PH6,XF     SUM OF CASH IN LOC. 11
43        LCCP        6PH,TOTAL
44        SAVEVALUE   11+,XF10,XF       ADD IN HEAD TELLER'S CASH
45        TERMINATE   1
          START       1
          END
```

```
480   ABSOLUTE CLOCK   480

RELATIVE CLOCK
BLOCK COUNTS
```

BLOCK	CURRENT	TOTAL	BLOCK	CURRENT	TOTAL	BLOCK	CURRENT	TOTAL	BLOCK	CURRENT	TOTAL	BLOCK	CURRENT	TOTAL
1	0	1	11	0	297	21	0	291	31	0	8	41	0	1
2	0	1	12	0	297	22	0	0	32	0	8	42	0	4
3	0	1	13	0	297	23	0	0	33	0	8	43	0	4
4	0	4	14	0	891	24	0	0	34	0	8	44	0	1
5	0	4	15	0	187	25	0	291	35	0	8	45	0	1
6	0	4	16	0	891	26	0	291	36	0	8			
7	3	1	17	3	297	27	0	291	37	0	8			
8	0	297	18	0	294	28	0	8	38	0	8			
9	0	297	19	0	294	29	0	8	39	0	8			
10	0	297	20	3	294	30	0	8	40	0	1			

```
113
114
115
116
117
118
119
120
121
122
123
124
125
126
127
128
129
130
131
132
133
134
135
136
137
138
```

```
********************
*                  *
*    FACILITIES    *
*                  *
********************
```

FACILITY	NUMBER ENTRIES	AVERAGE TIME/TRAN	-AVERAGE TOTAL TIME	UTILIZATION DURING- AVAIL. TIME	UNAVAIL. TIME	CURRENT STATUS	PERCENT AVAILABILITY	TRANSACTION NUMBER SEIZING	PREEMPTING
1	40	2.950	.245				100.0	15	
2	63	3.587	.470				100.0	12	
3	87	4.080	.739				100.0	16	
4	112	3.937	.918				100.0		

```
********************
*                  *
*      QUEUES      *
*                  *
********************
```

QUEUE	MAXIMUM CONTENTS	AVERAGE CONTENTS	TOTAL ENTRIES	ZERO ENTRIES	PERCENT ZEROS	AVERAGE TIME/TRANS	$AVERAGE TIME/TRANS	TABLE NUMBER	CURRENT CONTENTS
1	2	.102	40	26	64.9	1.224	3.500		
2	2	.243	64	30	46.8	1.828	3.441		1
3	3	.474	88	34	38.6	2.590	4.222		1
4	3	.754	113	31	27.4	3.203	4.414		1
10	1	.000	8	8	100.0	.000	.000		

$AVERAGE TIME/TRANS = AVERAGE TIME/TRANS EXCLUDING ZERO ENTRIES

```
***************************
*                         *
*   FULLWORD SAVEVALUES    *
*                         *
***************************
```

NUMBER - CONTENTS 1 2894   NUMBER - CONTENTS 2 3198   NUMBER - CONTENTS 3 1186   NUMBER - CONTENTS 4 1557   NUMBER - CONTENTS 10 92000   NUMBER - CONTENTS 11 101835

***** TOTAL RUN TIME (INCLUDING ASSEMBLY) = .06 MINUTES *****

END

facility would again become empty when the entity has completed its operations with the facility.

The PREEMPT statement has the format shown below:

PREEMPT A,B,C,D,E

where

A is the facility name

B is PR if priority preemption is desired; otherwise, B is not used

C,D,E are arguments that deal with aspects of preemption that are not discussed in this text; see the GPSS manual [3.1] for further information on the use of these arguments.

The two sample statements below illustrate nonpriority and priority preemption.

PREEMPT PH3

The entity executing this statement preempts the facility indicated by the value of its third half-word parameter. The entity preempted will regain control when the preempting entity has completed its operations with the facility.

PREEMPT CPU,PR

The priority of the entity executing this statement is compared against the priority of the entity holding the CPU facility. If the priority of the facility executing the statement is greater, control of the facility is given to that entity. Otherwise the entity waits at this statement block until the facility becomes empty or it has a higher priority than the entity holding the facility.

A preempting entity does not release a facility, but rather yields control via the RETURN statement. There is no difference to the programmer between RELEASE and RETURN. However, internally the two statements result in different actions to determine the entity to be given control of the facility. It is important to use RELEASE with SEIZE and RETURN with PREEMPT. Otherwise, GPSS produces an error message and terminates execution. The RETURN statement has the following format:

RETURN A

where

A is the facility name

Example 3.19 illustrates the use of nonpriority preemption.

EXAMPLE 3.19

In Example 3.18 an officer who had the need for a teller always moved to the front of the first teller's waiting line. Let us modify that model to include a less patient officer who immediately interrupts the first teller instead of waiting. When the officer's transaction is completed, the teller returns to process the interrupted customer.

```
JCK                                                               STATEMENT
MBER  *LOC   OPERATICN  A,B,C,D,E,F,G,H,I          COMMENTS        NUMBER
      *********************************************************************  1
      *     PROGRAM TO SIMULATE A BANK WITH A VARIABLE NUMBER OF TELLERS     2
      *   WITH SEPARATE WAITING LINES.  CUSTOMERS SELECT THE SHORTEST LINE.  3
      *   CUSTOMERS SELECT LAST TELLER IN CASE CF A TIE.                     4
      *     A BANK OFFICER ARRIVES WITH A TRANSACTION AND IMMEDIATELY        5
      *   INTERRUPTS THE FIRST TELLER.                                       6
      *     THE AMCUNT OF CASH ON HAND AT EACH TELLER STATION                7
      *   AND HELD BY THE HEAD TELLER IS MAINTAINED IN SAVEVALUES.           8
      *     THE TCTAL AMOUNT OF CASH AT THE END OF THE DAY IS PRINTED AS THE 9
      *   CONTENTS CF SAVEVALUE LOCATICN 11.                                10
      *                                                                     11
      *     PARAMETERS                                                      12
      *                                                                     13
      *     NUMBER CF TRANSACTIONS - 1 TO 5 PER CUSTCMER , AS SPECIFIED BY  14
      *          TRANS FUNCTION.  1 TRANSACTION PER OFFICER.                15
      *        CUSTCMER ARRIVALS - 2 MINUTES, EXPONENTIALLY DISTRIBUTED     16
      *        OFFICER ARRIVALS - 45 TC 75 MINUTES , UNIFORMLY DISTRIBUTED  17
      *        PROCESSING RATE -  SPECIFIED BY TYPE FUNCTION AND PROC VARIABLES 18
      *        TERMINATION CCNDITION - 8 HOURS                              19
      *        CASH WITHDRAWN PER CUSTOMER - FROM -499 TO 500 , UNIFORM DIST. 20
      *                                                                     21
      *********************************************************************  22
      *                                                                     23
      *     EXPONENTIAL FUNCTION                                            24
      *                                                                     25
      EXPO  FUNCTION    RN2,C24                                             26
      .0000,.000/.1000,.104/.2000,.222/.3000,.355/.4000,.509/.5000,.690/   27
      .6000,.915/.7C00,1.20/.7500,1.38/.8000,1.60/.8400,1.83/.8800,2.12/   28
      .9000,2.30/.9200,2.52/.9400,2.81/.9500,2.99/.9600,3.20/.970C,3.50/   29
      .9800,3.90/.9900,4.60/.9950,5.30/.9980,6.20/.9990,7.00/.9997,8.00/   30
      *                                                                     31
      *     TRANSACTION FUNCTION                                            32
      *                                                                     33
      TRANS FUNCTICN    RN3,D5                                              34
      .20,1/.45,2/.75,3/.90,4/1.0,5                                         35
      *                                                                     36
      *     TRANSACTICN TYPE FUNCTION                                       37
      *                                                                     38
      TYPE  FUNCTION    RN4,D6                                              39
      .20,1/.35,2/.55,3/.80,4/.95,5/1.0,6                                   40
      *                                                                     41
      *     PROCESSING TIME VARIABLES                                       42
      *                                                                     43
      PROC1 FVARIABLE   0.8*PH1                                             44
      PROC2 FVARIABLE   1.2*PH1                                             45
      PROC3 FVARIABLE   1.6*PH1                                             46
      PROC4 FVARIABLE   2.0*PH1                                             47
      PROC5 FVARIABLE   2.2*PH1                                             48
      PROC6 FVARIABLE   2.3*PH1                                             49
      *                                                                     50
      *     CASH WITHDRAWAL VARIABLE                                        51
      *                                                                     52
      CASH  VARIABLE    RN5-500                                            53
      *                                                                     54
      *     NUMBER OF TELLERS                                               55
```

```
        *                                                        50
        TELRS VARIABLE    4                    NUMBER CF TELLERS  5
        TELR1 VARIAELE    V$TELRS-1                               5
        *                                                        59
        *   INITIAL AMOUNT OF CASH PER TELLER                    60
        *                                                        61
        AMNT  VARIAELE    2000                                   62
        *                                                        63
        ************************************************************  64
        *                                                        65
        *    TELLER START UP SECTION                             66
        *                                                        6
        ************************************************************  68
        *                                                        6
              SIMULATE                                           70
1             GENERATE    ,,,1              GENERATE A DUMMY ENTITY  7
2             ASSIGN      6,V$TELRS,PH      PARM. 6 IS A LCCP INDEX  7
3             SAVEVALUE   10,100000,XF      LOC. 10 IS HEAD TELLER'S CASH  73
4       INIT  SAVEVALUE   PH6,V$AMNT,XF     EACH TELLER STARTS WITH V$AMNT  74
5             SAVEVALUE   10-,V$AMNT,XF     SUBTRACT FRCM HEAD TELLER'S CASH  7
6             LOOP        6PH,INIT          PROCESS ALL TELLERS  76
7             TERMINATE   0                 REMOVE CUMMY ENTITY  7
        *                                                        7
        ************************************************************  79
        *                                                        80
        *    CUSTOMER SECTION                                    81
        *                                                        82
        ************************************************************  83
        *                                                        84
8             GENERATE    2,FN$EXPC         CUSTOMER ARRIVES  85
9             ASSIGN      1,FN$TRANS,PH     SET NUMBER CF TRANSACTIONS  86
10            ASSIGN      2,FN$TYPE,PH      SET TRANSACTION TYPE  87
11            ASSIGN      5,V$CASH,PH       SET NET AMOUNT OF CASH TO BE WITHD  88
12            ASSIGN      3,V$TELRS,PH      SET LAST TELLER'S LINE AS SHORTEST  89
13            ASSIGN      4,V$TELR1,PH      P4 HAS CANDIDATE SHORTEST LINE  90
14      SHORT TEST L      Q*PF4,C*PH3,NLOOP TEST IF NEW SHORTEST LINE IS FOUND  91
15            ASSIGN      3,PH4,PH          SET NEW SHORTEST LINE IN PH3  92
16      NLOOP LOOP        4PH,SHORT         REPEAT FOR ALL LINES  93
17            QUEUE       PH3               CUSTOMER WAITS IN SHORTEST LINE  94
18            SEIZE       PH3               CUSTOMER REACHES TELLER  95
19            DEPART      PH3               REMOVE CUSTCMER FROM WAITING LINE  9
20            ADVANCE     V*PF2             TRANSACTIONS ARE PROCESSED  97
21            TEST L      X*PH3,PH5,CUST    TEST IF TELLER HAS ADEQUATE FUNDS  98
22            SAVEVALUE   PH3+,V$AMNT,XF    GIVE CASH TC TELLER  99
23            SAVEVALUE   10-,V$AMNT,XF     ADJUST HEAD TELLER'S CASH  100
24            ADVANCE     2                 2 MINUTES ARE NEEDED TO GET CASH  101
25      CUST  SAVEVALUE   PH3-,PH5          ADJUST TELLER'S CASH  102
26            RELEASE     PH3               CUSTOMER LEAVES TELLER  103
27            TERMINATE   0                                     104
        *                                                        105
        **********************                                  106
        *                                                        107
        *    OFFICER SECTION                                     108
        *                                                        109
        **********************                                  110
        *                                                        111
28            GENERATE    60,15             OFFICER ARRIVES WITH TRANSACTION  112
```

```
29      ASSIGN     1,1,PH            OFFICER HAS 1 TRANSACTION              113
30      ASSIGN     2,FN$TYPE,PH      SET TRANSACTION TYPE                   114
31      PREEMPT    1                 OFFICER INTERRUPTS FIRST TELLER        115
32      ADVANCE    V*PH2             OFFICER'S TRANSACTION IS PROCESSED     116
33      RETURN     1                 OFFICER LEAVES FIRST TELLER            117
34      TERMINATE  0                                                        118
                                                                            119
*                                                                          120
*********************************                                          121
*  TERMINATION SECTION                                                      122
*                                                                          123
*********************************                                          124
*                                                                          125
35      GENERATE   480                                                      126
36      ASSIGN     6,V$TELRS,PH      PARM. 6 IS LOOP INDEX                  127
37 TOTAL SAVEVALUE 11+,XF*PH6,XF     SUM OF CASH IN LOC. 11                 128
38      LOOP       6PH,TOTAL                                                129
39      SAVEVALUE  11+,XF10,XF       ADD IN HEAD TELLER'S CASH             130
40      TERMINATE  1                                                        131
        START      1                                                        132
        END                                                                133
```

RELATIVE CLOCK
BLOCK COUNTS

| | 480 RELATIVE CLOCK | | | 480 ABSOLUTE CLOCK | | | 48C | | | | |
BLOCK	CURRENT	TOTAL	BLOCK	CURRENT	TOTAL	BLOCK	CURRENT	TOTAL	BLOCK	CURRENT	TOTAL
1	0	1	11	0	297	21	0	291	31	0	8
2	0	1	12	0	297	22	●	0	32	0	8
3	0	1	13	0	297	23	0	0	33	0	8
4	0	4	14	0	891	24	0		34	0	8
5	0	4	15	0	187	25	0	291	35	0	1
6	0	4	16	0	891	26	0	291	36	0	1
7	0	1	17	3	297	27	0	291	37	0	4
8	0	297	18	0	294	28	0	8	38	0	4
9	0	297	19	0	294	29	0	8	39	0	1
10	0	297	20	3	294	30	0	8	40	0	1

```
****************************
*                          *
*       FACILITIES         *
*                          *
****************************

FACILITY   NUMBER    AVERAGE   -AVERAGE  UTILIZATION DURING-  CURRENT  PERCENT       TRANSACTION NUMBER
           ENTRIES   TIME/TRAN  TOTAL    AVAIL.  UNAVAIL.     STATUS   AVAILABILITY  SEIZING PREEMPTING
                                TIME     TIME    TIME
    1        4C       2.950      .245                                   100.0
    2        6?       3.587      .470                                   100.0          15
    3        87       4.080      .739                                   100.0          12
    4       112       3.937      .918                                   100.0          16

****************************************
*                                      *
*              QUEUES                  *
*                                      *
****************************************

QUEUE   MAXIMUM   AVERAGE   TOTAL    ZERC     PERCENT   AVERAGE     $AVERAGE
        CONTENTS  CONTENTS  ENTRIES  ENTRIES  ZEROS     TIME/TRANS  TIME/TRANS
   1       2       .102      32       18       56.2      1.531       3.500
   2       2       .243      64       30       46.8      1.828       3.441
   3       3       .474      88       34       38.6      2.590       4.222
   4       3       .754     113       31       27.4      3.203       4.414

$AVERAGE TIME/TRANS = AVERAGE TIME/TRANS EXCLUDING ZERC ENTRIES

****************************************
*                                      *
*        FULLWORD SAVEVALUES           *
*                                      *
****************************************

NUMBER - CONTENTS  NUMBER - CONTENTS  NUMBER - CONTENTS  NUMBER - CONTENTS  NUMBER - CONTENTS  NUMBER - CONTENTS
    1     3894         2     3198         3     1186         4     1557        10    92000        11    101835

***** TOTAL RUN TIME (INCLUDING ASSEMBLY) = .06 MINUTES *****

                                                                    TABLE    CURRENT
                                                                    NUMBER   CONTENTS
                                                                             1
                                                                             1
                                                                             1

END
```

Since the officer chooses the least active teller and the demands of the officer are very infrequent, there is little observable effect when the officer entity preempts rather than seizes the teller facility. The only difference in the statistics appears in the waiting line for teller 1. Since the officer does not wait for service, the queuing statistics for the first teller have changed slightly.

3.19 TABLES

The output produced by our GPSS examples has been determined by the type of statements used in the program. For example, facilities, storages, and queues each produce a particular set of statistics. The user has had no influence on the type of output generated. GPSS does provide the user with some flexibility as to the type of output produced, One such capability is the creation of tables that provide distributions as well as summary statistics on events in the model.

Tables must be defined explicitly, in a manner resembling storages, using the TABLE statement. Entries are made in the tables through the use of the TABULATE statement, which determines the numerical value to be stored. All tables are printed automatically upon successful program termination.

The definition of tables requires a complete specification of table size and contents. Since the size and number of intervals in a table are difficult to determine for an unknown distribution, many initial runs may result in tables with undesirable clustering of values. Often a second run is required to obtain a better picture of the distribution. The TABLE statement, which is used to define a table, has the following format:

TABLE A,B,C,D

where

A is the SNA to be tabulated, that is, used as the table's index

B is the lower limit

C is the interval size

D is the number of intervals

The range of values in the table is from B to B+C*D. Special intervals are created for values less than B or greater than B+C*D. The latter interval is labeled with OVERFLOW. The sample statement shown below defines a table that records the values assumed by half-word parameter 9.

RANGE TABLE PH9,0,100,10

The table RANGE will have 10 intervals, 1–100, 101–200,..., 901–1000.

Entries are made in tables by the execution of TABULATE statements. Whenever an entity executes a TABULATE statement for a given table, the table

index is evaluated and an entry made in the appropriate interval. The TABU-
LATE statement has the following form:

> TABULATE A,B

where

> A is the table in which an entry is to be made
>
> B is an optional argument indicating the number of entries to be made in the
> interval; the default value for B is 1

The use of the B argument permits weighing of the distribution based upon
events in the simulation.

The following two sample TABULATE statements illustrate its use in
conjunction with the previous sample TABLE statement.

> TABULATE RANGE

Half-word parameter 9 of the entity entering this statement block is
evaluated. An entry is made in the RANGE interval corresponding to the value of
the parameter.

> TABULATE RANGE,PH6

The action taken as a result of this statement is identical to that of the
previous sample except that half-word parameter 6 determines the number of
entries to be made in the appropriate interval of RANGE.

The statistics printed for a table include the number of entries, mean,
standard deviation, and sum for the entire table. For each interval, the upper limit
is printed, followed by the frequency, percentage of total entries in interval,
cumulative percentage, cumulative remainder (one minus cumulative percentage), multiple of mean (ratio of upper limit of interval to the mean), and deviation from mean. The output of Example 3.20 contains tables to familiarize the
reader with their content.

One piece of information that is important in many discrete simulation
models is the amount of time required for an entity to progress between two
points in the model. The time required to pass between two GPSS statements can
be recorded in table by use of MARK and TABULATE statements. The MARK
statement records the clock time in the transit time filed of the entity. The transit
time is a special field maintained as part of the information on each entity and
designated by the SNA M1. When the entity reaches a TABULATE statement
for a table indexed on transit time, the M1 value is subtracted from the current
clock time. The result is stored in M1 and used to determine the interval in which
a table entry should be made.

The MARK statement has no arguments. Whenever an entity enters a
MARK statement block, the clock time is placed in its M1 field. The use of
MARK statements is shown below.

> QTIME TABLE M1,100,200,50

.

MARK

.

.

TABULATE QTIME

If an entity executes MARK at clock time 2165 and then reaches the TABULATE statement at 3468, the value of M1 changes from 2165 to 1303 when the TABULATE statement is executed. Since the intervals in QTIME begin at 100 and increase in increments of 200, an entry will be made in the 1301–1500 interval.

EXAMPLE 3.20

Tables are inserted into the bank teller simulation model of Example 3.19 to obtain distributions of customer waiting time, total customer time in the bank, and teller cash on hand. Customer waiting-time data appear in the CUSTW table, customer time in bank information is in CUSTT, and CASHT holds the teller cash-on-hand distribution. Since the use of tables does not cause any alterations to the other portions of the program output, only the source code and tables are shown.

As shown by the output for CUSTW and CUSTT, GPSS terminates the printing of a table when all nonzero entries have been printed. The CASHT tables have overflow entries since on four occasions a teller had more than $3800 on hand. The only information given for the overflow entries is frequency and average value.

The CUSTW and CUSTT tables both measure time spent by customer entities in various parts of the model. However, only CUSTW uses M1 as its index. Since the waiting time measured in CUSTW is wholly contained in the time spent in the bank measured in CUSTT and there is only one M1 field per entity, the time of entrance to the bank had to be saved elsewhere. Thus, half-word parameter 7 holds the customer's time of entry to the bank. When the customer leaves, the total time in the bank is computed and stored in half-word parameter 7, which is used as the CUSTT table index.

3.20 DEBUGGING STATEMENTS

Two types of debugging aids, tracing and selective printing, are available to the GPSS programmer. The *tracing feature* produces dumps of the current and future events lists for all actions taken while it is enabled. The tracing feature is activated by the TRACE statement and deactivated by UNTRACE. The *selective printing option* permits the programmer to obtain portions of the standard GPSS

```
BLOCK                                                                    STATEM
NUMBER *LOC    OPERATICN  A,B,C,D,E,F,G,H,I         COMMENTS              NUMBE
       ***************************************************************************  1
       *       PROGRAM TO SIMULATE A BANK WITH A VARIABLE NUMBER OF TELLERS        2
       *    WITH SEPARATE WAITING LINES.  CUSTOMERS SELECT THE SHORTEST LINE.      3
       *    CUSTOMERS SELECT LAST TELLER IN CASE CF A TIE.                         4
       *       A BANK CFFICER ARRIVES WITH A TRANSACTION AND IMMEDIATELY           5
       *    INTERRUPTS THE FIRST TELLER.                                           6
       *       THE AMCLNT OF CASH ON HAND AT EACH TELLER STATICN                   7
       *    AND HELD BY THE HEAD TELLER IS MAINTAINED IN SAVEVALUES.               8
       *       THE TOTAL AMOUNT OF CASH AT THE END OF THE DAY IS PRINTED AS THE    9
       *    CONTENTS CF SAVEVALUE LCCATICN 11.                                    10
       *                                                                          11
       *       PARAMETERS                                                         12
       *                                                                          13
       *       NUMBER OF TRANSACTIONS - 1 TO 5 PER CUSTCMER , AS SPECIFIED BY     14
       *          TRANS FUNCTION.  1 TRANSACTICN PER CFFICER.                     15
       *       CUSTCMER ARRIVALS - 2 MINUTES, EXPONENTIALLY DISTRIBUTED           16
       *       CFFICER ARRIVALS - 45 TO 75 MINUTES , UNIFORMLY DISTRIBUTED        17
       *       PROCESSING RATE -  SPECIFIED BY TYPE FUACTICN AND PROC VARIABLES   18
       *       TERMINATION CONDITION - 8 HOURS                                    19
       *    CASH WITHDRAWN PER CUSTOMER - FROM -499 TO 500 , UNIFORM DIST.        20
       *                                                                          21
       ****************************************************************************  22
       *                                                                          23
       *    EXPCNENTIAL FUNCTION                                                  24
       *                                                                          25
       EXPO   FUNCTION   RN2,C 24                                                 26
       .0000,.000/.1000,.104/.2000,.222/.3000,.355/.40C0,.509/.500C,.690/        27
       .6000,.915/.7000,1.20/.7500,1.38/.8000,1.60/.8400,1.83/.8800,2.12/        28
       .9000,2.3C/.92C0,2.52/.9400,2.81/.9500,2.99/.9600,3.20/.9700,3.50/        29
       .9800,3.90/.9900,4.60/.9950,5.30/.9980,6.20/.999C,7.0C/.9997,8.00/        30
       *                                                                          31
       *    TRANSACTICN FUNCTION                                                  32
       *                                                                          33
       TRANS FUNCTICN   RN3,D5                                                    34
       .20,1/.45,2/.75,3/.90,4/1.0,5                                             35
       *                                                                          36
       *    TRANSACTION TYPE FUNCTION                                            37
       *                                                                          38
       TYPE  FUNCTICN   RN4,D6                                                    39
       .20,1/.35,2/.55,3/.80,4/.95,5/1.0,6                                       40
       *                                                                          41
       *    PROCESSINC TIME VARIABLES                                            42
       *                                                                          43
       PROC1 FVARIABLE   0.8*PH1                                                  44
       PROC2 FVARIABLE   1.2*PH1                                                  45
       PROC3 FVARIABLE   1.6*PH1                                                  46
       PROC4 FVARIABLE   2.0*PH1                                                  47
       PROC5 FVARIABLE   2.2*PH1                                                  48
       PROC6 FVARIABLE   2.3*PH1                                                  49
       *                                                                          50
       *       CASH WITHDRAWAL VARIABLE                                          51
       *                                                                          52
       CASH  VARIAELE   RN5-500                                                   53
       *                                                                          54
       *    NUMBER CF TELLERS                                                     55
```

```
*                                                                    56
  TELRS VARIABLE    4               NUMBER CF TELLERS                57
  TELR1 VARIABLE    V$TELRS-1                                        58
*                                                                    59
*   INITIAL AMCUNT OF CASH PER TELLER                               60
*                                                                    61
  AMNT  VARIABLE    2000                                            62
*                                                                    63
*   CUSTCMER TIME IN BANK                                           64
*                                                                    65
  CTIME VARIABLE    C1-PH7                                          66
*                                                                    67
*   TABLES                                                          68
*                                                                    69
  CUSTW TABLE       M1,0,1,20        CUSTOMER WAITING TIME          70
  CUSTT TABLE       PH7,0,1,20       CUTOMER TIME IN BANK           71
  CASHT TABLE       X*PH3,0,100,40   TELLER CASH ON HAND            72
*                                                                    73
******************************************************************  74
*                                                                    75
*   TELLER START UP SECTICN                                         76
*                                                                    77
******************************************************************  78
*                                                                    79
          SIMULATE                                                  80
1         GENERATE    ,,,1           GENERATE A DUMMY ENTITY        81
2         ASSIGN      6,V$TELRS,PH   PARM. 6 IS A LOOP INDEX        82
3         SAVEVALUE   10,100000,XF   LOC. 10 IS HEAD TELLER'S CASH  83
4   INIT  SAVEVALUE   PH6,V$AMNT,XF  EACH TELLER STARTS WITH V$AMNT 84
5         SAVEVALUE   10-,V$AMNT,XF  SUBTRACT FROM HEAD TELLER'S CASH 85
6         LOCP        6PH,INIT       PROCESS ALL TELLERS            86
7         TERMINATE   0              REMOVE CUMMY ENTITY            87
*                                                                    88
******************************************************************  89
*                                                                    90
*   CUSTOMER SECTION                                                91
*                                                                    92
******************************************************************  93
*                                                                    94
8         GENERATE    2,FN$EXPO      CUSTOMER ARRIVES               95
9         ASSIGN      1,FN$TRANS,PH  SET NUMBER OF TRANSACTIONS     96
10        ASSIGN      7,C1,PH        SAVE ARRIVAL TIME              97
11        ASSIGN      2,FN$TYPE,PH   SET TRANSACTION TYPE           98
12        ASSIGN      5,V$CASH,PH    SET NET AMOUNT OF CASH TO BE WITHD 99
13        ASSIGN      3,V$TELRS,PH   SET LAST TELLER'S LINE AS SHORTEST 100
14        ASSIGN      4,V$TELR1,PH   P4 HAS CANDIDATE SHORTEST LINE 101
15  SHORT TEST L      Q*PH4,Q*PH3,NLOOP TEST IF NEW SHCRTEST LINE IS FOUND 102
16        ASSIGN      3,PH4,PH       SET NEW SHORTEST LINE IN PH3   103
17  NLOOP LOCP        4PH,SHORT      REPEAT FOR ALL LINES           104
18        QUEUE       PH3            CUSTOMER WAITS IN SHORTEST LINE 105
19        MARK                       RECORD CUTOMER ENTRY TIME      106
20        SEIZE       PH3            CUSTOMER REACHES TELLER        107
21        DEPART      PH3            REMOVE CUSTOMER FROM WAITING LINE 108
22        TABULATE    CUSTW          RECORD WAITING TIME            109
23        ADVANCE     V*PH2          TRANSACTIONS ARE PROCESSED     110
24        TEST L      X*PH3,PH5,CUST TEST IF TELLER HAS ADEQUATE FUNDS 111
25        SAVEVALUE   PH3+,V$AMNT,XF GIVE CASH TC TELLER            112
```

```
26              SAVEVALUE     10-,V$AMNT,XF       ADJUST HEAD TELLER'S CASH                113
27              ADVANCE       2                   2 MINUTES ARE NEEDED TO GET CASH         114
28      CUST    SAVEVALUE     PH3-,PH5            ADJUST TELLER'S CASH                     115
29              TABULATE      CASHT               RECORD TELLER'S CASH ON HAND             116
30              RELEASE       PH3                 CUSTOMER LEAVES TELLER                   117
31              ASSIGN        7,V$C TIME,PH       DETERMINE TIME SPENT IN BANK             118
32              TABULATE      CUSTT               RECORD TIME SPENT IN BANK                119
33              TERMINATE     0                                                            120
        *                                                                                  121
        ****************************                                                       122
        *                                                                                  123
        *       OFFICER SECTION                                                            124
        *                                                                                  125
        ****************************                                                       126
        *                                                                                  127
34              GENERATE      60,15               OFFICER ARRIVES WITH TRANSACTION         128
35              ASSIGN        1,1,PH              OFFICER HAS 1 TRANSACTION                129
36              ASSIGN        2,FN$TYPE,PH        SET TRANSACTION TYPE                     130
37              PREEMPT       1                   OFFICER INTERRUPTS FIRST TELLER          131
38              ADVANCE       V*PH2               OFFICER'S TRANSACTION IS PROCESSED       132
39              RETURN        1                   OFFICER LEAVES FIRST TELLER              133
40              TERMINATE     0                                                            134
        *                                                                                  135
        ****************************                                                       136
        *                                                                                  137
        *   TERMINATION SECTION                                                            138
        *                                                                                  139
        ****************************                                                       140
        *                                                                                  141
41              GENERATE      480                                                          142
42              ASSIGN        6,V$TELRS,PH        PARM. 6 IS LOOP INDEX                    143
43      TOTAL   SAVEVALUE     11+,XF*PH6,XF       SUM OF CASH IN LOC. 11                   144
44              LOOP          6PH,TOTAL                                                    145
45              SAVEVALUE     11+,XF10,XF         ADD IN HEAD TELLER'S CASH                146
46              TERMINATE     1                                                            147
                START         1                                                            148
                END                                                                        149
```

```
                          *****************************************
                          *                                       *
                          *                TABLES                 *
                          *                                       *
                          *****************************************
```

TABLE CUSTW
ENTRIES IN TABLE   MEAN ARGUMENT   STANDARD DEVIATION   SUM OF ARGUMENTS
    294   2.537   2.941   746.000   NON-WEIGHTED

UPPER LIMIT	OBSERVED FREQUENCY	PER CENT OF TOTAL	CUMULATIVE PERCENTAGE	CUMULATIVE REMAINDER	MULTIPLE OF MEAN	DEVIATION FROM MEAN
0	113	38.43	38.4	61.5	-.000	-.862
1	23	7.82	46.2	53.7	.394	-.522
2	35	11.90	58.1	41.8	.788	-.182
3	38	12.92	71.0	28.9	1.182	.157
4	23	7.82	78.9	21.0	1.576	.497
5	15	5.10	84.0	15.9	1.970	.837
6	20	6.80	90.8	9.1	2.364	1.177
7	4	1.36	92.1	7.8	2.758	1.517
8	8	2.72	94.8	5.1	3.152	1.857
9	5	1.70	96.5	3.4	3.546	2.197
10	4	1.36	97.9	2.0	3.941	2.537
11	1	.34	98.2	1.7	4.335	2.877
12	3	1.02	99.3	.6	4.729	3.217
13	1	.34	99.6	.3	5.123	3.557
14	0	.00	99.6	.3	5.517	3.896
15	1	.34	100.0	.0	5.911	4.236

REMAINING FREQUENCIES ARE ALL ZERO

TABLE CUSTT
ENTRIES IN TABLE 291
MEAN ARGUMENT 6.408
STANDARD DEVIATION 4.105
SUM OF ARGUMENTS 1865.000
NON-WEIGHTED

UPPER LIMIT	OBSERVED FREQUENCY	PER CENT OF TOTAL	CUMULATIVE PERCENTAGE	CUMULATIVE REMAINDER	MULTIPLE OF MEAN	DEVIATION FROM MEAN
0	8	2.74	2.7	97.2	-.000	-1.561
1	14	4.81	7.5	92.4	.156	-1.317
2	28	9.62	17.1	82.8	.312	-1.073
3	23	7.90	25.0	74.9	.468	-.830
4	41	14.08	39.1	60.8	.624	-.586
5	27	9.27	48.4	51.5	.780	-.343
6	34	11.68	60.1	39.8	.936	-.099
7	19	6.52	66.6	33.3	1.092	.143
8	18	6.18	72.8	27.1	1.248	.387
9	18	6.18	79.0	20.9	1.404	.631
10	11	3.78	82.8	17.1	1.560	.874
11	10	3.43	86.2	13.7	1.716	1.118
12	10	3.43	89.6	10.3	1.872	1.361
13	11	3.78	93.4	6.5	2.028	1.605
14	6	2.06	95.5	4.4	2.184	1.849
15	2	.68	96.2	3.7	2.340	2.092
16	3	1.03	97.2	2.7	2.496	2.336
17	5	1.71	98.9	1.0	2.652	2.579
18	3	1.03	100.0	.0	2.808	2.823

REMAINING FREQUENCIES ARE ALL ZERO

TABLE CASHT
ENTRIES IN TABLE 291   MEAN ARGUMENT 2085.632   STANDARD DEVIATION 943.000   SUM OF ARGUMENTS 606919.000   NON-WEIGHTED

UPPER LIMIT	OBSERVED FREQUENCY	PER CENT OF TOTAL	CUMULATIVE PERCENTAGE	CUMULATIVE REMAINDER	MULTIPLE OF MEAN	DEVIATION FROM MEAN
0	0	.00	.0	100.0	-.000	-2.211
100	1	.34	.3	99.6	.047	-2.105
200	0	.00	.3	99.6	.095	-1.999
300	2	.68	1.0	98.9	.143	-1.893
400	1	.34	1.3	98.6	.191	-1.787
500	5	1.71	3.0	96.9	.239	-1.681
600	1	.34	3.4	96.5	.287	-1.575
700	4	1.37	4.8	95.1	.335	-1.469
800	10	3.43	8.2	91.7	.383	-1.363
900	7	2.40	10.6	89.3	.431	-1.257
1000	8	2.74	13.4	86.5	.479	-1.151
1100	10	3.43	16.8	83.1	.527	-1.045
1200	10	3.43	20.2	79.7	.575	-.939
1300	11	3.78	24.0	75.9	.623	-.833
1400	12	4.12	28.1	71.8	.671	-.727
1500	14	4.81	32.9	67.0	.719	-.621
1600	10	3.43	36.4	63.5	.767	-.514
1700	13	4.46	40.8	59.1	.815	-.408
1800	3	1.03	41.9	58.0	.863	-.302
1900	11	3.78	45.7	54.2	.910	-.196
2000	10	3.43	49.1	50.8	.958	-.090
2100	13	4.46	53.6	46.3	1.006	.015
2200	5	1.71	55.3	44.6	1.054	.121
2300	10	3.43	58.7	41.2	1.102	.227
2400	10	3.43	62.1	37.8	1.150	.333
2500	9	3.09	65.2	34.7	1.198	.439
2600	6	2.06	67.3	32.6	1.246	.545
2700	8	2.74	70.1	29.8	1.294	.651
2800	5	1.71	71.8	28.1	1.342	.757
2900	5	1.71	73.5	26.4	1.390	.863
3000	13	4.46	78.0	21.9	1.438	.969
3100	7	2.40	80.4	19.5	1.486	1.075
3200	14	4.81	85.2	14.7	1.534	1.181
3300	7	2.40	87.6	12.3	1.582	1.287
3400	6	2.06	89.6	10.3	1.630	1.393
3500	7	2.40	92.0	7.9	1.678	1.499
3600	6	2.06	94.1	5.8	1.726	1.605
3700	9	3.09	97.2	2.7	1.774	1.711
3800	4	1.37	98.6	1.3	1.821	1.817
OVERFLOW	4	1.37	100.0	.0		

AVERAGE VALUE OF OVERFLOW 3982.75

program output at intermediate points in the program. The PRINT statement is the mechanism by which the selective prints are obtained.

Tracing produces the same output that is obtained when a fatal run-time error occurs in a GPSS program. As long as the tracing feature is enabled, each time an entity enters a statement block, a message is printed indicating the statements between which the entity passed, the internal identifier of the entity, and the clock time. Following the message, the entries on the current and future events lists are dumped. A complete listing of the contents of the fields associated with each entity is produced including priority, mark time, and parameter values. The reader must be cautioned that the trace facility can result in a large amount of output. However, situations in which the programmer is totally befuddled occasionally arise. In those situations, tracing is the first step in the debugging procedure.

As with the MARK statement, TRACE and UNTRACE are used without arguments. These statements serve only to activate and deactivate the tracing facility. The programmer must be certain that an UNTRACE statement can be reached from a TRACE statement in order to prevent runaway output.

EXAMPLE 3.21

In order to illustrate the TRACE output, the tracing facility is enabled whenever an officer appears in the bank teller model of Example 3.20. Only the trace output is shown here since the remainder of the output is identical to that shown in the previous example, The output presented traces one officer entity from generation to termination.

The trace output permits us to follow the entity statement-by-statement as it moves through the officer section of code. The setting of the parameter values in statements 36 and 37 can be observed. The output also shows that the officer spent 1 minute with the teller.

The selective printing feature permits the programmer to obtain statistical information on any of the system attributes at intermediate points in the program. The information printed is identical in form to that printed upon normal program termination. Selective printing is produced by the PRINT statement, which has the following format:

> PRINT A,B,C,D

where

> A is the lower limit of the output
>
> B is the upper limit of the output
>
> C is the output code, as listed in Table 3.4
>
> D is the paging control; any alphabetic character will prevent the output from beginning on a new page

```
LOCK                                                                      STATEMENT
UMBER *LCC    OPERATION  A,B,C,D,E,F,G,H,I              COMMENTS            NUMBER
      **********************************************************************   1
      *      PROGRAM TO SIMULATE A BANK WITH A VARIABLE NUMBER OF TELLERS     2
      *   WITH SEPARATE WAITING LINES.  CUSTOMERS SELECT THE SHORTEST LINE.   3
      *   CUSTOMERS SELECT LAST TELLER IN CASE OF A TIE.                      4
      *      A BANK OFFICER ARRIVES WITH A TRANSACTION AND IMMEDIATELY        5
      *   INTERRUPTS THE FIRST TELLER.                                        6
      *      THE AMOUNT OF CASH ON HAND AT EACH TELLER STATION                7
      *   AND HELD BY THE HEAD TELLER IS MAINTAINED IN SAVEVALUES.            8
      *      THE TOTAL AMOUNT OF CASH AT THE END CF THE DAY IS PRINTED AS THE 9
      *   CONTENTS CF SAVEVALUE LOCATION 11.                                 10
      *                                                                      11
      *   PARAMETERS                                                         12
      *                                                                      13
      *      NUMBER OF TRANSACTIONS - 1 TO 5 PER CUSTOMER , AS SPECIFIED BY  14
      *         TRANS FUNCTICN.  1 TRANSACTION PER OFFICER.                  15
      *      CUSTOMER ARRIVALS - 2 MINUTES, EXPCNENTIALLY DISTRIBUTED        16
      *      OFFICER ARRIVALS - 45 TO 75 MINUTES , UNIFORMLY DISTRIBUTED     17
      *      PROCESSING RATE -  SPECIFIED BY TYPE FUNCTION AND PROC VARIABLES 18
      *      TERMINATION CCNDITION - 8 HOURS                                 19
      *      CASH WITHDRAWN PER CUSTOMER - FROM -499 TC 500 , UNIFCRM DIST.  20
      *                                                                      21
      **********************************************************************  22
      *                                                                      23
      *   EXPONENTIAL FUNCTION                                               24
      *                                                                      25
       EXPO   FUNCTICN    RN2,C24                                            26
      .0000,.000/.1C00,.104/.2C00,.222/.3000,.355/.4000,.509/.5000,.690/     27
      .6000,.915/.7000,1.20/.7500,1.38/.8000,1.60/.84CC,1.83/.880C,2.12/     28
      .9000,2.30/.9200,2.52/.9400,2.81/.9500,2.99/.9600,3.20/.9700,3.50/     29
      .9800,3.90/.9900,4.60/.9950,5.30/.9980,6.20/.9990,7.00/.9997,8.00/     30
      *                                                                      31
      *   TRANSACTION FUNCTION                                               32
      *                                                                      33
       TRANS  FUNCTICN    RN3,D5                                             34
      .20,1/.45,2/.75,3/.90,4/1.0,5                                          35
      *                                                                      36
      *      TRANSACTION TYPE FUNCTION                                       37
      *                                                                      38
       TYPE   FUNCTION    RN4,D6                                             39
      .20,1/.35,2/.55,3/.80,4/.95,5/1.0,6                                    40
      *                                                                      41
      *   PROCESSING TIME VARIABLES                                          42
      *                                                                      43
       PROC1  FVARIABLE   0.8*PH1                                            44
       PROC2  FVARIABLE   1.2*PH1                                            45
       PROC3  FVARIABLE   1.6*PH1                                            46
       PROC4  FVARIABLE   2.0*PH1                                            47
       PROC5  FVARIABLE   2.2*PH1                                            48
       PROC6  FVARIABLE   2.3*PH1                                            49
      *                                                                      50
      *      CASH WITHCRAWAL VARIABLE                                        51
      *                                                                      52
       CASH   VARIABLE    RN5-500                                           53
      *                                                                      54
      *   NUMBER CF TELLERS                                                  55
```

```
       *                                                                    56
       TELRS VARIABLE    4                   NUMBER OF TELLERS              57
       TELR1 VARIABLE    V$TELRS-1                                          58
       *                                                                    59
       *   INITIAL AMOUNT OF CASH PER TELLER                                60
       *                                                                    61
       AMNT  VARIABLE    2000                                               62
       *                                                                    63
       *   CUSTOMER TIME IN BANK                                            64
       *                                                                    65
       CTIME VARIABLE    C1-PH7                                             66
       *                                                                    67
       *   TABLES                                                           68
       *                                                                    69
       CUSTW TABLE       M1,0,1,20           CUSTOMER WAITING TIME          70
       CUSTT TABLE       PH7,0,1,20          CUTOMER TIME IN BANK           71
       CASHT TABLE       X*PH3,0,100,40      TELLER CASH ON HAND            72
       *                                                                    73
       **********************************************************************  74
       *                                                                    75
       *   TELLER START UP SECTION                                          76
       *                                                                    77
       **********************************************************************  78
       *                                                                    79
              SIMULATE                                                      80
  1           GENERATE    ,,,1               GENERATE A DUMMY ENTITY        81
  2           ASSIGN      6,V$TELRS,PH        PARM. 6 IS A LCOP INDEX       82
  3           SAVEVALUE   10, 100000,XF       LOC. 10 IS HEAD TELLER'S CASH 83
  4     INIT  SAVEVALUE   PH6,V$AMNT,XF       EACH TELLER STARTS WITH V$AMNT 84
  5           SAVEVALUE   10-,V$AMNT,XF       SUBTRACT FROM HEAD TELLER'S CASH 85
  6           LOOP        6PH,INIT            PROCESS ALL TELLERS           86
  7           TERMINATE   0                   REMOVE DUMMY ENTITY           87
       *                                                                    88
       **********************************************************************  89
       *                                                                    90
       *   CUSTOMER SECTION                                                 91
       *                                                                    92
       **********************************************************************  93
       *                                                                    94
  8           GENERATE    2,FN$EXPO           CUSTOMER ARRIVES              95
  9           ASSIGN      1,FN$TRANS,PH       SET NUMBER OF TRANSACTIONS    96
 10           ASSIGN      7,C1,PH             SAVE ARRIVAL TIME             97
 11           ASSIGN      2,FN$TYPE,PH        SET TRANSACTION TYPE          98
 12           ASSIGN      5,V$CASH,PH         SET NET AMOUNT OF CASH TO BE WITHD 99
 13           ASSIGN      3,V$TELRS,PH        SET LAST TELLER'S LINE AS SHORTEST 100
 14           ASSIGN      4,V$TELR1,PH        P4 HAS CANDIDATE SHORTEST LINE 101
 15     SHORT TEST L      Q*PH4,Q*PH3,NLOOP   TEST IF NEW SHORTEST LINE IS FOUND 102
 16           ASSIGN      3,PH4,PH            SET NEW SHORTEST LINE IN PH3  103
 17     NLOOP LOOP        4PH,SHORT           REPEAT FOR ALL LINES          104
 18           QUEUE       PH3                 CUSTOMER WAITS IN SHORTEST LINE 105
 19           MARK                            RECORC CUTOMER ENTRY TIME     106
 20           SEIZE       PH3                 CUSTOMER REACHES TELLER       107
 21           DEPART      PH3                 REMOVE CUSTOMER FROM WAITING LINE 108
 22           TABULATE    CUSTW               RECORD WAITING TIME           109
 23           ADVANCE     V*PH2               TRANSACTIONS ARE PROCESSED    110
 24           TEST L      X*PH3,PH5,CUST      TEST IF TELLER HAS ADEQUATE FUNDS 111
 25           SAVEVALUE   PH3+,V$AMNT,XF      GIVE CASH TO TELLER           112
```

```
26        SAVEVALUE   10-,V$AMNT,XF    ADJUST HEAD TELLER'S CASH
27        ADVANCE     2                2 MINUTES ARE NEEDED TO GET CASH
28   CUST SAVEVALUE   PH3-,PH5         ADJUST TELLER'S CASH
29        TABULATE    CASHT            RECORD TELLER'S CASH ON HAND
30        RELEASE     PH3              CUSTOMER LEAVES TELLER
31        ASSIGN      7,V$CTIME,PH     DETERMINE TIME SPENT IN BANK
32        TABULATE    CUSTT            RECORD TIME SPENT IN BANK
33        TERMINATE   0
     *
     *******************************
     *
     *    OFFICER SECTION
     *
     *******************************
     *
34        GENERATE    60,15            OFFICER ARRIVES WITH TRANSACTION
35        TRACE
36        ASSIGN      1,1,PH           OFFICER HAS 1 TRANSACTION
37        ASSIGN      2,FN$TYPE,PH     SET TRANSACTION TYPE
38        PREEMPT     1                OFFICER INTERRUPTS FIRST TELLER
39        ADVANCE     V*PH2            OFFICER'S TRANSACTION IS PROCESSED
40        RETURN      1                OFFICER LEAVES FIRST TELLER
41        UNTRACE
42        TERMINATE   0
     *
     *******************************
     *
     *    TERMINATION SECTION
     *
     *******************************
     *
43        GENERATE    480
44        ASSIGN      6,V$TELRS,PH     PARM. 6 IS LOOP INDEX
45  TOTAL SAVEVALUE   11+,XF*PH6,XF    SUM OF CASH IN LOC. 11
46        LOOP        6PH,TOTAL
47        SAVEVALUE   11+,XF10,XF      ADD IN HEAD TELLER'S CASH
48        TERMINATE   1
          START       1
          END
```

Line numbers (right margin): 113, 114, 115, 116, 117, 118, 119, 120, 121, 122, 123, 124, 125, 126, 127, 128, 129, 130, 131, 132, 133, 134, 135, 136, 137, 138, 139, 140, 141, 142, 143, 144, 145, 146, 147, 148, 149, 150, 151

```
TRANS    7 FROM  35 TO  35 CLOCK  36                  125 TERMINATIONS TO GO  125
```

*TRANS	CUR BLOCK	NEXT BLOCK	ADV BLK	DEPART	PRIORITY	MARK TIME	ASSEM SET	SEL	TRACE	DELAY	CHAIN	PREEMPT	COUNT/FLAG
7	35	36		125	0	125	1		X		C		

1	2	3	4	5	6	7	8	9	10
0	0	0	0	0	0	0	0	0	0

HALFWORD PARAMETERS

	1	2	3	4	5	6	7	8	9	10
1 - 10	0	0	0	0	0	0	0	0	0	0
11 - 12	0	0								

TRANS 7   FROM 36 TO 37   CLOCK 125
*TRANS 7

CUR BLOCK	NEXT BLOCK	ADV BLK DEPART	TERMINATIONS TO GO PRIORITY	MARK TIME	ASSEM SET	SEL TRACE	DELAY CHAIN	PREEMPT	COUNT/FLAG
36	37	125	0	125	1 / 7	x	C		

Parameters: 1 – 0   2 – 0   3 – 0   4 – 0   5 – 0   6 – 0   7 – 0   8 – 0   9 – 0   10 – 0

HALFWORD PARAMETERS
 1 – 10
11 – 12

TRANS 7   FROM 37 TO 38   CLOCK 125
*TRANS 7

CUR BLOCK	NEXT BLOCK	ADV BLK DEPART	TERMINATIONS TO GO PRIORITY	MARK TIME	ASSEM SET	SEL TRACE	DELAY CHAIN	PREEMPT	COUNT/FLAG
37	38	125	0	125	1 / 7	x	C		

Parameters: 1 – 0   2 – 0   3 – 0   4 – 0   5 – 0   6 – 0   7 – 0   8 – 0   9 – 0   10 – 0

HALFWORD PARAMETERS
 1 – 10
11 – 12

TRANS 7   FROM 38 TO 39   CLOCK 125
*TRANS 7

CUR BLOCK	NEXT BLOCK	ADV BLK DEPART	TERMINATIONS TO GO PRIORITY	MARK TIME	ASSEM SET	SEL TRACE	DELAY CHAIN	PREEMPT	COUNT/FLAG
38	39	125	0	125	1 / 7	x	C		

Parameters: 1 – 0   2 – 0   3 – 0   4 – 0   5 – 0   6 – 0   7 – 0   8 – 0   9 – 0   10 – 0

HALFWORD PARAMETERS
 1 – 10
11 – 12

TRANS 7   FROM 39 TO 40   CLOCK 126
*TRANS 7

CUR BLOCK	NEXT BLOCK	ADV BLK DEPART	TERMINATIONS TO GO PRIORITY	MARK TIME	ASSEM SET	SEL TRACE	DELAY CHAIN	PREEMPT	COUNT/FLAG
39	40	126	0	125	1 / 7	x	C		

Parameters: 1 – 0   2 – 0   3 – 0   4 – 0   5 – 0   6 – 0   7 – 0   8 – 0   9 – 0   10 – 0

HALFWORD PARAMETERS
 1 – 10
11 – 12

TRANS 7   FROM 40 TO 41   CLOCK 126
*TRANS 7

CUR BLOCK	NEXT BLOCK	ADV BLK DEPART	TERMINATIONS TO GO PRIORITY	MARK TIME	ASSEM SET	SEL TRACE	DELAY CHAIN	PREEMPT	COUNT/FLAG
40	41	126	0	125	1 / 7	x	C		

Parameters: 1 – 0   2 – 0   3 – 0   4 – 0   5 – 0   6 – 0   7 – 0   8 – 0   9 – 0   10 – 0

HALFWORD PARAMETERS
 1 – 10
11 – 12

When a PRINT statement is executed, argument C is used to select the attribute for which statistical information is to be printed. The first two arguments determine the number of attributes for which statistics are to be produced. The sample statements give instances of selective printing.

> PRINT 1,3,Q,D

The current statistics on the first three queues are printed without starting a new page whenever this statement is executed.

> PRINT 8,V$CARS,F

The current statistics for the facilities numbered 8 through the value of the variable CARS are printed on a new output page.

A perusal of Table 3.4 indicates that only system attributes and not entity attributes may be obtained using PRINT. No features are explicitly provided in PRINT to list parameter values. However, if the user has a need to observe the contents of a parameter, the parameter value can be stored in a savevalue location which is then available for printing using X as the third argument of PRINT.

Table 3.4   PRINT Statement Output Codes

Code	Output
MOV	Current Events Chain
FUT	Future Events Chain
C	Relative and Absolute Clock Time
B	Block Counts
S	Storage Statistics
Q	Queue Statistics
F	Facility Statistics
T	Table Statistics
XF	Contents of Full Word Savevalues
XH	Contents of Half Word Savevalues
XB	Contents of Byte Savevalues
XL	Contents of Floating-Point Savevalues
LG	Status of Logic Switches

EXAMPLE 3.22

The use of PRINT is illustrated by listing the waiting-line statistics for all tellers whenever an officer appears in the bank model of Example 3.20. As with the previous example, only the output generated by the PRINT statements is given, not the output produced upon termination.

The PRINT statement allows us to observe the behavior of the queues at intermediate points in the execution of the model. The output shows that the queuing behavior for the teller lines has little variation with time.

```
BLOCK                                                                         STATEMENT
NUMBER *LOC   OPERATION A,B,C,D,E,F,G,H,I          COMMENTS                    NUMBER
       *******************************************************************    1
       *       PROGRAM TO SIMULATE A BANK WITH A VARIABLE NUMBER OF TELLERS   2
       *    WITH SEPARATE WAITING LINES.  CUSTOMERS SELECT THE SHORTEST LINE. 3
       *    CUSTOMERS SELECT LAST TELLER IN CASE OF A TIE.                    4
       *       A BANK OFFICER ARRIVES WITH A TRANSACTION AND IMMEDIATELY      5
       *    INTERRUPTS THE FIRST TELLER.                                      6
       *       THE AMOUNT OF CASH ON HAND AT EACH TELLER STATION              7
       *    AND HELD BY THE HEAD TELLER IS MAINTAINED IN SAVEVALUES.          8
       *       THE TOTAL AMOUNT OF CASH AT THE END OF THE DAY IS PRINTED AS THE  9
       *    CONTENTS OF SAVEVALUE LOCATION 11.                               10
       *                                                                     11
       *       PARAMETERS                                                    12
       *                                                                     13
       *       NUMBER OF TRANSACTIONS - 1 TO 5 PER CUSTOMER , AS SPECIFIED BY  14
       *          TRANS FUNCTION.  1 TRANSACTION PER OFFICER.                15
       *       CUSTOMER ARRIVALS - 2 MINUTES, EXPONENTIALLY DISTRIBUTED      16
       *       OFFICER ARRIVALS - 45 TO 75 MINUTES , UNIFORMLY DISTRIBUTED   17
       *       PROCESSING RATE -  SPECIFIED BY TYPE FUNCTION AND PROC VARIABLES 18
       *       TERMINATION CONDITION - 8 HOURS                               19
       *    CASH WITHDRAWN PER CUSTOMER - FROM -499 TO 500 , UNIFORM DIST.   20
       *                                                                     21
       *******************************************************************   22
       *                                                                     23
       *    EXPONENTIAL FUNCTION                                             24
       *                                                                     25
        EXPO   FUNCTION   RN2,C24                                            26
       .0000,.000/.1000,.104/.2000,.222/.3000,.355/.4000,.509/.5000,.690/   27
       .6000,.915/.7000,1.20/.7500,1.38/.8000,1.60/.8400,1.83/.8800,2.12/   28
       .9000,2.30/.9200,2.52/.9400,2.81/.9500,2.99/.9600,3.20/.9700,3.50/   29
       .9800,3.90/.9900,4.60/.9950,5.30/.9980,6.20/.9990,7.00/.9997,8.00/   30
       *                                                                     31
       *    TRANSACTION FUNCTION                                             32
       *                                                                     33
        TRANS FUNCTION   RN3,D5                                             34
       .20,1/.45,2/.75,3/.90,4/1.0,5                                        35
       *                                                                     36
       *       TRANSACTION TYPE FUNCTION                                     37
       *                                                                     38
        TYPE   FUNCTION   RN4,D6                                            39
       .20,1/.35,2/.55,3/.80,4/.95,5/1.0,6                                  40
       *                                                                     41
       *    PROCESSING TIME VARIABLES                                        42
       *                                                                     43
        PROC1 FVARIABLE   0.8*PH1                                           44
        PROC2 FVARIABLE   1.2*PH1                                           45
        PROC3 FVARIABLE   1.6*PH1                                           46
        PROC4 FVARIABLE   2.0*PH1                                           47
        PROC5 FVARIABLE   2.2*PH1                                           48
        PROC6 FVARIABLE   2.3*PH1                                           49
       *                                                                     50
       *       CASH WITHDRAWAL VARIABLE                                      51
       *                                                                     52
        CASH   VARIABLE   RN5-500                                           53
       *                                                                     54
       *    NUMBER OF TELLERS                                                55
```

```
     *                                                              56
     TELRS VARIABLE    4                  NUMBER CF TELLERS          57
     TELR1 VARIAELE    V$TELRS-1                                     58
     *                                                              59
     *    INITIAL AMOUNT OF CASH PER TELLER                         60
     *                                                              61
     AMNT  VARIAELE    2000                                         62
     *                                                              63
     *    CUSTOMER TIME IN BANK                                     64
     *                                                              65
     CTIME VARIAELE    C1-PH7                                       66
     *                                                              67
     *    TABLES                                                    68
     *                                                              69
     CUSTW TABLE       M1,0,1,20          CUSTOMER WAITING TIME      70
     CUSTT TABLE       PH7,0,1,20         CUTOMER TIME IN BANK       71
     CASHT TABLE       X*PH3,0,100,40     TELLER CASH ON HAND        72
     *                                                              73
     **************************************************************  74
     *                                                              75
     *    TELLER START UP SECTION                                   76
     *                                                              77
     **************************************************************  78
     *                                                              79
           SIMULATE                                                 80
1          GENERATE    ,,,1               GENERATE A DUMMY ENTITY    81
2          ASSIGN      6,V$TELRS,PH       PARM. 6 IS A LOOP INDEX    82
3          SAVEVALUE   10,100000,XF       LOC. 10 IS HEAD TELLER'S CASH 83
4   INIT   SAVEVALUE   PH6,V$AMNT,XF      EACH TELLER STARTS WITH V$AMNT 84
5          SAVEVALUE   10-,V$AMNT,XF      SUBTRACT FROM HEAD TELLER'S CASH 85
6          LOOP        6PH,INIT           PROCESS ALL TELLERS        86
7          TERMINATE   0                  REMCVE DUMMY ENTITY        87
     *                                                              88
     **************************************************************  89
     *                                                              90
     *    CUSTOMER SECTION                                          91
     *                                                              92
     **************************************************************  93
     *                                                              94
8          GENERATE    2,FN$EXPO          CUSTOMER ARRIVES          95
9          ASSIGN      1,FN$TRANS,PH      SET NUMBER OF TRANSACTIONS 96
10         ASSIGN      7,C1,PH            SAVE ARRIVAL TIME         97
11         ASSIGN      2,FN$TYPE,PH       SET TRANSACTION TYPE      98
12         ASSIGN      5,V$CASH,PH        SET NET AMOUNT OF CASH TO BE WITHD 99
13         ASSIGN      3,V$TELRS,PH       SET LAST TELLER'S LINE AS SHORTEST 100
14         ASSIGN      4,V$TELR1,PH       P4 HAS CANDIDATE SHORTEST LINE 101
15  SHORT  TEST L      Q*PH4,Q*PH3,NLOOP  TEST IF NEW SHORTEST LINE IS FOUND 102
16         ASSIGN      3,PH4,PH           SET NEW SHORTEST LINE IN PH3 103
17  NLOOP  LOOP        4PH,SHORT          REPEAT FOR ALL LINES      104
18         QUEUE       PH3                CUSTOMER WAITS IN SHORTEST LINE 105
19         MARK                           RECORD CUTOMER ENTRY TIME 106
20         SEIZE       PH3                CUSTOMER REACHES TELLER   107
21         DEPART      PH3                REMOVE CUSTOMER FROM WAITING LINE 108
22         TABULATE    CUSTW              RECORD WAITING TIME       109
23         ADVANCE     V*PH2              TRANSACTIONS ARE PROCESSED 110
24         TEST L      X*PH3,PH5,CUST     TEST IF TELLER HAS ADEQUATE FUNDS 111
25         SAVEVALUE   PH3+,V$AMNT,XF     GIVE CASH TO TELLER       112
```

```
26              SAVEVALUE     10-,V$AMNT,XF      ADJUST HEAD TELLER'S CASH             113
27              ADVANCE       2                  2 MINUTES ARE NEEDED TO GET CASH     114
28      CUST    SAVEVALUE     PH3-,PH5           ADJUST TELLER'S CASH                 115
29              TABULATE      CASHT              RECORD TELLER'S CASH ON HAND         116
30              RELEASE       PH3                CUSTOMER LEAVES TELLER               117
31              ASSIGN        7,V$CTIME,PH       DETERMINE TIME SPENT IN BANK         118
32              TABULATE      CUSTT              RECORD TIME SPENT IN BANK            119
33              TERMINATE     0                                                       120
        *                                                                             121
        ****************************                                                  122
        *                                                                             123
        *    OFFICER SECTION                                                          124
        *                                                                             125
        *****************************                                                 126
        *                                                                             127
34              GENERATE      60,15              OFFICER ARRIVES WITH TRANSACTION     128
35              PRINT         1,V$TELRS,Q,K      PRINT WAITING LINE STATS             129
36              ASSIGN        1,1,PH             OFFICER HAS 1 TRANSACTION            130
37              ASSIGN        2,FN$TYPE,PH       SET TRANSACTION TYPE                 131
38              PREEMPT       1                  OFFICER INTERRUPTS FIRST TELLER      132
39              ADVANCE       V*PH2              OFFICER'S TRANSACTION IS PROCESSED   133
40              RETURN        1                  OFFICER LEAVES FIRST TELLER          134
41              TERMINATE     0                                                       135
        *                                                                             136
        *****************************                                                 137
        *                                                                             138
        * TERMINATION SECTION                                                         139
        *                                                                             140
        *****************************                                                 141
        *                                                                             142
42              GENERATE      480                                                     143
43              ASSIGN        6,V$TELRS,PH       PARM. 6 IS LOOP INDEX               144
44      TOTAL   SAVEVALUE     11+,XF*PH6,XF      SUM OF CASH IN LOC. 11              145
45              LOOP          6PH,TOTAL                                               146
46              SAVEVALUE     11+,XF10,XF        ADD IN HEAD TELLER'S CASH           147
47              TERMINATE     1                                                       148
                START         1                                                       149
                END                                                                   150
```

```
**********************
*                    *
*       QUEUES       *
*                    *
**********************

QUEUE   MAXIMUM   AVERAGE    TOTAL     ZERO     PERCENT    AVERAGE      $AVERAGE      TABLE     CURRENT
        CONTENTS  CONTENTS   ENTRIES   ENTRIES  ZEROS      TIME/TRANS   TIME/TRANS    NUMBER    CONTENTS
  1        1       .215        5         2       39.9       2.799        4.666
  2        1       .323        7         3       42.8       3.000        5.250
  3        1       .492       13         5       38.4       2.461        4.000                    1
  4        2       .969       15         5       33.3       4.199        6.299                    1

$AVERAGE TIME/TRANS = AVERAGE TIME/TRANS EXCLUDING ZERO ENTRIES


**********************
*                    *
*       QUEUES       *
*                    *
**********************

QUEUE   MAXIMUM   AVERAGE    TOTAL     ZERO     PERCENT    AVERAGE      $AVERAGE      TABLE     CURRENT
        CONTENTS  CONTENTS   ENTRIES   ENTRIES  ZEROS      TIME/TRANS   TIME/TRANS    NUMBER    CONTENTS
  1        1       .167       10         5       50.0       2.099        4.199
  2        1       .359       21         9       42.8       2.142        3.750
  3        1       .551       26         9       34.6       2.653        4.058                    1
  4        2       .887       27         7       25.9       4.111        5.549

$AVERAGE TIME/TRANS = AVERAGE TIME/TRANS EXCLUDING ZERO ENTRIES


**********************
*                    *
*       QUEUES       *
*                    *
**********************

QUEUE   MAXIMUM   AVERAGE    TOTAL     ZERO     PERCENT    AVERAGE      $AVERAGE      TABLE     CURRENT
        CONTENTS  CONTENTS   ENTRIES   ENTRIES  ZEROS      TIME/TRANS   TIME/TRANS    NUMBER    CONTENTS
  1        1       .107       11         6       54.5       1.909        4.199
  2        1       .255       26        12       46.1       1.923        3.571
  3        1       .423       38        17       44.7       2.184        3.952
  4        2       .775       47        13       27.6       3.234        4.470                    1

$AVERAGE TIME/TRANS = AVERAGE TIME/TRANS EXCLUDING ZERO ENTRIES
```

```
*********************************
*                               *
*           QUEUES              *
*                               *
*********************************

QUEUE  MAXIMUM   AVERAGE   TOTAL    ZERO    PERCENT  AVERAGE    $AVERAGE    TABLE   CURRENT
       CONTENTS  CONTENTS  ENTRIES  ENTRIES ZEROS    TIME/TRANS TIME/TRANS  NUMBER  CONTENTS
  1       1       .101      17        9      52.9     1.588      3.375
  2       1       .241      39       19      48.7     1.641      3.199                  1
  3       1       .486      56       21      37.5     2.303      3.685                  1
  4       2       .773      62       16      25.8     3.306      4.456

$AVERAGE TIME/TRANS = AVERAGE TIME/TRANS EXCLUDING ZERO ENTRIES


*********************************
*                               *
*           QUEUES              *
*                               *
*********************************

QUEUE  MAXIMUM   AVERAGE   TOTAL    ZERO    PERCENT  AVERAGE    $AVERAGE    TABLE   CURRENT
       CONTENTS  CONTENTS  ENTRIES  ENTRIES ZEROS    TIME/TRANS TIME/TRANS  NUMBER  CONTENTS
  1       1       .087      19       11      57.8     1.421      3.375
  2       1       .245      48       24      50.0     1.583      3.166
  3       1       .496      61       21      34.4     2.524      3.849
  4       2       .787      71       17      23.9     3.436      4.518                  1

$AVERAGE TIME/TRANS = AVERAGE TIME/TRANS EXCLUDING ZERO ENTRIES


*********************************
*                               *
*           QUEUES              *
*                               *
*********************************

QUEUE  MAXIMUM   AVERAGE   TOTAL    ZERO    PERCENT  AVERAGE    $AVERAGE    TABLE   CURRENT
       CONTENTS  CONTENTS  ENTRIES  ENTRIES ZEROS    TIME/TRANS TIME/TRANS  NUMBER  CONTENTS
  1       1       .075      21       13      61.9     1.285      3.375
  2       1       .229      51       26      50.9     1.607      3.279
  3       1       .477      68       24      35.2     2.514      3.886
  4       2       .754      82       20      24.3     3.292      4.354

$AVERAGE TIME/TRANS = AVERAGE TIME/TRANS EXCLUDING ZERO ENTRIES
```

```
********************************
*                              *
*            QUEUES            *
*                              *
********************************
```

QUEUE	MAXIMUM CONTENTS	AVERAGE CONTENTS	TOTAL ENTRIES	ZERO ENTRIES	PERCENT ZEROS	AVERAGE TIME/TRANS	$AVERAGE TIME/TRANS	TABLE NUMBER	CURRENT CONTENTS
1	2	.121	32	18	56.2	1.531	3.500		
2	2	.287	61	28	45.9	1.901	3.515		
3	3	.551	78	26	33.3	2.858	4.288		
4	3	.811	93	22	23.6	3.526	4.619		

$AVERAGE TIME/TRANS = AVERAGE TIME/TRANS EXCLUDING ZERO ENTRIES

```
********************************
*                              *
*            QUEUES            *
*                              *
********************************
```

QUEUE	MAXIMUM CONTENTS	AVERAGE CONTENTS	TOTAL ENTRIES	ZERO ENTRIES	PERCENT ZEROS	AVERAGE TIME/TRANS	$AVERAGE TIME/TRANS	TABLE NUMBER	CURRENT CONTENTS
1	2	.102	32	18	56.2	1.531	3.500		
2	2	.243	61	28	45.9	1.901	3.515		
3	3	.470	87	34	39.0	2.574	4.226		1
4	3	.752	113	31	27.4	3.168	4.365		1

$AVERAGE TIME/TRANS = AVERAGE TIME/TRANS EXCLUDING ZERO ENTRIES

3.21 CONCLUSION

GPSS is a very extensive language with a broader range of capabilities than those presented in this chapter. The material described here will permit a user to learn the GPSS language and develop a wide variety of simulation models of considerable complexity. Many powerful language features have not been discussed. If the reader feels that the implementation of a certain aspect of a model is very awkward or impossible using the GPSS subset presented in this chapter, References [3.1] and [3.2] should be consulted.

GPSS is an example of a discrete simulation language based upon the process interaction approach. It is one of the most widely used simulation languages. By providing powerful, high-level statements, GPSS permits the modeling of complex systems in a relatively small number of program statements. The reader can compare the flexibility and power of GPSS with the Simscript language described in the next chapter.

EXERCISES

(Use GPSS for all exercises. In all cases, collect queuing statistics.)

3.1 Simulate the behavior of the checkout lines in a supermarket given the following parameters:

> Customer arrivals (at checkout)—uniformly distributed from 1 to 5 minutes.
> Number of regular checkers—2.
> Number of express checkers—1.
> Percentage of customers using express checker—32%.
> Express checkout time—2 minutes per customer.
> Regular checkout time—uniformly distributed from 5 to 15 minutes per customer.
> Termination condition—200 customers processed.

3.2 Modify the supermarket model of the previous exercise by changing (or adding) the following parameters:

> Number of items per customer—exponentially distributed with mean 20.
> Express line selected if 7 items or less.
> Checkout time—3 items per minute.
> Termination condition—12 hours.

3.3 Simulate a doctor's office to measure patient waiting time using the following parameters:

> **a.** Patient arrivals—uniformly distributed between 5 and 15 minutes.
> Number of examination rooms—3.
> Examination time—uniformly distributed between 3 and 27 minutes per patient.
> Termination condition—20 patients examined.
> Prepare tables of patient waiting times in waiting room and examination room.

  b. After examining 20 patients, the doctor determines that she will be late for her golf match. She then reduces her examination time to 3 to 7 minutes per patient, uniformly distributed. Simulate as in 3.3(a).

  c. Repeat 3.3(a) and 3.3(b) with patient arrival time uniformly distributed between 5 and 11 minutes.

  d. Repeat 3.3(a) and 3.3(b) with patient arrival time uniformly distributed between 5 and 19 minutes.

3.4 Model a student registration environment described by the following parameters:

  Number of people processing registrations—5.

  Student arrival rate—1 to 5 minutes, uniformly distributed.

  Number of classes per student—50%, 5; 20%, 6; 75%, 4; 10%, 3; 5%, 7.

  Time to register a student—2 minutes per class.

  Students select a processing person by comparing the lengths of waiting lines and choosing the shortest.

  Every hour plus or minus 15 minutes, an athlete arrives and is registered immediately by the first processing person.

  Time of simulation—6 hours.

Execute the model four times using different random number generator seeds. Compute average queue length, waiting times, and utilization of registration personnel.

3.5 (This exercise is derived from a problem submitted to Reference [3.3] by Dr. Susan L. Solomon. For all parts of this problem, assume an 8-hour work night.) Xaviera operates an entertainment facility in Nevada. Xaviera's standard fee is $100. Her employees perform their services for $50, $20 of which is returned to Xaviera to cover operating expenses. Model Xaviera's receipts and the level of service offered her customers under the following alternative conditions:

  a. Xaviera is the only server. The average customer interarrival rate is 10 minutes, exponentially distributed. Determine the effects of the following service times:

   (1) Constant 15 minutes.

   (2) 15 ± 5 minutes, uniformly distributed.

   (3) Average of 15 minutes, exponentially distributed.

  b. Assume a second server is hired, and each server performs with a service time of 15 ± 5 minutes, uniformly distributed. What is the effect on service and profits?

  c. Assume that every hour (± 10 minutes), a customer arrives who requires both servers simultaneously. Measure the impact of service.

  d. Suppose a third server is hired, who serves customers in an average of 12 minutes (exponentially distributed). What is the effect on business if there are separate queues with customers entering the shortest queue? Only one queue?

  e. Suppose 60% of the customers want Xaviera; the other 40% have no preference. Investigate profits and queue behavior under these circumstances.

  f. If 10% of the customers require service that takes an average of 20 minutes (exponentially distributed), for a 50% price increment, what is the effect on the business?

  g. Assume Xaviera has submitted to pressure from the Equal Employment Opportunity Commission to avoid the loss of Federal contracts. She has hired a token male server who spends an average of 15 minutes (exponentially distributed) serving each of his customers. After completing a service, he is obliged to rest for 2 hours before he can take on another customer. Include this condition, assuming his customers arrive every 1 to 3 hours, uniformly distributed, and will not accept any of the other servers.

h. A parking lot on the premises has a capacity of 3 cars. If the lot is full, arriving customers take their business elsewhere. To what extent does this affect business?

3.6 Simulate the usage of elevators in a library under the following assumptions:

Number of elevators—2.

The interarrival rate at the first floor is uniformly distributed from 0 to 3 minutes.

Destination floor is given by 20%, 2; 30%, 3; 30%, 4; 20%, 5.

Time required to travel between adjacent floors—15 seconds.

Time to load or unload the elevator—30 seconds.

Elevator capacity—8 people each.

People return to the elevator at a rate that is exponentially distributed with a mean of 5 minutes; all people return to the first floor.

After 2 hours, the library staff ties up one elevator for 45 minutes.

Termination condition—4 hours.

Determine the average utilization of the elevators and the average waiting time for each floor.

3.7 Figure 3.1 shows the exits from a parking lot. Simulate the events of the parking lot during the evening rush hour. The model should be based upon the following assumptions:

Cars arrive at each lot exit every 30 seconds, exponentially distributed for a 20-minute period. After 20 minutes, arrivals cease.

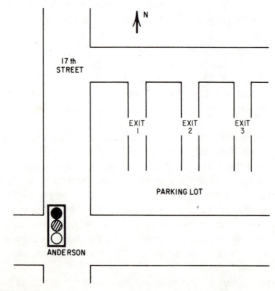

Figure 3.1 Parking Lot

90% of the cars turning onto 17th Street turn south.

1st lot exit is blocked if 3 cars are waiting to turn onto 17th Street. 2nd exit is blocked if 7 cars are waiting. 3rd exit is blocked if 11 cars are waiting.

No cutting in is permitted.

For first 15 minutes, cars arrive every minute, plus or minus 10 seconds, heading south on 17th Street. After that time, no further southbound cars appear.

For the entire simulation, cars arriving head north on 17th Street every minute, plus or minus 12 seconds.

The light at the intersection of 17th and Anderson changes every 2 minutes. A car requires 10 seconds to pass through the intersection. The light is initially red for 17th Street.

When 11 cars are waiting for the light, no car may turn south onto 17th Street.

Cars are removed from the model when they pass through the traffic light or turn north on 17th Street.

Termination condition—All cars have left the parking lot.

3.8 Simulate the behavior of the processor and memory of a computer system as described below:

Machine

Memory size—512K (512∗1024 bytes).

Time slice—1 second.

Task initiation overhead—100 milliseconds.

Jobs

Arrival rate—14 seconds, exponentially distributed.

CPU time—15 seconds, exponentially distributed.

Size—32K–128K, uniformly distributed.

When jobs arrive, they are loaded into memory using the memory allocation algorithms described below. Jobs are executed in a round-robin manner, given one CPU time slice at a time until their execution is complete. If a job completes execution prior to the end of a time slice, the CPU becomes available. Whenever a job completes its time slice, task initiation overhead is incurred by the CPU in order to execute the next job. All jobs have equal priority when contending for the CPU. When a job has completed execution, a new job is loaded into memory according to the allocation algorithm.

Execute the model using the allocation algorithms given below and compare the performance of the system.

a. First fit without priority.

b. Priority based on execution time.

c. Priority based on program size.

d. Priority based on execution time and program size.

REFERENCES

[3.1] IBM Corp., *General Purpose Simulation System V User's Manual,* 1975.

[3.2] Gordon, G., *The Application of GPSS V to Discrete System Simulation.* Englewood Cliffs, N.J.: Prentice-Hall, 1975.

[3.3] *ACM Simuletter,* vol. 7, no. 1, January 1976.

4

Simscript

4.1 ORGANIZATION OF SIMSCRIPT

The previous chapter described GPSS as a discrete simulation language. Another commonly used language for discrete simulation is Simscript, which differs considerably from GPSS in structure and capability. Simscript is a general-purpose programming language with built-in discrete simulation features. The material in this chapter focuses only upon those aspects of Simscript that are directly related to simulation. For a complete discussion of the full Simscript language, see References [4.1] and [4.2]. The particular language constructs discussed are found in Simscript II.5, which is the latest available version of the language. Throughout this text a reference to Simscript should be interpreted as a reference to Simscript II.5. Due to the richness of the Simscript language, not all simulation features can be presented in this chapter. The reader is referred to References [4.1] and [4.2] for further details.

Figure 4.1   Structure of Simscript Program

A Simscript program may consist of four types of routines ordered as shown in Figure 4.1. The preamble defines the structure of the model by describ-

146

ing the entities and their attributes, sets to which entities may belong, the events, and statistical information to be collected. The preamble consists wholly of definition and type declaration statements. All entities, sets of entities, events, and global variables must be defined in the preamble. The main routine initializes the model and initiates the execution by scheduling the first event. A simulation program written in Simscript must have one or more event routines that indicate the actions to be taken when an event occurs. Subprograms have the same function as in Fortran or PL/I and are included in a Simscript program at the option of the user whenever a computation is required at several points in the program or to improve the clarity of the program. A Simscript program may have any number of event routines and subprograms but only one preamble and a single main routine.

4.2 EVENTS

Simscript operates using the event scheduling technique discussed in Chapter 2. A Simscript model is developed by writing event routines that describe the actions taken by the system when a particular event occurs. Events are defined in the preamble and scheduled dynamically in the program. The main routine schedules the first series of events and then executes a START SIMULATION statement to initiate the simulation. An event routine may schedule several events. Recursion is permitted; that is, an event routine may schedule itself.

A Simscript model is driven by an event list that is ordered by time and priority. The system will execute the event routines for all events scheduled for a given time period in priority order. When no events scheduled for the current time remain in the event list, the internal clock is advanced to the time of the first event on the list.

The definition of events in the preamble consists of an EVENT NOTICES statement, which defines events that do not have parameters, optionally followed by some number of EVERY statements, which define events with parameters. An EVENT NOTICES statement has the following format:

      EVENT NOTICES INCLUDE *list of events*

where *list of events* is a collection of event names separated by commas and/or AND.

Consider the following sample statement:

      EVENT NOTICES INCLUDE ARRIVAL, EXPRESS.DEPARTURE,
      AND REGULAR.DEPARTURE

This statement defines three event names for the model. An event notice is the internal representation of a particular occurrence of an event in the model. Internally, Simscript schedules events by the manipulation of a list of event notices. This list is known as the event list.

This first sample statement demonstrates the English-like syntax of Simscript. Most statements are sentences and there is considerable flexibility in the use of connectives and articles. In the presentation of statement formats, the term *list of objects* means a collection of variable names, representing some type of object, joined by commas and/or the connective, AND.

Event routines with parameters are defined by a series of EVERY statements immediately following the EVENT NOTICES statement. If all event routines have parameters, then the EVENT NOTICES statement appears without the INCLUDE phrase.

The format of EVERY for the definition of an event with parameters is

EVERY *event* HAS *list of parameters*

For example, the following statements define two events: ARRIVAL, with no parameters, and DEPARTURE, with the variable TELLER.NO as the parameter.

EVENT NOTICES INCLUDE ARRIVAL
EVERY DEPARTURE HAS A TELLER.NO

For each event listed in the EVENT NOTICES or EVERY statements, an event routine must appear in the model. An EVENT statement indicates the start of the definition of the actions associated with the event.

Each Simscript routine, whether the main routine, an event routine, or a subroutine, must terminate with an END statement and contain at least one RETURN or STOP statement. The format of the EVENT statement is

EVENT *eventname* [*list of parameters*]

In the presentation of the Simscript statement formats, the use of brackets will denote optional sections, whereas the use of parentheses implies that one of the elements within the parentheses must appear in the statement. Thus the parameter list is optional in the EVENT statement.

The ARRIVAL and DEPARTURE event routines have the skeletal structures presented below:

EVENT ARRIVAL
⋮
RETURN
END

EVENT DEPARTURE (TELLER.NO)
⋮
RETURN
END

Event notices are placed into the event list by the SCHEDULE statement which specifies the event to be scheduled and the time at which the event routine is to be activated. The format of SCHEDULE is

$$\text{SCHEDULE} \left\{ \begin{array}{c} \text{AN} \\ \text{A} \end{array} \right\} \ \underline{event} \ [(\underline{\text{list of arguments}})] \ \left[\begin{array}{c} \text{IN} \\ \text{NOW} \end{array} \ \underline{\text{time-expression}} \right]$$

where

> AN or A is the appropriate article for the event name
>
> *event* is the event name
>
> *list of arguments* are the values to be used for the arguments for this occurrence of the event; it is important to distinguish between *parameters*, which are used in definition of an event, and *arguments*, which provide the values used in the execution of an event occurrence
>
> IN *time-expression* indicates that the event will be scheduled in some number of time units from the current time (representation of time is discussed in the next section)
>
> NOW indicates that the event routine to be executed before the internal clock is advanced

The following samples illustrate the use of the SCHEDULE statement.

> SCHEDULE AN EXPRESS DEPARTURE IN 2*NO.ITEMS MINUTES

The value of the expression 2*NO.ITEMS is evaluated and the event, EXPRESS.DEPARTURE, is scheduled with the time determined by adding the number of minutes indicated by the expression value to the current time.

> SCHEDULE A DEPARTURE (HEAD) NOW

An event notice for DEPARTURE is placed into the event list with the current time. The DEPARTURE routine will be executed before the clock time is advanced. The value of the variable HEAD at the time of execution of the SCHEDULE statement serves as the argument for DEPARTURE.

When several event notices in the event list have the same time of activation, they are executed in priority order. The PRIORITY statement indicates the event priorities by listing the events in an explicit priority ranking.

The format of the PRIORITY statement is

> PRIORITY ORDER IS *list of events*

For example, the statement

> PRIORITY ORDER IS ARRIVAL, EXPRESS.DEPARTURE,
> REGULAR.DEPARTURE

sets the relative priorities of the three events.

The flow of program control in Simscript is determined by the event list. Initially the MAIN routine is executed up to the START SIMULATION statement. The first event notice, in terms of time and priority, that was scheduled by the MAIN routine is removed from the event list and its corresponding event routine is executed. An event routine is executed until a RETURN statement is encountered. At this point, control returns to the event list to select the next event routine for execution. If a STOP statement is encountered, program execution terminates.

The scheduling of an event is not equivalent in function to a subroutine call since, upon completion of the event routine, control does not return necessarily to the scheduling routine. In particular, since the MAIN routine is never scheduled, it is executed only at program initiation and its last executable statement is START SIMULATION.

4.3 REPRESENTATION OF TIME

Simscript permits the user to be very explicit concerning the units of simulated time. The internal clock is represented by a system variable TIME.V that may be referenced, but not altered by the programmer. The default unit for TIME.V is days. Automatic conversion is provided for hours and minutes. Thus, time expressions using days, hours, or minutes, as in the sample SCHEDULE statements, may be used freely.

Other time units can be utilized by redefining the basic time unit. Time units are specified by the DEFINE statement, which appears in the PREAMBLE. In order to specify a new time unit, the following form of DEFINE is employed:

> DEFINE *identifier* TO MEAN [*expression*] UNITS

where

> *identifier* is the time unit.
>
> *expression* is an option that permits the time unit being defined to be expressed as a multiple of TIME.V. The expression consists of either an * or / followed by a constant.

The definition of new time units is shown in the following two samples:

> 1. DEFINE MILLISECS TO MEAN UNITS

The value of TIME.V is interpreted as MILLISECS by the program. Thus the statement

> SCHEDULE AN ENTRY IN 2 MILLISECS

causes an event notice for entry to be placed in the event list with a value of TIME.V + 2.

> 2. DEFINE YEARS TO MEAN *365.25 UNITS

The identifier YEARS is interpreted as 365.25 time units. The statement

> SCHEDULE A BIRTH IN 2 YEARS

places an event notice for BIRTH in the event list with a time of TIME.V + 730.50.

4.4 VARIABLES

The DEFINE statement is used to indicate the mode of arithmetic variables, which may be either integer or real. Any variable defined in the preamble can be referenced by all routines. A variable that is referenced only within an event routine must be defined explicitly in that routine. All event parameters are defined in the event routine. When utilized in the definition of variables, DEFINE has the following format:

$$\text{DEFINE } \underline{\text{list of identifiers}} \text{ AS } \begin{bmatrix} \text{A} \\ \text{AN} \end{bmatrix} \begin{Bmatrix} \text{REAL} \\ \text{INTEGER} \end{Bmatrix} \text{ VARIABLES}$$

The definition of variables is illustrated by the two sample statements.

    1. DEFINE CASH AS A REAL VARIABLE

This statement indicates that CASH is a real variable.

    2. DEFINE TELLER AND WINDOW AS INTEGER VARIABLES

TELLER and WINDOW are treated as integer variables.

    The Simscript identifier-naming convention is broader than in most languages. An identifier, which may be used as an event, variable, entity, or set, is any combination of letters, digits, and periods that is not a number. A number in Simscript may be an integer, a decimal fraction, or be represented in scientific notation, such as 100, 100.00, and 1.00E2, respectively. For example, the following are valid Simscript identifiers:

    4F

    . . .

    EXPRESS.LINE

    1.3.4

    A given implementation of Simscript may have a limitation on the length of global variable and event names. The IBM S/360 and S/370 implementations limit these identifiers to seven characters. Identifiers also may be assigned constant values in order to improve the readability of the program. Again, the DEFINE statement is utilized to assign a constant value to an identifier. The form of DEFINE for this application is

    DEFINE *identifier* TO MEAN *constant*

    A very common application to constant naming is to assign the values 0 and 1 to the identifiers IDLE and BUSY as shown in the next two statements:

    DEFINE IDLE TO MEAN 0

    DEFINE BUSY TO MEAN 1

4.5 COMPUTATIONS

Arithmetic computations are performed via the LET statement, which permits the same range of operations as Fortran. Any numeric variable may appear in a LET statement which has the general form

    LET *variable* = *expression*

where

    variable is a numeric variable

    expression is any valid arithmetic expression

The following are typical LET statements:

    LET REGULAR.CHECKER = IDLE

    LET X = SQRT ((A**2 + B**2)/4*A*C)

In the second statement above, A**2 means A to the second power, or A squared.

    An important feature in any simulation language is the mechanism for the introduction of randomness into the model. Simscript provides several built-in random distribution functions as listed in Table 4.1. The application of many of these distributions is discussed in Chapter 5. All functions in Table 4.1 are common statistical distributions except RANDI.F, which produces a random integer value in a given interval. The last argument of each of the functions in Table 4.1 is an integer indicating the random number generator from which a number is selected in order to produce a value from the specified distribution. Simscript provides ten random number generators, each producing numbers in the range from 0 to 1. Thus the last argument of a reference to a random distribution function is an integer from 1 to 10.

Table 4.1 Random Distribution Functions

Function	Arguments
BETA.F	(power of X, power of $(1-X)$, generator)
BINOMIAL.F	(trials, probability_of_success, generator)
ERLANG.F	(mean, K, generator)
EXPONENTIAL.F	(mean, generator)
GAMMA.F	(mean, K, generator)
LOG.NORMAL.F	(mean, standard_deviation, generator)
NORMAL.F	(mean, standard_deviation, generator)
POISSON.F	(mean, generator)
RANDI.F	(low_limit, up_limit, generator)
UNIFORM.F	(low_limit, up_limit, generator)
WEIBUL.F	(shape, scale, generator)

The following two statements depict the utilization of the random distribution functions.

1. SCHEDULE AN ARRIVAL IN UNIFORM.F (MIN.ARRIVAL, MAX.ARRIVAL, 8) MINUTES
2. LET X = Y**2 − EXPONENTIAL.F (BETA, 2)

The random number generators must be accessed directly through the use of the RANDOM.F function. The single argument to RANDOM.F is the number of the generator to be referenced. For example, a uniform random number between 0 and 1 is obtained from generator 4 in the statement

LET GRADE = 80 * RANDOM.F(4) + 20

so that the grade is given a value between 20 and 100.

4.6 TEMPORARY ENTITIES

Entities that enter and leave the model are known as *temporary* entities. The temporary entities and their attributes are explicitly defined in the preamble by a series of EVERY statements following a TEMPORARY ENTITIES statement. The format of an EVERY statement that defines a temporary entity and its attributes is

> EVERY *entity* HAS *list of attributes*

This group of sample statements defines the temporary entity, CUSTOMER, and its attributes

> TEMPORARY ENTITIES
> EVERY CUSTOMER HAS A TRANSACTION AND A
> WAITING.TIME

Each occurrence of a temporary entity enters the model by means of a CREATE statement and is removed by a DESTROY statement. There may be any number of temporary entities of a given type in the model at any time.

The formats for CREATE and DESTROY are straightforward.

$$\text{CREATE} \begin{bmatrix} \text{A} \\ \text{AN} \end{bmatrix} \underline{\text{entity}}$$

$$\text{DESTROY} \begin{bmatrix} \text{THE} \\ \text{THIS} \end{bmatrix} \underline{\text{entity}}$$

For example,

> CREATE A CUSTOMER
> DESTROY THIS CUSTOMER

The attributes of a temporary entity may be referenced directly using subscripted variables of the form

> ATTRIBUTE (ENTITY)

For example, a calculation involving customer waiting time is

> LET WAITING.TIME(CUSTOMER) = TIME.V −
> WAITING.TIME(CUSTOMER)

4.7 SETS

Temporary entities with some logical relationship can be grouped into ordered collections known as sets. Each set has one owner and zero or more members. Set members are temporary entities, whereas set owners may be temporary entities, permanent entities (see Section 4.12), or the system. Potential ownership or membership in a set by a temporary entity is declared in the preamble by listing in the EVERY statement the sets the entity may belong to or own. Temporary entities are dynamically inserted into and removed from sets by using the FILE and REMOVE statements.

In order to define set ownership and membership for a temporary entity, the phrases

              OWNS *list of sets*

and

              MAY BELONG TO *list of sets*

are added to the EVERY statement defining the temporary entity as shown in the following examples:

      EVERY CUSTOMER HAS A NUM.TRANSACTIONS AND
          WAITING.TIME AND MAY BELONG TO A WAITING.LINE AND
          OWNS A LIST.OF.TRANSACTIONS
      EVERY TRANSACTION HAS A PROC.TIME AND MAY BELONG TO
          A LIST.OF.TRANSACTIONS

Ownership by the system is a special case in which the set cannot be associated with any entity. If the system owns a set, there is only one set of that type in the model. Sets owned by the system are listed by using a THE SYSTEM statement, which has the following form:

      THE SYSTEM OWNS *list of sets*

For example, the statement

      THE SYSTEM OWNS A WAITING.LINE

defines a system-owned set.

    A set name is explicitly defined, and the order in which entities are inserted into and removed from the set is specified by the DEFINE SET statement. The options are FIFO (First In, First Out), LIFO (Last In, Last Out), and sorted by some attribute. If the set order is not defined, the default of FIFO is assumed. The programmer has the option in the FILE and REMOVE statements of altering the specified set order.

    The format of the DEFINE SET statement is

$$\text{DEFINE } \underline{\text{set}} \text{ AS A } \left[\begin{array}{c} \text{FIFO} \\ \text{LIFO} \end{array} \right] \text{SET} \left[\text{RANKED BY } \left\{ \begin{array}{c} \text{HIGH} \\ \text{LOW} \end{array} \right\} \underline{\text{attribute}} \right.$$

$$\left. \text{THEN BY } \left\{ \begin{array}{c} \text{HIGH} \\ \text{LOW} \end{array} \right\} \underline{\text{attribute}} \right] \Big]$$

where

      set is the set name
      attribute is an attribute by which the members of the set are sorted
      HIGH or LOW indicates descending or ascending order, respectively

    The various set orders are indicated by the following examples of DEFINE SET statements:

      DEFINE WAITING.LINE AS A FIFO SET
      DEFINE STACK AS A LIFO SET
      DEFINE ROSTER AS A SET RANKED BY LOW LAST.NAME THEN
        BY LOW FIRST.NAME

The set ROSTER is sorted in ascending order, first on last name and then on first name.

The insertion of a temporary entity into a set is accomplished using FILE. The format of FILE is

$$\text{FILE THE } \underline{entity1} \quad \left[\begin{array}{c} \text{FIRST} \\ \text{LAST} \\ \left\{ \begin{array}{c} \text{AFTER} \\ \text{BEFORE} \end{array} \right\} \underline{entity2} \end{array} \right] \quad \text{IN [THE] } \underline{set}$$

where

> *entity1* is the name of the temporary entity to be inserted into the set
>
> FIRST and LAST are optional positional indicators; if omitted, the entity is filed according to the order specified in the DEFINE SET statement
>
> *entity2* is the temporary entity in the set after (before) which *entity1* will be inserted
>
> *set* is the set name

The sample statement below illustrates the use of the FILE statement.

> FILE THE CUSTOMER IN THE WAITING.LINE

A CUSTOMER temporary entity is inserted in the WAITING.LINE set according to the order indicated in the DEFINE SET statement for WAITING.LINE.

> FILE THE CUSTOMER FIRST IN THE WAITING.LINE
> FILE CUSTOMER LAST IN WAITING.LINE
> FILE THE CUSTOMER BEFORE FRIEND IN WAITING.LINE

The position of the temporary entity FRIEND in the set WAITING.LINE is determined and the then temporary entity CUSTOMER is inserted immediately prior to FRIEND.

The deletion of a temporary entity from a set is accomplished by utilizing the REMOVE statement. REMOVE is similar to FILE in that either the first, last, or a particular member of the set may be extracted. However, with REMOVE, the user must specify the temporary entity to be removed explicitly. The option of defaulting to set order does not apply with the REMOVE statement.

REMOVE has the format pictured below:

$$\text{REMOVE} \left\{ \begin{array}{c} \text{FIRST} \\ \text{LAST} \\ \text{THIS} \end{array} \right\} \text{ } entity \text{ FROM [THE] } set$$

Some typical REMOVE statements are as follows:

> REMOVE FIRST CUSTOMER FROM THE WAITING.LINE
> REMOVE LAST DISH FROM THE STACK
> REMOVE THIS STUDENT FROM THE ROSTER

The identification of the temporary entity STUDENT must be established by the preceding statements in order for the third sample to execute properly.

All sets are initially empty. As indicated in Section 4.9, conditional expressions to test for set emptiness and membership are available in Simscript. At any given time a temporary entity may be a member of several sets of different types. However, a temporary entity may be a member of only one set of a given type.

4.8 TRANSFER STATEMENTS

The GO TO statement permits nonsequential execution within a routine. The format of the transfer statement is

    GO TO *label*

where *label* is a statement label within the same routine.

    Statements are labeled by an identifier enclosed within single quotes preceding the statement. The pair of sample statements shown below illustrate both the use of GO TO and the labeling of statements.

    GO TO WRONG.NUMBER
        :

    'WRONG.NUMBER' SCHEDULE A HANG.UP NOW

The effect of the GO TO statement can be obtained without the use of labels by means of the JUMP and HERE statements. The HERE statement simply marks a position in the program but indicates no action. JUMP is a special form of GO TO that transfers only to HERE statements. JUMP AHEAD causes a transfer to the immediately succeeding HERE statement, and JUMP BACK results in a transfer to the immediately preceding HERE.

    The statements below are equivalent to those used to illustrate GO TO if the HERE statement is the only such statement following JUMP.

    JUMP AHEAD
        :

    HERE
    SCHEDULE A HANG.UP NOW

It is important to note that if a HERE statement is inadvertently inserted between an existing JUMP AHEAD . . . HERE pair, the program will no longer function correctly.

4.9 CONDITIONAL STATEMENTS

Conditions are tested by the IF statement, which permits the execution of alternative groups of statements depending upon the result of the test. The conditional operators as listed in Table 4.2 include the standard relational operators used to compare numeric quantities as well as special set operators to test for emptiness or membership.

    The following examples of IF statements provide an illustration of the use of the conditional operators.

    IF X < Y,
    IF CUSTOMER IS IN WAITING.LINE,

IF WAITING.LINE IS NOT EMPTY,

IF EMP.SAL > 10000 AND EMP.DEPENDENTS <= 4,

The last sample shows the combination of conditional expressions using a Boolean operator. Conditions of arbitrary complexity can be stated by the use of AND and OR as connectives. As in most other high-level languages, parentheses may be utilized to clarify the precedence of the operators in a conditional expression.

Table 4.2   Conditional Operators

$$=$$
$$7 =$$
$$<$$
$$>$$
$$<=$$
$$>=$$

set IS EMPTY
set IS NOT EMPTY
entity IS IN *set*
entity IS NOT *set*

The most general form of conditional execution in Simscript occurs when either of two alternative actions is to be taken depending upon the truth or falsity of a condition. Figure 4.2 illustrates this situation in which the group of statements S_T is executed if the condition is true while the statements S_F are executed in the case of a false result. The beginning of the S_F group is indicated by the ELSE statement, which must be preceded by an unconditional transfer. The statements permitted in that position are either RETURN, JUMP, STOP, or GO TO.

This instance of conditional execution is realized through the use of JUMP

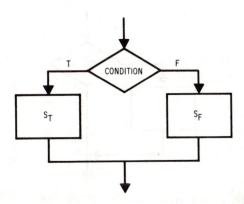

Figure 4.2   Conditional Execution: Case 1

AHEAD and HERE statements, or an equivalent GO TO statement, and has the form shown below:

> IF *condition*,
> ⠸ S_T
> JUMP AHEAD
> ELSE
> ⠸ S_F
> HERE

where *condition* is a conditional expression.

An example of this construct is given by the following statements:

> IF HEIGHT < 66.0,
> LET SHORT.PEOPLE = SHORT.PEOPLE + 1
> JUMP AHEAD
> ELSE
> LET NOT.SHORT = NOT.SHORT + 1
> HERE

A special case of conditional executing occurs when no action is to be taken if the condition is false. Figure 4.3 illustrates this situation. In this case, it is not necessary that S_T be followed by an unconditional transfer. The end of the S_T sequence is indicated by an ALWAYS statement as shown here.

> IF *condition*,
> ⠸ S_T
> ALWAYS

The second type of conditional execution is illustrated by the statements below:

> IF WITHDRAWAL > CASH(TELLER),
> LET CASH.HEAD = CASH.HEAD − 2000
> LET CASH(TELLER) = CASH(TELLER) + 2000
> ALWAYS
> LET CASH(TELLER) = CASH(TELLER) − WITHDRAWAL

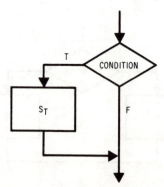

Figure 4.3 Conditional Execution: Case 2

The sequence of statements S_T or S_F may be any Simscript statements including IF statements. The use of IF statements within blocks of conditionally executed statements is known as *nesting*. IF statements can be nested to multiple levels. The only practical restriction is the programmer's ability to understand the complex logical structures resulting from multiple, nested IF statements. When nested IFs are used, it is necessary that a one-to-one correspondence between IF and ELSE (or ALWAYS) statements be maintained. Indenting the statements so that corresponding IF and ELSE statements are aligned is an excellent aid in maintaining the proper structure of complex conditional statements.

The use of nested IF statements is shown in the following sample:

```
IF HEIGHT < 66.0,
    LET SHORT.PEOPLE = SHORT.PEOPLE + 1
    JUMP AHEAD
ELSE
    IF HEIGHT > 75.0,
        LET TALL.PEOPLE = TALL.PEOPLE + 1
        JUMP AHEAD
    ELSE
        LET AVER.PEOPLE = AVER.PEOPLE + 1
HERE
```

4.10 INPUT/OUTPUT

Simscript provides easy-to-use and flexible input/output facilities. Input is accomplished by a free-form READ statement. Output can be obtained using either the LIST statement, which prints a variable name and its value, or the PRINT statement, which permits the use of headings and the specification of format. Typically, LIST is used for intermediate or debugging output and PRINT is employed to generate the final listing.

The READ statement assigns values from an input device to variables and attributes of temporary entities. The format of READ is shown below:

> READ *list of identifiers*

where the identifiers are either variables or attributes. The values on the data cards must be separated by blanks and are assigned sequentially to the data items named in the READ statement. For example, the statement

> READ NO.CUSTOMERS, NO.TELLERS

and the data card

> 100 3

will cause NO.CUSTOMERS to have a value of 100 and NO.TELLERS to be assigned a value of 3.

The LIST statement provides no format control. The output of a LIST statement begins a new output line and prints the quantities identified and then prints their values on the next line. The format of LIST is

LIST *list of identifiers*

where the identifiers are variables or attributes.

The sample LIST statement below illustrates its format and function:

LIST TIME.V, WAIT.TIME

The output generated by this statement would be (assuming the values shown)

TIME.V   WAIT.TIME

0.919   0.012

The preparation of the final program listing involves the application of the PRINT statement. PRINT permits the specification of the number of lines of output to be produced, the data items whose values will be printed, headings for each output line, and the format of each value printed. The form of the PRINT statement is

PRINT *count* LINES WITH *list of identifiers* THUS

⋮   *format of output lines*

where

count is the number of lines to be printed

list of identifiers indicates quantities to be printed

format of output lines consists of *count* lines each containing a combination of text and numeric formats

Two formats, standard and scientific, are available. The standard format consists of a series of asterisks, each indicating a digit with the decimal point inserted in the appropriate position. Scientific format, which prints a sign, mantissa, and exponent, is indicated by eight or more consecutive periods. The printed form of a number in scientific format is

± ddd.dddE±dd

The following sample PRINT statement shows its structure and that of the resulting output:

PRINT 5 LINES WITH NO. CUSTOMERS, TIME. V AND AVG. PROC. TIME THUS
BANKING MODEL
   TOTAL NUMBER OF CUSTOMERS   ***
   SIMULATED TIME   ** . ** HOURS
   AVERAGE CUSTOMER PROCESSING TIME   . . . . MIN
END OF SIMULATION

Again assuming the values shown below, the output produced by the PRINT statement is

BANKING MODEL
   TOTAL NUMBER OF CUSTOMERS   150
   SIMULATED TIME   8.23 HOURS
   AVERAGE CUSTOMER PROCESSING TIME   509.436E–02 MIN

EXAMPLE 4.1

The features of the Simscript language presented in this chapter can be assembled into a simple, yet complete, program. As in Chapter 3, a bank will serve as the system for which models are developed to illustrate the language constructs.

A drive-in banking window model is shown in the listing. The parameters of the model are

customer arrival time—uniformly distributed between MIN.ARRIVAL and MAX.ARRIVAL minutes

number of transactions per customer—exponentially distributed with mean AVG.TRANSACTIONS

transaction processing time—2 minutes

The values of all parameters of the random distributions are set by the READ statement, thus permitting easy modification. In the PRINT statement, MAX.WAIT is multiplied by 1440 in order to convert the default time unit of days into minutes.

The examples in this chapter are presented to illustrate the Simscript constructs presented in the preceding sections. It is quite natural for the reader to compare Simscript with GPSS since they are both discrete stochastic simulation languages. The basis for such a comparison should be the ease with which a programmer can develop models in a given language. Consequently, the examples used in this chapter will be similar to those of Chapter 3. However, since the main purpose of the examples is tutorial, not comparative, the example models of this chapter will differ slightly from those in the preceding chapter. The reader should not attempt to form an exact correspondence between any pair of examples from the two chapters.

4.11 STATISTICS

The analysis of a stochastic simulation model requires the evaluation of statistics describing the behavior of the stochastic variables of the model. Simscript contains mechanisms that permit the definition of statistical quantities in the preamble and the collection of these quantities throughout the course of the execution of the program. All statistical quantities must be defined explicitly by the programmer in the preamble and then printed as part of the user-generated output. However, the programmer need not be concerned with the computation of the statistical quantities in the program.

The statements utilized for the definition of statistical quantities are TALLY and ACCUMULATE. The purpose of TALLY is to collect statistics on

```
LINE  CACI SIMSCRIPT II.5  RELEASE 8G                    10/19/78  PAGE

   1   PREAMBLE
   2   THE SYSTEM OWNS A WAITING.LINE
   3   TEMPORARY ENTITIES
   4      EVERY CUSTOMER HAS A N.TRANSACTIONS AND AN ENTRY.TIME AND MAY
   5         BELONG TO THE WAITING.LINE
   6   EVENT NOTICES INCLUDE ARRIVAL, DEPARTURE, AND STOP.SIMULATICN
   7   PRIORITY CRDER IS STOP.SIMULATICN, DEPARTURE, ARRIVAL
   8   DEFINE IDLE TO MEAN 0
   9   DEFINE BUSY TO MEAN 1
  10   DEFINE WINDOW, N.ARRIVALS, N.DEPARTURES, AND N.TRANSACTICNS AS
  11      INTEGER VARIABLES
  12   DEFINE MAX.WAIT, MIN.ARRIVAL, MAX.ARRIVAL, AVG.TRANSACTICNS, AND
  13      ENTRY.TIME AS REAL VARIABLES
  14   DEFINE WAITING.LINE AS A FIFO SET
  15   END


   1   MAIN
   2   READ MIN.ARRIVAL, MAX.ARRIVAL, AVG.TRANSACTIONS
   3   LET WINDOW = IDLE
   4   LET N.ARRIVALS = 0
   5   LET N.DEPARTURES = 0
   6   LET MAX.WAIT = 0
   7   SCHEDULE AN ARRIVAL IN UNIFORM.F ( MIN.ARRIVAL, MAX.ARRIVAL, 1 )
   8      MINUTES
   9   SCHEDULE A STOP.SIMULATION IN 8 HOURS
  10   START SIMULATION
  11   END


   1   EVENT ARRIVAL
   2   SCHEDULE AN ARRIVAL IN UNIFORM.F ( MIN.ARRIVAL, MAX.ARRIVAL, 1 )
   3      MINUTES
   4   CREATE A CUSTCMER
   5   LET N.ARRIVALS = N.ARRIVALS + 1
   6   LET N.TRANSACTICNS ( CUSTOMER ) = EXPCNENTIAL.F ( AVG.TRANSACTICNS,
   7      2 )
   8   LET ENTRY.TIME ( CUSTOMER ) = TIME.V
   9   FILE THIS CUSTOMER IN THE WAITING.LINE
  10   IF WINDOW = IDLE,
  11      LET WINDOW = BUSY
  12      REMOVE FIRST CUSTOMER FROM THE WAITING.LINE
  13      LET WAIT = 0
  14      SCHEDULE A DEPARTURE IN N.TRANSACTIONS (CUSTCMER ) * MINUTES
  15      DESTROY THIS CUSTOMER
  16   ALWAYS
  17   RETURN
  18   END
```

```
LINE  CACI SIMSCRIPT II.5  RELEASE 8G                    1C/19/78  PAGE

   1    EVENT DEPARTURE
   2    LET N.DEPARTURES = N.DEPARTURES + 1
   3    IF WAITING.LINE IS EMPTY,
   4        LET WINDOW = IDLE
   5        JUMP AHEAD
   6    ELSE
   7        REMOVE FIRST CUSTOMER FROM WAITING.LINE
   8        LET WAIT = TIME.V - ENTRY.TIME ( CUSTOMER )
   9        IF WAIT > MAX.WAIT,
  10            LET MAX.WAIT = WAIT
  11        ALWAYS
  12        SCHEDULE A DEPARTURE IN N.TRANSACTIONS ( CUSTOMER ) * 2 MINUTES
  13        DESTROY THIS CUSTOMER
  14    HERE
  15    RETURN
  16    END


   1    EVENT STOP.SIMULATION
   2    PRINT 10 LINES WITH MIN.ARRIVAL, MAX.ARRIVAL, AVG.TRANSACTIONS,
   3        N.ARRIVALS, N.DEPARTURES, AND MAX.WAIT * 1440
   4        THUS
DRIVE-IN WINDOW MODEL
    PARAMETERS
        MINIMUM ARRIVAL TIME                    **.***  MINS.
        MAXIMUM ARRIVAL TIME                    **.***  MINS.
        AVERAGE TRANSACTICNS PER CUSTOMER       **.***
    RESULTS
        NUMBER CF ARRIVALS                      ***
        NUMBER OF DEPARTURES                    ***
        MAXIMUM WAIT                            **.***  MINS.
    END OF SIMULATION
   5    STOP
   6    END


    DRIVE-IN WINDOW MODEL
        PARAMETERS
            MINIMUM ARRIVAL TIME                 .250   MINS.
            MAXIMUM ARRIVAL TIME                5.750   MINS.
            AVERAGE TRANSACTICNS PER CUSTOMER   1.500
        RESULTS
            NUMBER OF ARRIVALS                  155
            NUMBER CF CEPARTURES                138
            MAXIMUM WAIT                        47.145  MINS.
        END OF SIMULATION
```

time-independent variables, whereas ACCUMULATE gathers statistics on time-dependent variables. The difference between the two statements is that the calculations made for the average, variance, and standard deviation of the statistical quantities defined by ACCUMULATE involve time as a weighting factor. For example, statistics regarding the number of elements in a set would be collected using ACCUMULATE since the amount of time spent by an entity in the set is used in the computation of the average. TALLY is appropriate for statistics on global variables because time does not figure in their computation.

One of the most common uses of ACCUMULATE is to garner statistics on the number of elements in a set. For each set there is a system variable of the form N.*setname* that indicates the number of elements in the set.

TALLY and ACCUMULATE have identical formats.

$$\left\{ \begin{array}{l} \text{TALLY} \\ \text{ACCUMULATE} \end{array} \right\} \textit{compute list} \text{ OF } \textit{name}$$

where

> *compute list* is a list of phrases of the form
> > *variable* AS THE *quantity*
>
> separated by commas and/or AND, with *quantity* a statistical quantity
> defined in Table 4.3 and *variable* any valid Simscript identifier
> *name* is the variable or attribute for which the statistics are gathered

The following samples show the use of TALLY and ACCUMULATE:

TALLY MAX.WAIT AS THE MAXIMUM OF WAIT

By defining MAX.WAIT in this fashion in the preamble, the two statements used to determine the value of MAX.WAIT could be eliminated from the DEPARTURE event routine of Example 4.1.

ACCUMULATE AVG.LENGTH AS THE MEAN AND MAX.LENGTH
AS THE MAXIMUM OF N.WAITING.LINE

The statement causes the average and maximum number of elements to be determined for the set, WAITING.LINE.

Table 4.3   Statistical Quantities for TALLY and ACCUMULATE

NUMBER
SUM
SUM.OF.SQUARES
MEAN
MEAN.SQUARE
VARIANCE
STD.DEV
MAXIMUM
MINIMUM

EXAMPLE 4.2

The drive-in window model of the previous example is expanded to include statistics on the number of customers waiting, the waiting times, and the utilization of the window. Note that the value for maximum wait that is computed using TALLY in this program is identical to the value computed explicitly in the previous example.

4.12 PERMANENT ENTITIES

Entities that remain in existence throughout the course of a simulation are termed *permanent* entities. The definition of permanent entities takes place in the preamble using a PERMANENT ENTITIES statement followed by a sequence of EVERY statements listing the attributes, set memberships, and set ownerships of every permanent entity. The form of the EVERY statement is identical for both permanent and temporary entities.

Permanent entities are allocated using a variant of the CREATE statement. By definition, permanent entities may not be destroyed. The number of permanent entities in a model may be fixed or may be a parameter of the model. In order to allocate a fixed number of permanent entities, a CREATE EVERY statement of the following form is used:

CREATE EVERY *entity(integer)*

where

entity is the name of the permanent entity

integer indicates the number of permanent entities of that type to be created

For example,

CREATE EVERY TELLER(5)

allocates five TELLER permanent entities.

If the number of permanent entities is a parameter of the model, then a value must be assigned to the system variable N.*entity* by a READ statement prior to the execution of the CREATE EVERY statement for that entity. In this case, CREATE EVERY has the form

CREATE EVERY *entity*

In order to establish a variable number of TELLER permanent entities, the following statements would be used:

READ N.TELLER

⋮

CREATE EVERY TELLER

With the previously noted exception of the DESTROY statement, permanent entities and their attributes may be operated upon in the same ways as temporary entities.

When TALLY and ACCUMULATE are defined for an attribute of a per-

```
LINE  CACI SIMSCRIPT II.5  RELEASE 8G                    10/19/78  PAGE

   1   PREAMBLE
   2    THE SYSTEM OWNS A WAITING.LINE
   3    TEMPORARY ENTITIES
   4       EVERY CUSTOMER HAS A N.TRANSACTIONS AND AN ENTRY.TIME AND MAY
   5          BELONG TO THE WAITING.LINE
   6    EVENT NOTICES INCLUDE ARRIVAL, DEPARTURE, AND STOP.SIMULATION
   7    PRIORITY ORDER IS STOP.SIMULATION, DEPARTURE, ARRIVAL
   8    DEFINE IDLE TO MEAN 0
   9    DEFINE BUSY TO MEAN 1
  10    DEFINE WINDOW, N.ARRIVALS, N.DEPARTURES, AND N.TRANSACTIONS AS
  11       INTEGER VARIABLES
  12    DEFINE MAX.WAIT, MIN.ARRIVAL, MAX.ARRIVAL, AVG.TRANSACTIONS,
  13       WAIT, AND ENTRY.TIME AS REAL VARIABLES
  14    DEFINE WAITING.LINE AS A FIFO SET
  15    TALLY MAX.WAIT AS THE MAXIMUM AND AVG.WAIT AS THE MEAN OF WAIT
  16    ACCUMULATE AVG.LENGTH AS THE MEAN AND MAX.LENGTH AS THE MAXIMUM OF
  17       N.WAITING.LINE
  18    ACCUMULATE UTILIZATION AS THE MEAN OF WINDOW
  19   END


   1   MAIN
   2    READ MIN.ARRIVAL, MAX.ARRIVAL, AVG.TRANSACTIONS
   3    LET WINDOW = IDLE
   4    LET N.ARRIVALS = 0
   5    LET N.DEPARTURES = 0
   6    SCHEDULE AN ARRIVAL IN UNIFORM.F ( MIN.ARRIVAL, MAX.ARRIVAL, 1 )
   7       MINUTES
   8    SCHEDULE A STOP.SIMULATION IN 8 HOURS
   9    START SIMULATION
  10   END


   1   EVENT ARRIVAL
   2    SCHEDULE AN ARRIVAL IN UNIFORM.F ( MIN.ARRIVAL, MAX.ARRIVAL, 1 )
   3       MINUTES
   4    CREATE A CUSTOMER
   5    LET N.ARRIVALS = N.ARRIVALS + 1
   6    LET N.TRANSACTIONS ( CUSTOMER ) = EXPONENTIAL.F ( AVG.TRANSACTIONS,
   7       2 )
   8    LET ENTRY.TIME ( CUSTOMER ) = TIME.V
   9    FILE THIS CUSTOMER IN THE WAITING.LINE
  10    IF WINDOW = IDLE,
  11       LET WINDOW = BUSY
  12       REMOVE FIRST CUSTOMER FROM THE WAITING.LINE
  13       LET WAIT = 0
  14       SCHEDULE A DEPARTURE IN N.TRANSACTIONS (CUSTOMER ) * 2 MINUTES
  15       DESTROY THIS CUSTOMER
  16    ALWAYS
  17    RETURN
  18   END
```

```
LINE  CACI SIMSCRIPT II.5  RELEASE 8G                    10/19/78   PAGE

    1     EVENT DEPARTURE
    2     LET N.DEPARTURES = N.DEPARTURES + 1
    3     IF WAITING.LINE IS EMPTY,
    4        LET WINDOW = IDLE
    5        JUMP AHEAD
    6     ELSE
    7        REMOVE FIRST CUSTOMER FROM WAITING.LINE
    8        LET WAIT = TIME.V - ENTRY.TIME ( CUSTOMER )
    9        SCHEDULE A DEPARTURE IN N.TRANSACTIONS ( CUSTOMER ) * 2 MINUTES
   10        DESTROY THIS CUSTOMER
   11     HERE
   12     RETURN
   13     END

    1     EVENT STOP.SIMULATION
    2     PRINT 14 LINES WITH MIN.ARRIVAL, MAX.ARRIVAL, AVG.TRANSACTIONS,
    3        N.ARRIVALS, N.DEPARTURES, MAX.WAIT * 1440, AVG.WAIT * 1440,
    4        AVG.LENGTH, MAX.LENGTH, AND UTILIZATION * 100
    5        THUS
DRIVE-IN WINDOW MODEL
     PARAMETERS
           MINIMUM ARRIVAL TIME                    **.***    MINS.
           MAXIMUM ARRIVAL TIME                    **.***    MINS.
           AVERAGE TRANSACTIONS PER CUSTOMER       **.***
     RESULTS
           NUMBER OF ARRIVALS                      ***
           NUMBER OF DEPARTURES                    ***
           MAXIMUM WAIT                            **.***    MINS.
           AVERAGE WAIT                            **.***    MINS.
           AVERAGE WAITING LINE LENGTH             **.***
           MAXIMUM WAITING LINE LENGTH             ***
           UTILIZATION OF WINDOW                   **.***%
     END OF SIMULATION
    6     STOP
    7     END


    DRIVE-IN WINDOW MODEL
     PARAMETERS
           MINIMUM ARRIVAL TIME                     .250    MINS.
           MAXIMUM ARRIVAL TIME                    5.750    MINS.
           AVERAGE TRANSACTIONS PER CUSTOMER       1.500
     RESULTS
           NUMBER OF ARRIVALS                      155
           NUMBER OF DEPARTURES                    138
           MAXIMUM WAIT                            47.145   MINS.
           AVERAGE WAIT                            15.758   MINS.
           AVERAGE WAITING LINE LENGTH             5.193
           MAXIMUM WAITING LINE LENGTH             17
           UTILIZATION OF WINDOW                   85.518%
     END OF SIMULATION
```

manent entity, an array of statistical entities is created. For example, if HEIGHT is the attribute of a permanent entity, CLASS, and the statement

TALLY AVG.HEIGHT AS A MEAN OF HEIGHT

appeared in the preamble, then AVG.HEIGHT would be an array with one entry for each CLASS entity. Then the statement

PRINT 1 LINE WITH AVG.HEIGHT(CLASS.NO)

prints the value of AVG.HEIGHT for the permanent entity CLASS identified by the variable CLASS.NO.

References to sets owned by permanent entities must be subscripted to indicate the particular parmanent entity owning the set as shown in the following sample.

REMOVE FIRST CUSTOMER FROM WAITING.LINE(TELLER.NO)

where WAITING.LINE is a set owned by a permanent entity.

EXAMPLE 4.3

The teller activity on the inside of a bank is modeled to illustrate the application of permanent entities. The number of tellers is a parameter of the model, as is the arrival rate of the customers and the number of transactions per customer. This model describes a banking facility with a single waiting line serviced by multiple tellers. Statistics are maintained on waiting-line behavior and teller activity.

4.13 LOOPS

One of the most powerful and frequently used features of programming languages is the construction of program loops that permit the repetitive execution of a group of statements. The FOR statement provides this capability in Simscript. In general, a loop consists of two parts:

a specification statement, which identifies a variable whose value is modified for each iteration along with the initiation and termination conditions

a loop body consisting of the statements to be executed

A Simscript loop has the following structure:

FOR *specifications*
    DO
        ⋮ *loop body*
    LOOP

If the loop body consists of only one statement, DO and LOOP may be omitted.

Three types of specifications—numeric, set, and entity—can be used. Numeric specifications are similar to those found in most high-level programming

```
LINE  CACI SIMSCRIPT II.5  RELEASE 8G                    10/19/78  PAGE
   1    PREAMBLE
   2     THE SYSTEM OWNS A WAITING.LINE
   3     PERMANENT ENTITIES
   4        EVERY TELLER HAS A STATUS
   5     TEMPORARY ENTITIES
   6        EVERY CUSTOMER HAS AN ENTRY.TIME, AND A
   7           N.TRANSACTIONS AND MAY BELONG TO THE WAITING.LINE
   8     DEFINE WAITING.LINE AS A FIFO SET
   9     EVENT NOTICES INCLUDE ARRIVAL, AND
  10        STOP.SIMULATION
  11        EVERY DEPARTURE HAS A TELLER.NO
  12     PRIORITY ORDER IS STOP.SIMULATION, DEPARTURE, AND
  13        ARRIVAL
  14     DEFINE IDLE TC MEAN 0
  15     DEFINE BUSY TO MEAN 1
  16     DEFINE MIN.ARRIVAL, MAX.ARRIVAL, AVG.TRANSACTIONS, ENTRY.TIME, AND
  17        WAIT AS VARIABLES
  18     DEFINE BUSY.TELLERS, N.ARRIVALS, N.DEPARTURES, N.TRANSACTIONS,
  19        STATUS, NUM.TELLER, AND TELLER.NO AS INTEGER VARIABLES
  20     TALLY AVG.WAIT AS THE MEAN AND MAX.WAIT AS THE MAXIMUM OF WAIT
  21     ACCUMULATE AVG.LENGTH AS THE MEAN AND MAX.LENGTH AS THE MAXIMUM OF
  22        N.WAITING.LINE
  23     ACCUMULATE AVG.BUSY AS THE MEAN OF BUSY.TELLERS
  24     ACCUMULATE AVG.STATUS AS THE MEAN OF STATUS
  25    END

   1    MAIN
   2     READ MIN.ARRIVAL, MAX.ARRIVAL, AVG.TRANSACTIONS, N.TELLER
   3     CREATE EVERY TELLER
   4     LET BUSY.TELLERS = 0
   5     LET N.ARRIVALS = 0
   6     LET N.DEPARTURES = 0
   7     SCHEDULE AN ARRIVAL IN UNIFORM.F ( MIN.ARRIVAL, MAX.ARRIVAL, 1 )
   8        MINUTES
   9     SCHEDULE A STOP.SIMULATION IN 8 HOURS
  10     START SIMULATION
  11    END
```

```
LINE  CACI SIMSCRIPT II.5  RELEASE 8G                      10/19/78  PAGE

  1   EVENT ARRIVAL
  2     LET N.ARRIVALS = N.ARRIVALS + 1
  3     SCHEDULE AN ARRIVAL IN UNIFORM.F ( MIN.ARRIVAL, MAX.ARRIVAL, 1 )
  4       MINUTES
  5     CREATE A CUSTCMER
  6     LET N.TRANSACTIONS ( CUSTOMER ) = EXPCNENTIAL.F ( AVG.TRANSACTICNS,
  7       2 )
  8     LET ENTRY.TIME ( CUSTOMER ) = TIME.V
  9     FILE THE CUSTOMER IN THE WAITING.LINE
 10     IF BUSY.TELLERS < N.TELLER,
 11       LET BUSY.TELLERS = BUSY.TELLERS  + 1
 12       LET NUM.TELLER = 1
 13     HERE
 14       IF STATUS ( NUM.TELLER ) = IDLE,
 15           LET STATUS ( NUM.TELLER ) = BUSY
 16           JUMP AHEAD
 17       ELSE
 18           LET NUM.TELLER = NUM.TELLER + 1
 19           JUMP BACK
 20     HERE
 21       REMOVE FIRST CUSTOMER FROM THE WAITING.LINE
 22       LET WAIT = 0
 23       SCHEDULE A DEPARTURE ( NUM.TELLER ) IN N.TRANSACTICNS ( CUSTCMER )
 24         * 2 MINUTES
 25       DESTROY THE CUSTOMER
 26     ALWAYS
 27     RETURN
 28   END

  1   EVENT DEPARTURE ( TELLER.NO )
  2     DEFINE TELLER.NO AS AN INTEGER VARIABLE
  3     LET N.DEPARTURES = N.DEPARTURES + 1
  4     IF WAITING.LINE IS EMPTY,
  5       LET STATUS ( TELLER.NC ) = IDLE
  6       LET BUSY.TELLERS = BUSY.TELLERS - 1
  7       JUMP AHEAD
  8     ELSE
  9       REMOVE THE FIRST CUSTOMER FRCM THE WAITING.LINE
 10       LET WAIT = TIME.V - ENTRY.TIME ( CUSTOMER )
 11       SCHEDULE A DEPARTURE ( TELLER.NO ) IN N.TRANSACTICNS ( CUSTOMER )
 12         * 2 MINUTES
 13       DESTRCY THIS CUSTCMER
 14     HERE
 15     RETURN
 16   END
```

```
LINE  CACI SIMSCRIPT II.5  RELEASE 8G                    1C/19/78  PAGE

  1    EVENT STOP.SIMULATION
  2     PRINT 14 LINES WITH MIN.ARRIVAL, MAX.ARRIVAL, AVG.TRANSACTICNS,
  3        N.TELLER, N.ARRIVALS, N.DEPARTURES, AVG.WAIT * 1440, MAX.WAIT
  4        * 1440, AVG.LENGTH, MAX.LENGTH, AVG.BUSY
  5         THUS
         BANK TELLER MODEL
             PARAMETERS
                     MINIMUM CUSTCMER ARRVIAL TIME          **.*** MINS.
                     MAXIMUM CUSTOMER ARRIVAL TIME          **.*** MINS.
                     AVERAGE TRANSACTION PER CLSTCMER       **.***
                     NUMBER OF TELLERS                      ***
             RESULTS
                     NUMBER OF ARRIVALS                     ****
                     NUMBER OF DEPARTURES                   ****
                     AVERAGE WAITING TIME                   **.*** MINS.
                     MAXIMUM WAITING TIME                   **.*** MINS.
                     AVERAGE LINE LENGTH                    **.***
                     MAXIMUM LINE LENGTH                    **
                     AVERAGE NUMBER CF BUSY TELLERS         **.***
  6    LET NUM.TELLER = 1
  7    HERE
  8     IF NUM.TELLER <= N.TELLER,
  9        PRINT 1 LINE WITH NUM.TELLER AND AVG.STATUS ( NUM.TELLER )
 10             THUS
                     UTILIZATION CF TELLER**                **.***%
 11        LET NUM.TELLER = NUM.TELLER + 1
 12        JUMP BACK
 13    ALWAYS
 14    PRINT 1 LINE
 15        THUS
         END OF SIMULATICN
 16    STOP
 17    END


       BANK TELLER MODEL
           PARAMETERS
                   MINIMUM CUSTOMER ARRIVAL TIME        .250 MINS.
                   MAXIMUM CUSTOMER ARRIVAL TIME       2.750 MINS.
                   AVERAGE TRANSACTION PER CLSTOMER    1.500
                   NUMBER OF TELLERS                   2
           RESULTS
                   NUMBER OF ARRIVALS                  312
                   NUMBER OF DEPARTURES                278
                   AVERAGE WAITING TIME                18.461 MINS.
                   MAXIMUM WAITING TIME                56.211 MINS.
                   AVERAGE LINE LENGTH                 12.471
                   MAXIMUM LINE LENGTH                 36
                   AVERAGE NUMBER OF BUSY TELLERS      1.857
                   UTILIZATICN OF TELLER 1              .945%
                   UTILIZATICN CF TELLER 2              .912%
       END OF SIMULATION
```

language. However, Simscript also permits looping through sets without requiring the programmer to determine the number of entities in the set beforehand, and iteratively processing all permanent entities without specifying the exact number of entities.

A FOR statement with numeric specifications has the form

FOR *variable* = *initial* TO *final* [BY *incr*]

where

variable is the control variable of the loop

initial is an expression indicating the value of the variable used in the first execution of the loop

final is an expression used to indicate the maximum value of the variable in the loop

incr is an optional expression indicating the amount by which the value of the variable is to be increased after each loop iteration; the default value is 1.0

Consider the sample loops:

```
FOR K = 1 TO 10
    DO
      IF CASH(K) > 2000
        LET EXCESS.CASH = CASH(K) − 2000 + EXCESS.CASH
        LET CASH(K) = 2000
      ALWAYS
          PRINT 1 LINE WITH CASH(K) THUS ****.**
    LOOP
```

The FOR statement will execute the statements between DO and LOOP 10 times with K assuming the values 1, 2, ..., 9, 10.

```
FOR HEIGHT = X*2 TO MAX.HEIGHT BY .05
    PRINT 1 LINE WITH WIDTH*HEIGHT THUS ***.**
```

These two statements are equivalent to the following group of statements:

```
LET HEIGHT = X*2
HERE
  IF HEIGHT > MAX.HEIGHT
    JUMP AHEAD
  ELSE
    PRINT 1 LINE WITH WIDTH*HEIGHT THUS ***.**
    LET HEIGHT = HEIGHT + .05
    JUMP BACK
HERE
```

The set specification of FOR has the following format:

$$
\text{FOR} \left\{ \begin{array}{l} \text{EACH} \\ \text{ALL} \\ \text{EVERY} \end{array} \right\} \underline{\text{entity}} \left\{ \begin{array}{l} \text{IN} \\ \text{OF} \\ \text{ON} \\ \text{AT} \end{array} \right\} \text{[THE]} \underline{\text{set}}
$$

The statements below provide an example of a loop through a set:

```
FOR EACH CUSTOMER IN THE WAITING.LINE
    DO
        IF ENTRY.TIME(CUSTOMER) < TIME.V -15.0
            REMOVE THIS CUSTOMER FROM WAITING.LINE
            LET DISGUSTED = DISGUSTED + 1
            DESTROY THIS CUSTOMER
        ALWAYS
    LOOP
```

The entity specification allows the iterative processing of the attributes of a permanent entity. The format is

```
FOR EVERY entity
```

where *entity* is a permanent entity.

A typical loop using the entity specification is as follows:

```
FOR EVERY TELLER
    LET TOT.WAIT = N.WAITING.LINE(TELLER) + TOT.WAIT
```

Loops may be nested by using FOR statements in the loop body. The programmer must take care to ensure that all DO and LOOP statements are properly balanced. The use of indention is a very convenient method of clearly indicating the structure of a nested loop. An example of a nested loop is as follows:

```
FOR EACH CUSTOMER IN THE WAITING.LINE
    DO
        LET TOTAL.TIME(CUSTOMER) = 0
        FOR EACH TRANS IN TRANS.LIST(CUSTOMER)
            LET TOTAL.TIME(CUSTOMER) = TIME(TRANS) +
                TOTAL.TIME(CUSTOMER)
    LOOP
```

EXAMPLE 4.4

In the preceding example, loops were constructed using IF and JUMP statements in the ARRIVAL and STOP SIMULATION routines. The same logical effect can be achieved with FOR statements as shown in the accompanying listing.

4.14 SELECTIVITY

The specifications of a FOR statement can be expanded to specify explicitly the conditions under which the statements in the loop body are to be executed (or not executed). This feature permits the execution of a loop including only selected elements of a set or a collection of attributes or excluding specified elements.

Selection is indicated by the use of a conditional expression preceded by the key words WITH or WHEN. Exclusion is designated by either EXCEPT

```
LINE   CACI SIMSCRIPT II.5  RELEASE 8G                    10/19/78   PAGE

 1    PREAMBLE
 2    THE SYSTEM OWNS A WAITING.LINE
 3    PERMANENT ENTITIES
 4        EVERY TELLER HAS A STATUS
 5    TEMPORARY ENTITIES
 6        EVERY CUSTOMER HAS AN ENTRY.TIME, AND A
 7           N.TRANSACTICNS AND MAY BELCNG TO THE WAITING.LINE
 8    DEFINE WAITING.LINE AS A FIFO SET
 9    EVENT NOTICES INCLUDE ARRIVAL,   AND
10        STOP.SIMULATICN
11        EVERY DEPARTURE HAS A TELLER.NC
12    PRIORITY ORDER IS STOP.SIMULATICN, DEPARTURE, AND
13        ARRIVAL
14    DEFINE IDLE TO MEAN 0
15    DEFINE BUSY TO MEAN 1
16    DEFINE MIN.ARRIVAL, MAX.ARRIVAL, AVG.TRANSACTIONS, ENTRY.TIME, AND
17        WAIT AS REAL VARIABLES
18    DEFINE BUSY.TELLERS, N.ARRIVALS, N.CEPARTURES, N.TRANSACTICNS,
19        STATUS, NUM.TELLER, AND TELLER.NC AS INTEGER VARIABLES
20    TALLY AVG.WAIT AS THE MEAN AND MAX.WAIT AS THE MAXIMUM CF WAIT
21    ACCUMULATE AVG.LENGTH AS THE MEAN AND MAX.LENGTH AS THE MAXIMUM OF
22        N.WAITING.LINE
23    ACCUMULATE AVG.BUSY AS THE MEAN CF BUSY.TELLERS
24    ACCUMULATE AVG.STATUS AS THE MEAN OF STATUS
25    END

 1    MAIN
 2    READ MIN.ARRIVAL, MAX.ARRIVAL, AVG.TRANSACTIONS, N.TELLER
 3    CREATE EVERY TELLER
 4    LET BUSY.TELLERS = 0
 5    LET N.ARRIVALS = 0
 6    LET N.DEPARTURES = 0
 7    SCHEDULE AN ARRIVAL IN UNIFCRM.F ( MIN.ARRIVAL, MAX.ARRIVAL, 1 )
 8        MINUTES
 9    SCHEDULE A STOP.SIMULATICN IN 8 HOURS
10    START SIMULATICN
11    END
```

```
LINE  CACI SIMSCRIPT II.5  RELEASE 8G                        1C/19/78  PAGE

   1    EVENT ARRIVAL
   2    LET N.ARRIVALS = N.ARRIVALS + 1
   3    SCHEDULE AN ARRIVAL IN UNIFCRM.F ( MIN.ARRIVAL, MAX.ARRIVAL, 1 )
   4       MINUTES
   5       CREATE A CUSTCMER
   6    LET N.TRANSACTIONS ( CUSTOMER ) = EXPCNENTIAL.F ( AVG.TRANSACTIONS,
   7       2 )
   8    LET ENTRY.TIME ( CUSTCMER ) = TIME.V
   9    FILE THE CUSTOMER IN THE WAITING.LINE
  10    IF BUSY.TELLERS < N.TELLER,
  11       LET BUSY.TELLERS = BUSY.TELLERS  + 1
  12       FOR NUM.TELLER = 1 TO N.TELLER
  13             DO
  14                    IF STATUS ( NUM.TELLER ) = IDLE,
  15                         LET STATUS ( NUM.TELLER ) = BLSY
  16                       JUMP AHEAC
  17                    ALWAYS
  18             LOOP
  19      HERE
  20      REMOVE FIRST CUSTOMER FRCM THE WAITING.LINE
  21      LET WAIT = 0
  22      SCHEDULE A DEPARTURE ( NUM.TELLER ) IN N.TRANSACTICNS ( CUSTOMER )
  23         * 2 MINUTES
  24      DESTRCY THIS CUSTCMER
  25    ALWAYS
  26    RETURN
  27    END

   1    EVENT DEPARTURE ( TELLER.NO )
   2    DEFINE TELLER.NO AS AN INTEGER VARIABLE
   3    LET N.DEPARTURES = N.DEPARTURES + 1
   4    IF WAITING.LINE IS EMPTY,
   5       LET STATUS ( TELLER.NO ) = IDLE
   6       LET BUSY.TELLERS = BUSY.TELLERS − 1
   7       JUMP AHEAC
   8    ELSE
   9       REMOVE THE FIRST CUSTCMER FRCM THE WAITING.LINE
  10       LET WAIT = TIME.V − ENTRY.TIME ( CLSTOMER )
  11       SCHEDULE A DEPARTURE ( TELLER.NO ) IN N.TRANSACTICNS ( CUSTCMER )
  12          * 2 MINUTES
  13       DESTROY THIS CUSTOMER
  14    HERE
  15    RETURN
  16    END
```

```
LINE  CACI SIMSCRIPT II.5  RELEASE 8G                    10/19/78  PAGE

   1    EVENT STOP.SIMULATICN
   2     PRINT 14 LINES WITH MIN.ARRIVAL, MAX.ARRIVAL, AVG.TRANSACTICNS,
   3        N.TELLER, N.ARRIVALS, N.DEPARTURES, AVG.WAIT * 144C, MAX.WAIT
   4        * 1440, AVG.LENGTH, MAX.LENGTH, AVG.BUSY
   5     THUS
         BANK TELLER MODEL
              PARAMETERS
                        MINIMUM CUSTOMER ARRVIAL TIME       **.*** MINS.
                        MAXIMUM CUSTOMER ARRIVAL TIME       **.*** MINS.
                        AVERAGE TRANSACTICN PER CUSTOMER    **.***
                        NUMBER OF TELLERS                   ***
              RESULTS
                        NUMBER OF ARRIVALS                  ****
                        NUMBER CF DEPARTURES                ****
                        AVERAGE WAITING TIME                **.*** MINS.
                        MAXIMUM WAITING TIME                **.*** MINS.
                        AVERAGE LINE LENGTH                 **.***
                        MAXIMUM LINE LENGTH                 **
                        AVERAGE NUMBER OF BUSY TELLERS      **.***
   6    FOR NUM.TELLER = 1 TC N.TELLER
   7      PRINT 1 LINE WITH NUM.TELLER AND AVG.STATUS ( NUM.TELLER )
   8          THUS
                        UTILIZATICN OF TELLER**             **.***%
   9    PRINT 1 LINE
  10      THUS
          END OF SIMULATICN
  11    STOP
  12    END
```

WHEN or UNLESS, followed by a conditional expression. The following statements show selection and then exclusion:

```
FOR EVERY PERSON WITH HEIGHT(PERSON) < 66.0
LET SHORT.PEOPLE = SHORT.PEOPLE + 1

FOR EACH CUSTOMER IN THE WAITING.LINE
   EXCEPT WHEN(ENTRY.TIME(CUSTOMER) >=TIME.V −15.0
   DO
      REMOVE THIS CUSTOMER FROM WAITING.LINE
      LET DISGUSTED = DISGUSTED + 1
      DESTROY THIS CUSTOMER
   LOOP
```

The second loop is functionally equivalent to the second sample loop in the preceding section.

EXAMPLE 4.5

The bank teller model of the previous example is expanded so that customers who wait more than 15 minutes in line leave the bank without completing their business. This activity is simulated by an event, IMPATIENT, which occurs every 5 minutes after the first 15 minutes of banking. Whenever the IMPATIENT event occurs, any customers waiting for more than 15 minutes leave the bank. In order to simplify the computations involved, the time unit of the model is changed from days to minutes. The number of customers departing without service is represented by the variable DISGUSTED.

4.15 SEARCHING

The selection option of the FOR statement can be combined with a FIND statement to create a searching facility to locate an entity with a specified property. Searching is performed on a set to identify the first entity that satisfies the selection criterion. A special conditional key word, NONE, permits testing for the failure of the search.

The statements comprising a search have the organization shown below:

```
FOR EACH entity IN set WITH condition
FIND THE FIRST CASE
IF NONE,
   ⋮
ELSE
   ⋮
```

```
LINE   CACI SIMSCRIPT II.5  RELEASE 8G                    10/19/78  PAGE

   1    PREAMBLE
   2    THE SYSTEM OWNS A WAITING.LINE
   3    PERMANENT ENTITIES
   4       EVERY TELLER HAS A STATUS
   5    TEMPORARY ENTITIES
   6       EVERY CUSTOMER HAS AN ENTRY.TIME, AND A
   7          N.TRANSACTICNS AND MAY BELONG TO THE WAITING.LINE
   8    DEFINE WAITING.LINE AS A FIFO SET
   9    EVENT NOTICES INCLUDE ARRIVAL,
  10       IMPATIENT, AND STCP.SIMULATICN
  11       EVERY DEPARTURE HAS A TELLER.NC
  12    PRIORITY CRDER IS STOP.SIMULATICN, DEPARTURE,
  13       ARRIVAL, AND IMPATIENT
  14    DEFINE ICLE TO MEAN O
  15    DEFINE BUSY TC MEAN 1
  16    DEFINE MINUTES TO MEAN UNITS
  17    DEFINE HCURS TC MEAN * 60 MINUTES
  18    DEFINE MIN.ARRIVAL, MAX.ARRIVAL, AVG.TRANSACTIONS, ENTRY.TIME, ANC
  19       WAIT AS REAL VARIABLES
  20    DEFINE BUSY.TELLERS, N.ARRIVALS, N.DEPARTURES, N.TRANSACTICNS,
  21       STATUS, DISGUSTED, NUM.TELLER, AND TELLER.NO AS
  22       INTEGER VARIABLES
  23    TALLY AVG.WAIT AS THE MEAN AND MAX.WAIT AS THE MAXIMUM CF WAIT
  24    ACCUMULATE AVG.LENGTH AS THE MEAN AND MAX.LENGTH AS THE MAXIMUM CF
  25       N.WAITING.LINE
  26    ACCUMULATE AVG.BUSY AS THE MEAN CF BUSY.TELLERS
  27    ACCUMULATE AVG.STATUS AS THE MEAN OF STATUS
  28    END

   1    MAIN
   2    READ MIN.ARRIVAL, MAX.ARRIVAL, AVG.TRANSACTIONS, N.TELLER
   3    CREATE EVERY TELLER
   4    LET BUSY.TELLERS = 0
   5    LET DISGUSTED = 0
   6    LET N.ARRIVALS = 0
   7    LET N.DEPARTURES = 0
   8    SCHEDULE AN ARRIVAL IN UNIFORM.F ( MIN.ARRIVAL, MAX.ARRIVAL, 1 )
   9       MINUTES
  10    SCHEDULE AN IMPATIENT IN 15 MINUTES
  11    SCHEDULE A STOP.SIMULATICN IN 8 HOURS
  12    START SIMULATICN
  13    END
```

```
 1     EVENT ARRIVAL
 2     LET N.ARRIVALS = N.ARRIVALS + 1
 3     SCHEDULE AN ARRIVAL IN UNIFORM.F ( MIN.ARRIVAL, MAX.ARRIVAL, 1 )
 4        MINUTES
 5     CREATE A CUSTCMER
 6     LET N.TRANSACTICNS ( CUSTOMER ) = EXPCNENTIAL.F ( AVG.TRANSACTIONS,
 7        2 )
 8     LET ENTRY.TIME ( CUSTOMER ) = TIME.V
 9     FILE THE CUSTOMER IN THE WAITING.LINE
10     IF BUSY.TELLERS < N.TELLER,
11        LET BUSY.TELLERS = BUSY.TELLERS  + 1
12        FOR NUM.TELLER = 1 TO N.TELLER
13           DO
14                  IF STATUS ( NUM.TELLER ) = ICLE,
15                     LET STATLS ( NUM.TELLER ) = BUSY
16                     JUMP AHEAD
17                  ALWAYS
18              LOOP
19        HERE
20        REMOVE FIRST CUSTCMER FROM THE WAITING.LINE
21        LET WAIT = 0
22        SCHEDULE A DEPARTURE ( NUM.TELLER ) IN N.TRANSACTICNS ( CUSTCMER )
23           * 2 MINUTES
24        DESTROY THIS CUSTOMER
25     ALWAYS
26     RETURN
27     END
```

```
 1     EVENT DEPARTURE ( TELLER.NO )
 2        DEFINE TELLER.NO AS AN INTEGER VARIABLE
 3        LET N.DEPARTURES = N.DEPARTURES + 1
 4        IF WAITING.LINE IS EMPTY,
 5           LET STATUS ( TELLER.NO ) = ICLE
 6           LET BUSY.TELLERS = BUSY.TELLERS - 1
 7           JUMP AHEAD
 8        ELSE
 9           REMOVE THE FIRST CUSTOMER FRCM THE WAITING.LINE
10           LET WAIT = TIME.V - ENTRY.TIME ( CLSTOMER )
11           SCHEDULE A DEPARTURE ( TELLER.NO ) IN N.TRANSACTICNS ( CUSTOMER )
12              * 2 MINUTES
13           DESTROY THIS CUSTCMER
14        HERE
15        RETURN
16     END
```

```
 1     EVENT IMPATIENT
 2     SCHEDULE AN IMPATIENT IN 5 MINUTES
 3     FOR EVERY CUSTOMER IN THE WAITING.LINE EXCEPT WHEN ( ENTRY.TIME
 4        ( CUSTCMER ) >= TIME.V - 15.0 )
 5        DO
 6              REMOVE THIS CUSTCMER FROM THE WAITING.LINE
 7              LET DISGUSTED = DISGUSTED + 1
 8              DESTROY THIS CUSTCMER
 9        LCCP
10     RETURN
11     END
```

```
'LINE  CACI SIMSCRIPT II.5  RELEASE 8G                 10/19/78  PAGE

      1   EVENT STOP.SIMULATICN
      2     PRINT 15 LINES WITH MIN.ARRIVAL, MAX.ARRIVAL, AVG.TRANSACTICNS,
      3       N.TELLER, N.ARRIVALS, N.DEPARTURES, CISGUSTED, AVG.WAIT,
      4       MAX.WAIT, AVG.LENGTH, MAX.LENGTH, AVG.EUSY
      5       THUS
            BANK TELLER MCDEL
                PARAMETERS
                            MINIMUM CLSTOMER ARRIVAL TIME       **.*** MINS.
                            MAXIMUM CUSTCMER ARRIVAL TIME       **.*** MINS.
                            AVERAGE TRANSACTION PER CUSTOMER    **.***
                            NUMBER OF TELLERS                   ***
                RESULTS
                            NUMBER OF ARRIVALS                  ****
                            NUMBER OF SERVED CLSTCMERS          ****
                            NUMBER OF UNSERVED CUSTOMERS        ****
                            AVERAGE WAITING TIME                **.*** MINS.
                            MAXIMUM WAITING TIME                **.*** MINS.
                            AVERAGE LINE LENGTH                 **.***
                            MAXIMUM LINE LENGTH                 **
                            AVERAGE NUMBER CF EUSY TELLERS      **.***
      6     FOR NUM.TELLER = 1 TO N.TELLER
      7       PRINT 1 LINE WITH NUM.TELLER AND AVG.STATUS ( NUM.TELLER )
      8           THUS
                            UTILIZATION CF TELLER**             **.***%
      9     PRINT 1 LINE
     10         THUS
            END OF SIMULATION
     11     STOP
     12   END


    BANK TELLER MODEL
        PARAMETERS
                    MINIMUM CUSTOMER ARRIVAL TIME        .250 MINS.
                    MAXIMUM CUSTCMER ARRIVAL TIME       2.750 MINS.
                    AVERAGE TRANSACTICN PER CLSTCMER    1.50C
                    NUMBER OF TELLERS                   2
        RESULTS
                    NUMBER OF ARRIVALS                   312
                    NUMBER OF SERVED CUSTCMERS           279
                    NUMBER OF UNSERVED CUSTCMERS          26
                    AVERAGE WAITING TIME                 8.812 MINS.
                    MAXIMUM WAITING TIME                18.851 MINS.
                    AVERAGE LINE LENGTH                  6.124
                    MAXIMUM LINE LENGTH                  14
                    AVERAGE NUMBER OF EUSY TELLERS       1.857
                    UTILIZATICN OF TELLER 1              .945%
                    UTILIZATICN CF TELLER 2              .912%
    END OF SIMULATION
```

The following statements search for the first PLAYER entity in the DRAFT.LIST set who is taller than 6 feet 9 inches. If such a player is found, he is removed from the draft list and contract negotiations begin.

```
FOR EACH PLAYER IN DRAFT LIST WITH HEIGHT(PLAYER) > 81.0
    FIND THE FIRST CASE
    IF NONE,
        JUMP AHEAD
    ELSE
        REMOVE THIS PLAYER FROM THE DRAFT.LIST
        SCHEDULE A NEGOTIATION(PLAYER) NOW
        RETURN
```

EXAMPLE 4.6

The bank teller model can be further expanded to include an officer who periodically requires the services of a teller. The officer enters the waiting line but is served by the first free teller, even if customers are ahead of the officer.

A new event, ARR.OFFICER, is introduced to bring the officers into the system. The DEPARTURE event now includes a search for an officer in the waiting line. Officers are distinguished from customers by means of a TYPE attribute associated with each CUSTOMER entity. The program output is expanded to provide statistics on officer behavior.

The presence of the officers in the model produces only a minor increase in teller utilization and waiting-line length.

4.16 USER-DEFINED DISTRIBUTIONS

The built-in statistical distributions available to the Simscript programmer were shown in Table 4.1. Although this collection of distributions is extensive, the behavior of many stochastic variables may not conform to a built-in distribution and hence require definition by the user. For example, an experimentally determined distribution that is not statistically representable by a built-in distribution would be defined by the user. A user-defined distribution is represented by a random variable in a Simscript program. Two types of random variables are permitted:

STEP for discrete distributions
LINEAR for continuous distributions

User-defined distributions are represented as attributes of the system and are thus defined using THE SYSTEM HAS statement, as follows:

```
LINE  CACI SIMSCRIPT II.5  RELEASE 8G                         10/19/78  PAGE

   1    PREAMBLE
   2    THE SYSTEM OWNS A WAITING.LINE
   3    PERMANENT ENTITIES
   4       EVERY TELLER HAS A STATUS
   5    TEMPORARY ENTITIES
   6       EVERY CUSTOMER HAS AN ENTRY.TIME, A TYPE, AND A
   7          N.TRANSACTIONS AND MAY BELONG TO THE WAITING.LINE
   8    DEFINE WAITING.LINE AS A FIFO SET
   9    EVENT NOTICES INCLUDE ARRIVAL, ARR.OFFICER,
  10       IMPATIENT, AND STOP.SIMULATION
  11       EVERY DEPARTURE HAS A TELLER.NO
  12    PRIORITY ORDER IS STOP.SIMULATION, DEPARTURE,
  13       ARRIVAL, ARR.OFFICER, AND IMPATIENT
  14    DEFINE IDLE TO MEAN 0
  15    DEFINE BUSY TO MEAN 1
  16    DEFINE REG TO MEAN 2
  17    DEFINE OFF TO MEAN 3
  18    DEFINE MINUTES TO MEAN UNITS
  19    DEFINE HOURS TO MEAN * 60 MINUTES
  20    DEFINE MIN.ARRIVAL, MAX.ARRIVAL, AVG.TRANSACTIONS, ENTRY.TIME,
  21       WAIT, MIN.OFFICER.ARRIVAL, MAX.OFFICER.ARRIVAL, AND WAIT.OFFICER
  22       AS REAL VARIABLES
  23    DEFINE BUSY.TELLERS, N.ARRIVALS, N.DEPARTURES, N.TRANSACTIONS,
  24       STATUS, DISGUSTED, N.OFFICERS, NUM.TELLER, AND
  25       TELLER.NO AS INTEGER VARIABLES
  26    TALLY AVG.WAIT AS THE MEAN AND MAX.WAIT AS THE MAXIMUM OF WAIT
  27    TALLY AVG.O.WAIT AS THE MEAN AND MAX.C.WAIT AS THE MAXIMUM
  28       OF WAIT.OFFICER
  29    ACCUMULATE AVG.LENGTH AS THE MEAN AND MAX.LENGTH AS THE MAXIMUM OF
  30       N.WAITING.LINE
  31    ACCUMULATE AVG.BUSY AS THE MEAN OF BUSY.TELLERS
  32    ACCUMULATE AVG.STATUS AS THE MEAN OF STATUS
  33    END

   1    MAIN
   2    READ MIN.ARRIVAL, MAX.ARRIVAL, AVG.TRANSACTIONS, N.TELLER,
   3       MIN.OFFICER.ARRIVAL, MAX.OFFICER.ARRIVAL
   4    CREATE EVERY TELLER
   5    LET BUSY.TELLERS = 0
   6    LET DISGUSTED = 0
   7    LET N.ARRIVALS = 0
   8    LET N.DEPARTURES = 0
   9    LET N.OFFICERS = 0
  10    SCHEDULE AN ARRIVAL IN UNIFORM.F ( MIN.ARRIVAL, MAX.ARRIVAL, 1 )
  11       MINUTES
  12    SCHEDULE AN ARR.OFFICER IN UNIFORM.F ( MIN.OFFICER.ARRIVAL,
  13       MAX.OFFICER.ARRIVAL, 3 ) MINUTES
  14    SCHEDULE AN IMPATIENT IN 15 MINUTES
  15    SCHEDULE A STOP.SIMULATION IN 8 HOURS
  16    START SIMULATION
  17    END
```

```
    1    EVENT ARRIVAL
    2     LET N.ARRIVALS = N.ARRIVALS + 1
    3     SCHEDULE AN ARRIVAL IN UNIFORM.F ( MIN.ARRIVAL, MAX.ARRIVAL, 1 )
    4         MINUTES
    5     CREATE A CUSTOMER
    6     LET N.TRANSACTIONS ( CUSTOMER ) = EXPONENTIAL.F ( AVG.TRANSACTICNS,
    7         2 )
    8     LET ENTRY.TIME ( CUSTOMER ) = TIME.V
    9     LET TYPE ( CUSTOMER ) = REG
   10     FILE THE CUSTCMER IN THE WAITING.LINE
   11     IF BUSY.TELLERS < N.TELLER,
   12        LET BUSY.TELLERS = BUSY.TELLERS  + 1
   13        FOR NUM.TELLER = 1 TO N.TELLER
   14             DO
   15                   IF STATUS ( NUM.TELLER ) = IDLE,
   16                       LET STATUS ( NUM.TELLER ) = BUSY
   17                       JUMP AHEAD
   18                   ALWAYS
   19             LOOP
   20     HERE
   21       REMOVE FIRST CUSTOMER FROM THE WAITING.LINE
   22       LET WAIT = 0                                           •
   23       SCHEDULE A DEPARTURE ( NUM.TELLER ) IN N.TRANSACTIONS ( CUSTCMER )
   24         * 2 MINUTES
   25       LET N.DEPARTURES = N.DEPARTURES + 1
   26       DESTROY THIS CUSTOMER
   27     ALWAYS
   28     RETURN
   29    END

    1    EVENT DEPARTURE ( TELLER.NO )
    2     DEFINE TELLER.NO AS AN INTEGER VARIABLE
    3     IF WAITING.LINE IS EMPTY,
    4        LET STATUS ( TELLER.NO ) = IDLE
    5        LET BUSY.TELLERS = BUSY.TELLERS - 1
    6        GO TO END.EVENT
    7     ELSE
    8        FOR EACH CUSTCMER IN THE WAITING.LINE WITH ( TYPE ( CUSTCMER ) =
    9             OFF )
   10             FIND THE FIRST CASE
   11             IF NCNE,
   12                   JUMP AHEAD
   13             ELSE
   14                   REMCVE THIS CUSTOMER FROM THE WAITING.LINE
   15                   LET WAIT.CFFICER = TIME.V - ENTRY.TIME ( CUSTOMER )
   16                   SCHEDULE A DEPARTURE ( TELLER.NO ) IN 2 MINUTES
   17                   LET N.OFFICERS = N.CFFICERS + 1
   18                   DESTROY THIS CUSTOMER
   19                   GO TC END.EVENT
   20        HERE
   21       REMOVE THE FIRST CUSTOMER FRCM THE WAITING.LINE
   22       LET WAIT = TIME.V - ENTRY.TIME ( CUSTOMER )
   23       SCHEDULE A DEPARTURE ( TELLER.NO ) IN N.TRANSACTICNS ( CUSTOMER )
   24         * 2 MINUTES
   25       LET N.DEPARTURES = N.DEPARTURES + 1
   26       DESTROY THIS CUSTOMER
   27    'END.EVENT'
   28     RETURN
   29    END
```

```
LINE  CACI SIMSCRIPT II.5  RELEASE 8G                    10/19/78  PAGE

   1    EVENT IMPATIENT
   2    SCHEDULE AN IMPATIENT IN 5 MINUTES
   3    FOR EVERY CUSTOMER IN THE WAITING.LINE EXCEPT WHEN ( ENTRY.TIME
   4       ( CUSTOMER ) >= TIME.V - 15.0 )
   5       DO
   6             REMOVE THIS CUSTOMER FROM THE WAITING.LINE
   7             LET DISGUSTED = DISGUSTED + 1
   8             DESTROY THIS CUSTOMER
   9          LOOP
  10    RETURN
  11    END

   1    EVENT ARR.OFFICER
   2    SCHEDULE AN ARR.OFFICER IN UNIFORM.F ( MIN.OFFICER.ARRIVAL,
   3       MAX.OFFICER.ARRIVAL, 3 ) MINUTES
   4    CREATE A CUSTOMER
   5    LET ENTRY.TIME ( CUSTOMER ) = TIME.V
   6    LET TYPE ( CUSTOMER ) = OFF
   7    FILE THE CUSTOMER IN THE WAITING.LINE
   8    IF BUSY.TELLERS < N.TELLER,
   9       LET BUSY.TELLERS = BUSY.TELLERS + 1
  10       FOR NUM.TELLER = 1 TO N.TELLER
  11          DO
  12             IF STATUS ( NUM.TELLER ) = IDLE,
  13                LET STATUS ( NUM.TELLER ) = BUSY
  14                JUMP AHEAD
  15             ALWAYS
  16          LOOP
  17      HERE
  18       REMOVE FIRST CUSTOMER FROM THE WAITING.LINE
  19       LET WAIT.OFFICER = 0
  20       SCHEDULE A DEPARTURE ( NUM.TELLER ) IN 2 MINUTES
  21       LET N.OFFICERS = N.OFFICERS + 1
  22       DESTROY THIS CUSTOMER
  23    ALWAYS
  24    RETURN
  25    END
```

```
LINE  CACI SIMSCRIPT II.5  RELEASE 8G                    1C/19/78  PAGE

  1    EVENT STOP.SIMULATION
  2     PRINT 20 LINES WITH MIN.ARRIVAL, MAX.ARRIVAL, AVG.TRANSACTICNS,
  3        N.TELLER, MIN.CFFICER.ARRIVAL, MAX.OFFICER.ARRIVAL, N.ARRIVALS,
  4        N.DEPARTURES, DISGUSTED, N.OFFICERS, AVG.WAIT,
  5        MAX.WAIT, AVG.C.WAIT, MAX.O.WAIT, AVG.LENGTH,
  6        MAX.LENGTH, AVG.BUSY
  7        THUS
         BANK TELLER MCDEL
              PARAMETERS
                        MINIMUM CUSTOMER ARRVIAL TIME          **.*** MINS.
                        MAXIMUM CUSTCMER ARRIVAL TIME          **.*** MINS.
                        AVERAGE TRANSACTICN PER CUSTCMER       **.***
                        NUMBER OF TELLERS                      ***
                        MINIMUM CFFICER ARRIVAL TIME           **.*** MINS.
                        MAXIMUM OFFICER ARRIVAL TIME           **.*** MINS.
              RESULTS
                        NUMBER OF ARRIVING CUSTCMERS           ****
                        NUMBER OF SERVED CUSTCMERS             ****
                        NUMBER OF UNSERVED CUSTCMERS           ****
                        NUMBER OF OFFICERS SERVED              ***
                        AVERAGE CUSTCMER WAITING TIME          **.*** MINS.
                        MAXIMUM CUSTCMER WAITING TIME          **.*** MINS
                        AVERAGE CFFICER WAITING TIME           **.*** MINS.
                        MAXIMUM CFFICER WAITING TIME           **.*** MINS.
                        AVERAGE LINE LENGTH                    **.***
                        MAXIMUM LINE LENGTH                    **
                        AVERAGE NUMBER CF BUSY TELLERS         **.***
  8    FOR NUM.TELLER = 1 TC N.TELLER
  9      PRINT 1 LINE WITH NUM.TELLER AND AVG.STATUS ( NUM.TELLER )
 10          THUS
                        UTILIZATICN CF TELLER**                **.***%
 11    PRINT 1 LINE
 12        THUS
         END OF SIMULATICN
 13    STOP
 14    END

BANK TELLER MODEL
     PARAMETERS
                   MINIMUM CLSTOMER ARRVIAL TIME          .250 MINS.
                   MAXIMUM CUSTCMER ARRIVAL TIME         2.750 MINS.
                   AVERAGE TRANSACTION PER CLSTOMER      1.500
                   NUMBER OF TELLERS                     2
                   MINIMUM OFFICER ARRIVAL TIME         15.000 MINS.
                   MAXIMUM CFFICER ARRIVAL TIME         45.000 MINS.
     RESULTS
                   NUMBER OF ARRIVING CUSTCMERS         312
                   NUMBER OF SERVED CUSTOMERS           312
                   NUMBER OF UNSERVED CUSTOMERS           0
                   NUMBER OF OFFICERS SERVED            17
                   AVERAGE CUSTOMER WAITING TIME         1.642 MINS.
                   MAXIMUM CUSTCMER WAITING TIME        13.877 MINS
                   AVERAGE CFFICER WAITING TIME          .902 MINS.
                   MAXIMUM CFFICER WAITING TIME         3.450 MINS.
                   AVERAGE LINE LENGTH                  1.099
                   MAXIMUM LINE LENGTH                  9
                   AVERAGE NUMBER OF BUSY TELLERS       1.505
                   UTILIZATICN CF TELLER 1               .813%
                   UTILIZATICN CF TELLER 2               .693%
END CF SIMULATICN
```

```
LINE  CACI SIMSCRIPT II.5  RELEASE 8G                    10/19/78  PAGE

  1    EVENT STOP.SIMULATION
  2     PRINT 20 LINES WITH MIN.ARRIVAL, MAX.ARRIVAL, AVG.TRANSACTICNS,
  3        N.TELLER, MIN.OFFICER.ARRIVAL, MAX.OFFICER.ARRIVAL, N.ARRIVALS,
  4        N.DEPARTURES, DISGUSTED, N.OFFICERS, AVG.WAIT,
  5        MAX.WAIT, AVG.C.WAIT, MAX.O.WAIT, AVG.LENGTH,
  6        MAX.LENGTH, AVG.BUSY
  7         THUS
          BANK TELLER MODEL
             PARAMETERS
                        MINIMUM CUSTCMER ARRIVAL TIME        **.*** MINS.
                        MAXIMUM CUSTCMER ARRIVAL TIME        **.*** MINS.
                        AVERAGE TRANSACTION PER CUSTOMER     **.***
                        NUMBER OF TELLERS                    ***
                        MINIMUM CFFICER ARRIVAL TIME         **.*** MINS.
                        MAXIMUM OFFICER ARRIVAL TIME         **.*** MINS.
             RESULTS
                        NUMBER OF ARRIVING CUSTCMERS         ****
                        NUMBER OF SERVED CUSTCMERS           ****
                        NUMBER OF UNSERVED CUSTOMERS         ****
                        NUMBER OF CFFICERS SERVED            ***
                        AVERAGE CUSTCMER WAITING TIME        **.*** MINS.
                        MAXIMUM CUSTCMER WAITING TIME        **.*** MINS
                        AVERAGE OFFICER WAITING TIME         **.*** MINS.
                        MAXIMUM CFFICER WAITING TIME         **.*** MINS.
                        AVERAGE LINE LENGTH                  **.***
                        MAXIMUM LINE LENGTH                  **
                        AVERAGE NUMBER OF BUSY TELLERS       **.***
  8    FOR NUM.TELLER = 1 TC N.TELLER
  9      PRINT 1 LINE WITH NUM.TELLER AND AVG.STATUS ( NUM.TELLER )
 10         THUS
                        UTILIZATION OF TELLER**              **.***%
 11    PRINT 1 LINE
 12        THUS
          END OF SIMULATICN
 13    STOP
 14    END

BANK TELLER MODEL
     PARAMETERS
                MINIMUM CUSTOMER ARRIVAL TIME          .250 MINS.
                MAXIMUM CUSTCMER ARRIVAL TIME         2.750 MINS.
                AVERAGE TRANSACTION PER CLSTOMER      1.500
                NUMBER OF TELLERS                     2
                MINIMUM OFFICER ARRIVAL TIME         15.000 MINS.
                MAXIMUM CFFICER ARRIVAL TIME         45.000 MINS.
     RESULTS
                NUMBER OF ARRIVING CUSTCMERS           312
                NUMBER OF SERVED CUSTOMERS             276
                NUMBER OF UNSERVED CUSTOMERS            31
                NUMBER OF OFFICERS SERVED               17
                AVERAGE CUSTOMER WAITING TIME         8.944 MINS.
                MAXIMUM CUSTOMER WAITING TIME        18.048 MINS
                AVERAGE CFFICER WAITING TIME          1.410 MINS.
                MAXIMUM CFFICER WAITING TIME          5.524 MINS.
                AVERAGE LINE LENGTH                   6.318
                MAXIMUM LINE LENGTH                   15
                AVERAGE NUMBER OF BUSY TELLERS        1.870
                UTILIZATION CF TELLER 1                .945%
                UTILIZATICN OF TELLER 2                .924%
END OF SIMULATICN
```

THE SYSTEM HAS A COIN.TOSS RANDOM STEP VARIABLE AND A
PROCESSING.TIME RANDOM LINEAR VARIABLE

This statement defines the discrete distribution, COIN.TOSS, and a continuous distribution, PROCESSING.TIME, as system attributes.

The mode of the function is specified in a DEFINE statement. All RANDOM LINEAR VARIABLES must be real. RANDOM STEP VARIABLES may be real or integer. In addition to specifying the mode, the DEFINE statement also indicates the random number generator, called a *stream,* used to select values from the distribution. Thus, the following mode definitions are valid for the two sample distributions:

DEFINE COIN.TOSS AS AN INTEGER, STREAM 1 VARIABLE

DEFINE PROCESSING.TIME AS A REAL, STREAM 6 VARIABLE

The data points of a user-defined distribution are obtained by a READ statement. A data point for a user-defined distribution consists of an ordered pair (X,Y) where X is the cumulative probability and Y is the value. The cumulative probability is the sum of the probabilities of all previous points in the distribution. See Chapter 5 for an explanation. The end of the data points for a user-defined distribution is marked by an asterisk.

The data points shown below correspond to the distribution of Table 4.4, which indicates the probability of observing an exact number of tails in three tosses of a fair coin.

0.125   0   0.500   1   0.875   2   1.000   3   *

The values shown above are assigned to the COIN.TOSS random variable by the statement

READ COIN.TOSS

A reference to a random variable results in a value being computed from the data points provided by the user. A random number between 0 and 1 is generated by the system using the random number generator indicated in the DEFINE statement. The method of computing the value of the random variable differs for continuous (LINEAR) and discrete (STEP) variables.

In the discrete case, only the values specified as data points may be assigned to the random variable. The value selected is the Y component of the data point whose X value is the first cumulative probability greater than or equal to the random number from stream 1.

For example, the following statement references the COIN.TOSS distribution:

LET N.TAILS(PLAYER) = COIN.TOSS

If on three successive executions of this statement, the random numbers .760, .076, .942 were generated from generator 1, the values assigned to N.TAILS(PLAYER) would be 2, 0, and 3.

The assignment of values to continuous random variables employs the technique of linear interpolation, which is discussed in detail in Chapter 5. Whenever a generated random number falls between two data points, the applica-

Table 4.4 Probability Distribution of Number of Tails in Three Coin Tosses

Number of Tails	Probability	Cumulative Probability
0	.125	.125
1	.375	.500
2	.375	.875
3	.125	1.000

tion of linear interpolation involves constructing a straight line between the two points and then computing the point on the line whose X coordinate is the generated random number. Again, see Chapter 5 for an example of linear interpolation.

EXAMPLE 4.7

In all previous bank teller models of this chapter, it was assumed that a teller required 2 minutes to process each transaction. In this model, the constant is replaced by a continuous distribution which indicates the variation in processing time for each customer. The distribution is depicted by the graph of Figure 4.4, which plots processing time per transaction against the cumulative probability.

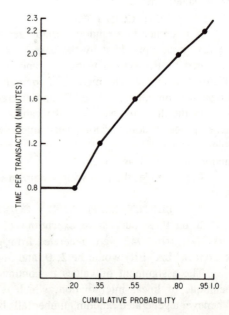

Figure 4.4 Transaction Processing Distribution

In the program, the transaction processing time distribution is represented by the random variable, TRANS.TIME, which is defined as a system attribute. TRANS.TIME is referenced whenever a departure is scheduled.

The output indicates that the tellers are less busy and the lines shorter when transactions are processed according to the TRANS.TIME distribution. The reason for the decrease in processing time is that the mean of the TRANS.TIME distribution is less than 2.

4.17 EXTERNAL EVENTS

In a simulation model using the event scheduling approach, as Simscript does, one of the prime determinants of model behavior is the sequence of events. By use of the SCHEDULE statement, events can be made to occur at fixed intervals, at intervals described by some common statistical distribution, or at intervals described by a user-defined distribution. The statistical distributions are employed to approximate the interevent times of the real system. This approximation is necessary in many models because actual data on interevent times may not be available to the modeler.

Simscript permits, through the external event feature, the specification of exact event times as input data. Thus, if exact data on event occurrence times is available, the event can be declared as external and its occurrences scheduled by input data.

In the preamble, the statement EXTERNAL EVENTS signifies the presence of externally scheduled events. Those external events without parameters are listed in the EXTERNAL EVENTS statement. External events with parameters are defined by EVERY statements, which immediately follow the EXTERNAL EVENTS statement.

The format of the EXTERNAL EVENTS statement is

EXTERNAL EVENTS [ARE *list of events*]

The following statements illustrate the definition of external events:

EXTERNAL EVENTS ARE ARR.OFFICER

EVERY LUNCH.BREAK HAS A N.EMPLOYEES

These statements define two external events, ARR.OFFICER and LUNCH.BREAK. The LUNCH.BREAK event has the variable N.EMPLOYEES as a parameter.

External events are scheduled by input data rather than by the SCHEDULE statement. The format of input data used to schedule an external event is

event name   *time*   *list of argument values* *

where

event name is the name of an external event

time is the time at which the event is to occur in the same units as TIME.V

list of argument values is a list of numeric values separated by commas which are to be read by the external event routine

```
   1    PREAMBLE
   2    THE SYSTEM OWNS A WAITING.LINE AND HAS A TRANS.TIME RANDOM LINEAR
   3        VARIABLE
   4    PERMANENT ENTITIES
   5        EVERY TELLER HAS A STATUS
   6    TEMPORARY ENTITIES
   7        EVERY CUSTOMER HAS AN ENTRY.TIME, A TYPE,
   8            AND A N.TRANSACTIONS AND MAY BELONG TO THE
   9            WAITING.LINE
  10    DEFINE WAITING.LINE AS A FIFO SET
  11    EVENT NOTICES INCLUDE ARRIVAL, ARR.OFFICER,
  12        IMPATIENT, AND STOP.SIMULATION
  13        EVERY DEPARTURE HAS A TELLER.NO
  14    PRIORITY ORDER IS STOP.SIMULATION, DEPARTURE,
  15        ARRIVAL, ARR.OFFICER, AND IMPATIENT
  16    DEFINE IDLE TO MEAN 0
  17    DEFINE BUSY TO MEAN 1
  18    DEFINE REG TO MEAN 2
  19    DEFINE OFF TO MEAN 3
  20    DEFINE MINUTES TO MEAN UNITS
  21    DEFINE HOURS TO MEAN * 60 MINUTES
  22    DEFINE MIN.ARRIVAL, MAX.ARRIVAL, AVG.TRANSACTIONS, ENTRY.TIME,
  23        WAIT, MIN.OFFICER.ARRIVAL, MAX.OFFICER.ARRIVAL, AND
  24        WAIT.OFFICER AS REAL VARIABLES
  25    DEFINE BUSY.TELLERS, N.ARRIVALS, N.DEPARTURES, N.TRANSACTIONS,
  26        STATUS, DISGUSTED, N.OFFICERS, NUM.TELLER, AND
  27        TELLER.NO AS INTEGER VARIABLES
  28    DEFINE TRANS.TIME AS A REAL, STREAM 4 VARIABLE
  29    TALLY AVG.WAIT AS THE MEAN AND MAX.WAIT AS THE MAXIMUM OF WAIT
  30    TALLY AVG.O.WAIT AS THE MEAN AND MAX.O.WAIT AS THE MAXIMUM
  31        OF WAIT.OFFICER
  32    ACCUMULATE AVG.LENGTH AS THE MEAN AND MAX.LENGTH AS THE MAXIMUM OF
  33        N.WAITING.LINE
  34    ACCUMULATE AVG.BUSY AS THE MEAN OF BUSY.TELLERS
  35    ACCUMULATE AVG.STATUS AS THE MEAN OF STATUS
  36    END

   1    MAIN
   2    READ MIN.ARRIVAL, MAX.ARRIVAL, AVG.TRANSACTIONS, N.TELLER,
   3        MIN.OFFICER.ARRIVAL, MAX.OFFICER.ARRIVAL
   4    READ TRANS.TIME
   5    CREATE EVERY TELLER
   6    LET BUSY.TELLERS = 0
   7    LET DISGUSTED = 0
   8    LET N.ARRIVALS = 0
   9    LET N.DEPARTURES = 0
  10    LET N.OFFICERS = 0
  11    SCHEDULE AN ARRIVAL IN UNIFORM.F ( MIN.ARRIVAL, MAX.ARRIVAL, 1 )
  12        MINUTES
  13    SCHEDULE AN ARR.OFFICER IN UNIFORM.F ( MIN.OFFICER.ARRIVAL,
  14        MAX.OFFICER.ARRIVAL, 3 ) MINUTES
  15    SCHEDULE AN IMPATIENT IN 15 MINUTES
  16    SCHEDULE A STOP.SIMULATION IN 8 HOURS
  17    START SIMULATION
  18    END
```

```
LINE  CACI SIMSCRIPT II.5  RELEASE 8G                        1C/19/78  PAGE

  1   EVENT ARRIVAL
  2   LET N.ARRIVALS = N.ARRIVALS + 1
  3   SCHEDULE AN ARRIVAL IN UNIFORM.F ( MIN.ARRIVAL, MAX.ARRIVAL, 1 )
  4       MINUTES
  5   CREATE A CUSTCMER
  6   LET N.TRANSACTIONS ( CUSTOMER ) = EXPCNENTIAL.F ( AVG.TRANSACTICNS,
  7       2 )
  8   LET ENTRY.TIME ( CUSTOMER ) = TIME.V
  9   LET TYPE ( CUSTOMER ) = REG
 10   FILE THE CUSTCMER IN THE WAITING.LINE
 11   IF BUSY.TELLERS < N.TELLER,
 12       LET BUSY.TELLERS = BUSY.TELLERS + 1
 13       FOR NUM.TELLER = 1 TO N.TELLER
 14           DO
 15                   IF STATUS ( NUM.TELLER ) = IDLE,
 16                       LET STATUS ( NUM.TELLER ) = BUSY
 17                       JUMP AHEAD
 18                   ALWAYS
 19           LOOP
 20       HERE
 21       REMOVE FIRST CUSTOMER FRCM THE WAITING.LINE
 22       LET WAIT = 0
 23       SCHEDULE A DEPAPTURE ( NUM.TELLER ) IN N.TRANSACTICNS ( CUSTCMER )
 24           * TRANS.TIME MINUTES
 25       DESTROY THIS CUSTOMER
 26       LET N.DEPARTURES = N.DEPARTURES + 1
 27   ALWAYS
 28   RETURN
 29   END

  1   EVENT DEPARTURE ( TELLER.NO )
  2   DEFINE TELLER.NO AS AN INTEGER VARIABLE
  3   IF WAITING.LINE IS EMPTY,
  4       LET STATUS ( TELLER.NO ) = IDLE
  5       LET BUSY.TELLERS = BUSY.TELLERS - 1
  6       GO TO END.EVENT
  7   ELSE
  8       FOR EACH CUSTCMER IN THE WAITING.LINE WITH ( TYPE ( CUSTCMER ) =
  9           OFF )
 10               FIND THE FIRST CASE
 11               IF NONE,
 12                   JUMP AHEAD
 13               ELSE
 14                   REMOVE THIS CUSTOMER FROM THE WAITING.LINE
 15                   LET WAIT.CFFICER = TIME.V - ENTRY.TIME ( CUSTCMER )
 16                   SCHEDULE A DEPARTURE ( TELLER.NO ) IN TRANS.TIME
 17                       MINUTES
 18                   DESTROY THIS CUSTOMER
 19                   LET N.OFFICERS = N.OFFICERS + 1
 20                   GO TC END.EVENT
 21       HERE
 22       REMOVE THE FIRST CUSTOMER FROM THE WAITING.LINE
 23       LET WAIT = TIME.V - ENTRY.TIME ( CUSTOMER )
 24       SCHEDULE A DEPARTURE ( TELLER.NO ) IN N.TRANSACTICNS ( CUSTOMER )
 25           * TRANS.TIME MINUTES
 26       DESTROY THIS CUSTCMER
 27       LET N.DEPARTURES = N.DEPARTURES + 1
 28   'END.EVENT'
 29   RETURN
 30   END
```

```
LINE  CACI SIMSCRIPT II.5  RELEASE 8G                    10/19/78  PAGE

    1    EVENT IMPATIENT
    2    SCHEDULE AN IMPATIENT IN 5 MINUTES
    3    FOR EVERY CUSTOMER IN THE WAITING.LINE EXCEPT WHEN ( ENTRY.TIME
    4       ( CUSTOMER ) >= TIME.V - 15.0 )
    5       DO
    6            REMOVE THIS CUSTOMER FROM THE WAITING.LINE
    7            LET DISGUSTED = DISGUSTED + 1
    8            DESTROY THIS CUSTOMER
    9       LOOP
   10    RETURN
   11    END


    1    EVENT ARR.OFFICER
    2    SCHEDULE AN ARR.OFFICER IN UNIFORM.F ( MIN.OFFICER.ARRIVAL,
    3       MAX.OFFICER.ARRIVAL, 3 ) MINUTES
    4    CREATE A CUSTOMER
    5    LET ENTRY.TIME ( CUSTOMER ) = TIME.V
    6    LET TYPE ( CUSTOMER ) = OFF
    7    FILE THE CUSTOMER IN THE WAITING.LINE
    8    IF BUSY.TELLERS < N.TELLER,
    9       LET BUSY.TELLERS = BUSY.TELLERS + 1
   10       FOR NUM.TELLER = 1 TO N.TELLER
   11          DO
   12               IF STATUS ( NUM.TELLER ) = IDLE,
   13                    LET STATUS ( NUM.TELLER ) = BUSY
   14                    JUMP AHEAD
   15               ALWAYS
   16          LOOP
   17       HERE
   18       REMOVE FIRST CUSTOMER FROM THE WAITING.LINE
   19       LET WAIT.OFFICER = 0
   20       SCHEDULE A DEPARTURE ( NUM.TELLER ) IN TRANS.TIME
   21          MINUTES
   22       DESTROY THIS CUSTOMER
   23       LET N.OFFICERS = N.OFFICERS + 1
   24    ALWAYS
   25    RETURN
   26    END
```

The data below define four occurrences of the external events specified in the prior sample statements:

ARR.OFFICER	32.767	*
LUNCH.BREAK	240.000	1 *
ARR.OFFICER	271.214	*
ARR.OFFICER	437.642	*

The data defining external events are read by the system and inserted into the event list in the appropriate position based upon its time of activation and priority.

An event routine for an external event is identical in structure to that of an internally defined event. If the external event has arguments, values for the arguments must be obtained via a READ statement. For the sample events of this section, the event routine for LUNCH.BREAK would include a statement

        READ N.EMPLOYEES

which would result in a value of 1 being assigned to N.EMPLOYEES for the sample data shown.

EXAMPLE 4.8

In Example 4.7 the arrival of officers is uniformly distributed over the interval from 15 to 45 minutes. Instead of describing the arrival times by a statistical distribution, exact arrivals are specified by external events in the following program.

The event ARR.OFFICER is changed to external and is scheduled via user input. For illustrative purposes, the officer arrival times are printed in the ARR.OFFICER event.

Since the officer arrival distribution is altered in this model, the statistics obtained differ slightly from those of the prior model. Overall, the system exhibits a very minor increase in activity in the current model. The reason for the difference in the results between the current and previous examples is that the officer arrival pattern is less uniform in this case, and thus customer service is occasionally slowed.

4.18 SUBPROGRAMS

In Section 4.1 the structure of a Simscript simulation program was stated to be a preamble, a main routine, one or more event routines, and an optional number of subprograms. As evidenced by the programs in the first eight examples of this chapter, a Simscript program need not contain any subprograms. However, if the program contains a sequence of code that is common to several event routines or if for purposes of modularity the programmer feels a routine should be divided into smaller components, the use of subprograms is appropriate.

```
1    EVENT ARRIVAL
2      LET N.ARRIVALS = N.ARRIVALS + 1
3      SCHEDULE AN ARRIVAL IN UNIFORM.F ( MIN.ARRIVAL, MAX.ARRIVAL, 1 )
4          MINUTES
5      CREATE A CUSTOMER
6      LET N.TRANSACTIONS ( CUSTOMER ) = EXPCNENTIAL.F ( AVG.TRANSACTIONS,
7          2 )
8      LET ENTRY.TIME ( CUSTOMER ) = TIME.V
9      LET TYPE ( CUSTOMER ) = REG
10     FILE THE CUSTOMER IN THE WAITING.LINE
11     IF BUSY.TELLERS < N.TELLER,
12         LET BUSY.TELLERS = BUSY.TELLERS  + 1
13         FOR NUM.TELLER = 1 TO N.TELLER
14                 DO
15                         IF STATUS ( NUM.TELLER ) = IDLE,
16                             LET STATUS ( NUM.TELLER ) = BUSY
17                             JUMP AHEAD
18                         ALWAYS
19                 LOOP
20         HERE
21         REMOVE FIRST CUSTOMER FROM THE WAITING.LINE
22         LET WAIT = 0
23         SCHEDULE A DEPARTURE ( NUM.TELLER ) IN N.TRANSACTICNS ( CUSTCMER )
24             * TRANS.TIME MINUTES
25         DESTRCY THIS CUSTCMER
26         LET N.DEPARTURES = N.DEPARTURES + 1
27     ALWAYS
28     RETURN
29   END
```

```
1    EVENT DEPARTURE ( TELLER.NO )
2      DEFINE TELLER.NO AS AN INTEGER VARIABLE
3      IF WAITING.LINE IS EMPTY,
4          LET STATUS ( TELLER.NO ) = IDLE
5          LET BUSY.TELLERS = BUSY.TELLERS - 1
6          GO TO END.EVENT
7      ELSE
8          FOR EACH CUSTCMER IN THE WAITING.LINE WITH ( TYPE ( CUSTOMER ) =
9              OFF )
10                 FIND THE FIRST CASE
11                 IF NCNE,
12                     JUMP AHEAD
13                 ELSE
14                     REMOVE THIS CUSTOMER FRCM THE WAITING.LINE
15                     LET WAIT.OFFICER = TIME.V - ENTRY.TIME ( CUSTCMER )
16                     SCHECULE A DEPARTURE ( TELLER.NO ) IN TRANS.TIME
17                         MINUTES
18                     DESTROY THIS CUSTOMER
19                     LET N.OFFICERS = N.CFFICERS + 1
20                     GO TO END.EVENT
21         HERE
22         REMOVE THE FIRST CUSTOMER FRCM THE WAITING.LINE
23         LET WAIT = TIME.V - ENTRY.TIME ( CLSTOMER )
24         SCHEDULE A DEPARTURE ( TELLER.NO ) IN N.TRANSACTICNS ( CUSTOMER )
25             * TRANS.TIME MINUTES
26         DESTRCY THIS CUSTCMER
27         LET N.DEPARTURES = N.DEPARTURES + 1
28     'END.EVENT'
29     RETURN
30   END
```

```
 1    EVENT IMPATIENT
 2     SCHEDULE AN IMPATIENT IN 5 MINUTES
 3     FOR EVERY CUSTOMER IN THE WAITING.LINE EXCEPT WHEN ( ENTRY.TIME
 4        ( CUSTOMER ) >= TIME.V - 15.0 )
 5        DO
 6               REMOVE THIS CUSTOMER FROM THE WAITING.LINE
 7               LET DISGUSTEC = DISGUSTEC + 1
 8               DESTROY THIS CUSTOMER
 9        LCOP
10     RETURN
11    END

 1    EVENT ARR.CFFICER
 2     PRINT 1 LINE WITH TIME.V
 3        THUS
        OFFICER ARRIVAL AT ****.*** MINS.
 4     CREATE A CUSTOMER
 5     LET ENTRY.TIME ( CUSTOMER ) = TIME.V
 6     LET TYPE ( CUSTOMER ) = OFF
 7     FILE THE CUSTOMER IN THE WAITING.LINE
 8     IF BUSY.TELLERS < N.TELLER,
 9        LET BUSY.TELLERS = BUSY.TELLERS + 1
10        FOR NUM.TELLER = 1 TO N.TELLER
11               DO
12                    IF STATUS ( NUM.TELLER ) = IDLE,
13                         LET STATUS ( NUM.TELLER ) = BUSY
14                    JUMP AHEAD
15                    ALWAYS
16               LOOP
17      HERE
18      REMOVE FIRST CUSTOMER FROM THE WAITING.LINE
19      LET WAIT.CFFICER = 0
20      SCHEDULE A DEPARTURE ( NUM.TELLER ) IN TRANS.TIME
21         MINUTES
22      DESTROY THIS CUSTCMER
23      LET N.OFFICERS = N.OFFICERS + 1
24     ALWAYS
25     RETURN
26    END

 1    EVENT STOP.SIMULATICN
 2     SKIP 2 LINES
 3     PRINT 18 LINES WITH MIN.ARRIVAL, MAX.ARRIVAL, AVG.TRANSACTICNS,
 4        N.TELLER, N.ARRIVALS,
 5        N.DEPARTURES, CISGUSTED, N.OFFICERS, AVG.WAIT,
 6        MAX.WAIT, AVG.C.WAIT, MAX.O.WAIT, AVG.LENGTH,
 7        MAX.LENGTH, AVG.BUSY
 8        THUS
        BANK TELLER MODEL
              PARAMETERS
                        MINIMUM CUSTOMER ARRVIAL TIME        **.*** MINS.
                        MAXIMUM CUSTOMER ARRIVAL TIME        **.*** MINS.
                        AVERAGE TRANSACTION PER CUSTOMER     **.***
                        NUMBER OF TELLERS                    ***
              RESULTS
                        NUMBER OF ARRIVING CUSTCMERS         ****
                        NUMBER OF SERVED CUSTOMERS           ****
                        NUMBER OF UNSERVED CUSTOMERS         ****
                        NUMBER OF OFFICERS SERVED            ***
                        AVERAGE CUSTCMER WAITING TIME        **.*** MINS.
                        MAXIMUM CUSTOMER WAITING TIME        **.*** MINS
                        AVERAGE OFFICER WAITING TIME         **.*** MINS.
                        MAXIMUM OFFICER WAITING TIME         **.*** MINS.
                        AVERAGE LINE LENGTH                  **.***
                        MAXIMUM LINE LENGTH                  **
                        AVERAGE NUMBER OF BUSY TELLERS       **.***
 9     FOR NUM.TELLER = 1 TC N.TELLER
10        PRINT 1 LINE WITH NUM.TELLER AND AVG.STATUS ( NUM.TELLER )
11               THUS
                    UTILIZATICN OF TELLER**               **.***%
12     PRINT 1 LINE
13        THUS
        END OF SIMULATICN
14     STOP
15    END
```

```
OFFICER ARRIVAL AT     30.000 MINS.
OFFICER ARRIVAL AT     60.000 MINS.
OFFICER ARRIVAL AT     61.229 MINS.
OFFICER ARRIVAL AT     96.783 MINS.
OFFICER ARRIVAL AT    157.249 MINS.
OFFICER ARRIVAL AT    173.208 MINS.
OFFICER ARRIVAL AT    233.999 MINS.
OFFICER ARRIVAL AT    234.000 MINS.
OFFICER ARRIVAL AT    256.460 MINS.
OFFICER ARRIVAL AT    301.010 MINS.
OFFICER ARRIVAL AT    314.786 MINS.
OFFICER ARRIVAL AT    409.409 MINS.
OFFICER ARRIVAL AT    432.872 MINS.
OFFICER ARRIVAL AT    457.002 MINS.
OFFICER ARRIVAL AT    478.213 MINS.
OFFICER ARRIVAL AT    479.999 MINS.


BANK TELLER MODEL
     PARAMETERS
               MINIMUM CUSTCMER ARRIVAL TIME          .250 MINS.
               MAXIMUM CUSTOMER ARRIVAL TIME         2.750 MINS.
               AVERAGE TRANSACTICN PER CUSTOMER      1.5CC
               NUMBER OF TELLERS                     2
     RESULTS
               NUMBER OF ARRIVING CUSTCMERS          312
               NUMBER OF SERVED CUSTCMERS            310
               NUMBER OF UNSERVED CUSTCMERS          2
               NUMBER OF OFFICERS SERVED             16
               AVERAGE CUSTCMER WAITING TIME         2.301 MINS.
               MAXIMUM CUSTCMER WAITING TIME        16.708 MINS
               AVERAGE CFFICER WAITING TIME          .560 MINS.
               MAXIMUM CFFICER WAITING TIME         5.58C MINS.
               AVERAGE LINE LENGTH                   1.570
               MAXIMUM LINE LENGTH                  12
               AVERAGE NUMBER OF BUSY TELLERS        1.519
               UTILIZATICN CF TELLER 1               .800%
               UTILIZATICN CF TELLER 2               .719%
END OF SIMULATICN
```

As in most high-level programming languages, there are two types of subprograms: the subroutine subprogram and the function subprogram.

Subroutine subprograms are not defined in the preamble, but rather by a ROUTINE statement followed by the statements indicating the actions performed by the routine. The body of a subroutine is terminated by an END statement and must contain at least one RETURN statement.

The format of the ROUTINE statement is

> ROUTINE *name* [GIVEN *list1 of parameters*]
> [YIELDING *list2 of parameters*]

where

> *name* is the subroutine name
> *list1 of parameters* is an optional list of input parameters
> *list2 of parameters* is an optional list of output parameters

For example, the statement

> ROUTINE PROCESS GIVEN X YIELDING Y AND Z

indicates the beginning of a subroutine definition for the routine PROCESS which has a single input parameter, X, and two output parameters, Y and Z.

Subroutines are referenced using the CALL statement that matches the actual arguments supplied by the calling routine to the parameters defined in the subroutine definition. A CALL results in a transfer to the first executable statement of the subroutine. When a RETURN statement in the subroutine is executed, control transfers to the statement following the CALL.

The format of CALL is identical to that of ROUTINE beyond the first word.

> CALL *name* [GIVEN *list1 of arguments*]
> [YIELDING *list2 of arguments*]

where

> *name* is the subroutine name
> *list1 of arguments* is a list of variables and/or constants whose values are passed to the corresponding subroutine parameters
> *list2 of arguments* is a list of variables that will receive the values assigned to the corresponding subroutine parameters

The sample statement

> CALL PROCESS GIVEN ALPHA YIELDING BETA AND GAMMA

supplies the value of the variable ALPHA to the X parameter of routine PROCESS. The values computed in the subroutine for Y and Z are assigned to BETA and GAMMA, respectively.

A CALL statement must have the same number of input and output parameters as the corresponding ROUTINE statement. A subroutine may have no input or output parameters, if appropriate.

Function subprograms operate in a fashion very similar to subroutine subprograms with some minor differences in definition and reference. The function subprograms are defined in the preamble explicitly by statements of the form

DEFINE *name* AS A FUNCTION.

The body of the function subprogram is preceded by a ROUTINE statement without a YIELDING clause. The format of a ROUTINE statement defining a function subprogram is shown below.

ROUTINE *name* [GIVEN *list of parameters*]

where

name is the function name as specified in the DEFINE statement

list of parameters is an optional list of input parameters of the function

The execution of a function subprogram terminates via a RETURN WITH statement that indicates the value of the function. As is the case of the RETURN statement, a function subprogram must have at least one RETURN WITH statement. The format of RETURN WITH is

RETURN WITH *expression*

where *expression* is an arithmetic expression indicating the function value.

Function subprograms are referenced in a manner identical to the built-in statistical distributions. The values of the arguments used in a given function reference are assigned to the corresponding parameters of the function subprogram.

The statements below illustrate the definition and utilization of function subprograms.

```
PREAMBLE
    DEFINE TOTAL.EX.WGHT AS A FUNCTION
        ⋮
ROUTINE TOTAL.EX.WGHT GIVEN CUT.OFF
    DEFINE TOT AND CUT.OFF AS REAL VARIABLES
        ⋮
    RETURN WITH TOT
END
    ⋮
    LET MIN.WEIGHT = INIT.WEIGHT + INC
    LET TARIFF = TOTAL.EX.WGHT(MIN.WEIGHT)*RATE +
        BASE.FARE
```

EXAMPLE 4.9

In Example 4.8 the ARRIVAL and ARR.OFFICER routines both have similar sections of code for determining the teller which will process the customer or officer if there is no waiting. This code is extracted from the arrival routines and formed into the subroutine, FIND.TELLER, with one output and no input arguments. The use of the subroutine eliminates some redundant code from the model but has no effect upon the results of the simulation.

```
  1     PREAMBLE
  2     THE SYSTEM OWNS A WAITING.LINE AND HAS A TRANS.TIME RANDCM LINEAR
  3        VARIABLE
  4     PERMANENT ENTITIES
  5        EVERY TELLER HAS A STATUS
  6     TEMPCRARY ENTITIES
  7        EVERY CUSTOMER HAS AN ENTRY.TIME, A TYPE,
  8           AND A N.TRANSACTIONS AND MAY BELONG TO THE
  9           WAITING.LINE
 10     DEFINE WAITING.LINE AS A FIFO SET
 11     EVENT NOTICES INCLUDE ARRIVAL,
 12        IMPATIENT, AND STCP.SIMULATICN
 13        EVERY DEPARTURE HAS A TELLER.NO
 14     EXTERNAL EVENTS ARE ARR.OFFICER
 15     PRIORITY ORDER IS STOP.SIMULATION, DEPARTURE,
 16        ARRIVAL, ARR.OFFICER, AND IMPATIENT
 17     DEFINE IDLE TC MEAN 0
 18     DEFINE BUSY TO MEAN 1
 19     DEFINE REG TC MEAN 2
 20     DEFINE OFF TO MEAN 3
 21     DEFINE MINUTES TO MEAN UNITS
 22     DEFINE HCURS TO MEAN * 60 MINUTES
 23     DEFINE MIN.ARRIVAL, MAX.ARRIVAL, AVG.TRANSACTIONS, ENTRY.TIME,
 24        WAIT, AND
 25        WAIT.CFFICER AS REAL VARIABLES
 26     DEFINE BUSY.TELLERS, N.ARRIVALS, N.DEPARTURES, N.TRANSACTICNS,
 27        STATUS, DISGUSTED, N.OFFICERS, NUM.TELLER, AND
 28        TELLER.NO AS INTEGER VARIABLES
 29     DEFINE TRANS.TIME AS A REAL, STREAM 4 VARIABLE
 30     TALLY AVG.WAIT AS THE MEAN AND MAX.WAIT AS THE MAXIMUM CF WAIT
 31     TALLY AVG.O.WAIT AS THE MEAN AND MAX.O.WAIT AS THE MAXIMUM
 32        OF WAIT.OFFICER
 33     ACCUMULATE AVG.LENGTH AS THE MEAN AND MAX.LENGTH AS THE MAXIMUM OF
 34        N.WAITING.LINE
 35     ACCUMULATE AVG.BUSY AS THE MEAN OF BUSY.TELLERS
 36     ACCUMULATE AVG.STATUS AS THE MEAN OF STATUS
 37     END

  1     MAIN
  2     READ MIN.ARRIVAL, MAX.ARRIVAL, AVG.TRANSACTIONS, N.TELLER
  3     READ TRANS.TIME
  4     CREATE EVERY TELLER
  5     LET BUSY.TELLERS = 0
  6     LET DISGUSTED = 0
  7     LET N.ARRIVALS = 0
  8     LET N.DEPARTURES = 0
  9     LET N.OFFICERS = 0
 10     SCHEDULE AN ARRIVAL IN UNIFORM.F ( MIN.ARRIVAL, MAX.ARRIVAL, 1 )
 11        MINUTES
 12     SCHEDULE AN IMPATIENT IN 15 MINUTES
 13     SCHEDULE A STCP.SIMULATICN IN 8 HOURS
 14     START SIMULATICN
 15     END
```

```
 1    EVENT ARRIVAL
 2      LET N.ARRIVALS = N.ARRIVALS + 1
 3      SCHEDULE AN ARRIVAL IN UNIFORM.F ( MIN.ARRIVAL, MAX.ARRIVAL, 1 )
 4         MINUTES
 5      CREATE A CUSTCMER
 6      LET N.TRANSACTIONS ( CUSTOMER ) = EXPONENTIAL.F ( AVG.TRANSACTIONS,
 7         2 )
 8      LET ENTRY.TIME ( CUSTOMER ) = TIME.V
 9      LET TYPE ( CUSTOMER ) = REG
10      FILE THE CUSTCMER IN THE WAITING.LINE
11      IF BUSY.TELLERS < N.TELLER,
12         CALL FIND.TELLER YIELDING NUM.TELLER
13         REMOVE FIRST CUSTCMER FRCM THE WAITING.LINE
14         LET WAIT = 0
15         SCHEDULE A DEPARTURE ( NUM.TELLER ) IN N.TRANSACTICNS ( CUSTCMER )
16            * TRANS.TIME MINUTES
17         DESTROY THIS CUSTOMER
18         LET N.DEPARTURES = N.DEPARTURES + 1
19      ALWAYS
20      RETURN
21    END


 1    EVENT DEPARTURE ( TELLER.NO )
 2      DEFINE TELLER.NO AS AN INTEGER VARIABLE
 3      IF WAITING.LINE IS EMPTY,
 4         LET STATUS ( TELLER.NO ) = IDLE
 5         LET BUSY.TELLERS = BUSY.TELLERS - 1
 6         GO TO END.EVENT
 7      ELSE
 8         FOR EACH CUSTCMER IN THE WAITING.LINE WITH ( TYPE ( CUSTCMER ) =
 9            OFF )
10            FIND THE FIRST CASE
11            IF NONE,
12               JUMP AHEAC
13            ELSE
14               REMOVE THIS CUSTOMER FROM THE WAITING.LINE
15               LET WAIT.CFFICER = TIME.V - ENTRY.TIME ( CUSTCMER )
16               SCHEDULE A DEPARTURE ( TELLER.NO ) IN TRANS.TIME
17                  MINUTES
18               DESTROY THIS CUSTCMER
19               LET N.OFFICERS = N.CFFICERS + 1
20               GO TC END.EVENT
21         HERE
22         REMOVE THE FIRST CUSTOMER FROM THE WAITING.LINE
23         LET WAIT = TIME.V - ENTRY.TIME ( CUSTOMER )
24         SCHEDULE A DEPARTURE ( TELLER.NO ) IN N.TRANSACTICNS ( CUSTOMER )
25            * TRANS.TIME MINUTES
26         DESTRCY THIS CUSTCMER
27         LET N.DEPARTURES = N.DEPARTURES + 1
28      'END.EVENT'
29      RETURN
30    END
```

```
 1    EVENT IMPATIENT
 2      SCHEDULE AN IMPATIENT IN 5 MINUTES
 3      FOR EVERY CUSTOMER IN THE WAITING.LINE EXCEPT WHEN ( ENTRY.TIME
 4         ( CUSTCMER ) >= TIME.V - 15.0 )
 5         DO
 6            REMOVE THIS CUSTOMER FROM THE WAITING.LINE
 7            LET DISGUSTEC = CISGUSTEC + 1
 8            DESTROY THIS CLSTOMER
 9         LCCP
10      RETURN
11    END
```

```
1     EVENT ARR.OFFICER
2      PRINT 1 LINE WITH TIME.V
3         THUS
       OFFICER ARRIVAL AT ****.*** MINS.
4      CREATE A CUSTOMER
5      LET ENTRY.TIME ( CUSTOMER ) = TIME.V
6      LET TYPE ( CUSTOMER ) = OFF
7      FILE THE CUSTOMER IN THE WAITING.LINE
8      IF BUSY.TELLERS < N.TELLER,
9        CALL FIND.TELLER YIELDING NUM.TELLER
10       REMOVE FIRST CUSTOMER FROM THE WAITING.LINE
11       LET WAIT.OFFICER = 0
12       SCHEDULE A DEPARTURE ( NUM.TELLER ) IN TRANS.TIME MINUTES
13       DESTROY THIS CUSTOMER
14       LET N.OFFICERS = N.OFFICERS + 1
15     ALWAYS
16     RETURN
17     END


1     ROUTINE FIND.TELLER YIELDING NUM.TELLER
2      DEFINE NUM.TELLER AS AN INTEGER VARIABLE
3      LET BUSY.TELLERS = BUSY.TELLERS + 1
4      FOR NUM.TELLER = 1 TO N.TELLER
5         DO
6               IF STATUS ( NUM.TELLER ) = IDLE,
7                   LET STATUS ( NUM.TELLER ) = BUSY
8                   JUMP AHEAD
9               ALWAYS
10       LOOP
11     HERE
12      RETURN
13     END


1     EVENT STOP.SIMULATION
2      SKIP 2 LINES
3      PRINT 18 LINES WITH MIN.ARRIVAL, MAX.ARRIVAL, AVG.TRANSACTIONS,
4        N.TELLER, N.ARRIVALS,
5        N.DEPARTURES, DISGUSTED, N.OFFICERS, AVG.WAIT,
6        MAX.WAIT, AVG.C.WAIT, MAX.O.WAIT, AVG.LENGTH,
7        MAX.LENGTH, AVG.BUSY
8         THUS
       BANK TELLER MODEL
           PARAMETERS
                   MINIMUM CUSTOMER ARRIVAL TIME          **.*** MINS.
                   MAXIMUM CUSTOMER ARRIVAL TIME          **.*** MINS.
                   AVERAGE TRANSACTION PER CUSTOMER       **.***
                   NUMBER OF TELLERS                      ***
           RESULTS
                   NUMBER OF ARRIVING CUSTOMERS           ****
                   NUMBER OF SERVED CUSTOMERS             ****
                   NUMBER OF UNSERVED CUSTOMERS           ****
                   NUMBER OF OFFICERS SERVED              ***
                   AVERAGE CUSTOMER WAITING TIME          **.*** MINS.
                   MAXIMUM CUSTOMER WAITING TIME          **.*** MINS
                   AVERAGE OFFICER WAITING TIME           **.*** MINS.
                   MAXIMUM OFFICER WAITING TIME           **.*** MINS.
                   AVERAGE LINE LENGTH                    **.***
                   MAXIMUM LINE LENGTH                    **
                   AVERAGE NUMBER OF BUSY TELLERS         **.***
9      FOR NUM.TELLER = 1 TO N.TELLER
10       PRINT 1 LINE WITH NUM.TELLER AND AVG.STATUS ( NUM.TELLER )
11               THUS
                   UTILIZATION OF TELLER**                **.***%
12     PRINT 1 LINE
13        THUS
       END OF SIMULATION
14     STOP
15     END
```

4.19 CONCLUSION

This chapter describes the basic Simscript simulation program language. Simscript is a general-purpose, high-level language enhanced with special simulation features. Those simulation-oriented Simscript facilities presented in this chapter are a subset of those available in the language. However, after mastering the material of this chapter, the reader should be capable of synthesizing rather complex Simscript models. The reader interested in further details on the Simscript simulation capabilities should consult References [4.1] and [4.2].

EXERCISES

(Use Simscript for all exercises. In all cases, collect maximum and average waiting times and waiting-line lengths, indicate percentage utilization of activities, and count the number of entities passing through the various parts of the models.)

4.1 Model the student registration environment described by the following parameters:
Number of people processing registrations—3.
Student arrival rate—3 minutes, exponentially distributed.
Number of classes per student—60%, 5; 15%, 6; 15%, 3; 7%, 4; 3%, 7.
Time to register a student—2 minutes per class.
A single waiting line is employed.
Time of simulation—9 hours.

4.2 (This exercise is derived from a problem submitted to Reference [4.3] by Dr. Susan L. Solomon. For all parts of this problem, assume an 8-hour work night and a customer arrival rate of 10 minutes exponentially distributed.)
Xaviera operates an entertainment facility in Nevada. Xaviera's standard fee is $100. Her employees perform their services for $50, $20 of which is returned to Xaviera to cover operating expenses. Model Xaviera's receipts and the level of service offered her customers under the following alternative conditions:

a. Xaviera is the only server. Determine the effects of the following service times:
    1. Constant 15 minutes.
    2. Normally distributed, with mean of 15 minutes and standard deviation of 3 minutes.
    3. Uniformly distributed from 9 to 21 minutes.

b. Assume a second server is hired with a services time uniformly distributed from 12 to 18 minutes. For this and the remaining subproblems, assume Xaviera's service time is that given in a(3) above. What is the effect upon service and profits of the second server?

c. Assume that every 45 minutes, exponentially distributed, a customer who requires both servers simultaneously arrives. Measure the impact of this service.

d. Suppose a third server is hired who serves customers in an average of 18 minutes, exponentially distributed. What is the effect on business if there are separate queues, with customers entering the shortest queue? Only one queue?

e. Suppose 50% of the customers want Xaviera, 30% want the second server, and the rest prefer the third server. Investigate profits and queue behavior under these circumstances.

f. If 15% of the customers require service that takes from 20 to 30 minutes, uniformly distributed, and costs 50% more, what is the effect upon the business?

g. Assume Xaviera has submitted to pressure from the Equal Employment Opportunity Commission to avoid the loss of federal contracts. She has hired a token male server who spends an average of 15 minutes, exponentially distributed, serving each of his customers. After completing a service, he is obliged to rest for 1.75 hours before he can engage another customer. Include this condition, assuming his customers arrive every 1 to 2 hours, uniformly distributed, and will not accept any of the other servers.

h. A parking lot on the premise has a capacity of 3 cars. If the lot is full, arriving customers take their business elsewhere. To what extent does this affect business?

4.3 a. Model the checkout lines at a supermarket under the following assumptions:
1. Number of regular checkers—2.
2. Number of express checkers—1.
3. Customer arrivals at regular checkouts—5 minutes, exponentially distributed.
4. Customer arrivals at express checkout—1 to 5 minutes, uniformly distributed.
5. Time required at express checkout—2 minutes.
6. Time required at regular checkout—normally distributed, with mean 10 and standard deviation 5.
7. Termination condition—10 hours.

Collect statistics on waiting time for regular and express checkouts and on utilization of checkout counters.

b. What is the effect of adding a third regular checker?

4.4 Simulate a doctor's office in which patients enter a waiting room and then one of several examination rooms before seeing the doctor. Use the following parameters:
1. Patient arrivals—5 to 15 minutes, uniformly distributed.
2. Age of patient—uniformly distributed from 0 to 80.
3. Examination time of patient—20% of age plus 10.
4. Number of examination rooms—3.
5. Every 2 hours, exponentially distributed, an emergency occurs, which requires the doctor's attention for a time that is normally distributed with a mean of 30 minutes and a standard deviation of 10 minutes; during the emergency, no patients are admitted to the examination rooms.
6. Termination condition—6 hours.

Collect queuing statistics on the waiting lines for the examination rooms, the waiting times in the examination room, and the amount of time from arrival to departure spent in the doctor's office by each patient.

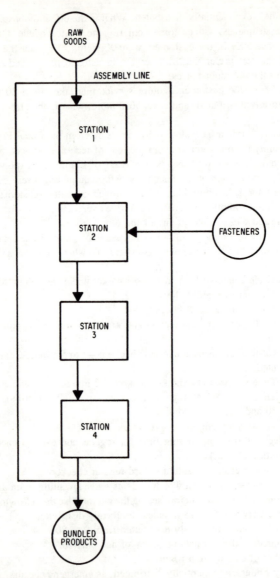

Figure 4.5 Simplified Manufacturing Process

4.5 Figure 4.5 illustrates a simplified manufacturing process. Simulate the manufacturing process given the following parameters:

1. Transfer between stations requires 30 seconds.
2. Raw goods arrive at Station 1 in lots of 50 every 2 hours.

3. At Station 1, raw goods are processed at a rate of 30 per hour and passed to Station 2.
4. Fasteners arrive at Station 2 in lots of 30 every 15 minutes.
5. At Station 2, 5 fasteners are attached to each processed item in 3 minutes, exponentially distributed. The fastened items then pass to Station 3.
6. At Statiuon 3, 5 fastened items are assembled into a finished product in 12 ± 4 minutes, uniformly distributed. Finished products are moved to Station 4.
7. At Station 4, the finished products are bundled into lots of 10 in a process that requires 25 ± 11 minutes, uniformly distributed, whenever 10 items are available.
8. If processed items wait for fastening at Station 2 for more than 1 hour, they must be discarded.
9. Termination condition—24 hours.

Determine the activity and waiting at each station and the number of items delivered, manufactured, and discarded.

4.6 Simulate the usage of elevators in a library under the following assumptions:
1. Number of elevators—2.
2. The passenger arrival rate at the first floor is uniformly distributed from 0 to 3 minutes.
3. Destination floor is given by 20%, 2; 30%, 3; 30%, 4; 20%, 5.
4. Time required to travel between adjacent floors—15 seconds.
5. Time required to load or unload elevator—30 seconds.
6. Elevator capacity—8 people each.
7. People return to the elevator at a rate that is exponentially distributed with a mean of 5 minutes; all people return to the first floor.
8. After 2 hours, the library staff ties up one elevator for 45 minutes.
9. Termination condition—4 hours.

Determine the average utilization of the elevators and the average waiting time on each floor.

4.7 Simulate the behavior of the processor and memory of a computer system as described below.

Machine
> Memory size—1 M (one million bytes).
> Time slice—1 second.
> Task initiation overhead—75 milliseconds.

Jobs
> Arrival rate—27 seconds, exponentially distributed.
> CPU time—30 seconds, exponentially distributed.
> Size—a mean of 128 K with a standard deviation of 32 K.

When jobs arrive, they are loaded into memory using the memory allocation algorithms described below. Jobs are executed in a round-robin manner, given one CPU time slice each until their execution is complete. If a job completes execution prior to the end of a time slice, the CPU becomes available. Whenever a job begins its time slice, task initiation overhead is incurred by the CPU. All jobs have equal priority when contending for the CPU. When a job has completed execution, a new job is loaded into memory according to the allocation algorithm.

Execute the model using the allocation algorithms given below and compare the performance of the system.

a. First fit—Select the first job waiting to enter memory that will fit into the available space.

b. Best fit—Select the job waiting to enter memory with the memory requirement closest to the available space (i.e., select the job with the largest memory requirements that will fit).

c. Worst fit—Select the job waiting to enter memory with the memory requirement least close to the available space (i.e., select the job with the smallest memory requirements).

REFERENCES

[4.1] Kiviat, P. J.; Villanueva, R.; and Markowitz, H. M., *SIMSCRIPT II.5 Programming Language*. New York: CACI, Inc., 1975.

[4.2] *SIMSCRIPT II.5 Reference Handbook*. New York: CACI, Inc., 1976.

[4.3] *ACM Simuletter,* vol. 7, no. 1, January 1976.

5 Probability and Statistics in Simulation

5.1 INTRODUCTION

As defined in Chapter 1, a stochastic system behaves in a random manner. The randomness may be inherent to the system structure or derived from a random input sequence. This chapter presents methods for quantitatively describing randomness in stochastic systems. The basic terminology of those aspects of probability and statistics important to simulation studies is established here. Randomness in a digital computer simulation of a stochastic system is generally introduced by means of stochastic variables. The generation of sequences of values for stochastic variables and the testing of such sequences for randomness is an important simulation topic that is covered in this chapter. In addition, discussions are presented of the generation of uniformly distributed stochastic variables and also stochastic variables fitting nonuniform distributions of both the continuous and discrete variety.

The material in this chapter is intended to provide the simulation programmer with sufficient background to apply and understand the basic and most frequently used concepts in probability and statistics.

5.2 PROBABILITY FUNCTIONS

The result of a stochastic activity is represented by a stochastic variable. The range of possible values for a stochastic variable is predefined. However, the exact sequence of values to be assumed by a stochastic variable during an experiment is unknown. Stochastic variables are described by probability functions which indicate the probability of a random variable taking on specific values within its range.

In Chapter 1, the concepts of discrete and continuous systems were introduced. Stochastic variables which describe the behavior of these classes of systems have either discrete or continuous probability functions. A discrete probability function can be represented by a finite set of points and can be graphed with a stairstep representation. A continuous function has an infinite number of points and is represented by a smooth curve.

Definition 5.1

If the range of a stochastic variable, X, contains k values $[X_1, X_2, \ldots, X_k]$ and the probability of the ith value being assumed by X is $p(X_i)$, $1 \leq i \leq k$, then the set of numbers $[p(X_1), p(X_2), \ldots, p(X_k)]$ is a *discrete probability function* if

$$\sum_{i=1}^{k} p(X_i) = 1, p(X_i) \geq 0, \qquad 1 \leq i \leq k$$

This definition conforms to our intuitive feeling for probability functions. There are two restrictions placed upon a set of numbers in order for them to define a discrete probability function. First, all numbers (called probability measures) must be nonnegative. Thus, the concept of an event occurring with negative probability is not considered. Stating that all probability measures must sum to one implies that the probability of a stochastic activity producing a result in its range is one.

EXAMPLE 5.1

Table 5.1 shows the probability function for the number of tails in four tosses of a fair coin. The T variable indicates the exact number of tails obtained in the four tosses, and $p(T)$ is the probability of obtaining the given number of tails.

Table 5.1 indicates the probability of a stochastic variable assuming a particular value in a coin toss experiment. In many situations, it is necessary to determine the probability of a stochastic variable assuming a value

Table 5.1 Probability Function for Number of Tails in Four Tosses

T	$p(T)$
0	1/16
1	1/4
2	3/8
3	1/4
4	1/16

within a specific range. The mechanism used to compute such a probability is the cumulative probability function.

Definition 5.2

The *cumulative probability function* for a discrete stochastic variable is

$$P_c(X_j) = \sum_{i=1}^{j} p(X_i)$$

The cumulative probability function, $P_c(X_j)$, indicates the probability of a stochastic variable attaining a value less than or equal to X_j. Table 5.2 gives the cumulative probability function for the number of tails in four coin tosses.

Definitions 5.1 and 5.2 are limited to discrete systems. In these definitions, the assumption has been made that the stochastic variable has a finite range. When this restriction is removed, the summation operation in Definitions 5.1 and 5.2 must be replaced by integration, thus resulting in the following definitions for continuous stochastic variables.

Table 5.2   Cumulative Probability Function for Number of Tails in Four Tosses

T	$p(T)$	$P_c(T)$
0	1/16	1/16
1	1/4	5/16
2	3/8	11/16
3	1/4	15/16
4	1/16	1

Definition 5.3

The *probability density function* of a continuous stochastic variable, X, is $f(X)$, where

$$1 = \int_{-\infty}^{\infty} f(X)dX, \ f(X) \geq 0$$

In the previous definition, the limits of the integral are set to negative and positive infinity to represent the general case. In most situations a continuous stochastic variable will be positive over some finite interval and have a zero value outside the interval. However, for reasons of generality, all subsequent definitions of continuous stochastic variables will have infinite limits on the integrals.

Definition 5.4

The *probability distribution function* of a continuous stochastic variable is $F(y)$, where

$$F(y) \int_{-\infty}^{y} f(X)\,dX$$

The probability density function $f(x)$ indicates the probability of the stochastic variable assuming a particular value. The probability distribution function $F(y)$ is the probability of the stochastic variable assuming a value less than or equal to y.

EXAMPLE 5.2

Perhaps the simplest continuous stochastic variable is one that is uniformly distributed over an interval. The probability density function for a uniformly distributed stochastic variable over the interval from a to b is

$$f(X) = \left[\begin{array}{c} \dfrac{1}{b-a} \qquad a \le X \le b \\ 0 \end{array} \right.$$

$$\text{otherwise}$$

$$\int_{-\infty}^{\infty} f(X)\,dX = \int_{a}^{b} \frac{1}{b-a}\,dX$$

$$= \frac{1}{b-a}\int_{a}^{b} dX$$

$$= \frac{1}{b-a}[1]_{a}^{b} = \left[\frac{1}{b-a}\right]\left[b-a\right] = 1 \Bigg]$$

The probability distribution function for a uniformly distributed stochastic variable is

$$F(y) = \int_{-\infty}^{y} f(X)\,dX$$

$$= \int_{a}^{y} \frac{1}{b-a}\,dX$$

$$= \frac{1}{b-a}\int_{a}^{y} dX = \frac{1}{b-a}[1]_{a}^{y} = \frac{y-a}{b-a}$$

Consider a stochastic variable uniformly distributed between 0 and 10. Then

$$F(6) = \int_0^6 \frac{1}{10-0} dX = .60$$

The relationship between probability functions and event distributions in stochastic simulations is extremely important. An event distribution is represented by a stochastic variable indicating the time until the next occurrence of the event. The probability of the stochastic event variable assuming a particular value is defined by a probability density function. Consider a customer arrival event that can be described by a probability function indicating the probability of an arrival in X minutes. If customer arrivals are uniformly distributed from 0 to 10 minutes, then the probability functions of Example 5.2 describe the event distribution. As shown in the example, the probability of the next customer arrival occurring in 6 minutes or less is .60. The probability of the next arrival occurring in exactly 6 minutes is .10, assuming minutes as the atomic time unit.

A very important descriptor of a probability density function is its mean (or expected value). The mean can be thought of as the most likely value to appear in a sample taken from the probability density function.

Definition 5.5

The mean, μ_x, of the probability density function, $f(x)$, is

$$\mu_x = \int_{-\infty}^{\infty} xf(x) \, dx$$

If the mean is referred to as the expected value, it is denoted by $E(X)$.

The mean of a probability density function is a descriptor that aids in the characterization of the function's behavior. Later in this chapter, definitions are presented for other descriptors of probability function behavior, that is, standard deviation and variance. Such descriptors are termed *statistical parameters* of the probability functions.

Definition 5.6

The sample mean, M_x (or mean of a discrete probability density function), is

$$M_x = \sum_{i=1}^{k} x_i p(x_i)$$

where $p(x_i)$ is the probability of x_i in the sample (or the probability of x_i according to the discrete probability distribution).

EXAMPLE 5.3

If $f(X)$ is the number of tails in four tosses of a fair coin as shown in Table 5.1, then

$$M_x = \sum_{T=0}^{4} Tp(T)$$

$$= 0(1/16) + 1(1/4) + 2(3/8) + 3(1/4) + 4(1/16)$$

$$= 0 + 1/4 + 3/4 + 3/4 + 1/4 = 2$$

If $f(X)$ is the uniform distribution between a and b, then

$$\mu_x = \int_{a}^{b} \frac{X}{b-a} dX$$

$$= \frac{1}{b-a} \left[\frac{X^2}{2} \right]_{a}^{b}$$

$$= \frac{b^2 - a^2}{2(b-a)} = \frac{(b+a)(b-a)}{2(b-a)} = \frac{b+a}{2}$$

5.3 CONDITIONAL AND JOINT PROBABILITY FUNCTIONS

The probability density function indicates the probability of a single event. In many models it is important to determine the probability of two events occurring in a specific or arbitrary sequence. For example, in a bank teller model, the customer arrival rate in the morning may differ from the afternoon rate. Thus the event distribution for customer arrivals is dependent upon the event represented by the simulated time passing noon. Since the probability density function of the customer arrival stochastic variable is dependent upon the occurrence of the noon time event, the function is termed a *conditional* probability density function.

Definition 5.7

The *conditional probability density function* $f(X_1/X_2)$ is the probability of event X_1 occurring, given that event X_2 has occurred.

The conditional probability function cannot be computed, in general, from the probability density functions of the stochastic variable. Instead, the conditional probability function must be evaluated separately.

EXAMPLE 5.4

The probability of exactly three tails in four tosses of a fair coin is

$f(3T4) = \frac{1}{4}$

The probability of exactly two tails in three tosses of a fair coin is

$f(2T3) = \frac{3}{8}$

The conditional probability of getting exactly three tails in four tosses, given that exactly two tails were obtained in the first three tosses, is

$f(3T4/2T3) = \frac{1}{2}$

The value of the conditional probability is $\frac{1}{2}$, since the situation reduces to the need to obtain one tail in one coin toss. Under the fair coin assumption, the probability is $\frac{1}{2}$, no matter how many tails have been obtained in previous tosses.

The conditional probability function indicates the probability of two events occurring in a given sequence. If the sequence is not critical, the *joint* probability function is applicable.

Definition 5.8

The *joint probability density function*, $f(X_1, X_2)$, is the probability of events X_1 and X_2 occurring; that is,

$$f(X_1, X_2) = f(X_1/X_2)f(X_2) = f(X_2/X_1)f(X_1)$$

The above definition states that the probability of two events occurring is the product of the probability of the first event times the conditional probability of the second event occurring, given that the first event has already taken place.

EXAMPLE 5.6

In Example 5.4 the following probability functions were shown:

$f(2T3) = \frac{3}{8}$
$f(3T4/2T3) = \frac{1}{2}$

Using Definition 5.7, the probability of obtaining exactly two tails in the first three tosses of a fair coin and exactly three tails in four tosses can be computed.

$f(2T3, 3T4) = f(3T4/2T3)f(2T3)$
$= (\frac{3}{8})(\frac{1}{2}) = \frac{3}{16}$

It was previously stated that a conditional probability function cannot be computed in general using only the density functions of events. However, conditional probability functions and density functions are related as shown in the following theorem.

Theorem 5.1 (Bayes' theorem)

$$f(X_1/X_2) = \frac{f(X_2/X_1)f(X_1)}{f(X_2)} \quad \text{where } f(X_2) \neq 0$$

Proof

From Definition 5.8,

$$f(X_1/X_2)f(X_2) = f(X_2/X_1)f(X_1)$$

Therefore,

$$f(X_1/X_2) = \frac{f(X_2/X_1)f(X_1)}{f(X_2)}$$

Bayes' theorem provides the basis for a large body of statistical decision-making theory [5.1–5.4].

EXAMPLE 5.7

Bayes' theorem can be used to determine the conditional probability that exactly two tails were obtained in the first three tosses, given that exactly three tails were obtained in four tosses.

$$f(2T3/3T4) = \frac{f(3T4/2T3)f(2T3)}{f(3T4)}$$

$$= \frac{(1/2)(3/8)}{(1/4)} = 3/4$$

This result can be confirmed by testing the four combinations of tosses that can lead to three tails in four and observing that three of the combinations have two tails in the first three tosses.

5.4 STATISTICAL INDEPENDENCE

One of the most common questions to be answered by a simulation study is, "Are two events related?" From a statistical viewpoint, the relationship between events is indicated by a *dependence* between the stochastic variables that characterize the events. Stochastic variables that have no relationship between them are said to be *independent*.

Definition 5.9

Two events are *independent* if

$$f(X_1/X_2) = f(X_1) \quad \text{and} \quad f(X_2/X_1) = f(X_2)$$

The above definition states that two events are independent if the occurrence of either event has no effect on the probability of occurrence of the other event.

EXAMPLE 5.8

Let X_1 be the event that is the obtaining three tails in four coin tosses and X_2 be the event that is the drawing an ace out of a deck of standard playing cards.

$f(X_1) = \frac{1}{4}$
$f(X_2) = \frac{1}{13}$
$f(X_1/X_2) = \frac{1}{4}$
$f(X_2/X_1) = \frac{1}{13}$

Thus X_1 and X_2 are independent.

For independent events, the following expression can be employed to compute the joint probability.

Lemma 5.1

If X_1 and X_2 are independent, then

$$f(X_1, X_2) = f(X_1)f(X_2)$$

Proof

From Definition 5.8,

$$f(X_1, X_2) = f(X_1/X_2)f(X_2)$$

Since X_1 and X_2 are independent,

$$f(X_1/X_2) = f(X_1)$$

Thus

$$f(X_1, X_2) = f(X_1)f(X_2)$$

Stochastic variables that are not independent are said to be *dependent*. Dependent variables fail to satisfy Definition 5.9; the occurrence of one event affects the probability of occurrence of the second event.

5.5 CORRELATION

In many simulation studies it is important to determine whether events are dependent upon each other and, if so, to quantify the dependence. The amount of dependence between stochastic variables is characterized by the *correlation* between the variables. A high correlation between stochastic variables means that a change in one variable is reflected in the behavior of the other variable. A first step in determining the correlation between two stochastic variables is to compute the *variance* of the individual variables. The variance measures the dispersion of the probability density function around its mean.

Definition 5.10

The *variance* of a stochastic variable X is

$$V_x = E(X - \mu_x)^2$$

For continuous variables,

$$V_x = \int_{-\infty}^{\infty} (X - \mu_x)^2 f(X)\, dX$$

EXAMPLE 5.9

For a uniform distribution between a and b with $a \leq b$,

$$V_x = \int_a^b \left(X - \frac{b+a}{2} \right)^2 \left(\frac{1}{b-a} \right) dX$$

$$= \frac{1}{b-a} \int_a^b \left[X^2 - X(b+a) + \frac{(b+a)^2}{4} \right] dX$$

$$= \frac{1}{b-a} \left[\frac{X^3}{3} - \frac{X^2(b+a)}{2} + \frac{X(b+a)^2}{4} \right]_a^b$$

$$= \frac{1}{b-a} \left[\frac{b^3}{3} - \frac{b^2(b+a)}{2} + \frac{b(b+a)^2}{4} \right.$$

$$\left. - \frac{a^3}{3} + \frac{a^2(b+a)}{2} - \frac{a(b+a)^2}{4} \right]$$

$$= \frac{1}{b-a} \left[\frac{b^3}{12} - \frac{ab^2}{4} + \frac{a^2 b}{4} - \frac{a^3}{12} \right]$$

$$= \frac{1}{12(b-a)} (b^3 - 3ab^2 + 3a^2 b - a^3)$$

$$= \frac{(b-a)^3}{12(b-a)} = \frac{(b-a)^2}{12}$$

Since the variance is a measure of the amount of dispersion in a distribution, it can be used along with the mean to characterize a collection of sample data. Here again, the difference between the sample variance and the variance of the distribution (or population) must be emphasized. The variance of the distribution is defined in Definition 5.10; the expression for the sample variance is provided in the following definition.

Definition 5.11

The sample variance, or variance of a discrete distribution, R_{xx}, is

$$R_{xx} = \frac{1}{k-1} \sum_{i=1}^{k} (X_i - M_x)^2$$

The reader might have expected the term $1/k$ instead of $1/(k-1)$ in the equation for the sample variance. However, if k is used in the computation of the sample variance, then the resulting value will be a biased estimate of the variance. An estimate of a statistical parameter of a distribution is unbiased if the expected value of the estimate is equal to the true parameter of the distribution.

Let R be an estimate of the variance of a distribution where

$$R = \frac{1}{k} \sum_{i=1}^{k} (X_i - M_x)^2$$

It can be shown [5.5] that

$$E(R) = V_x - V_{M_x}$$

where V_{M_x} is the variance of the sample mean, which can be computed by replacing x with M_x in Definition 5.10.

The expected value of R is equal to the difference between the variance of the distribution and the variance of the sample mean. Since the sample size cannot be infinitely large, the variance of the sample mean cannot be 0. Thus

$$E(R) \neq V_x - V_{M_x}$$

and R is a biased estimate of the variance.

Chao [5.5] shows that a correction factor of $k/(k-1)$ can be applied to R to produce an unbiased estimate. Hence,

$$R_{xx} = \frac{k}{k-1} R$$

is the correct representation of the sample variance.

EXAMPLE 5.10

Assume that 100 samples are taken from two populations to determine life expectancy. From population P_1, all 100 samples yield a value of 50. In population P_2, 50 samples have a value of 80, while the other 50 samples all yield a value of 20.

The means of the two samples are identical.

$$M_1 = \frac{100(50)}{100} = 50$$

$$M_2 = \frac{50(20) + 50(80)}{100} = 50$$

However, the sample variances are considerably different.

$$R_{11} = \frac{1}{99} \sum_{S=1}^{100} (S - M_1)^2$$

$$= \frac{1}{99} \sum_{S=1}^{100} (50 - 50)^2 = 0$$

$$R_{22} = \frac{1}{99} \left[\sum_{S=1}^{100} (S - M_2)^2 \right]$$

$$= \frac{1}{99} (50(20 - 50)^2 + 50(80 - 50)^2)$$

$$= \frac{1}{99}(50(900) + 50(900))$$

$$= \frac{1}{99}(90,000) = 909.091$$

The variance is a measure of dispersion in a distribution of a single stochastic variable. Since the variance is computed using the square of the difference of the data points and the mean (in order to prevent positive and negative differences from canceling out), it is expressed in square units. In order to measure dispersion in terms of original units, the standard deviation is used.

Definition 5.12

The *standard deviation* of a stochastic variable is the positive square root of the variance.

$$\sigma_x = \sqrt{V_x}$$

The standard deviation of a sample, S_{xx}, is

$$S_{xx} = \sqrt{R_{xx}}$$

The standard deviation is the average variation per observation of the stochastic variable.

EXAMPLE 5.11

For the population samples of Example 5.10,

$$S_{11} = \sqrt{R_{11}} = 0$$
$$S_{22} = \sqrt{R_{22}}$$
$$= \sqrt{909.091} = 30.151$$

Whereas the variance measures dispersion of a single stochastic variable, the covariance measures the relative dispersion of two stochastic variables.

Definition 5.13

The covariance of two stochastic variables, X and Y, is

$$V_{xy} = V_{yx} = E[(X - \mu_x)(Y - \mu_y)]$$

For continuous variables,

$$V_{xy} = \int_{-\infty}^{\infty} \int_{-\infty}^{\infty} (X - \mu_x)(Y - \mu_y)f(X,Y)\ dx\ dy$$

For discrete variables, or sample covariance,

$$R_{xy} = \frac{1}{k-1} \sum_{i=1}^{k} (X_i - M_x)(Y_i - M_y)$$

EXAMPLE 5.12

Consider the climatic and population data given in Table 5.3. This data describes the weather and population of a university town in the Midwest. The change in population is due to the exodus of students for various holidays. Using Definition 5.13, the relationships between maximum temperature and minimum temperature, precipitation, and population can be indicated by the following covariances:

$R_{12} = 107.0$ (max. temp. vs. min. temp.)
$R_{13} = 33.3$ (max. temp. vs. precipitation)
$R_{14} = -38.1$ (max. temp. vs. population)

Note that covariances R_{12} and R_{13} are positive, while R_{14} is negative. The sign of the covariance indicates the type of correlation between the stochastic variables. *Positive correlation* indicates that both variables tend to increase (or decrease) at the same time. *Negative correlation* indicates that the variables tend to behave in opposite manners with respect to time. Figure 5.1 illustrates the behavior of the maximum temperature, minimum temperature, precipitation, and population variables of Table 5.3. If the covariance of two stochastic variables is 0, the variables are *uncorrelated*.

Example 5.12 indicates that minimum temperature and precipitation are both positively correlated to maximum temperature. In many situations it is important to determine the strength of the correlation. Since the magnitude of the covariance is partially dependent upon the magnitude of the stochastic variables, it cannot be used fairly to compare the amount of correlation between pairs of stochastic variables. A ratio is required to remove the influence of the magnitude of the variables. The *correlation* coefficient, which is a ratio of the covariance and variances of stochastic variables, indicates the strength (or weakness) of the correlation of the variables.

Definition 5.14

The correlation coefficient ρ_{xy} of two stochastic variables X and Y is

$$\rho_{xy} = \frac{V_{xy}}{\sqrt{V_x V_y}}$$

Table 5.3 Sample Climatic and Population Data

Month	X_1 Max. Temp., °C	X_2 Min. Temp., °C	X_3 Precip., cm	X_4 Population, Thousands
J	4	−7	2	35
F	4	−8	3	45
M	9	−4	5	40
A	13	1	7	45
M	23	8	11	40
J	28	14	14	25
J	32	19	11	25
A	33	19	8	25
S	31	15	10	45
O	26	9	6	45
N	19	4	2	40
D	10	−3	3	35
M_x	19.3	5.6	6.8	37.1

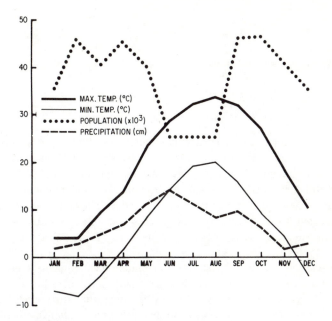

Figure 5.1 Positive and Negative Correlation

Fishman [5.6] demonstrates that $-1 \leq \rho_{xy} \leq 1$. The larger the magnitude of ρ_{xy}, the more strongly X and Y are correlated. Note that the sign of the correlation coefficient also indicates whether the correlation is positive or negative. The sample correlation coefficient, C_{xy}, is

$$C_{xy} = \frac{R_{xy}}{\sqrt{R_{xx}R_{xy}}}$$

C_{xy} has the same bounds and interpretation as ρ_{xy}.

EXAMPLE 5.13

Let us compute the correlation coefficients for the maximum temperature and the other three variables of Example 5.12. First the variances must be computed.

$$R_{11} = 120.1 \qquad R_{22} = 97.2 \qquad R_{33} = 16.1 \qquad R_{44} = 65.7$$

The correlation coefficients can then be computed using Definition 5.14.

$$C_{12} = \frac{R_{12}}{\sqrt{R_{11}R_{22}}} = .990$$

$$C_{13} = \frac{R_{13}}{\sqrt{R_{11}R_{33}}} = .757$$

$$C_{14} = \frac{R_{14}}{\sqrt{R_{11}R_{44}}} = -.429$$

The correlation coefficients indicate a very strong positive correlation between maximum and minimum temperature. The positive correlation between maximum temperature and precipitation is not quite as strong, but still substantial. The negative correlation of maximum temperature and population is weaker than the other two cases. The correlation strengths as indicated by the correlation coefficients conform to intuitive feelings of correlation that can be obtained by observing Table 5.3 and Figure 5.1.

Correlation is used in the analysis of simulation experiments to measure the effect that a change in an attribute has upon other attributes. In particular, the experiment may be repeated several times varying an input parameter and then computing the correlation coefficient to determine the relationship between the input parameter and the attributes for which statistics are maintained. In the banking model, if several executions were made using different customer arrival rates, the effect of arrival rate upon teller utilization could be measured by computing the correlation coefficient.

5.6 INDEPENDENCE AND CORRELATION

The correlation statistics quantify the dependence between stochastic variables. Let us examine more closely the relationship between statistical independence and correlation.

Lemma 5.2

If two stochastic variables are independent, then they are uncorrelated.

Proof

Let X and Y be stochastic variables. From Definition 5.13,

$$V_{xy} = \int_{-\infty}^{\infty} \int_{-\infty}^{\infty} (X - \mu_x)(Y - \mu_y) f(X,Y) \, dX \, dY$$

$$= \int_{-\infty}^{\infty} (X - \mu_x)f(X) \left[\int_{-\infty}^{\infty} (Y - \mu_y)f(Y/X) \, dY \right] dX$$

If X and Y are independent,

$$f(Y/X) = f(Y)$$

Thus

$$V_{xy} = \int_{-\infty}^{\infty} (X - \mu_x)f(X)\left[\int_{-\infty}^{\infty} (Y - \mu_y)f(Y)\, dY\right] dX$$

$$= \int_{-\infty}^{\infty} (X - \mu_x)f(X)\left[\int_{-\infty}^{\infty} Yf(Y)\, dY - \mu_y \int_{-\infty}^{\infty} f(X)\, dY\right] dX$$

$$= \int_{-\infty}^{\infty} (X - \mu_x)f(X)[\mu_y - \mu_y(1)]\, dX$$

Then from the definitions of the mean and of probability density functions,

$$V_{xy} = \int_{-\infty}^{\infty} (X - \mu_x)f(X)(0)\, dX$$

$$= 0$$

Therefore, X and Y are uncorrelated.

Lemma 5.2 states that independence implies no correlation. However, it does not follow that no correlation implies independence. It may be possible to obtain a zero covariance for dependent variables. The following example shows that if two events are mutually exclusive, they are uncorrelated but not independent.

EXAMPLE 5.14

Let X and Y be a pair of mutually exclusive events. Then

$$f(Y) = 1 - f(X),\ 0 < f(X) < 1$$

where $f(X)$ is some probability density function.

Since X and Y are mutually exclusive, $f(X,Y) = 0$. According to Definition 5.13,

$$V_{xy} = \int_{-\infty}^{\infty} \int_{-\infty}^{\infty} (X - \mu_x)(Y - \mu_y)f(X,Y)\, dX\, dY$$

$$= 0$$

Since events X and Y are mutually exclusive, the events are uncorrelated. However,

$$0 = f(Y/X) \neq f(Y)$$

Thus X and Y are not independent.

5.7 RANDOM NUMBERS

In order to simulate stochastic systems, some method of inserting randomness into the model is necessary. In digital computer simulations, this is generally accomplished with *random numbers*. A random number is a stochastic variable that may assume any value over a given range. A value assumed by a random variable is independent of the previous values assumed. The GPSS and Simscript models of the bank tellers both relied upon random numbers to derive the values for the stochastic variables representing customer arrivals, number of transactions per customer, and transaction processing time.

Before the advent of computers, random numbers were generated using tables of random digits. Table 5.4 [5.7] lists 2100 random units. The procedure for random number generation from a table involves first defining a method of selecting the five-digit entries, i.e., first line, second column; second line, third column; etc. Once an entry is selected, the random number is formed by extracting and/or operating on specific digits of the entry. For example, a three-digit random number could be created from the first, fourth, and third digits of a five-digit table entry.

Actually digital computers are not capable of generating truly random numbers due to their deterministic nature. If a digital computer is operating properly, for a given input it should always yield the same results. Thus digital computers produce pseudorandom numbers using functions that are carefully constructed to give the appearance of random behavior.

The problem of generating random numbers by means of a computer program can be approached using either a table or an algorithm. A tabular method would resemble the technique used by a human working with a table such as Table 5.4. From a given starting point in the table, digits can be selected according to some specified procedure. Since digital computers operate deterministically, a specific starting point in the table will always produce the same number. In order to generate a new number a different point in the table must be selected. Again, the next starting point must be generated by the digital computer using some algorithm.

From the above discussion, it can be seen that some algorithm is necessary to select random digits from a table. Since the execution of an algorithm by a digital computer is not a random process, this leads to the conclusion that truly random numbers cannot be produced by a digital computer. Hence, digital computers are limited to the generation of pseudorandom numbers. In all subsequent discussions, the qualifier *pseudo* will be implied whenever random numbers are mentioned.

The algorithmic approach to the generation of random number involves the use of a programmed procedure to produce random numbers directly rather than table indices as in the previous method. As with the tabular method, an initial value, or *seed,* must be supplied to the algorithm as a starting point. The algorithm generates a random number from the seed value and then uses the

Table 5.4 2100 Random Units

Line/Col.	(1)	(2)	(3)	(4)	(5)	(6)	(7)	(8)	(9)	(10)	(11)	(12)	(13)	(14)
1	10480	15011	01536	02011	81647	91646	69179	14194	62590	36207	20969	99570	91291	90700
2	22368	46573	25595	85393	30995	89198	27982	53402	93965	34095	52666	19174	39615	99505
3	24130	48360	22527	97265	76393	64809	15179	24830	49340	32081	30680	19655	63348	58629
4	42167	93093	06243	61680	07856	16276	39440	53537	71341	57004	00849	74917	97758	16379
5	37570	39975	81837	16656	06121	91782	60468	81305	49684	60672	14110	06927	01263	54613
6	77921	06907	11008	42751	27756	53498	18002	70659	90655	15053	21916	81825	44394	42880
7	99562	72905	56420	69994	98872	31016	71194	18728	44013	48840	63213	21069	10634	12952
8	96301	91977	05463	08982	18876	20922	94505	56809	60914	60045	18425	84903	42508	32307
9	89579	14342	63661	10291	17453	18103	57740	84278	25331	12566	58678	44947	05585	56941
10	85475	36857	53342	53988	53060	59333	38867	62300	08158	17983	16439	11458	18593	64952
11	28918	69578	88231	33276	70997	79936	56965	95859	90196	31595	91547	85590	91510	78188
12	63553	40961	48235	03427	49626	69445	18663	72695	52180	20847	12234	90511	33703	90322
13	09429	93969	52636	92737	88974	33488	36329	17617	39915	08272	84115	27156	30613	74952
14	10365	61129	87529	85689	48237	52267	56589	93394	01511	26358	85104	20285	29975	89808
15	07119	97336	71048	08178	77233	13916	47564	81056	97735	85977	29372	74461	29551	90707
16	51085	12765	51821	51259	77452	16308	60756	92144	49442	53900	70960	63990	75601	40719
17	02368	21382	52404	60268	89368	19885	55322	44819	01188	65255	64835	44919	05944	55157
18	01011	54092	33362	94904	31273	04146	18594	29852	71585	85030	51132	01915	92747	64951
19	52162	53916	46369	58586	23216	14513	83149	98736	23495	64350	94738	17752	35156	35749
20	07056	97628	33787	09998	42698	06691	76988	13602	51851	46104	88916	19509	25625	58104
21	48663	91245	85828	14346	09172	30168	90229	04734	59193	22178	30421	61666	99904	32812
22	54164	58492	22421	74103	47070	25306	76468	26384	58151	06646	21524	15227	96909	44592
23	32639	32363	04497	24200	13363	38055	94342	28728	35806	06912	17012	64161	18296	22851
24	29334	27001	87627	87308	58731	00256	45834	15398	46557	41135	10367	07684	36188	18510
25	02488	33062	28834	67351	19731	92420	60952	61280	50001	67658	32586	86679	50720	94953
26	81525	72295	04839	96423	24878	82651	66566	14778	76797	14780	13300	87074	79666	95725
27	29787	29501	79097	27432	47061	20849	89768	81536	86645	12649	92259	46102	80428	25280
28	00742	57392	39064	66432	84673	40027	32832	61362	98947	96067	64760	64584	96096	92853
29	05366	04213	25669	26422	44407	44048	36936	63904	45766	66134	75470	66502	34693	90449
30	91921	26418	64117	94305	26766	25940	39962	22209	71500	64568	91402	42416	07844	69618

generated random number to produce the next value. In general, the $(K + 1)$th random number is derived from the Kth random number. Different sequences of random numbers can be produced by supplying distinct seed values. A sequence of random numbers generated in this manner is not independent. However, it is reproducible. Reproducibility is important in simulation experiments in which a model is exercised several times. The ability to generate the same sequence of random numbers allows a proper analysis of the effect of changing an input parameter, since the random elements of a simulation model will be identical over the set of executions.

5.8 CONGRUENCE METHOD OF RANDOM NUMBER GENERATION

Generation of random numbers is of sufficient complexity and importance to produce a substantial body of literature on the topic. Detailed treatments of this subject can be found in References [5.6] and [5.8] through [5.12]. These highly sophisticated methods produce sequences that are very close to being truly random in terms of uniformity and independence. However, excellent results (in terms of uniformity) can be obtained using very simple methods. One such approach is the *congruence* (or residue) method. Given three constants ($i, j,$ and m), the $(K + 1)$th random number is derived from the Kth random number using the following equation:

$$r_{k+1} = (ir_k + j) \text{ modulo } M \tag{5.1}$$

The modulo function in Eq. (5.1) divides the expression $ir_k + j$ by M and returns the remainder as the value. Thus, r_{k+1} will always be in the range from 0 to $M - 1$. Generally, the value of M is a constraint of the problem. Often, $M = 10^d$ or 2^b, where d is the number of digits (or b is the number of bits) of the random numbers. The performance of a random number generator based upon the congruence method is strongly dependent upon the relationship among $i, j,$ and m. The ideal situation is to select values of i and j such that all random numbers in the interval $[0, m - 1]$ will be generated before the sequence begins to repeat. Since the generation algorithm is deterministic, whenever a number is generated that previously appeared as input, the sequence will begin to cycle. Since there is a finite range of random numbers, $[0, m - 1]$, possible for a given generator, each generator must eventually cycle. The length of the cycle is an important characteristic of a random number generation algorithm.

There are some interesting special cases of congruence random number generators. If $i = 1$, the random number generator is *additive*. If $j = 0$, the random number generator is *multiplicative*. If neither of the previous two conditions holds, the random number generator is said to be *mixed*. In terms of the approximate randomness of the various types of congruence random number generators, mixed gives the best results, followed by multiplicative, and then additive.

The following example illustrates the performance of a very simple multiplicative congruence random number generator.

EXAMPLE 5.15

In the program, the actual generation of random numbers is carried out by the first two assignment statements within the DO Loop that terminates at the statement labeled 300. The remaining statements deal primarily with counting the frequencies of the two-digit random numbers and printing the frequencies.

The output of the program consists of a listing of the 1000 one-digit random numbers, followed by a frequency count of each number. All one-digit numbers in the range from 0 to 9 were generated from 78 to 119 times each. In Section 5.12, a method of testing the randomness of a sequence of numbers is presented.

In all subsequent discussions we will assume that we can generate uniformly distributed random numbers over the interval [0,1]. For notational convenience, let r, $0 \leq r \leq 1$, be uniformly distributed. Using r as a basis, any type of stochastic distribution can be produced.

5.9 GENERATION OF DISCRETE STOCHASTIC DISTRIBUTIONS

In order to generate a value for a discrete stochastic variable, X, that is uniformly distributed over an interval $[A,B]$, the following equation is used:

$$X = A + (B - A)r \tag{5.2}$$

EXAMPLE 5.16

Let X be a uniformly distributed random integer in the range of 1 to 400. Then

$$A = 1 \text{ and } B = 400$$

If a value for r of .43 is generated, then using Eq. (5.2) and truncating the final result to an integer value yields

$$
\begin{aligned}
X &= 1 + (400 - 1) * .43 \\
&= 1 + 399 * .43 \\
&= 1 + 128.57 \\
&= 129
\end{aligned}
$$

FILE: RANDOM1C FORTRAN A1   KANSAS STATE UNIVERSITY - CMS V5 PLC 2

```
      INTEGER RANDOM(40) , COUNT (10) , SEED              RANOCC10
C                                                         RAN00020
COMMENT :  INITIALIZE FREQUENCY COUNTS                    RAN00030
C                                                         RAN00040
      DO 100 K = 1 , 10                                   RAN00050
      COUNT(K) = 0                                        RANOCC60
100   CONTINUE                                            RANOCC70
C                                                         RAN00080
CCMMENT :  SET INITIAL VALUES AND CONSTANTS               RAN0CC90
COMMENT :  19727 IS A SEED VALUE KNOWN TO YIELD A LONG CYCLE  RAN00100
COMMENT :  20403 IS A MULTIPLIER KNOWN TO PRODUCE A LONG CYCLE  RAN00110
COMMENT :  32768 IS 2**15                                 RAN00120
C                                                         RAN00130
      SEED = 19727                                        RAN00140
      I = 20403                                           RAN00150
      M = 32768                                           RAN00160
C                                                         RAN00170
COMMENT : GENERATE 40 GROUPS OF 25 RANDOM NUMBERS EACH    RAN00180
C                                                         RANOC190
      WRITE ( 9 , 200 )                                   RAN00200
200   FORMAT ('1)00  1 DIGIT RANDOM NUMBERS')             RANOO210
C                                                         RAN00220
      DO 500 L = 1 , 40                                   RAN00230
C                                                         RAN00240
COMMENT : GENERATE 25 RANDOM NUMBERS IN  THE RANGE OF 0 TO 9.  RAN00250
COMMENT :  AN INTERMEDIATE RANDOM NUMBER IN THE RANGE OF  RAN00260
COMMENT :  0 TO 2**15 - 1 IS GENERATED.                   RAN00270
COMMENT :  THE FREQUENCY OF EACH RANDOM DIGIT IS COUNTED. RAN00280
C                                                         RAN00290
      DO 300 K = 1 , 25                                   RAN00300
      SEED = MOD(I * SEED , M)                            RAN00310
      RANDOM(K) = SEED * 10 / M                           RANOC320
      INDEX = RANDOM(K) + 1                               RAN00330
      COUNT(INDEX) = COUNT(INDEX) + 1                     RAN00340
300   CONTINUE                                            RANCC350
C                                                         RAN00360
      WRITE (9 , 400) (RANDOM(K) , K = 1 , 25 )           RAN00370
400   FORMAT ( 25 ( I2 , 1X ) )                           RAN00380
500   CONTINUE                                            RAN00390
C                                                         RAN00400
      WRITE (9 , 600)                                     RAN00410
600   FORMAT ( 'NUMBER' , 3X , 'FREQUENCY' , 6X )         RAN00420
C                                                         RAN00430
COMMENT : PRINT FREQUENCIES                               RAN00440
C                                                         RANOC450
      DO 800 K = 1, 10                                    RAN00460
      I = K - 1                                           RAN00470
      WRITE (9 , 700) ( I , COUNT(K) )                    RANOC480
700   FORMAT ( 3X , I1 , 8X , I3 )                        RAN00490
800   CONTINUE                                            RAN00500
C                                                         RAN00510
      STOP                                                RAN00520
      END                                                 RAN00530
```

FILE: FILE   FT09F001 A1   KANSAS STATE UNIVERSITY - CMS V5 PLC 2

```
1000   1 DIGIT RANDOM NUMBERS
 0  6  0  5  9  0  5  9  0  6   2  6  8  3  7  6  9  8  7  8   C  2  6  9  7
 3  2  9  7  9  2  6  5  0  0   0  7  3  3  8  1  9  9  0  2   5  2  5  6  0
 9  0  1  3  7  6  1  3  1  0   3  9  9  2  4  9  5  0  0  2   7  2  7  7  0
 9  1  2  1  8  9  6  7  8  6   9  3  8  0  9  5  6  5  4  1   2  9  3  5  4
 8  5  5  2  8  9  7  2  5  4   6  6  6  8  0  0  7  0  4  4   3  9  4  7  2
 3  8  8  9  2  0  4  1  4  8   6  4  7  8  1  5  1  6  9  9   5  7  8  2  6
 9  6  2  4  8  4  4  8  0  8   4  6  1  9  9  7  7  5  5  0   5  5  9  3  0
 7  6  6  0  0  3  7  0  3  5   4  7  5  0  8  7  4  4  5  6   9  2  5  0  0
 2  8  6  4  8  0  0  0  8  3   8  7  8  3  6  5  4  0  1  1   2  2  5  5  9
 9  6  4  0  9  8  9  3  0  2   7  2  3  4  8  6  4  0  0  9   4  7  2  8  0
 0  2  9  2  6  0  9  8  1  4   3  7  2  3  9  8  4  6  2  0   4  1  8  1  8
 7  4  0  3  4  6  5  4  8  1   6  8  1  4  2  1  9  1  1  C   3  C  1  C  0
 6  2  8  9  5  2  1  0  5  0   4  0  0  5  3  0  7  6  5  6   4  1  7  9  4
 9  3  7  6  9  2  8  5  9  8   2  8  9  9  7  C  6  9  2  9   1  7  6  9  1
 7  7  8  5  7  4  2  2  2  6   7  2  8  2  9  1  3  0  5  0   1  0  1  7  0
 9  2  1  6  7  6  0  4  3  8   4  2  4  5  1  5  1  3  9  C   1  9  8  2  3
 9  7  9  7  6  3  6  1  1  6   0  3  8  5  6  3  3  8  2  9   3  4  3  0  5
 2  6  5  3  0  7  2  5  8  2   0  7  4  7  8  4  7  9  5  5   5  3  9  3  7
 7  9  6  3  7  4  1  0  8  3   2  8  6  5  7  5  9  7  2  C   3  0  3  2  3
 1  6  9  5  9  8  1  8  4  4   6  5  4  2  3  4  7  7  0  1   3  5  6  2  0
 3  1  3  6  7  2  2  2  3  9   3  5  8  0  3  4  7  4  8  8   8  0  5  6  6
 7  0  6  7  3  0  7  8  7  9   8  5  7  6  8  5  4  5  5  3   4  3  5  5  8
 7  7  9  3  2  9  0  9  5  4   5  4  2  0  9  8  0  5  9  8   4  9  2  3  2
 1  3  3  8  9  8  6  0  2  5   1  3  8  9  6  5  7  7  1  0   7  4  3  6  7
 8  3  8  6  3  8  4  2  7  7   8  4  6  0  8  1  6  4  0  2   4  8  9  5  4
 2  3  9  5  4  7  4  1  3  7   7  0  8  1  7  7  6  3  4  9   8  2  5  2  1
 1  1  3  6  9  8  7  9  0  7   0  0  3  6  0  8  1  3  2  2   3  8  2  0  4
 9  7  1  0  5  4  4  8  4  7   8  3  6  4  0  3  9  1  1  3   2  4  9  0  4
 9  2  0  3  2  9  9  9  0  0   3  9  0  2  9  3  6  5  3  9   6  7  1  7  0
 7  9  4  2  4  4  0  0  7  2   4  7  3  9  4  8  3  1  8  1   5  6  7  1  7
 7  7  4  8  4  9  7  8  0  1   6  4  3  2  7  6  9  0  7  2   4  4  1  2  5
 3  7  3  7  5  0  4  7  1  6   5  1  7  2  4  6  3  4  0  7   8  5  1  1  0
 2  6  4  9  9  5  3  2  8  5   3  9  4  6  2  9  4  7  4  5   3  5  7  0  8
 0  6  9  6  0  8  6  2  5  0   9  2  3  6  6  4  3  5  8  3   3  1  2  6  3
 2  7  8  1  2  2  7  5  0  5   7  5  0  6  7  9  0  4  0  7   5  6  5  6  1
 2  8  6  6  0  3  5  4  9  9   2  3  9  0  5  9  7  4  5  7   2  6  8  5  4
 3  5  8  0  2  4  3  0  7  3   5  3  6  1  2  7  4  7  9  0   9  1  3  3  6
 9  9  3  1  2  5  8  1  9  6   9  3  6  9  4  1  5  0  1  3   3  5  9  5  8
 0  7  3  1  2  4  3  9  7  8   1  1  0  8  4  7  0  4  9  4   1  3  C  2  9
 4  5  9  2  7  0  4  6  9  1   6  6  0  4  4  9  9  6  6  1   3  2  0  8  3
```

NUMBER	FREQUENCY
0	119
1	78
2	96
3	105
4	101
5	98
6	95
7	107
8	95
9	116

The cumulative probability function is required for the generation of nonuniform discrete stochastic variables. Using r and the cumulative probability function of a nonuniform discrete distribution, a random value corresponding to the distribution can be generated by the following rule:

If $P_c(X_{i-1}) < r \leq P_c(X_i)$, then X_i is the value selected.
If $r \leq P_c(X_1)$, then X_1 is the value selected.

EXAMPLE 5.17

Consider the cumulative probability function for customer transaction type in Table 5.5. Assume that the simulation program requires three transaction types. If the uniform random number generator produced the values $r = .51, .12, .22$, then the three transaction types produced would be:

1. Checking Deposit, since $.35 < r \leq .55$;
2. Savings Deposit, since $r < .20$;
3. Savings Withdrawal, since $.20 < r \leq .35$.

Table 5.5 Sample Cumulative Probability Distribution

X (*Transaction Type*)	$P(X)$	$P_c(X)$
Savings Deposit	.20	.20
Savings Withdrawal	.15	.35
Checking Deposit	.20	.55
Check Cashing	.25	.80
Christmas Club Payment	.15	.95
Other	.05	1.00

5.10 GENERATION OF CONTINUOUS STOCHASTIC DISTRIBUTIONS

In simulation models, many of the stochastic variables describing attribute and event distributions are continuous in nature. Consider the arrival of customers in a banking model, the acceleration of a rocket, or the rate of fuel consumption by an airliner as examples of continuous stochastic variables in simulation models. The value of an attribute for a particular entity or the time of the next event is determined by generating a value according to the appropriate continuous distribution.

Values for continuous stochastic variables that are uniformly distributed are generated using Eq. (5.2) without truncation. Generation using nonuniform continuous random distributions is a more complex operation.

Let $f(X)$ be the probability density function from which the random values are to be generated. Let $F(X)$ be the corresponding probability distribution function. Recall from Definition 5.4 that $0 \leq F(X) \leq 1$ and that $F(X)$ is monotonically nondecreasing. In order to generate a random value for the stochastic variable, X, distributed according to $f(X)$, a uniform random number r, $0 \leq r \leq 1$, is produced, and then X is selected such that $F(X) = r$. That is, the inverse function

$$F^{-1}(r) = X \qquad (5.3)$$

must be solved. Figure 5.2 illustrates the use of the inverse probability distribution function to generate a random value from a given distribution.

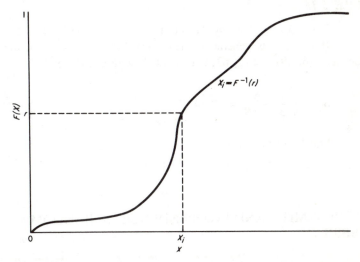

Figure 5.2 Generation of Random Value Using Inverse Probability Distribution Function

In general, it is very difficult to solve Eq. (5.3). The inverse probability distribution functions have been solved (or approximated) for many common probability density functions. Several of these functions are presented later in this chapter.

In cases where the probability distribution has been determined experimentally, a method similar to the discrete case can be used. In the continuous case, some form of interpolation is necessary. Assume that $F(X)$ is specified as a finite number of points. The simplest interpolation technique is linear interpolation, which assumes that all points are connected by straight lines. Between any two points, (X_i, Y_i) and (X_{i+1}, Y_{i+1}), the slope of the line is given by

$$S_i = \frac{X_{i+1} - X_i}{Y_{i+1} - Y_i} \tag{5.4}$$

where $Y_j = F(X_j)$.

In order to generate a random value for the stochastic variable, X_q, using the experimentally determined distribution function, first generate r, $0 \leq r \leq 1$.

If $r = F(X_i)$, then $X_q = X_i$ is the generated value.

Otherwise, for $Y_i < r < Y_{i+1}$ compute S_i from Eq. (5.4).

Since $S_i = \dfrac{X_q - X_i}{r - Y_i}$, it follows that $X_q = X_i + S_i(r - Y_i)$. (5.5)

EXAMPLE 5.18

Let $F(X)$ be given by the set of points shown in Table 5.6.

If $r = .50$ is generated, then since $F(6) < r < F(7)$, the slope between $(6, .49)$ and $(7, .63)$ is computed using Eq. (5.4).

$$S = \frac{7 - 6}{.63 - .49} = 7.14$$

Equation (5.5) yields

$$X_q = 6 + 7.14(.50 - .49) = 6.07$$

5.11 UNIFORMITY AND INDEPENDENCE OF RANDOM NUMBERS

As mentioned several times in earlier sections of this chapter, digital computers generate pseudorandom numbers. Consequently, techniques are required for measuring the randomness of numbers produced by pseudorandom number generators. In order for a sequence of numbers to be truly random, they must be uniformly distributed over the interval and the value of a given number must be independent of its predecessors and successors. A considerable body of knowledge on the topic of tests of randomness exists. We will only present one relatively straightforward test in this chapter. More detailed information can be obtained from References [5.6], [5.8], and [5.10] through [5.12].

Table 5.6 Sample Experimental Probability Distribution Function

X	0	1	2	3	4	5	6	7	8	9	10
F(X)	0	.03	.20	.27	.34	.40	.49	.63	.69	.75	1.00

5.12 CHI-SQUARE TEST

The chi-square test is a generalized goodness-of-fit test with a wide range of applications. Here we present the chi-square test as a mechanism for measuring the uniformity of a sample set of random numbers. Since the random number generator can produce an infinite quantity of random numbers and the observed sample is finite, the sample set cannot be truly representative of the universe of random numbers from which it was extracted. We therefore must hypothesize that the sample set was not selected from a universe of uniformly distributed random numbers. The chi-square test estimates the probability that this hypothesis, known as the *null hypothesis,* does not hold.

In general, the chi-square test measures the closeness of an observed sample set to a hypothesized probability distribution from which the sample may have been collected. The sample set is divided into mutually exclusive classes. For the random numbers generated in Example 5.15 it is convenient to use ten classes, each corresponding to the digits 0 through 9. The probability distribution indicates the probability of a single observation from that distribution falling into each class. For uniformly distributed random numbers, if there are K classes, then the probability of an observation falling in any given class is $1/K$. If the total number of observations in a sample set is M, then for each class the expected number of occurrences is given by $X_i = M * p_i$. For uniformly distributed random numbers, $X_i = M/K$. Let $S = (f_1, f_2, \ldots, f_k)$ be the set of observed occurrences, where f_i is the number of observations in the ith class. Using S and the corresponding X_i values, a number can be computed that indicates the closeness of the observed frequencies and expected number of occurrences. This number is known as the *chi-square statistic* and is defined by the following equation.

Definition 5.15

Let $\chi_0{}^2$ be the chi-square statistic, where

$$\chi_0{}^2 = \sum_{i=1}^{K} (f_i - M * p_i)^2 / M * p_i \qquad (5.6)$$

The chi-square statistic is equal to the square of the difference of the observed frequency and the expected number of occurrences divided by the expected number of occurrences. The squaring operation is necessary to prevent positive and negative differences between observed and expected values from canceling each other. The division permits the chi-square statistic to be represented in units rather than units squared.

Note that for uniformly distributed random numbers, the chi-square statistic is computed by

$$\chi_0^2 = \sum_{i=1}^{K} \left(f_i - \frac{M}{K} \right)^2 \Big/ \frac{M}{K}$$

$$= \frac{K}{M} \sum_{i=1}^{K} \left(f_i - \frac{M}{K} \right)^2 \tag{5.7}$$

The chi-square statistic is used to determine the probability of the null hypothesis, which stated that the observed sample was not drawn from the particular distribution. If a good fit between the sample set and the distribution exists, then the probability of the null hypothesis being true is low. The probability of rejection of the null hypothesis when it is true is known as the *significance level* of the chi-square test. The significance level provides the degree of confidence with which the goodness of fit of the sample to the distribution can be accepted. Commonly used values for the significance level are .10, .05, and .01 [5.13].

The significance level for the chi-square test is computed from a probability distribution, known as the chi-square distribution. The two parameters of the chi-square distribution are the chi-square statistic (which is defined in Definition 5.15) and the number of degrees of freedom.

Many statistical tests have the number of degrees of freedom as a parameter [5.14–5.17]. In statistical applications, the number of degrees of freedom is the number of free variables entering into a problem. For the chi-square test, there are $K - 1$ independent frequencies being compared. There are only $K - 1$ independent pairs since

$$\sum_{i=1}^{K} x_i = M \quad \text{and} \quad \sum_{i=1}^{K} p_i = 1$$

Using the above relationships, the observed frequency and expected number of occurrences for the Kth class can be computed from the values of the other $K - 1$ classes.

The significance level of the chi-square test can be obtained from the chi-square statistic and number of degrees of freedom either using a statistical table, such as Table 5.7, or computed analytically [5.18]. The significance level has the following relationship with the chi-square distribution.

Let $\chi_{q,d}^2$ be the point on the chi-square distribution with d degrees of freedom and significance level q. When the number of samples is large and the

Table 5.7 χ^2 Table

Degrees of Freedom	P = 0.99	0.98	0.95	0.90	0.80	0.70	0.50	0.30	0.20	0.10	0.05	0.02	0.01
1	0.000157	0.000628	0.00393	0.0158	0.0642	0.148	0.455	1.074	1.642	2.706	3.841	5.412	6.635
2	0.0201	0.0404	0.103	0.211	0.446	0.713	1.386	2.408	3.219	4.605	5.991	7.824	9.210
3	0.115	0.185	0.352	0.584	1.005	1.424	2.366	3.665	4.642	6.251	7.815	9.837	11.341
4	0.297	0.429	0.711	1.064	1.649	2.195	3.357	4.878	5.989	7.779	9.488	11.668	13.277
5	0.554	0.752	1.145	1.610	2.343	3.000	4.351	6.064	7.289	9.236	11.070	13.388	15.086
6	0.872	1.134	1.635	2.204	3.070	3.828	5.348	7.231	8.558	10.645	12.592	15.033	16.812
7	1.239	1.564	2.167	2.833	3.822	4.671	6.346	8.383	9.803	12.017	14.067	16.622	18.475
8	1.646	2.032	2.733	3.490	4.594	5.527	7.344	9.524	11.030	13.362	15.507	18.168	20.090
9	2.088	2.532	3.325	4.168	5.380	6.393	8.343	10.656	12.242	14.684	16.919	19.679	21.666
10	2.558	3.059	3.940	4.865	6.179	7.267	9.342	11.781	13.442	15.987	18.307	21.161	23.209
11	3.053	3.609	4.575	5.578	6.989	8.148	10.341	12.899	14.631	17.275	19.675	22.618	24.725
12	3.571	4.178	5.226	6.304	7.807	9.034	11.340	14.011	15.812	18.549	21.026	24.054	26.217
13	4.107	4.765	5.892	7.052	8.634	9.926	12.340	15.119	16.985	19.812	22.362	25.472	27.688
14	4.660	5.368	6.571	7.790	9.467	10.821	13.339	16.222	18.151	21.064	23.685	26.873	29.141
15	5.229	5.985	7.261	8.547	10.307	11.721	14.339	17.322	19.311	22.307	24.996	28.259	30.578
16	5.812	6.614	7.962	9.312	11.152	12.624	15.338	18.418	20.465	23.542	26.296	29.633	32.000
17	6.408	7.255	8.672	10.085	12.002	13.531	16.338	19.511	21.615	24.769	27.587	30.995	33.409
18	7.015	7.906	9.390	10.865	12.857	14.440	17.338	20.601	22.760	25.989	28.869	32.346	34.805
19	7.633	8.567	10.117	11.651	13.716	15.352	18.338	21.689	23.900	27.204	30.144	33.687	36.191
20	8.260	9.237	10.851	12.443	14.578	16.266	19.337	22.775	25.038	28.412	31.410	35.020	37.566
21	8.897	9.915	11.591	13.240	15.445	17.182	20.337	23.858	26.171	29.615	32.671	36.343	38.932
22	9.542	10.600	12.338	14.041	16.314	18.101	21.337	24.939	27.301	30.813	33.924	37.659	40.289
23	10.196	11.293	13.091	14.848	17.187	19.021	22.337	26.018	28.429	32.007	35.172	38.968	41.638
24	10.856	11.992	13.848	15.659	18.062	19.943	23.337	27.096	29.553	33.196	36.415	40.270	42.980
25	11.524	12.697	14.611	16.473	18.940	20.867	24.337	28.172	30.675	34.382	37.652	41.566	44.314
26	12.198	13.409	15.379	17.292	19.820	21.792	25.336	29.246	31.795	35.563	38.885	42.856	45.642
27	12.879	14.125	16.151	18.114	20.703	22.719	26.336	30.319	32.912	36.741	40.113	44.140	46.963
28	13.565	14.847	16.928	18.939	21.588	23.647	27.336	31.391	34.027	37.916	41.337	45.419	48.278
29	14.256	15.574	17.708	19.768	22.475	24.577	28.336	32.461	35.139	39.087	42.557	46.693	49.588
30	14.953	16.306	18.493	20.599	23.364	25.508	29.336	33.530	36.250	40.256	43.773	47.962	50.892

samples have been taken from the tested distribution, then the probability that the chi-square statistic, χ_0^2, is greater than $\chi_{q,d}^2$ is q. That is, $p(\chi_0^2 > \chi_{q,d}^2) = q$ if the null hypothesis is false and the sample was obtained from the distribution. The reason for the chi-square statistic being greater than the point on the distribution when the null hypothesis is actually false is the randomness of the sample.

For a particular significance level, if the chi-square statistic of a sample is greater than $\chi_{q,d}^2$, then the sample shows a significant deviation for the hypothetical distribution. Thus, the null hypothesis is accepted as true and the statement that the sample was taken from the distribution must be rejected. Since the probability that the observed difference was due to the randomness of the sample is q, we say that the probability of false rejection is q. If the chi-square statistic is less than $\chi_{q,d}^2$, then the statement that the sample was taken from the distribution is accepted at significance level q. The reader must keep in mind that the chi-square is a statistical test that specifies acceptance with a significance, or confidence, level. The chi-square test is based upon the data supplied, and its result must be interpreted properly and acceptance not taken as a statement of infallible doctrine.

The following observations can be made on the behavior of the χ^2 distribution:

1. $\chi_{q,d}^2 < \chi_{q,e}^2$ if $d < e$.
2. $\chi_{q,d}^2 < \chi_{p,d}^2$ if $p < q$.

These observations indicate that for a given significance level the value of the chi-square distribution increases with the number of degrees of freedom. Also, for a fixed number of degrees of freedom, the value of chi-square distribution decreases with the significance level. Thus we can conclude that for a given theoretical distribution, a sample with a low chi-square statistic is a better fit than a sample with a higher chi-square statistic.

EXAMPLE 5.19

In Example 5.15, 1000 one-digit random numbers were produced by a simple random number generator. The chi-square test can be applied to measure the uniformity of the generated digits. In this case, $M = 1000$ and $K = 10$.

In Example 5.15, the following frequency distribution was observed:

f_0	f_1	f_2	f_3	f_4	f_5	f_6	f_7	f_8	f_9
119	78	96	105	101	88	95	107	95	116

The chi-square statistic is

$$\chi_0^2 = \frac{10}{1000} \sum_{i=0}^{9} \left(f_i - \frac{1000}{10} \right)^2$$

$$= .01 [(119 - 100)^2 + (78 - 100)^2 + (96 - 100)^2 + (105 - 100)^2$$
$$+ (101 - 100)^2 + (88 - 100)^2 + (95 - 100)^2 +$$
$$(107 - 100)^2 + (95 - 100)^2 + (116 - 100)^2]$$
$$100)^2 + (116 - 100)^2$$
$$= .01 (1386) = 13.86$$

For a confidence level of .05 with 9 degrees of freedom, $\chi^2_{.05,9} = 16.919$ according to Table 5.7.

Since $\chi_0^2 < \chi^2_{.05,9}$, we accept at the .05 level the statement that the random number generator produces uniformly distributed random digits.

5.13 GENERATION OF EXPONENTIALLY DISTRIBUTED RANDOM NUMBERS

In Section 10 of this chapter, the difficulty of the general problem of generating nonuniform continuous random numbers was discussed briefly. In the next two sections in this chapter, solutions for certain common probability distributions will be presented. A similar analysis for a much wider range of distributions can be found in Fishman's text [5.6].

Perhaps the most common assumption in a simulation program is that the occurrences of a stochastic variable are randomly distributed about some mean. In many situations when only the mean value is given, the assumption of complete randomness is the only valid assumption. In the next chapter we will discuss methods of estimating distributions from observations of their behavior.

If a stochastic variable is truly random, the time of the next event occurrence is independent of the previous occurrence. Thus, the probability of an event in a time interval t is proportional to t.

Let β be the mean interevent time.
The expected number of events in t is t/β.

Under these assumptions, the probability of exactly K events occurring within an interval t when the mean interevent time is β is given by

$$p(K) = \frac{(t/\beta)^K e^{-t/\beta}}{K!} \tag{5.8}$$

The above distribution is known as the Poisson distribution. For a derivation of the Poisson distribution see Reference [5.19].

From Eq. (5.8) and the definition of probability density and probability distribution functions, the distribution of the time to the next event can be computed for a stochastic variable conforming to the Poisson distribution. Let T be the time until the next event and t be a stochastic variable with a Poisson

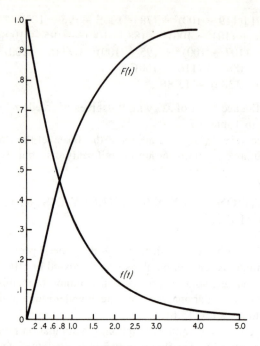

Figure 5.3   Exponential Density and Distribution Functions

distribution. The probability distribution function for an event occurring at time T or less, $F(T)$, is given by

$$F(T) = p(T \leq t)$$
$$= 1 - p(T > t)$$

If T is greater than t, there would be no arrivals in the time interval t. Thus,

$$p(T > t) = p(0)$$

where $p(0)$ can be computed from Eq. (5.8). Hence,

$$F(T) = 1 - p(0)$$
$$= 1 - e^{-t/\beta} \tag{5.9}$$

from Eq. (5.8). From Definition 5.4 it follows that

$$f(t) = \frac{dF(T)}{dt} = \frac{e^{-t/\beta}}{\beta} \tag{5.10}$$

The probability density function described by Eq. (5.10) is known as the *exponential distribution*. Figure 5.3 illustrates the exponential density and distribution functions when $\beta = 1$.

EXAMPLE 5.20

Consider a model of job submittals to a computer system. Assume that jobs arrive every 2 seconds on the average and that their arrival pattern is completely random (described by an exponential distribution). In any 5-second period, the probabilities of exactly 0 through 10 jobs arriving are computed using Eq. (5.10) with $t = 5$, $\beta = 2$, and $K = 0, 1, \ldots, 10$. The results are shown in Table 5.8.

Table 5.8 Probabilities of Exactly K Jobs in a 5-Second Interval

K	0	1	2	3	4	5	6	7	8	9	10
$P(K)$	.082	.205	.257	.214	.134	.067	.028	.010	.003	.001	.0002

In order to generate a series of exponentially distributed random numbers we first generate r, which is uniformly distributed between 0 and 1, and then let $F(X) = r$ and solve for X. Thus,

$$r = F(X) = 1 - e^{-X/\beta}$$

$$\frac{X}{\beta} = -\log(1 - r)$$

We can observe that if r is uniformly distributed, then so is $1 - r$. Therefore, $1 - r$ can be replaced by r, yielding

$$\frac{X}{\beta} = -\ln r$$

or

$$X = -\beta \ln r \tag{5.11}$$

As previously mentioned, the exponential distribution is an exception since it can be generated in a straightforward manner given a uniform random number generator.

EXAMPLE 5.21

For the model in Example 5.20, let us generate the arrival times of the first 1000 jobs. Recall that $\beta = 2$.

```
      INTEGER FREQ(50) , STARS(115), FIVES(24), CLASS , OVER , STAR   EXP00010
      INTEGER SEED                                                    EXP00020
      DATA STAR /1H*/                                                 EXP00030
C                                                                     EXP00040
COMMENT: INITIALIZE MEAN AND RANDOM NUMBER SEED VALUES AND CONSTANTS  EXP00050
COMMENT: INITIALIZE FREQUENCY COUNTS                                  EXP00060
C                                                                     EXP00070
      BETA = 2.0                                                      EXPOCC80
      SEED = 19727                                                    EXP00090
      I = 20403                                                       EXP00100
      M = 32768                                                       EXP00110
      REALM = 32768.0                                                 EXP00120
      DO 100 K = 1,50                                                 EXP00130
         FREQ(K) = 0                                                  EXP00140
100   CONTINUE                                                        EXP00150
C                                                                     EXP00160
COMMENT: GENERATE EXPONENTIALLY DISTRIBUTED RANDOM NUMBERS WITH       EXP00170
COMMENT:    MEAN BETA.                                                EXP00180
COMMENT: FREQUNCY COUNTS ARE MAINTAINED FOR INTERVALS OF SIZE .2      EXP0C190
COMMENT:    BETWEEN 0 AND 5.                                          EXPJ0200
COMMENT: A FREQUENCY COUNT FOR THOSE NUMBERS GREATER THAN 5 IS ALSO   EXP00210
COMMENT:    MAINTAINED.                                               EXP00220
C                                                                     EXPJ0230
      DO 300 K = 1, 1000                                              EXP00240
         SEED = MOD( I * SEED , M )                                   EXP00250
         R = SEED / REALM                                            EXP00260
         EXPO = - BETA * ALOG ( R )                                  EXP0C270
         CLASS = EXPO * 5 + 1                                        EXP00280
         IF ( CLASS .LE. 50 ) GO TO 200                              EXP00290
             OVER = OVER + 1                                         EXP00300
             GO TO 300                                               EXP0031J
200          FREQ(CLASS) = FREQ(CLASS) + 1                           EXP0C320
300   CONTINUE                                                        EXP00330
C                                                                     EXP00340
COMMENT: INITIALIZE FOR OUTPUT                                        EXP00350
C                                                                     EXP00360
      DO 400 K = 1, 115                                               EXP00370
         STARS(K) = STAR                                              EXP00380
400   CONTINUE                                                        EXPJ0390
C                                                                     EXP00400
      DO 500 K = 1,24                                                 EXP00410
         FIVES(K) = ( K - 1 ) * 5                                     EXP00420
500   CONTINUE                                                        EXP00430
C                                                                     EXP00440
COMMENT: PRINT HEADINGS                                               EXP00450
C                                                                     EXP00460
      WRITE( 9 , 600 ) (FIVES(K) , K = 1,24 )                        EXPJ0470
600   FORMAT( 10X , I1 , 4X , I1 , 4X , 18( I2 , 3X) , 4 ( I3 , 2X)) EXP00480
      WRITE( 9 , 700 )                                                EXP00490
700   FORMAT( 10X , 115 ( '_' ) )                                     EXP00500
C                                                                     EXP00510
COMMENT: PRINT FREQUENCIES                                            EXP00520
C                                                                     EXP00530
      POINT = -0.2                                                    EXP00540
      DO 1100 K = 1 ,50                                               EXP00550
         POINT = POINT + 0.2                                          EXP00560
         IF ( FREQ(K) .EQ. 0 ) GO TO 900                             EXP00570
```

FILE: EXPOC   FORTRAN A1   KANSAS STATE UNIVERSITY - CMS V5 PLC 2

```
          KOUNT = FREQ(K)                                          EXP00580
          WRITE( 9 , 800 ) POINT , ( STARS(I) , I = 1 , KCUNT)     EXP00590
800       FORMAT( F4.1 , 5X , '|' , 115 ( A1 ) )                   EXP0C600
          GO TO 1100                                               EXP00610
900       WRITE( 9 , 1000 ) POINT , STAR                           EXP00620
1000      FORMAT( F4.1 , 5X , A1 )                                 EXP00630
1100  CONTINUE                                                     EXP0C640
C                                                                  EXP0C650
COMMENT: PRINT OVERFLOW FREQUENCY                                  EXP00660
C                                                                  EXP00670
      IF ( OVER .EQ. 0 ) GO TO 1300                                EXP00680
      WRITE( 9 , 1200) ( STARS(I) , I = 1 , OVER )                 EXP00690
1200      FORMAT( 'OVER' , 5X , '|' , 115 ( A1 ) )                 EXP0C700
          GO TO 1500                                               EXP00710
1300      WRITE( 9 , 1400 ) STAR                                   EXP00720
1400      FORMAT( 'OVER' , 5X , A1 )                               EXP00730
1500  CONTINUE                                                     EXP00740
C                                                                  EXP00750
      STOP                                                         EXP00760
      END                                                          EXP00770
```

```
        0    5    10   15   20   25   30   35   40   45   50   55   60   65   70   75   80   85   90   95   100  105  110  115

0.0  |*********************************************************************************************************************
0.2  |*****************************************************
0.4  |*******************************************************************************
0.6  |**********************************************************************************
0.8  |***********************************************************************************
1.0  |***********************************************
1.2  |*************************************************
1.4  |*****************************************************
1.6  |**********************************************
1.8  |***********************************
2.0  |*************************************
2.2  |*********************************
2.4  |****************************
2.6  |*******************
3.0  |********************
3.2  |**************
3.4  |*****************
3.6  |*************
3.8  |**********
4.0  |*************
4.2  |*********
4.4  |*******
4.6  |*************
4.8  |***********
5.0  |*******
5.2  |*********
5.4  |********
5.6  |*************
5.8  |******
6.0  |*******
6.2  |*******
6.4  |******
6.6  |****
7.0  |***
7.2  |*****
7.4  |****
7.6  |**
7.8  |*
8.0  |**
8.2  |****
8.4  |***
8.6  |**
8.8  |*
9.0  |*
9.2  |*
9.4  |****
9.6  |
9.8  |***
OVER |*
```

5.14 NORMALLY DISTRIBUTED RANDOM NUMBERS

Another commonly used distribution is the normal distribution in which the frequencies are symmetric about the mean. The normal distribution is often described as a "bell-shaped curve." Two parameters, the mean and standard deviation, are used to describe a normal distribution. The mean and standard deviation were defined in Definitions 5.5 and 5.12, respectively.

Graphically, the value of standard deviation indicates the width of the bell-shaped curve. As depicted in Figure 5.4, a larger value of σ_x indicates a wider curve.

Let X be a normally distributed random number with mean μ_x and standard deviation σ_x. Let

$$Z = (X - \mu_x)\sigma_x \tag{5.12}$$

Note that Z is normally distributed, with mean 0 and standard deviation 1.

The probability density function for Z is

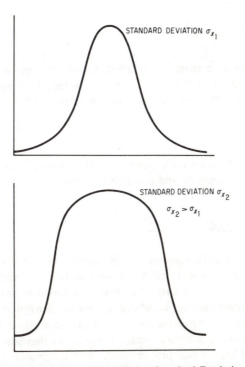

Figure 5.4   Normal Distributions with Differing Standard Deviations

$$f(Z) = \frac{e^{-Z^2/2}}{(2\pi)^{1/2}} \tag{5.13}$$

In order to generate X, a random number is produced using the equation for $f(Z)$. Equation (5.13) is then solved for X. That is,

$$X = \mu_x + \sigma_x Z \tag{5.14}$$

It is very difficult to solve the inverse of $F(Z)$ in order to generate a normally distributed random number. However, the inverse function can be approximated by generating several uniformly distributed random numbers and solving

$$Z = \frac{\left(\sum_{k=1}^{m} r_k\right) - m/2}{\left(\dfrac{m}{12}\right)^{1/12}} \tag{5.15}$$

The distribution of Z approximates the normal distribution as m approaches infinity. Equation (5.15) is fairly difficult to compute except for the case of $m = 12$. Then, the equation

$$Z = \left(\sum_{k=1}^{m} r_k\right) - 6 \tag{5.16}$$

can be used to generate normally distributed random numbers with zero mean and standard deviation of 1. Equation (5.14) can then be used to produce normally distributed random numbers with arbitrary means and standard deviations.

EXAMPLE 5.22

The program shown generates 1000 normally distributed random numbers with mean 20 and standard deviation 2.

5.15 CONCLUSION

The mathematical material discussed in this chapter provides a basis for understanding the statistical aspects of stochastic simulations. Practical rather than theoretical properties are emphasized so that a programmer or the designer of a simulation experiment can feel comfortable with the constructs and apply them properly. This chapter is by no means an exhaustive discussion of the subjects of probability and statistics or even of their application to simulation. However, the material presented here should provide sufficient background to simulate a wide variety of systems. Additional information on probability and statistics in simulation can be found in the references.

```
FILE:  NORMALC  FORTRAN  A1            KANSAS STATE UNIVERSITY - CMS V5 PLC 2


       INTEGER FREQ(49) , STARS(115), FIVES(24), CLASS , OVER , STAR   NORJJJ1J
       INTEGER SEED                                                    NCRJ0020
       REAL MEAN , NORMAL                                              NORO0030
       DATA STAR /1H*/                                                 NCRJJ04J
C                                                                      NGROCC5J
COMMENT: INITIALIZE RANDOM NUMBER SEEDS AND CONSTANTS                  NORJ0060
COMMENT: INITIALIZE MEAN , STANDARD DEVIATION , AND FREQUENCY          NCRJCC7J
CCMMENT:    CCUNTS                                                     NOROCC8J
C                                                                      NCRJCJ9J
       SEED = 19727                                                    NCRO010J
       I = 20403                                                       NJROC11J
       M = 32768                                                       NCRJJ12J
       REALM = 32768.0                                                 NGRO0130
       OVER = 0                                                        NURO0140
       NDER = J                                                        NGRO0150
       BETA = 20.0                                                     NGRJ016J
       STD = 2.0                                                       NCRJJ17J
       DO 100 K = 1,49                                                 NCRU0180
          FREQ(K) = 0                                                  NJROC19J
100    CONTINUE                                                        NCRJ02JJ
C                                                                      NCRO0210
COMMENT: GENERATE NORMALLY DISTRIBUTED RANDOM NUMBERS WITH             NORCC220
COMMENT:    MEAN BETA.                                                 NCRJJ230
CCMMENT: FREQUENCY CCUNTS ARE MAINTAINED FOR INTERVALS OF SIZE .5      NGRCC24J
COMMENT:    BETWEEN 8 AND 32.                                          NCRJJ25J
C                                                                      NCRJ026J
       DO 300 K = 1, 1000                                              NURJ027J
          R =0.0                                                       NCRU0230
          DO 200 L = 1 , 12                                            NCRJC290
             SEED = MOD( I * SEED , M )                                NORJJ3JJ
             R = SEED / REALM + R                                      NCRU031J
200    CONTINUE                                                        NCRO0320
       Z = R - 6.0                                                     NCRJJ33J
       NORMAL = BETA + STD * Z                                         NCRJC34J
       CLASS = NORMAL + NORMAL - 15                                    NUROJ35J
       FREQ(CLASS)= FREQ(CLASS) + 1                                    NGRJ036J
300    CONTINUE                                                        NCRO0370
C                                                                      NORO0380
COMMENT: INITIALIZE FOR OUTPUT                                         NCROC390
C                                                                      NGRO040J
       DO 400 K = 1, 115                                               NCRJC41J
          STARS(K) = STAR                                              NCRJ0420
400    CONTINUE                                                        NORU0430
C                                                                      NCRJJ44J
       DO 500 K = 1,24                                                 NCRO0450
          FIVES(K) = ( K - 1 ) * 5                                     NOROO46J
500    CONTINUE                                                        NCRJJ47J
C                                                                      NCRCJ48J
COMMENT: PRINT HEADINGS                                                NCRJ049J
C                                                                      NCRJ0500
       WRITE( 9 , 600 ) (FIVES(K) , K = 1,24 )                         NJRO0510
600    FORMAT( 10X , I1 , 4X , I1 , 4X , 18( I2 , 3X) , 4 ( I3 , 2X))  NCRJJ52J
       WRITE( 9 , 700 )                                                NORO0530
700    FORMAT( 10X , 115 ( '_' ) )                                     NORO0540
C                                                                      NCRO0550
COMMENT: PRINT FREQUENCIES                                             NGROC56J
C                                                                      NCRJJ57J
```

```
FILE:  NORMALC  FCRTRAN  A1              KANSAS STATE UNIVERSITY - CMS V5 PLC 2


       POINT = 7.5                                        NCR)058)
       DO 1100 K = 1 ,49                                  NCRJC590
          POINT = POINT + 0.5                             NOROC60J
          IF ( FREQ(K) .EQ. 0 ) GO TO 90J                 NCRO0610
          KCUNT = FREQ(K)                                 NUROC620
             WRITE( 9 , 800 ) POINT , ( STARS(I) , I = 1 , KCUNT)  NOROC630
800          FORMAT( F4.1 , 5X , '|' , 115 ( A1 ) )       NCRJC640
             GO TO 1100                                   NOR00650
900          WRITE( 9 , 1)00 ) PCINT , STAR               NCR)066J
1000         FORMAT( F4.1 , 5X , A1 )                     NCROC670
1100   CONTINUE                                           NGRUC680
C                                                         NGRJ069)
CCMMENT: PRINT OVERFLCW FREQUENCY                         NOROC7CO
C                                                         NORO0710
       STOP                                               NCRJO720
       END                                                NCROC730
```

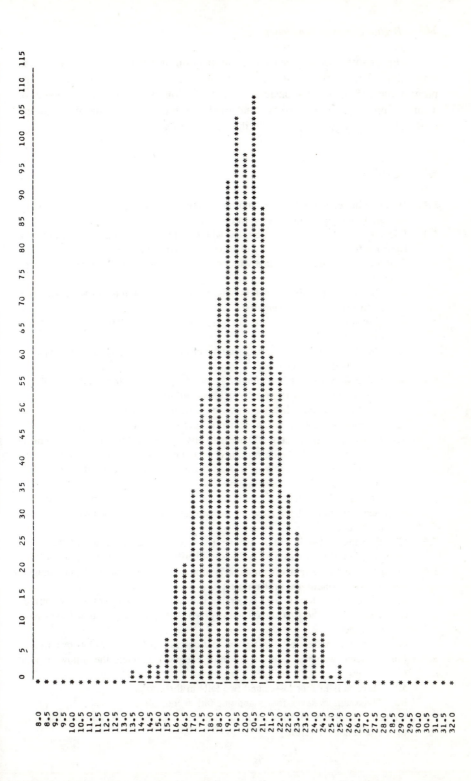

This chapter has emphasized the application of probability and statistics in simulation. This is the most important aspect from the point of view of the programmer. However, the designer of a simulation experiment or a manager of a simulation project must also be concerned with the interpretation of simulation statistics. That subject is treated in the next chapter.

EXERCISES

5.1   Write additive, multiplicative, and mixed random number generators to produce two-digit random numbers between 0.00 and 1.00.

5.2   Use the chi-square test to determine whether the random number generators of Exercise 5.1 generate uniformly distributed random numbers.

5.3   Assume that a coin is weighted with an 80% probability of obtaining a head in a single toss.

    a.   Give the cumulative probability distribution for the number of heads expected in five tosses of the weighted coin.

    b.   Use your own random number generator. Generate 100 sequences of five tosses each.

    c.   Use the chi-square test to measure the closeness of the observed and expected coin toss distributions.

5.4   **a.**   Using your own random number generator, produce 500 normally distributed random numbers with mean 5 and standard deviation 6.

    b.   Plot the frequency distribution of the generated numbers.

    c.   Compute the sample mean, variance, and standard deviation.

    d.   Generate a second set of 500 normally distributed random numbers with mean 5 and standard deviation 6 using $1 - r$ wherever r (a random number uniformly distributed between 0 and 1) was used to produce the first set of normally distributed random numbers.

    e.   Compute the correlation coefficient of the two samples of normally distributed random numbers. Describe the dependence between the random numbers in the two sets.

5.5   Calculate the probability of K arrivals ($K = 0, 1, \ldots, 15$) in an interval of 10 seconds when the arrivals have a Poisson distribution with a mean value of 2.5.

5.6   For a coin that is weighted with an 80% probability of obtaining a head, compute the following conditional probabilities:

    a.   Three tails in four tosses, given that two tails in three tosses have occurred.

    b.   Two tails in the first three tosses, given that three tails in four tosses have occurred.

    c.   Three tails in seven tosses, given that one tail in four tosses has occurred.

5.7   For the same weighted coin of the prior exercise, compute the following joint probabilities:

    a.   Three tails in four tosses and two tails in three tosses.

    b.   Three tails in seven tosses and one tail in four tosses.

5.8   Given the sample probability distribution function taken from a continuous stochastic variable shown below.

    a. Using your random number generator, generate 100 values according to the experimental distribution.

    b. Construct a sample probability distribution function from the generated values.

X	0	1	2	3	4	5	6	7
$F(X)$	.49	.50	.65	.69	.74	.79	.95	1.00

REFERENCES

[5.1] Hogg, R. V., and Tanis, E. A., *Probability and Statistical Inference*. New York: Macmillan, 1977.

[5.2] Larson. H. J., *Introduction to Probability Theory and Statistical Inference*. New York: Wiley, 1969.

[5.3] Pratt, J. W., Raiffo, A. H., and Schlaifer, R., *Introduction to Statistical Decision Theory*. New York: McGraw-Hill, 1965.

[5.4] Weiss, L., *Statistical Decision Theory*. New York: McGraw-Hill, 1961.

[5.5] Chao, L. L., *Statistics: Methods and Analyses*. New York: McGraw-Hill, 1969.

[5.6] Fishman, G. S., *Concepts and Methods in Discrete Event Digital Simulation*. New York: Wiley-Interscience, 1973.

[5.7] Hodgman, C. S. (ed.), *Standard Mathematical Tables*, 12th ed. Cleveland: Chemical Rubber Publishing Company, 1963.

[5.8] Knuth, D. E., *The Art of Computer Programming*, vol. 2. Reading, Mass.: Addison-Wesley, 1969.

[5.9] von Mises, R., *Probability, Statistics, and Truth*. New York: Macmillan, 1957.

[5.10] Madaren, M. D., and Marsaglia, G., "Uniform Random Number Generators," *Journal of the ACM*, vol. 12, no. 1, January 1965, pp. 83–89.

[5.11] Marsaglia, G., "Random Numbers Fall Mainly in the Planes," *Proceedings of the National Academy of Science*, vol. 61, September 1968, pp. 25–28.

[5.12] Whittlesey, J., "A Comparison of Correlational Behavior of Random Number Generators," *Communications of the ACM*, vol. 11, no. 9, September 1968, pp. 641–644.

[5.13] Cochrane, W. G., "The χ^2 Test of Goodness of Fit," *Annals of Mathematical Statistics*, vol. 23, 1952, pp. 315–345.

[5.14] Cramér, H., *Mathematical Methods of Statistics*. Princeton, N.J.: Princeton University Press, 1946.

[5.15] Freund, J. E., *Mathematical Statistics*. Englewood Cliffs, N.J.: Prentice-Hall, 1962.

[5.16] Hoel, P. G., *Introduction to Mathematical Statistics*, 2nd ed. New York: Wiley, 1954.

[5.17] Barr, D. R., and Zehna, P. W., *Probability*. Monterey, Calif.: Brooks/Cole, 1971.

[5.18] Goldstein, R. B., "Chi-Square Quantiles," Algorithm 451, *Communications of the ACM*, vol. 16, no. 8, August 1973, pp. 483–485.

[5.19] Morse, P. M., *Queues, Inventories, and Maintenance*. New York: Wiley, 1958.

6 Design and Analysis of Simulation Experiments

6.1 INTRODUCTION

Thus far the text has emphasized the description and implementation of simulation models. Once a simulation model has been synthesized, it must be exercised in an orderly manner to provide some insight into the system being modeled. A collection of runs of a simulation program comprises a simulation *experiment*. As in the case of any scientific experiment, considerable attention must be devoted to the selection of the input parameters and the analysis of the experimental output.

This chapter describes methods for estimating the parameters of a simulation model and testing the accuracy of the estimates. A number of potential error sources for simulation experiments are enumerated along with guidelines for avoiding the errors. General rules for the interpretation of simulation results are provided along with techniques for improving the accuracy of the statistics produced by the simulation model. The final topic in the chapter is a discussion of model validation, which is one of the most difficult tasks facing the designer of a simulation experiment.

6.2 ESTIMATION OF SYSTEM PARAMETERS

Most simulation models contain several parameters that must be set to describe a specific system or class of systems. In a simulation experiment, certain parameters are varied in order to determine their effect upon system behavior. The values assigned to these parameters are set by the designer using experimental measurements, intuition, sound judgment, etc. ("Etc." includes darts, dice, I Ching, and asking a friend.) This class of parameters is known as *experimental parameters*.

The other class of parameters consists of those whose behavior is described in a consistent manner throughout the course of the simulation experiment. These parameters are termed *system parameters* since a change in their values indicates a substantial change in the system being modeled. A system parameter may be described by a probability distribution; however, the same probability distribution must be used for all runs in the experiment.

For different simulation experiments on the same basic model the classification of parameters as either experimental or system may vary. Consider, as an example, a simulation model of an automobile with a parameter indicating tire pressure. If the purpose of the simulation experiment is to determine the effect of tire pressure on gas mileage, then the tire pressure parameter would be an experimental parameter assigned different values throughout the runs. If the simulation experiment is intended to project the effects of fuels with varying octane counts upon gas mileage, then tire pressure would be treated as a system variable. In this case a value for tire pressure would be determined prior to the beginning of the experiment and held constant through all simulation runs.

There are two problems in describing a system parameter:

1. Selection of the correct probability distribution.
2. Assignment of numerical values to the statistical descriptor (i.e., mean, standard deviation, etc.) of the distribution.

In a purely abstract case, the designer may assume (guess) a distribution and its parameters. Naturally, any such assumptions must be clearly indicated in the analysis of results and should be justified to as great an extent as possible.

When a physical system from which experimental data can be obtained is being modeled, it is generally desirable to use a probability distribution to describe the parameter in the simulation model. Under such circumstances the simulation designer must determine the amount of data to be collected. From an economic point of view, the cost of data collection for the purpose of parameterization should remain at least an order of magnitude less than the expected benefits to be accrued from the simulation study. A statistical test to determine when sufficient data have been collected is presented later in this chapter.

Once a body of data has been accumulated, a probability distribution that describes the data as closely as possible must be selected. The selection of the distribution must be performed by the designer using his/her experience or judgment. When the distribution has been determined, the values of the parameters must be estimated. One of the most powerful estimation techniques is maximum likelihood estimation.

6.3 MAXIMUM LIKELIHOOD PARAMETER ESTIMATION

The maximum likelihood estimation technique produces the set of parameters that have the highest probability of obtaining a given sample of observed data from a specified probability density function.

Assume n independent experimental observations $(X_1, X_2, \ldots, X_n)$ and a probability density function $f(X: q_1, q_2, \ldots, q_m)$ where $Q = q_1, q_2, \ldots, q_m$ are the parameters to be estimated. The likelihood function, L, can be defined as the joint probability function of obtaining the experimental data from the probability density function with parameters $q_1, q_2, \ldots, q_m$.

Hence,

$$L = \prod_{j=1}^{n} f(X_j : q_1, q_2, \ldots, q_m) \tag{6.1}$$

Note that

$$\log L = \sum_{j=1}^{n} \log(f(X_j : q_1, q_2, \ldots, q_m)) \tag{6.2}$$

To compute a maximum likelihood estimate of the parameters Q, the value of the likelihood function L must be maximized. It can be observed that L and $\log L$ have the same relative behavior. That is, $\log L$ increases as L increases and decreases as L decreases. Thus if $\log L$ is maximized for a set of values for Q, then L is also maximized. In order to maximize Eqs. (6.1) and (6.2), the functions can be differentiated with respect to Q and set to 0. In general, derivatives are easier to compute for $\log L$ than for L.

Hence,

$$\frac{\partial \log L}{\partial q_k} = \sum_{j=1}^{n} \frac{\partial f(X_j : q_1 \cdots q_m)/\partial q_k}{f(X_j : q_1 \cdots q_m)} = 0 \qquad K = 1, \ldots, m$$

yields a system of m equations.

If $\bar{Q} = (\bar{q}_1, \bar{q}_2, \ldots, \bar{q}_m)$ is a solution to these equations, then $\bar{Q}$ is a maximum likelihood estimator of Q.

EXAMPLE 6.1

The exponential distribution has one parameter, β (the mean). See Section 5.13 for a discussion of the exponential distribution. In order to determine the maximum likelihood estimate of β, the following steps are necessary. For the probability density function,

$$f(X_\beta) = \frac{e^{-X/\beta}}{\beta}$$

The logarithm of the likelihood function is

$$\sum_{j=1}^{n} \log(f(X_j : \beta)) = \sum_{j=1}^{n} \log \frac{e^{-X_j/\beta}}{\beta}$$

$$= \sum_{j=1}^{n} \left(\log\frac{1}{\beta} + \log e^{-X_j/\beta} \right)$$

$$= \sum_{j=1}^{n} \left[\log\frac{1}{\beta} - \frac{X_j}{\beta} \right]$$

$$= \sum_{j=1}^{n} \log\frac{1}{\beta} - \sum_{j=1}^{n} \frac{X_j}{\beta}$$

$$= n \log\frac{1}{\beta} - \frac{1}{\beta}\sum_{j=1}^{n} X_j$$

In order to maximize the logarithm of the likelihood function, we must set the derivative to 0.

$$0 = \frac{\partial \left[\sum\limits_{j=1}^{n} \log [f(X_j : \beta)] \right]}{\partial\beta}$$

$$= \frac{\partial \left[n \log\frac{1}{\beta} - \frac{1}{\beta}\sum\limits_{j=1}^{n} X_j \right]}{\partial\beta}$$

$$= n\beta \left[\frac{-1}{\beta^2} \right] + \frac{1}{\beta^2}\sum_{j=1}^{n} X_j$$

$$= \frac{-n}{\beta} + \frac{1}{\beta^2}\sum_{j=1}^{n} X_j$$

$$n = \frac{1}{\beta}\sum_{j=1}^{n} X_j$$

$$\beta = \frac{1}{n}\sum_{j=1}^{n} X_j$$

Example 6.1 indicates that the maximum likelihood estimator for the mean of the exponential distribution is obtained by summing all observations and dividing by the total number of observations.

Maximum likelihood estimators can be derived for any function. Naturally, the derivation increases in complexity as the distribution function becomes more complex. A table of maximum likelihood estimators for a large number of distributions can be found in Reference [6.1]. Since the normal distribution was discussed in Chapter 5, it should be mentioned that the maximum likelihood estimate of the standard deviation is

$$\sigma_x = \sqrt{\frac{\sum\limits_{j=1}^{n} X_j{}^2 - \frac{1}{n}\left[\sum\limits_{j=1}^{n} X_j \right]^2}{n}}$$

However, according to Definition 5.11,

$$\sigma_x = \sqrt{\frac{\sum\limits_{j=1}^{n} X_j^2 - \dfrac{1}{n}\left[\sum\limits_{j=1}^{n} X_j\right]^2}{n-1}}$$

(6.3)

is an unbiased estimator of the standard deviation. When an estimate of standard deviation is required, Eq. (6.3) should be used.

There are two notes of caution on maximum likelihood estimators:

1. Parameters estimated from a finite number of samples from a distribution are *estimated* and *not* true parameters.

2. If a poor choice of distributions is made, a maximum likelihood estimate will not produce good results. For example, if one estimated the parameters of a normal distribution for a set of exponentially distributed random numbers, the parameters would describe the closest normal distribution to the data. However, the estimated distribution would not be a close approximation to the distribution from which the samples were taken.

6.4 GOODNESS OF FIT OF ESTIMATED DISTRIBUTIONS

The maximum likelihood estimation technique will yield the best possible set of parameters for fitting a selected distribution to a set of data points. However, use of the maximum likelihood method does not guarantee that the estimated distribution will be an acceptable approximation of the data. A "goodness of fit" test is required to determine the closeness of an approximation. In Chapter 5 the chi-square test was presented as a means of validating the uniformity of random number generators. That application of the chi-square test is a special case of its more general function as a goodness-of-fit test.

When the chi-square test is applied to a distribution with estimated parameters, the calculation of the number of degrees of freedom changes. If S parameters are estimated, then the number of degrees of freedom becomes $K - S - 1$. For a given value of the chi-square statistic, decreasing the number of degrees of freedom makes the acceptance test more strict. Statisticians disagree as to whether $K - 1$ or $K - S - 1$ degrees of freedom should be used when parameters are estimated. The following guidelines represent a compromise between the conflicting viewpoints:

1. If $\chi_0^2 > \chi_{\alpha,K-1}^2$, reject at the α confidence level.
2. If $\chi_0^2 < \chi_{\alpha,K-S-1}^2$, accept at the α confidence level.
3. If $\chi_{\alpha,K-S-1}^2 < \chi_0^2 < \chi_{\alpha,K-1}^2$, then the result is uncertain at the α confidence level.

EXAMPLE 6.2

Assume that a normal distribution is to be estimated from a collection of data points. Recall that the normal distribution has two parameters: the mean and the standard deviation. If the points were grouped in 20 classes and a significance level of .05 employed, one of the following decisions can be made, based upon the value of the chi-square statistic, χ_0^2.

If $\chi_0^2 > \chi^2_{.05,19}$, reject the hypothesis that the points conform to the normal distribution.

If $\chi_0^2 < \chi^2_{.05,17}$, accept the hypothesis that the points conform to the normal distribution.

If $\chi^2_{.05,17} < \chi_0^2 < \chi^2_{.05,19}$, gather more data before making a decision.

6.5 SELECTION OF INTERVALS FOR THE CHI-SQUARE TEST

In order to apply the chi-square test to verify the hypothesis that sample data fit a distribution whose parameters have been estimated, it is necessary to establish the number and size of the intervals to be used in the test. The rule of thumb for selecting intervals is that each interval should be expected to contain the same number of points and that the expected number of occurrences in each interval should exceed 5. For an arbitrary distribution, requiring the intervals to contain the same expected number of points does not imply that the intervals will be uniform in size.

If n is the number of observations and K is the number of intervals, then $n > 5K$ should hold.

If there are K intervals, with identical expected numbers of occurrences, then the probability of an observation falling in any given interval is $1/K$.

Let $q_0, q_1, q_2, \ldots, q_K$ be the boundary points of the intervals. Then

$$F(q_j) = \sum_{i=q_0}^{qj} P(q_i) = \frac{j}{K} \tag{6.4}$$

In order to select the interval boundaries, Eq. (6.4) must be solved for q_j, j = 1, 2, ..., K.

This problem is similar to that of generating random numbers according to some probability density function since the inverse probability distribution function must be solved.

EXAMPLE 6.3

Let us consider the selection of intervals for the exponential distribution.

$$F(q_j) = 1 - e^{-q_j/\beta}$$

From Eq. (6.4) we know that

$$F(q_j) = \frac{j}{K} = 1 - e^{-q_j/\beta}$$

$$e^{-q_j/\beta} = 1 - \frac{j}{K} = \frac{K - j}{K}$$

$$\frac{-q_j}{\beta} = \log \frac{K - j}{K}$$

$$q_j = -\beta \log \frac{K - j}{K}$$

$$= \beta \log \frac{K}{K - j}$$

Table 6.1 lists the interval boundaries for $K = 10$ and $\beta = 2$. Figure 6.1 illustrates the intervals defined in Table 6.1 on a graph of the exponential distribution with mean of 2.

Table 6.1   Sample Intervals for Chi-Square Test—Exponential Distribution

j	q_j
0	0
1	0.211
2	0.446
3	0.713
4	1.022
5	1.386
6	1.833
7	2.408
8	3.219
9	4.605
10	∞

EXAMPLE 6.4

In Example 5.20 we generated 1000 random numbers exponentially distributed with mean 2. Let us apply the chi-square test to determine how closely the 1000 random numbers approximate exponential distributions with means of 2 and 4.

The program shown computes the chi-square statistic for the two means. If we set $\alpha = 0.05$, we can accept the hypothesis that the mean of the generated numbers is 2.0 since $\chi^2(.05,18) = 28.869$. The hypothesis that the mean is 4.0 must be rejected.

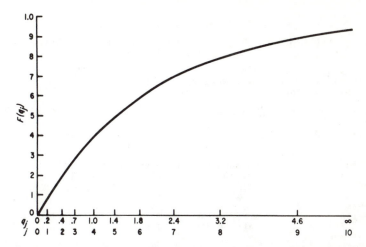

Figure 6.1   Sample Intervals for Chi-Square Test—Exponential Distribution

6.6 POTENTIAL ERRORS IN SIMULATION STUDIES

All projects that involve programming are subject to a large number of potential error sources. However, in a simulation study the designer is faced with perhaps the greatest variety of hazards of any software project. Many of these pitfalls have already been discussed in the text. These problems and their remedies are collected here along with some new difficulties whose solutions are discussed in the succeeding sections.

Among the errors that can lead to incorrect or misinterpreted simulation results are the following:

1. *Bad Random Number Generation.* This source of error can be avoided by using a random number generator built into a programming language. If the randomness of the generator is suspect or if it is user-written, tests such as the chi-square can be performed. One very useful technique is to run the experiment several times using different initial values, or *seeds,* for the random number generator. Techniques for testing random number generators are described in References [6.1] through [6.5].

2. *Incorrect Stochastic Variable Generation.* If a stochastic variable conforms to a particular distribution, care must be taken to ensure that the proper equations are used to describe the distribution. The exponential and normal distributions are treated in Chapter 5. Approximations for other probability distributions can be found in the literature [6.1].

3. *Misrepresentation of System Parameters.* Values assigned to system parameters have a strong bearing upon the output of a simulation experiment. System parameters should only be assigned values that are intrinsic to the system, determined by the designer's experience with or knowledge of the system,

FILE: CHIC   FCRTRAN   A1   KANSAS STATE UNIVERSITY CMS V5 PLC 2

```
      INTEGER FREQ(2,20) , SEED                                    CHI00010
      REAL INTR(2,19) , CHI(2) , BETA(2) , MEAN                    CHI00020
      DATA INFINT /4HINFI/ , N /1HN/                               CHIO0C30
C                                                                  CHI00040
COMMENT: INITIALIZE THE MEAN VALUES                               CHIO0C50
C                                                                  CHI00060
      BETA(1) = 2.0                                                CHI00070
      BETA(2) = 4.0                                                CHIOCC80
C                                                                  CHI00090
COMMENT: GENERATE 20 INTERVALS EACH FOR MEANS CF 2.0 AND 4.0      CHI00100
COMMENT: NOTE THAT THE UPPER BCUND FCR THE 20TH INTERVAL IS       CHI00110
COMMENT: INFINITY.                                                CHI00120
C                                                                  CHI00130
      DO 200 K = 1 , 2                                             CHI00140
         DO 100 J = 1 , 19                                         CHI00150
            INTR(K,J) = BETA(K) * ALOG ( 20.0 / ( 20.0 - J ) )    CHIOC160
100      CONTINUE                                                  CHIO0170
200   CONTINUE                                                     CHI00180
C                                                                  CHI00190
COMMENT: INITIALIZE FOR RANDOM NUMBER GENERATICN                  CHIO0200
C                                                                  CHIO0210
      MEAN = 2.0                                                   CHI00220
      SEED = 19727                                                 CHIU0230
      I = 20403                                                    CHI00240
      M = 32768                                                    CHIO0250
      REALM = 32768.0                                             CHI00260
      DO 400 K = 1 , 2                                             CHI00270
         DO 300 J = 1 , 20                                         CHIO028J
            FREQ(K,J) = 0                                          CHI00290
300      CONTINUE                                                  CHIOC300
400   CONTINUE                                                     CHI00310
C                                                                  CHI00320
COMMENT: GENERATE 1000 EXPONENTIALLY DISTRIBUTED RANDOM NUMBERS   CHI00330
COMMENT: WITH MEAN 2.0.                                           CHI00340
COMMENT: FOR EACH OF THE THREE DISTRIBUTICNS BEING TESTED , THE   CHI00350
COMMENT: FREQUENCY COUNT FOR THE INTERVAL INTO WHICH THE          CHI00360
COMMENT: RANDOM NUMBER FALLS IS INCREMENTED                       CHI00370
C                                                                  CHI00380
      DO 800 L = 1 , 1000                                          CHI00390
         SEED = MOD ( I * SEED , M )                               CHIOC400
         R = SEED / REALM                                          CHI30410
         EXPO = - MEAN * ALOG ( R )                                CHI00420
         DO 700 K = 1 , 2                                          CHI00430
            DO 500 J = 1 , 19                                      CHIO044J
               IF ( EXPC .LE. INTR(K,J) ) GO TO 600               CHI00450
500         CONTINUE                                               CHIO0460
            J = 20                                                 CHI00470
600         FREQ(K,J) = FREC(K,J) + 1                             CHIOC480
700      CONTINUE                                                  CHIJ0490
800   CONTINUE                                                     CHIU0500
C                                                                  CHI00510
COMMENT: INITIALIZE FOR COMPUTATICN OF CHI-SQUARE STATISTIC       CHI00520
C                                                                  CHIOC530
      DO 900 K = 1 , 2                                             CHI00540
         CHI(K) = 0.0                                              CHIOC550
900   CONTINUE                                                     CHIOC560
C                                                                  CHIJ0570
```

```
FILE:  CHIC      FORTRAN  A1                    KANSAS STATE UNIVERSITY CMS V5 PLC 2

COMMENT: COMPUTE CHI-SQUARE STATISTIC.                                     CHI00580
COMMENT: NOTE THAT EACH INTERVAL IS EXPECTED TO CONTAIN 50 ELEMENTS        CHI00590
C                                                                          CHI00600
         DO 1100 K = 1 , 2                                                 CHI00610
            DO 1000 J = 1 , 20                                             CHI00620
               CHI (K) = CHI(K) + ( ABS ( FREC(K,J) - 50.0 ) ** 2.0 ) /    CHI00630
C                        50.0                                              CHI00640
1000        CONTINUE                                                       CHI00650
1100     CONTINUE                                                          CHI00660
C                                                                          CHI00670
COMMENT: OUTPUT RESULTS                                                    CHI00680
C                                                                          CHI00690
         DO 1500 K = 1 , 2                                                 CHI00700
            WRITE( 9 , 1200 ) ( INTR(K,J) , J = 1 , 19 ) , INFINT , N      CHI00710
1200        FORMAT( ' INTERVAL ' , 19 F6.2 , 1X , A4 , A1 )                CHI00720
            WRITE( 9 , 1300 ) ( FREQ(K,J) , J = 1 ,20 )                    CHI00730
1300        FORMAT( ' FREQUENCY' , 20 ( 3X , I3 ) )                        CHI00740
            WRITE( 9 , 1400 ) BETA(K) , CHI(K)                            CHI00750
1400        FORMAT ( 10X , 'THE CHI-SQUARE STATISTIC FOR MEAN ' ,F8.6,     CHI00760
C                     ' IS ' , E15.8 )                                     CHI00770
1500     CONTINUE                                                          CHI00780
C                                                                          CHI00790
         STOP                                                              CHI00800
         END                                                              CHI00810
```

```
INTERVAL   0.10  0.21  0.33  0.45  0.58  0.71  0.86  1.02  1.20  1.39  1.60  1.83
FREQUENCY   61    55    55    40    47    60    54    41    43    45    56    45

           2.10  2.41  2.77  3.22  3.79  4.61  5.99 INFIN
            58    47    46    50    39    39    61    58

THE CHI-SQUARE STATISTIC FOR MEAN 2.000000 IS  0.22559937E 02


INTERVAL   0.21  0.42  0.65  0.89  1.15  1.43  1.72  2.04  2.39  2.77  3.19  3.67
FREQUENCY  115    90    88    91    64    62    65    78    53    47    46    36

           4.20  4.82  5.55  6.44  7.59  9.21 11.98 INFIN
            30    31    31    27    24    13     8     1

THE CHI-SQUARE STATISTIC FOR MEAN 4.000000 IS  0.36779907E 03
```

or estimated by statistical methods. The procedure for statistical parameter estimation is as follows:

    a.   Select the distribution to describe the system parameter.
    b.   Estimate the parameters of the distribution (e.g., maximum likelihood estimation).
    c.   Test the closeness of the estimated parameters and available data.

4. *Programming Errors.* The implementation of the simulation model in a programming language is perhaps the most error-prone portion of the simulation process. Detection of programming errors still remains an art form in spite of the effort of workers in the area of software engineering. The most practical method for program checking in simulation is manually "walking through" the program using simple numerical values. If the program is organized in a modular fashion as recommended in Chapter 1, the "walk-through" process is facilitated considerably. When the program is in its initial execution test stages, intermediate results should be printed at various points in the program to aid in the checking of the model. An output trace of program behavior is often an invaluable debugging tool. It is the consensus of most people with considerable software experience that the number of execution time errors can be reduced by a careful, well-structured design that produces a modular program [6.6–6.9].

5. *Invalid Model.* Although in terms of frequency most errors arise in the programming portion of the simulation experiment, the most significant and most difficult to detect errors arise in the modeling phase. Modeling is certainly the most subjective step of the simulation. Errors in the model can be avoided by careful preparation and adherence to system specifications and close communication with and verification by persons knowledgeable with the details of the system behavior.

6. *Data Collection Errors.* Errors in data collection can occur either by a mechanical or human failure, which produces an incorrect number, or by poor collection methodology. Errors of the first type can be minimized (but not eliminated) without much difficulty. In terms of data collection techniques, one important rule is to collect data at regular intervals, not sporadically when an event occurs. A rather difficult question is the determination of the amount of data to be collected. Economically, a balance between the cost of data collection and the value of the simulation must be maintained. Statistically, sufficient data should be collected to describe the observed process accurately. The material in Sections 6.10 and 6.11 is applicable to the sample data size problem.

7. *Poor Selection of System Parameters.* The selection of system parameters is a simulation experiment design decision. Parameters are classified as either experimental or system, depending upon the goal of the simulation experiment and the nature of the system under study. Parameters should receive the

system designation only if a representative distribution is known or can be estimated or if preliminary simulation runs have indicated that the precise values assumed by the parameter are not critical to the output of the simulation.

8. *Improper Parameter Estimation.* The estimation of system parameter values from experimental data is a key factor in simulation procedure. An error in this phase could invalidate the entire experiment. Use of the maximum likelihood estimate will provide the best fit for a given distribution. Care must be taken that the correct estimation method is used.

9. *Numerical Errors.* The effect of numerical errors depends upon the complexity of the computations and the precision of the data in the model. The values of the output parameters cannot be given a greater precision than the precision of the input parameters from which they are derived. One must be aware of the effects of truncation and roundoff in digital computations when the final output is interpreted.

10. *Influence of Initial Conditions.*

11. *Influence of Final Conditions.*

12. *Poor Validation Techniques.*

The last three problem areas are discussed in Sections 6.8, 6.9, and 6.12, respectively.

6.7 SIMULATION OUTPUT ANALYSIS

When a simulation run is complete, its output is generally a set of numeric values for certain variables. By exercising the model several times using different random number seeds, a collection of values for each output variable can be obtained. The simulation designer must now analyze this collection of numbers to determine the conclusion of the simulation experiment. One approach toward reducing the simulation output to a more meaningful and understandable form is to represent the behavior of the output variables with probability distributions. The same methods (i.e., maximum likelihood and chi-square) that are applicable to estimation of input distributions can be employed to estimate the distributions of the output variables. As in the input case, the number of data points is an important consideration. The determination of sample size is discussed in Section 6.10.

The method of describing the behavior of output variables discussed in the previous paragraph is known as static output analysis, since the initial state of the system was fixed. In many systems the initial state is invariant; hence a static analysis is completely acceptable. However, if the initial conditions of the real system may vary, the initial state of the model must be altered using an appropriate range of values. The output variables must then be represented as conditional probability distributions, dependent upon the initial state. The analysis of output variables with varying initial conditions is known as *dynamic output analysis*.

6.8 EFFECT OF INITIAL CONDITIONS ON SIMULATION RESULTS

The dependence between initial conditions and final results exists to a certain extent in all simulation models. In some cases, a precise set of initial conditions is required to describe the system correctly. For example, in a model of bank teller utilization, all lines are empty at the beginning of banking hours. Thus it is valid to initialize the simulation model with empty queues and idle tellers. However, the telephone system for a large city, while completely idle when first installed many years ago, is never idle in any normal situation. Therefore, if a simulation run of a telephone system model started with empty queues and idle lines, the initial condition would improperly influence the statistics produced.

In order to obtain meaningful statistics, the bias introduced by the initial condition must be reduced. One approach to reducing this type of statistical bias is to ignore the statistics collected at the beginning of the run until the model reaches a state more closely corresponding to the real system. This can be accomplished by delaying the activation of the statistical routines for a brief period of time. In this manner the initial measurements of queue lengths and facility utilization, which would be unrealistically low, are eliminated from the computation of the final statistics.

6.9 EFFECT OF FINAL CONDITIONS ON SIMULATION RESULTS

The final state of a simulation model can adversely affect the results of a simulation run in a similar manner to the initial state. If, at termination of the simulation, entities remain in queues and the queue times of these entities are used in the statistical analysis, then the statistics will be biased. If the entities that have not received service are included in the final statistics, the implicit assumption is made that these entities were serviced at the termination of the simulation run. As indicated in Section 2.10, the mean waiting time for a queue must be computed using the information on only those entities that have been serviced; see Eq. (2.5). The unbiased value of the mean queue length is computed by monitoring the queue length and averaging queue length with respect to time; see Eq. (2.2).

6.10 DETERMINATION OF SAMPLE SIZE

In all stochastic simulation experiments a model of the real system is exercised some number of times in an attempt to obtain a sufficient number of data points to describe the behavior of the system accurately. Even if the model were a totally accurate portrayal of a random system, an infinite number of data points would be required to simulate the system correctly. Since it is impossible to generate an infinite number of points in a computer simulation, some guidelines are necessary to determine when a sufficient number of simulation runs have been made.

The first consideration must be economic; a simulation study is an investment that returns an increase in knowledge of the behavior or structure of the system as its dividend. The cost of the simulation study must remain in balance with the expected value of the information obtained. For example, if an organization is considering the purchase of a large quantity of computer equipment and software, a simulation study is appropriate for determining the most suitable structure of the computing system (large mainframe vs. network of minicomputers, data base management system vs. information retrieval system, etc.). The maximum cost of the simulation study should be approximately 10% of the budgeted cost of the computer system. An upper limit on simulation cost in the range of 10% should be used in all simulation studies.

In academic simulation studies the investigator may not have a financial value placed upon the results of the study. Even in an academic environment, however, simulation studies must be governed by constraints such as computer and personnel time.

Once the upper limit on the cost of the simulation study has been determined, a maximum number of possible simulation runs can be computed. However, the designer of the simulation experiment should not make the maximum number of runs immediately, since it may be possible to obtain sufficient accuracy with a smaller number of executions. The guideline that can be applied to determine the necessary number of iterations is to repeat the experiment until the variance of the estimated parameters of the output distribution is less than some preset values. Figure 6.2 presents a flowchart of the process of estimating the output values of a simulation model given a minimum acceptable variance of the sample means.

6.11 VARIANCE REDUCTION

The argument of the preceding section indicates that a technique for reducing the variance of the output statistics obtained from a series of simulation runs has both economic and statistical value. One such variance reduction technique is known as *antithetic sampling*. The basic idea of antithetic sampling is to execute pairs of simulation runs where if r is used as a random number at a point in the first run, then $1 - r$ is used at the same point in the second run.

It can be shown that antithetic sampling does reduce variance. Let e_i be the estimate of a variable obtained on the ith replication of the simulation experiment. Then over k experiments the estimate of the parameter is

$$e = \frac{1}{k}\sum_{i=1}^{k} e_i$$

The sample variance of the estimates is

$$R_{ee} = \frac{1}{k}\left[\sum_{i=1}^{k} R_{ii} + 2\sum_{\substack{j=1 \\ j\neq 1}}^{k} R_{ij} \right] \tag{6.5}$$

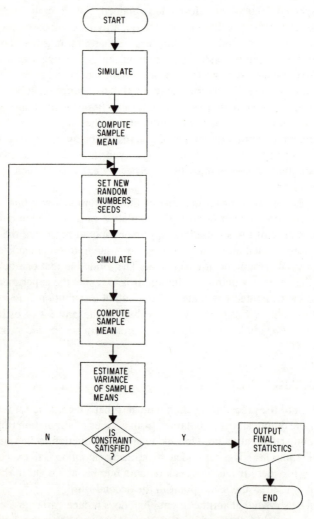

Figure 6.2 Determination of Required Number of Simulation Runs

For a given run of the simulation model the variance of the estimate, R_{ii}, cannot be reduced. Therefore, if the result of Eq. (6.5) is to be reduced, the covariance between the estimates, R_{ij}, must be minimized. Lemma 5.2 states that if two stochastic variables are independent, their covariance is zero. However, according to Definition 5.11, the covariance can be negative. A negative covariance is more desirable than a zero covariance for reducing the variance of the estimates. Therefore it is desirable that the estimates of the output variables be strongly negatively correlated.

Antithetic sampling is intended to yield negative correlation of output variables produced on successive runs. By using r as a random number in one run and $1 - r$ at the same point in the second run, the stochastic variables in the simulation model will be negatively correlated. The degree of negative correlation of the output variables depends upon the form of their probability distributions [6.1]. Antithetic sampling can be applied to generate negatively correlated stochastic variables. Example 6.5 illustrates the effect of antithetic sampling on uniformly distributed stochastic variables.

EXAMPLE 6.5

Let X be a stochastic variable between b and $b + a$. Thus $X = ar + b$, where r is a uniformly distributed random number between 0 and 1. If on the ith replication of the simulation experiment

$$X_i = ar + b$$

then using antithetic sampling, on the $(i + 1)$th. run,

$$X_{i+1} = a(1 - r) + b$$

The correlation coefficient of X_i and X_{i+1} will indicate the type of correlation between the two variables. In order to compute the correlation coefficient, the expected value, sample variance, and sample covariance are necessary.

Since $E(r) = E(1 - r) = \frac{1}{2}$, then

$$E(X_i) = E(X_{i+1}) = \frac{a}{2} + b$$

The sample variances of X_i and X_{i+1} can be computed by

$$R_{ii} = E(X_i - E(X_i))^2$$

$$= E\left(ar_i + b - \frac{a}{2} - b \right)^2$$

$$= E\left(a^2 r_i^2 - a^2 r_i + \frac{a}{4}\right)^2$$

$$= a^2 E\left(r_i^2 - r_i + \frac{1}{4}\right)$$

$$= a^2 \int_0^1 \left(r_i^2 - r_i + \frac{1}{4}\right) dr_i$$

$$= a^2 \left[\frac{r_i^3}{3} - \frac{r_i^2}{2} + \frac{r_i}{4}\right]_0^1$$

$$= a^2 \left(\frac{1}{3} - \frac{1}{2} + \frac{1}{4}\right) = \frac{a^2}{12}$$

The value $R_{i+1\,i+1} = a^2/12$ can be derived in a similar manner. The sample covariance of X_i and X_{i+1} can now be computed.

$$R_{i\,i+1} = E((X_i - E(X_i))(X_{i+1} - E(X_{i+1})))$$

$$= E\left(ar_i + b - \frac{a}{2} - b\right)\left(a(1 - r_i) + b - \frac{a}{2} - b\right)$$

$$= E\left(\left(ar_i - \frac{a}{2}\right)\left(\frac{a}{2} - ar_i\right)\right)$$

$$= E\left(-a^2 r_i^2 + a^2{}_i - \frac{a^2}{4}\right)$$

$$= -a^2 E\left(r_i^2 + r_i - \frac{1}{4}\right)$$

From the derivation of the variance, we know that

$$E\left(r_i^2 + r_i - \frac{1}{4}\right) = \frac{1}{12}$$

$$R_{i\,i+1} = -\frac{a^2}{12}$$

The type and strength of the correlation can be determined from the correlation coefficient.

$$C_{i\,i+1} = \frac{R_{i\,i+1}}{\sqrt{R_{ii}\,R_{i+1\,i+1}}} = \frac{-a^2/12}{\sqrt{(a^2/12)(a^2/12)}} = -1$$

Thus the two successive values of the stochastic variable are perfectly negatively correlated.

6.12 VALIDATION

One of the principal emphases of this chapter is the development of techniques that ensure accuracy of the simulation statistics. Methods have been presented for reducing bias due to initial and final conditions, for estimating the proper number of samples to collect and simulation runs to perform, and for reducing the variance of stochastic variables in the simulation model. Since the benefits of all of these methods can be invalidated by a single programming error in the model, great care must be taken to ensure that the model has been properly implemented. Even if a simulation program is proved to be a "correct" representation of the model, there may be a basic flaw in the concept of the model that prevents the faithful replication of the real system.

It is imperative that the designer of a simulation experiment realize that simulation results must be analyzed and conclusions formulated from an imperfect model of a real system. The designer of the experiment must not state that the behavior of the system projected by the model will occur with absolute certainty. However, it is possible to establish confidence intervals for certain statistical values. Determination of confidence intervals is one of the topics in this section.

There are several levels of validation for a simulation study. The level of validation for a given study is dependent upon the amount of information available on the system being studied.

The first check is to determine whether the model behaves in a "reasonable" manner. This is, of course, a highly subjective method of validation. However, very gross errors can be eliminated at this level. For instance, it was quite evident to a programmer that his submarine model contained an error since it would fly instead of dive. The programmer must not form preconceived notions of the result of the simulation study and then attempt to force the model to behave in a corresponding manner. For example, the designer of a simulation study for the bank teller simulation may be convinced, prior to the simulation, that no more than two tellers are necessary to handle the bank's transactions. However, the design, parameterization, and implementation of the teller model must not reflect this prejudice.

A model of a stochastic system should produce different results on any given run because of its inherent randomness. Several repetitions of the experiment are required to reduce the effects of randomness. One must never accept the results of a single simulation run as an acceptable approximation of the behavior of a stochastic system. In Section 6.10 a method for determining the number of iterations of the experiment was described. This method involves repeating the experiment until the variance of the output variables is less than some acceptable value. If the variance increases rather than decreases with the number of iterations, the correctness of the simulation model must then be suspect.

When an acceptable number of iterations have been made, the average values of the output values can be presented as the results of the simulation program. Again, due to the randomness of the system, these values must be treated as approximations. It is possible to establish confidence intervals for the output values by using the t-test. Only the utilization of the t-test is explained in this section. A theoretical treatment of the t-test can be found in References [6.10] through [6.12].

Table 6.2 contains the values of the t statistic for given degrees of freedom and significance level. Let $t_{\alpha,d}$ represent the t statistic for d degrees of freedom and significance level α. For example, $t_{.05,9} = 2.262$.

If a simulation experiment has been replicated k times, and for the stochastic variable X, the sample mean m_X and sample variance R_{XX} have been computed, the confidence interval for the true mean can be obtained from the following equation:

$$m_X \pm t_{\alpha, K-1} \sqrt{\frac{R_{XX}}{K}}$$

or

$$m_X - t_{\alpha,K-1} \sqrt{\frac{R_{XX}}{K}} \leq \mu_X \leq m_X + t_{\alpha, K-1} \sqrt{\frac{R_{XX}}{K}} \qquad (6.6)$$

Equation (6.6) gives a $1 - \alpha$ confidence interval for the mean of X.

EXAMPLE 6.6

In the simulation model of the bank, assume that the amount of time that all tellers were idle is measured. Table 6.3 is a collection of these idle times from nine simulation runs. The sample mean and variance can be computed for the idle times by

Table 6.3 Sample Idle Times

.008
.003
.012
.009
.009
.008
.004
.011
.008

Table 6.2 Table for t-Test of Significance between Two Sample Means

Degree of Freedom	P = 0.9*	0.8	0.7	0.6	0.5	0.4	0.3	0.2	0.1	0.05	0.02	0.01
1	0.158	0.325	0.510	0.727	1.000	1.376	1.963	3.078	6.314	12.706	31.821	63.657
2	0.142	0.289	0.445	0.617	0.816	1.061	1.386	1.886	2.920	4.303	6.965	9.925
3	0.137	0.277	0.424	0.584	0.765	0.978	1.250	1.638	2.353	3.182	4.541	5.841
4	0.134	0.271	0.414	0.569	0.741	0.941	1.190	1.533	2.132	2.776	3.747	4.604
5	0.132	0.267	0.408	0.559	0.727	0.920	1.156	1.476	2.015	2.571	3.365	4.032
6	0.131	0.265	0.404	0.553	0.718	0.906	1.134	1.440	1.943	2.447	3.143	3.707
7	0.130	0.263	0.402	0.549	0.711	0.896	1.119	1.415	1.895	2.365	2.998	3.499
8	0.130	0.262	0.399	0.546	0.706	0.889	1.108	1.397	1.860	2.306	2.896	3.355
9	0.129	0.261	0.398	0.543	0.703	0.883	1.100	1.383	1.833	2.262	2.821	3.250
10	0.129	0.260	0.397	0.542	0.700	0.879	1.093	1.372	1.812	2.228	2.764	3.169
11	0.129	0.260	0.396	0.540	0.697	0.876	1.088	1.363	1.796	2.201	2.718	3.106
12	0.128	0.259	0.395	0.539	0.695	0.873	1.083	1.356	1.782	2.179	2.681	3.055
13	0.128	0.259	0.394	0.538	0.694	0.870	1.079	1.350	1.771	2.160	2.650	3.012
14	0.128	0.258	0.393	0.537	0.692	0.868	1.076	1.345	1.761	2.145	2.624	2.977
15	0.128	0.258	0.393	0.536	0.691	0.866	1.074	1.341	1.753	2.131	2.602	2.947
16	0.128	0.258	0.392	0.535	0.690	0.865	1.071	1.337	1.746	2.120	2.583	2.921
17	0.128	0.257	0.392	0.534	0.689	0.863	1.069	1.333	1.740	2.110	2.567	2.898
18	0.127	0.257	0.392	0.534	0.688	0.862	1.067	1.330	1.734	2.101	2.552	2.878
19	0.127	0.257	0.391	0.533	0.688	0.861	1.066	1.328	1.729	2.093	2.539	2.861
20	0.127	0.257	0.391	0.533	0.687	0.860	1.064	1.325	1.725	2.086	2.528	2.845
21	0.127	0.257	0.391	0.532	0.686	0.859	1.063	1.323	1.721	2.080	2.518	2.831
22	0.127	0.256	0.390	0.532	0.686	0.858	1.061	1.321	1.717	2.074	2.508	2.819
23	0.127	0.256	0.390	0.532	0.685	0.858	1.060	1.319	1.714	2.069	2.500	2.807
24	0.127	0.256	0.390	0.531	0.685	0.857	1.059	1.318	1.711	2.064	2.492	2.797
25	0.127	0.256	0.390	0.531	0.684	0.856	1.058	1.316	1.708	2.060	2.485	2.787
26	0.127	0.256	0.390	0.531	0.684	0.856	1.058	1.315	1.706	2.056	2.479	2.779
27	0.127	0.256	0.389	0.531	0.684	0.855	1.057	1.314	1.703	2.052	2.473	2.771
28	0.127	0.256	0.389	0.530	0.683	0.855	1.056	1.313	1.701	2.048	2.467	2.763
29	0.127	0.256	0.389	0.530	0.683	0.854	1.055	1.311	1.699	2.045	2.462	2.756
30	0.127	0.256	0.389	0.530	0.683	0.854	1.055	1.310	1.697	2.042	2.457	2.750
∞	0.12566	0.25335	0.38532	0.52440	0.67449	0.84162	1.03643	1.28155	1.64485	1.95996	2.32634	2.57582

$$m_X = \frac{1}{9} \sum_{i=1}^{9} X_i = \frac{.072}{9} = .008$$

$$R_{XX} = \frac{1}{8} \sum_{i=1}^{9} (X_i - m_X)^2 = \frac{.68 \times 10^{-4}}{8} = .85 \times 10^{-5}$$

From Table 6.2, $t_{.05,8} = 2.306$. Thus the 95% confidence interval for the mean idle time is

$$.008 - 2.306\sqrt{\frac{.85 \times 10^{-5}}{9}} \leq \mu_X \leq .008 + 2.306\sqrt{\frac{.85 \times 10^{-5}}{9}}$$

$$.008 - 2.306\,(.9718 \times 10^{-3}) \leq \mu_X \leq .008 + 2.306\,(.9718 \times 10^{-3})$$
$$.008 - .0022 \leq \mu_X \leq .008 + .0022$$
$$.0058 \leq \mu_X \leq .0102$$

The test described above provides a confidence measure for the value of an output parameter of the simulation. The test does not measure the closeness of the simulation model to the real system. If statistics on the behavior of the real system are available, the t-test can be used in the verification of the simulation model. The t-test can test the hypothesis that the simulated and measured means are significantly different at level α. Let M_r and R_r be the means and variance of the measurements of the real system. Let M_s and R_s be their counterparts for the results of the simulation experiment. Also let K_r and K_s be the number of sample points for the real system and simulation model, respectively.

The standard error of difference between the sample means is given by

$$S_D = \sqrt{\frac{K_r R_r + K_s R_s}{K_r + K_s - 2}}\sqrt{\frac{K_r + K_s}{K_r K_s}} \tag{6.7}$$

The standard error of difference is then used to determine the t ratio

$$t = \frac{|M_r - M_s|}{S_D} \tag{6.8}$$

The number of degrees of freedom for this test is $d = K_r + K_s - 2$. In order to apply the t-test at level α, t is compared against $t_{(\alpha,d)}$.

If $t < t_{(\alpha,d)}$, then we accept the hypothesis that the means are equal at significance level α. Otherwise, the hypothesis is rejected.

Accepting the hypothesis at level α means that the probability that the differences between the means is not due to randomness is α.

EXAMPLE 6.7

Let us assume that measurements are available on the teller idle times used in Example 6.6. Assume that 14 measurements were taken yielding a mean of 0.095 with variance $.50 \times 10^{-5}$. In the notation of Eqs. (6.7) and (6.8),

$$K_r = 14 \quad m_r = .0095 \quad R_r = .50 \times 10^{-5}$$
$$K_s = 9 \quad m_s = .0080 \quad R_s = .85 \times 10^{-6}$$

Thus

$$
\begin{aligned}
S_D &= \sqrt{\frac{(14)(.50 \times 10^{-5}) + (9)(.85 \times 10^{-5})}{14 + 9 - 2}} \sqrt{\frac{14 + 9}{(14)(9)}} \\
&= \sqrt{\frac{.1465 \times 10^{-3}}{21}} \sqrt{\frac{23}{126}} = \sqrt{.6976 \times 10^{-5}} \sqrt{.1825} \\
&= (.2641 \times 10^{-2})(.4272) = .1128 \times 10^{-2}
\end{aligned}
$$

and

$$
t = \frac{|.0095 - .0080|}{.1128 \times 10^{-2}} = 1.330
$$

For 21 degrees of freedom and .05 significance level, 1.330 is below the t statistic, 2.080. Thus we accept the hypothesis at the .05 significance level that the means are statistically close. Therefore, we can consider the simulation model to be an acceptable representation of the real system.

Some caution about the use of the t-test is necessary. The t-test does assume that the underlying distributions of the two populations are normal. Therefore, some justification of this assumption is necessary.

6.13 CONCLUSION

The point of view of the simulation experiment designer is stressed in this chapter. The problems involved in the design of a simulation experiment are emphasized. Particular attention has been paid to the collection, estimation, and verification of input parameters, potential errors in a simulation study, and the analysis and validation of simulation output. One final point that must be repeated for the designer of a simulation experiment or the manager of a simulation project is that one must at all times retain the distinction between a model and the real system when digesting the results of a simulation study.

EXERCISES

6.1 Generate 1000 normally distributed random numbers using mean 5 and standard deviation 1 as parameters of your generation routine. Use the maximum likelihood method to estimate the mean and standard deviation of the generated numbers.

6.2 Use the chi-square test at the .05 level to determine whether the numbers generated in the previous exercise are normally distributed with mean 5 and standard deviation 1.

6.3 Generate 500 exponentially distributed random numbers with mean 15. Compute the interval boundaries for the chi-square test when K (the number of intervals) is equal to 20. Use the chi-square test at the .05 level to determine whether the sample numbers are exponentially distributed with mean 15. Repeat for $K = 5$, 10, 50, 100.

6.4 Generate 1000 exponentially distributed random numbers with mean 3.5; then generate a second set of 1000 exponentially distributed random numbers with mean 3.5 such that whenever r (a uniform random number between 0 and 1) is used in generating the first set of numbers, $1 - r$ is used in the generation of the second set. Using the two sample sets, estimate the mean of the generated random numbers and compute the sample variance of the estimates.

6.5 Generate 15 sets of normally distributed random numbers with mean 2 and standard deviation 1. For both the mean and the standard deviation, compute the sample mean and sample variance. Determine the 95% confidence interval, based upon the t-test, for the mean and standard deviation of the generated numbers.

6.6 In the process of validating a simulation model of a tire manufacturing plant, the following measurements on the number of radial tires produced daily were obtained:

3261	3098	3814	3229
3747	3462	3352	3104
3529	3911	3478	3615

The simulation model yielded the following projected daily yields:

3914	3753	3013	3811	4001
3826	3519	3064	3779	3104
3084	3642	3991	3679	3829

Can we accept the hypothesis that the means are statistically close, using the t-test at the .05 significance level?

REFERENCES

[6.1] Fishman, G. S., *Concepts and Methods in Discrete Event Digital Simulation*. New York: Wiley-Interscience, 1973.

[6.2] Knuth, D. E., *The Art of Computer Programming,* vol. 2. Reading, Mass.: Addison-Wesley, 1969.

[6.3] Madaren, M. D., and Marsaglia, G., "Uniform Random Number Generators," *Journal of the ACM,* vol. 12, no. 1, January 1965, pp. 83–89.

[6.4] Marsaglia, G., "Random Numbers Fall Mainly in the Planes," *Proceedings of the National Academy of Sciences,* vol. 61, September 1968, pp. 25–28.

[6.5] Whittlesey, J., "A Comparison of Correlational Behavior of Random Number Generators," *Communications of the ACM,* vol. 11, no. 9, September 1968, pp. 641–644.

[6.6] Aron, J. D., *The Program Development Process.* Reading, Mass.: Addison-Wesley, 1974.

[6.7] Dahl, O. J., Dijkstra, E. W., and Hoare, C. A. R., *Structured Programming.* New York: Academic Press, 1972.

[6.8] McGowan, C. L., and Kelly, J. R., *Top-Down Structured Programming Techniques.* New York: Petrocelli/Charter, 1975.

[6.9] Van Tassell, D., *Program Style Design, Efficiency, Debugging, and Testing.* Englewood Cliffs, N.J.: Prentice-Hall, 1974.

[6.10] Blakeslee, D. W., and Chinn, W. G., *Introductory Statistics and Probability: A Basis for Decision Making.* Boston: Houghton Mifflin, 1971.

[6.11] Blum, J. B., and Rosenblatt, J. I., *Probability and Statistics.* Philadelphia: Saunders, 1972.

[6.12] Chao, L. L., *Statistics: Methods and Analyses.* New York: McGraw-Hill, 1969.

7 The Continuous Simulation Modeling Program (CSMP)

7.1 CONTINUOUS SIMULATION

In the first chapter, simulation models are classified as either continuous or discrete depending upon the manner in which changes occur within the system. A continuous system simulation model describes the rates at which the values of the attributes change with respect to time. The behavior of the variables in these models is depicted by continuous functions rather than by a finite set of points as in the discrete case.

A continuous system model consists of a set of equations specifying the values of the variable attributes, the entities, and the activities of the system. The state of the system at a particular time is determined by evaluating the equations. A set of equations with common variables is known as a system of *simultaneous* equations.

An important piece of information in a continuous simulation model is the rate of change of an attribute. Derivatives describe the rates of change of variables. An equation specifying the derivative of a variable is a *differential* equation. If a continuous system is modeled by defining the rates of change of its variable attributes, then the model consists of a system of simultaneous differential equations.

Methods for the solution of systems of simultaneous differential equations have been studied by mathematicians for many years. The advent of digital computers and the application of these systems of equations as continuous simulation models have fostered considerable research efforts to discover efficient numerical techniques for differential equation solution. The principal difficulty in solving a system of simultaneous differential equations using a digital computer is that derivatives and integrals of continuous functions are also continuous and may require the evaluation of an infinite number of points to determine their precise value. Thus, solutions obtained using numerical techniques on digital computers are only approximations of the true solutions. The approximations made by digital computers are similar to those made whenever physical mea-

274

surements are taken in the scientific or business world. These measures are approximations rather than true values because of the limitations of mechanical accuracy. This does not imply that digital computers are useless in the modeling of continuous systems. Software packages have been developed that can produce accurate approximations to extremely complex systems of equations using surprisingly little computer time [7.1–7.3].

The proper use of these powerful differential equation evaluation techniques requires considerable mathematical sophistication on the part of the user. Consequently, the details of these techniques are not treated here. The interested reader is referred to the references at the end of this chapter. However, many simulation languages have been developed that provide easy-to-use, reasonably accurate, differential equation evaluation methods. Depending upon the mathematical inclinations of the user, a choice exists between a language that permits the selection of one of several methods for evaluating integrals and one that attempts to disguise integrals and derivatives as simpler mathematical expressions. Two continuous simulation languages are presented in this text— CSMP, which is engineering-oriented and is quite mathematical in its representation, and Dynamo, which tends to be used more in the social and behavioral sciences and is less explicit about the underlying mathematical operations. CSMP is the subject of this chapter, whereas Dynamo is described in Chapter 8.

7.2 ANALOG COMPUTERS

Before embarking upon the presentation of CSMP, analog computers will be presented as a brief, yet relevant, diversion. In the discussion of the numerical solution of simultaneous differential equations, several references were made to *digital* computers. To many readers, this distinction as to the type of computer may have seemed unnecessary. However, another type of computer, the *analog* computer, does exist. Whereas digital computers operate internally on actual numbers and can accept and produce character strings as input and output, analog computers operate strictly upon electronic signals. Although digital computers perform discrete computations, analog computers can operate in a continuous fashion. Circuitry has been developed to perform operations such as summation, multiplication, negation, inversion, differentiation, and integration in analog computers. By relating the variables of a system of simultaneous differential equations to a set of electronic signals, an analog computer can be used to solve the system of equations. Analog computers further differ from their digital counterparts in that analog devices operate upon continuous signals, whereas digital computers are designed to operate in a discrete manner. The continuous nature of analog devices permits the simultaneous operation of distinct processing units, thus allowing the evaluation of a system of equations in a truly simultaneous manner. A traditional digital computer is limited to a sequential evaluation of a set of equations. Due to these characteristics, analog computers have been used in the modeling of continuous systems.

Analog computers do have some drawbacks not found in digital machines:

1. The range of values represented by the voltages acceptable to analog computers is considerably smaller than the range of numeric values that can be obtained in a large digital computer.

2. People understand numbers and not voltages. Thus a conversion between digital values and analog signals is required, resulting in some approximations.

3. The memory capacity of digital computers far exceeds that available in analog machines, thus permitting the representation of more complex systems of equations.

4. Digital computers are more flexible in their application and are far more common. This has reduced the relative price of digital machines as compared to analog computers. Consequently, a digital computer is more likely to be available to a researcher in the continuous simulation area.

Since both analog and digital computers have features that facilitate continuous simulation, their technologies have been merged to create *hybrid* computers. In these machines, the analog arithmetic operations are joined with the input/output and memory capabilities of the digital computers to form a computer tailored for continuous system modeling. Hybrid computers have become more plentiful than pure analog machines. At the present time, very few pure analog computers are manufactured. Although hybrid machines represent a small percentage of the world's computers, they do support a substantial number of continuous simulation efforts.

7.3 ORGANIZATION OF CSMP

The Continuous Simulation Modeling Program (CSMP) is an engineering-oriented language that has its foundation in analog simulation. An analog computer is programmed by wiring together various functional blocks such as integrators, adders, inverters, and so on. A CSMP model is constructed by forming a system of simultaneous equations using Fortran assignment statements plus a special collection of built-in functions derived by modeling those available on analog computers.

A CSMP program is written in three sections. Each section contains statements of a particular type. The three types of CSMP statements are

1. *Structural statements,* whose purpose is to define the set of equations which model the system being simulated.

2. *Data statements,* which are used to initialize the model by assigning numerical values to constants and parameters.
3. *Control statements,* which specify the execution options and the choice of output.

The remainder of the chapter describes the structural, data, and control statements. As with GPSS and Simscript in Chapters 3 and 4, this chapter does not attempt to provide a full discussion of all the features of CSMP. Sufficient information is provided to allow the reader to become familiar with the language and to develop reasonable system models. The reader seeking additional information is referred to the manuals listed in References [7.4] through [7.6].

7.4 STRUCTURAL STATEMENTS

A CSMP model is built from a collection of mathematical equations. CSMP provides an extensive library of built-in functions tailored for continuous simulation applications. These functions are utilized in the specification of the structure of the model. Table 7.1 contains a partial list of the CSMP functions.

EXAMPLE 7.1

Let us model the flight of a hobbyist's rocket as our sample system. We will develop a set of CSMP equations that describe the changes in the rocket's altitude with respect to time. Three variables are necessary to describe the rocket's flight—acceleration, velocity, and altitude. The mnemonics ACC, VEL, ALT will be used to represent the three variables. According to the basic laws of physics:

VEL = ∫ACCdt + IVEL

where IVEL is the initial velocity, and

ALT = ∫VELdt + IALT

where IALT is the initial altitude. If we assume that the only acceleration is the negative influence of gravity, then the following CSMP statements define the rocket's flight:

ACC = −16.0
VEL = INTGRL(IVEL,ACC)
ALT = INTGRL(IALT,VEL)

Values for IVEL and IALT can be specified by other structure statements or by data statements.

The majority of the functions are mathematically oriented. A few do permit some limited decision making. Two functions of this type are LIMIT

Table 7.1   CSMP Built-in Functions

Function	Statement	Interpretation
1. Integral	Y=INTGRL (IC,X)	$Y = \int Xdt + IC$
2. Derivative	Y=DERIV(IC,X)	$Y = \dfrac{dX}{dt} + IC$
3. Limit	Y=LIMIT(P1,P2,X)	$Y=P1,\ X<P1$ $Y=P2,\ X>P2$ $Y=X,\ P1 \leqslant X \leqslant P2$
4. Step	Y=STEP(P)	$Y=0,\ t<P$ $Y=1,\ t \geqslant P$
5. Comparison	Y=COMPAR(X1,X2)	$Y=0,\ X1<X2$ $Y=1,\ X1 \geqslant X2$
6. NOT	Y=NOT(X)	$Y=1,\ X \leqslant 0$ $Y=0,\ X>0$
7. AND	Y=AND(X1,X2)	$Y=1,\ X1>0,\ X2>0$ $Y=1,$ otherwise
8. NOT AND	Y=NAND(X1,X2)	$Y=0,\ X1>0,\ X2>0$ $Y=0,$ otherwise
9. Inclusive OR	Y=IOR(X1,X2)	$Y=0,\ X1 \leqslant 0,\ X2 \leqslant 0$ $Y=1,$ otherwise
10. NOT OR	Y=NOR(X1,X2)	$Y=1,\ X1 \leqslant 0,\ X2 \leqslant 0$ $Y=0,$ otherwise
11. Exclusive OR	Y=EOR(X1,X2)	$Y=1,\ X1 \leqslant 0,\ X2>0$ $Y=1,\ X1>0,\ X2 \leqslant 0$ $Y=0,$ otherwise
12. Equivalence	Y=EQUIV(X1,X2)	$Y=1,\ X1 \leqslant 0,\ X2 \leqslant 0$ $Y=1,\ X1>0,\ X2>0$ $Y=0,$ otherwise
13. Exponential	Y=EXP(X)	$Y=e^X$
14. Natural Log	Y=ALOG(X)	$Y=\ln(X)$
15. Common Log	Y=ALOGN(X)	$Y=\log_{10}(X)$
16. Square Root	Y=SQRT(X)	$Y=\sqrt{X}$
17. Sine	Y=SIN(X)	$Y=\sin(X)$
18. Cosine	Y=COS(X)	$Y=\cos(X)$
19. Arctangent	Y=ATAN(X)	$Y=\tan^{-1}(X)$
20. Hyperbolic Tangent	Y=TANH(X)	$Y=\tanh(X)$
21. Absolute Value	Y=ABS(X)	$Y=X$
22. Maximum	Y=AMAX1(X1,X2,... XN)	$Y=\max(X1,X2,... XN)$
23. Minimum	Y=AMIN1(X1,X2,... XN)	$Y=\min(X1,X2,...XN)$

and STEP. The purpose of LIMIT is to set bounds on the range of values assumed by a variable. STEP permits time-dependent changes in variables.

The format of the LIMIT function is

LIMIT (X1, X2, X3)

where

X1 is a lower bound

X2 is an upper bound

X3 is the bounded variable

The value of the LIMIT function is in the interval (X1, X2). If the value of X3 is less than X1, the value of LIMIT is set to X1. If X3 is greater than X2, LIMIT is given the value of X2. IF X3 falls between X1 and X2, then LIMIT takes the value of X3. Figure 7.1 illustrates the determination of the value of Y = LIMIT (X1, X2, X3).

STEP is a binary function with the format shown below:

STEP (X1)

where X1 is a value such that if the current simulation time is less than X1, STEP has a 0 value. Once the simulated time exceeds X1, STEP has a value of 1 for the remainder of the simulation.

EXAMPLE 7.2

The rocket model can be enhanced to permit firing of two stages during its flight and also to stop the flight of the rocket when it eventually hits the ground.

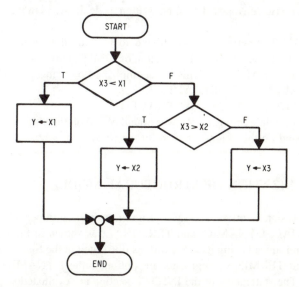

Figure 7.1   Evaluation of Y = LIMIT (X1, X2, X3)

The STEP function is employed to model the firing of the stages. Let the initial acceleration of the rocket be 30 ft/s^2. At 10 seconds, the second stage fires, causing an acceleration of 120 ft/s^2. The third stage fires at 15 seconds, causing an acceleration of 90 ft/s^2. Each firing causes a 1-second change in acceleration. At times when a stage is not firing, the -16 ft/s^2 acceleration of gravity is in effect.

In CSMP, as in GPSS, the internal time can be interpreted as any unit by the user. For this model, we will assume that 1 simulation time unit is equivalent to 1 second. The CSMP statement for acceleration in this model is

$$ACC = 30.0 - 46.0 * STEP(1.0) + 136.0 * STEP(10.0) - 136.0$$
$$* STEP(11.0) + 106.0 * STEP(15.0) - 106.0 * STEP(16.0)$$

The preceding statement causes the value of ACC to change with time. Initially, the values of all the STEP functions are 0 and ACC is equal to 30.0. At time 1.0, the first STEP function is set to 1 and then the value of ACC becomes 30.0 minus 46.0, or -16.0. ACC retains this value until the second STEP function attains a value of 1 at time 10.0. At this point, ACC assumes a value of 120. At time 11.0, the third STEP function causes ACC to return to the -16.0 value. The final two STEP functions result in ACC having a value of 90 between times 15.0 and 16.0, and then maintaining a value of -16.0 for the remainder of the simulation. Figure 7.2 illustrates the behavior of ACC as specified by the preceding statement.

Since a CSMP model is executed as a FORTRAN program with real variables, numeric constants should be written as decimals as in the equation for ACC.

The LIMIT function can be utilized to halt the downward flight of the rocket when it hits the ground. The function of LIMIT in this model is to hold the minimum value of ALT to 0. This is accomplished by using

ALT1 = INTGRL(IALT,VEL)
ALT = LIMIT(0.0,ALT1,ALT1)

This statement, while imposing a lower bound of 0.0 on the altitude, does not set an upper bound on the height attained by the rocket.

7.5 ORGANIZATION OF STRUCTURAL MODEL

The structure statements of a CSMP program may be grouped into three segments, INITIAL, DYNAMIC, and TERMINAL, as shown in Figure 7.3. Each segment is introduced using its key word, as illustrated in the figure. Whereas the INITIAL and TERMINAL segments are optional, the DYNAMIC segment is mandatory. The statements in the INITIAL section are evaluated sequentially at

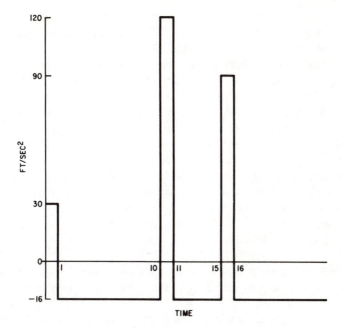

Figure 7.2   Acceleration in Rocket Model

the beginning of the execution of the model. The TERMINAL statements are similarly processed at the completion of the model's execution.

The structural statements in the DYNAMIC segment comprise the main body of the model. The CSMP translator builds a system of simultaneous equations from these statements. These statements are sorted by CSMP and then executed repetitively until a termination condition is met. CSMP sorts the structure statements to ensure that the variables are evaluated in the proper order.

Figure 7.3   Organization of Structure Segments

Since the statements are evaluated as simultaneous equations, it is necessary that the values of the variables to be used in the evaluation of an integral are established before the integration is performed. Because the proper sequencing of the statements in a complex model can be difficult, CSMP automatically reorders the statements internally. Therefore the order of the statements in the DYNAMIC section is unimportant except for the clarity of the model and program.

Due to the discrete nature of digital computers, the computations of a continuous simulation model must be approximated by a sequence of discrete calculations. CSMP attempts this approximation by evaluating the model's system of simultaneous equations over a large number of very small time intervals. The system of equations defined by the DYNAMIC segment is ordered so that each equation can be evaluated using the correct value of each variable on the right-hand side. For example, the statements

    ACC = 16.0
    VEL = INTGRL(IVEL,ACC)
    ALT = INTGRL(IALT,VEL)

are executed in the order shown so that the current velocity can be computed from the current acceleration, and the current altitude computed from the current velocity.

This ordering implies that a variable cannot appear on the left side of an equation and also on the right side of any equation used to compute the value of the first equation. For example, the statement

    X = X + 1

will cause the error message

    "INPUT NAME SAME AS OUTPUT NAME"

to be generated since the variable X appears on both sides of the equation. However, the same error message would be obtained from this set of statements:

    X1 = X
    X = X1 + 1

The use of the dummy variable X1 will not "trick" the CSMP translator since the evaluation of the equation for X requires that the equation for X1 be evaluated first, while the evaluation of X1 requires the prior evaluation of X.

The reason CSMP cannot tolerate a variable whose value is a function of itself is that CSMP statements are interpreted as equations with the left side equal to the right side. At any given time in the simulation, a variable can have but one value. Thus

    X = X + 1

is interpreted as "X is equal to X + 1," which can never be true.

7.6 DATA STATEMENTS

The function of the data statements is to assign fixed values to variables. In this section the definition of constants, initial conditions, and experimental parameters by means of data statements is discussed. The more complex uses of data statements are described in the CSMP manuals [7.4–7.6].

The CONSTANT statement is employed to assign a value to a variable that will remain fixed throughout the simulation. The CONSTANT statement is used either to improve the clarity of the program or for variables that may be modified in later simulation experiments.

The format of a CONSTANT statement is

CONSTANT *variable* = *numeric*{,*variable* = *numeric* . . .}

Several equations, separated by commas, may appear in a CONSTANT statement. If a large number of constants are necessary, multiple CONSTANT statements may be used.

EXAMPLE 7.3

The value of gravity in the rocket model of Example 7.1 can be treated as a constant.

```
ACC = GRAVTY
VEL = INTGRL(IVEL,ACC)
ALT = INTGRL(IALT,VEL)
CONSTANT GRAVITY = -16.0
```

The PARAMETER data statement permits the programmer to specify several values of an experimental parameter, which are used on successive iterations of the model. A variable named in a PARAMETER statement followed by a sequence of values is treated in the same manner as a variable in a CONSTANT statement except that the entire model is executed once for each of the values specified in the statement. Only one variable in the model may have a sequence of values in a PARAMETER statement. A PARAMETER statement may have variables that are assigned single values. These variables are treated exactly as variables in a CONSTANT statement.

The format of the PARAMETER statement is

PARAMETER *variable* = (*numeric*{,*numeric, numeric* . . .})

The sequence of numeric values to be assigned to the variable is contained with parentheses with commas separating the individual variables.

EXAMPLE 7.4

The rocket model of Example 7.2 can be run using different initial accelerations by including a PARAMETER statement and changing the ACC as shown here.

```
PARAMETER IACC = (25.0,30.0,40.0,50.0,80.0)
ACC = IACC - (IACC + 16.0) * STEP(1.0) + 136.0 * STEP(10.0)
    - 136.0 * STEP(11.0) + 106.0 * STEP(15.0) - 106.0
    * STEP(16.0)
```

7.7 TERMINATION CONTROL STATEMENTS

The termination conditions of a CSMP model and the output produced are specified by the control statements. Two options exist for establishing termination conditions in a CSMP program:

a time constraint
the occurrence of a specified condition in the model

The time constraint is indicated by the FINTIM field of the TIMER statement. The FINISH statement permits testing for the occurrence of a set of logical termination conditions in the model. The use of FINTIM is mandatory, whereas FINISH is optional. If FINISH is used in conjunction with FINTIM, the simulation will terminate due to elapsed time unless a logical termination condition occurs first. Termination due to either FINTIM or FINISH results in the execution of the TERMINAL segment of the model, if one is present.

In addition to specifying the maximum simulation time, the TIMER statement may also specify the printing interval (PRDEL), the print/plot option interval (OUTDEL), and the integration interval (DELT). PRDEL and OUTDEL are optional fields indicating the frequency at which variables in PRINT and PRTPLOT statements are to have their values appear as output. DELT determines the lapse in simulation time between successive evaluations of the system of equations comprising the DYNAMIC segment of the model. The value of DELT affects both the execution time and accuracy of the results. A decrease in the value of DELT will increase both run time and accuracy since more iterations through the DYNAMIC segment occur.

The format of the TIMER statement is

TIMER *field* = *numeric*{,*field* = *numeric* . . .}

where

field is either FINTIM, PRDEL, OUTDEL, or DELT
and *numeric* is a decimal constant

The fields may appear in any order. Only FINTIM is required on the TIMER statement.

EXAMPLE 7.5

The following TIMER statement could be utilized in the rocket model:

TIMER PRDEL = 1.0, OUTDEL = 2.0, FINTIM = 100.0, DELT = 0.1

The FINISH statement can be optionally used to provide termination conditions in addition to the elapsed time set by FINTIM. The conditions that may be specified by FINISH are arithmetic equalities. It is possible to terminate a simulation when a variable has a certain value or when two variables are equal. Checks for inequalities are not permitted.

The format of FINISH is

$$\text{FINISH variable } = \begin{bmatrix} \text{variable} \\ \hline \text{numeric} \end{bmatrix}, \left\{ \text{ variable } = \begin{bmatrix} \text{variable} \\ \hline \text{numeric} \end{bmatrix} \right\}$$

There may be several equalities per FINISH statement and multiple FINISH statements in a program.

EXAMPLE 7.6

The TIMER statement of the previous example will halt the rocket simulation after 100 seconds. However, if the rocket crashes, continuing the simulation has no value. The FINISH statement can be employed to terminate the simulation if the rocket should hit the ground. A TERMINAL segment is included to set the velocity and acceleration to zero and the conclusion of the simulation.

```
           TERMINAL
                  VEL = 0.0
                  ACC = 0.0
           FINISH  ALT = 0.0
```

7.8 OUTPUT CONTROL STATEMENTS

As mentioned in the explanation of the TIMER card option, CSMP provides two types of output: printing and a print/plot feature. (A graphics capability has been added to CSMP-III, but this is not discussed here.) The print facility produces a table, indexed by time of the values of a specified set of variables. The increment of time in the table is given in the PRTDEL field of the TIMER statement. The variables whose values are listed are specified in a PRINT statement. The print/plot output produces a graph of the behavior of a variable with respect to time. The graph intervals are specified in the OUTDEL field of TIMER. The variables to be plotted are listed individually in PRTPLT statements.

Each plot may be labeled using the LABEL statement, which contains text to be printed as a header for each plot. The LABEL statement must immediately follow the PRTPLT statement for which it is providing a header.

All output pages may be labeled with a program header specified by the TITLE statement. Each program may have only one TITLE statement.

EXAMPLE 7.7

The following statements will print the acceleration, velocity, and altitude while plotting the altitude for the rocket model. The plot is labeled and the program is titled.

TITLE ROCKET MODEL
PRINT ALT, VEL, ACC
PRTPLT ALT
LABEL ALTITUDE OF ROCKET

7.9 EXECUTION CONTROL STATEMENT

CSMP requires control statements to indicate the end of the model definition and end of program. The END statement marks the completion of the structural definition of the model and initiates program execution. END sets the internal variable TIME to zero and resets the initial conditions. Data and control statements may be modified between successive executions of a model by the use of multiple END statements. The modified data and control statements appear between each pair of END statements.

The STOP statement follows the last END statement in the program to signify the termination of the model executions. The end of the program is denoted by ENDJOB. For the subset of CSMP features presented in this chapter, ENDJOB will immediately follow the STOP statement.

7.10 COMMENTS AND CONTINUATIONS

Two CSMP features, comments and continuations, improve the ease of program preparation and the readability of the finished product. Comments are inserted into a CSMP program by placing an asterisk (*) in the first column of a line of text. Comments may appear at any point in a CSMP program. The use of comments is illustrated in the subsequent example.

The continuation feature is employed to allow an equation to be split over several lines. Continuation is indicated by ''...'' appearing as the last three characters in a statement line. The equation is continued starting from the first nonblank character on the next line. The equation for acceleration of the model rocket requires the use of continuation since it cannot be written in a single statement line. The acceleration equation, with continuation, is shown below:

ACC = IACC − (IACC + 16.0) + STEP(1.0) + 136.0 *...
     STEP(10.0) − 136.0 * STEP(11.0) + 106.0 + STEP(15.0)...
     − 106.0 * STEP(16.0)

Continuation marks can be inserted only between operands and operators. Identifier or function names may not be split over two lines.

```
TITLE   ROCKET MODEL
*      PROGRAM TO SIMULATE THE FLIGHT CF A MODEL ROCKET
*       THE INITIAL ALTITUE AND INITIAL VELOCITY CF THE ROCKET
*         ARE SPECIFIEC IN THE CONSTANT STATEMENTS.
*       THE INITIAL ACCELERATION IS GIVEN AS A PARAMETER.
*      THE ROCKET FIRES IN THREE STAGES
*          THE SECOND STAGE FIRES AT TIME 10.0 AND CAUSES AN
*          ACCELERATICN OF 120.0
*          THE THIRD STAGE FIRES AT TIME 15.0 , PRODUCING AN A
*          ACCELERATION OF 90.0.
*       THE VELOCITY AND ALTITUDE OF THE ROCKET ARE DERIVED FROM
*          THE ACCELERATION BY INTEGRATICN
INITIAL
        ALT = IALT
        VEL = IVEL
DYNAMIC
        ACC = IACC - ( IACC + 16.0 ) * STEP (1.0) + 136.0 * ...
              STEP (10.0) - 136.0 * STEP (11.0) + 106.0 * STEP (15.0) ...
              - 106.0 * STEP (16.0)
        VEL = INTGRL ( IVEL , ACC )
        ALT1 = INTGRL ( IALT , VEL )
        ALT = LIMIT ( 0.0 , ALT1 , ALT1 )
*
CONSTANT    IALT = 6.0 , IVEL = 50.0
PARAMETER   IACC = ( 25.0 , 40.0 )
TIMER       PRDEL = 1.0 , OUTDEL = 1.0 , FINTIM = 100.0 , DELT = 0.1
FINISH      ALT = 0.C
PRINT       ALT , VEL , ACC
PRTPLT      ALT
LABEL       ALTITUDE CF ROCKET
END
CONSTANT    IALT = 60.0 , IVEL = 50.0
END
STOP
```

```
                ROCKET MODEL

                IACC  =      25.000

                TIME         ALT          VEL          ACC
                0.0          6.0CCC       50.000       25.000
                1.00000      68.500       75.000      -16.000
                2.00000      135.50       59.000      -16.000
                3.00000      186.5C       43.000      -16.000
                4.00000      221.50       27.000      -16.000
                5.00000      240.50       11.000      -16.000
                6.00000      243.50       -5.0001     -16.000
                7.00000      230.5C       -21.C00     -16.000
                8.00000      201.50       -37.000     -16.000
                9.00000      156.50       -53.000     -16.000
                10.0000      95.499       -69.C00      120.00
                11.0000      86.499       51.000      -16.000
                12.0000      129.50       35.000      -16.000
                13.0000      156.50       19.000      -16.000
                14.0000      167.50       2.9999      -16.000
                15.0000      162.50       -13.000      90.000
                16.0000      194.50       77.000      -16.000
                17.0000      263.5C       61.000      -16.000
                18.0000      316.50       45.000      -16.000
                19.0000      353.50       29.000      -16.000
                20.0000      374.5C       13.C00      -16.000
                21.0000      379.50       -3.0001     -16.000
                22.0000      368.50       -19.000     -16.000
                23.0000      341.49       -35.000     -16.000
                24.0000      298.49       -51.000     -16.000
                25.0000      239.49       -67.000     -16.000
                26.0000      164.49       -83.000     -16.000
                27.0000      73.454       -99.000     -16.000
                28.0000      0.0          -115.00     -16.000
```

```
ROCKET MODEL

IACC  =     40.0C0

TIME          ALT           VEL           ACC
0.0           6.0000        50.000        40.000
1.00000       76.0CC        90.000        -16.000
2.00000       158.CC        74.000        -16.000
3.00000       224.00        58.000        -16.000
4.00000       274.00        42.000        -16.000
5.00000       3C8.CC        26.000        -16.000
6.00000       326.00        9.9999        -16.000
7.00000       328.00        -6.0001       -16.000
8.000C0       314.C0        -22.000       -16.000
9.00000       284.CC        -38.000       -16.000
10.0000       238.00        -54.000       120.00
11.0000       244.C0        66.000        -16.000
12.0000       3C2.CC        50.000        -16.000
13.0000       344.00        34.000        -16.000
14.0000       370.00        18.000        -16.000
15.0000       379.SS        1.9999        90.000
16.0000       426.99        92.000        -16.00C
17.0000       510.99        76.000        -16.000
18.0000       578.S9        60.000        -16.000
19.0000       630.S9        44.000        -16.000
20.0000       666.99        28.000        -16.000
21.00C0       686.S9        12.000        -16.000
22.0000       6S0.SS        -4.0C01       -16.000
23.0000       678.S9        -20.000       -16.000
24.0000       650.99        -36.000       -16.000
25.0000       606.SS        -52.000       -16.000
26.0000       546.99        -68.000       -16.000
27.0000       470.99        -84.000       -16.000
28.0000       378.S9        -100.00       -16.000
29.0000       270.SS        -116.00       -16.000
30.0000       146.99        -132.00       -16.000
31.0000       6.9877        -148.00       -16.000
32.0000       0.C           -164.00       -16.000
```

ALTITUDE OF ROCKET

IACC =   25.000

800.0

'+'=ALT

0.0

TIME	ALT
0.0	6.0CCC
1.0000	68.500
2.0000	135.50
3.0000	186.50
4.0000	221.50
5.0000	240.50
6.0000	243.50
7.0000	230.5C
8.0000	201.50
9.0000	156.5C
10.000	95.4S
11.000	86.499
12.000	129.50
13.000	156.5C
14.000	167.50
15.000	162.50
16.000	194.50
17.000	263.50
18.000	316.50
19.000	353.50
20.000	374.5C
21.000	379.50
22.000	368.50
23.000	341.4S
24.000	298.49
25.000	239.49
26.000	164.4S
27.000	73.494
28.000	0.0

ALTITUDE OF ROCKET

IACC = 40.000

'+'=ALT

0.0   800.0

TIME	ALT
0.0	6.0000
1.0000	76.0CC
2.0000	158.CC
3.0000	224.00
4.0000	274.00
5.0000	308.CC
6.0000	326.00
7.0000	328.00
8.0000	314.CO
9.0000	284.CC
10.000	238.00
11.000	244.CO
12.000	302.CC
13.000	344.00
14.000	370.00
15.000	379.99
16.000	426.99
17.000	510.99
18.000	578.99
19.000	630.99
20.000	666.99
21.000	686.99
22.000	650.99
23.000	678.99
24.000	650.99
25.000	606.99
26.000	546.99
27.000	470.99
28.000	378.99
29.000	270.99
30.000	146.99
31.000	6.9877
32.000	0.0

$$$** CONTINUOUS SYSTEM MODELING PROGRAM III   V1M3   EXECUTION OUTPUT **$$$

CONSTANT   IALT = 6C.C , IVEL = 50.0
END

TIMER VARIABLES   RKS   INTEGRATION   START TIME = 0.0
    DELT   DELMIN   FINTIM   PRDEL   OUTDEL   DELMAX
1.000000-01 1.00000C-05 100.00   1.0000   1.C000   1.0000

ROCKET MODEL

IACC =   25.0C0

TIME	ALT	VEL	ACC
0.0	6C.0CC	50.000	25.000
1.00000	122.5C	75.000	-16.000
2.00000	189.50	59.000	-16.000
3.00000	240.50	43.000	-16.000
4.00000	275.5C	27.C00	-16.000
5.00000	294.50	11.000	-16.000
6.00000	297.50	-5.0001	-16.000
7.00000	284.5C	-21.000	-16.000
8.00000	255.5C	-37.000	-16.000
9.00000	210.50	-53.000	-16.000
10.00C0	149.50	-69.000	120.00
11.0000	140.5C	51.C00	-16.000
12.0000	183.50	35.000	-16.000
13.0000	210.50	19.000	-16.000
14.0000	221.5C	2.9999	-16.000
15.0000	216.50	-13.000	90.000
16.0000	248.50	77.000	-16.000
17.0CC0	317.50	61.000	-16.000
18.0000	370.5C	45.000	-16.000
19.0000	407.49	29.000	-16.000
20.0000	428.49	13.000	-16.000
21.0000	433.4S	-3.0001	-16.000
22.0000	422.49	-19.000	-16.000
23.0000	395.49	-35.000	-16.000
24.0000	352.4S	-51.C00	-16.000
25.0000	293.49	-67.000	-16.000
26.0000	218.49	-83.000	-16.000
27.0CC0	127.49	-99.000	-16.000
28.0000	2C.4S2	-115.00	-16.000
29.0000	0.0	-131.00	-16.000

```
ROCKET MCDEL

IACC   =     40.000

TIME          ALT           VEL           ACC
0.0           60.000        50.000        40.000
1.00000       130.C0        90.000        -16.000
2.00000       212.CC        74.C00        -16.000
3.00000       278.00        58.000        -16.000
4.00000       328.00        42.000        -16.000
5.00000       362.CC        26.C00        -16.000
6.00000       380.00        9.9999        -16.000
7.00000       382.00        -6.0001       -16.000
8.000C0       368.C0        -22.000       -16.000
9.00000       338.CC        -38.000       -16.000
10.0000       292.00        -54.000       120.00
11.0000       298.C0        66.000        -16.000
12.0000       356.CC        50.000        -16.000
13.0000       397.99        34.000        -16.000
14.0000       423.99        18.000        -16.000
15.0000       433.SS        1.9999        90.000
16.0000       480.99        92.000        -16.000
17.0000       564.99        76.000        -16.000
18.00C0       632.SS        60.000        -16.000
19.0000       684.SS        44.000        -16.000
20.0000       720.99        28.000        -16.000
21.0000       740.SS        12.000        -16.000
22.0000       744.SS        -4.0001       -16.000
23.0000       732.99        -20.000       -16.000
24.0000       704.99        -36.000       -16.000
25.0000       660.SS        -52.000       -16.000
26.0000       600.99        -68.000       -16.000
27.0000       524.99        -84.000       -16.000
28.0000       432.SS        -100.00       -16.000
29.0000       324.SS        -116.00       -16.000
30.0000       200.99        -132.00       -16.000
31.0000       60.986        -148.00       -16.000
32.0000       0.C           -164.00       -16.000
```

ALTITUDE OF RCCKET

IACC =   25.000

'+'=ALT

0.0   800.0

TIME	ALT
0.0	60.CCC
1.0000	122.50
2.0000	189.50
3.0000	240.5C
4.0000	275.50
5.0000	294.50
6.0000	297.50
7.0000	284.50
8.0000	255.50
9.0000	210.50
10.000	149.5C
11.000	140.50
12.000	183.50
13.000	210.5C
14.000	221.50
15.000	216.50
16.000	248.5C
17.000	317.50
18.000	370.50
19.000	407.49
20.000	428.49
21.000	433.49
22.000	422.49
23.000	395.49
24.000	352.49
25.000	293.49
26.000	218.49
27.000	127.49
28.000	20.492
29.000	0.0

ALTITUDE OF ROCKET

IACC = 40.000

'+'=ALT

0.0   800.0

TIME	ALT
0.0	60.0C0
1.0000	130.CC
2.0000	212.00
3.0000	278.00
4.0000	328.CC
5.0000	362.00
6.0000	380.00
7.0000	382.C0
8.0000	368.00
9.0000	338.00
10.0C0	292.CC
11.000	2S8.CC
12.000	356.C0
13.000	397.S9
14.000	423.99
15.000	433.99
16.000	480.99
17.000	564.99
18.000	632.99
19.000	684.99
20.000	720.S9
21.000	740.SS
22.000	744.99
23.000	732.S9
24.000	704.SS
25.000	660.99
26.000	600.99
27.000	524.SS
28.000	432.99
29.000	324.99
30.000	200.S9
31.000	60.S86
32.000	0.0

EXAMPLE 7.8

All of the CSMP features discussed in this chapter can be combined to produce a program that simulates the flight of the rocket. The model is executed with two values of the parameter IACC and two END statements which utilize different values of IALT. Thus, a total of four executions is made. The output indicates that changing the initial acceleration from 25.0 to 40.0 causes the rocket to fly longer and higher. However, a change in the initial altitude has little bearing on the rocket's flight.

7.11 CONCLUSION

CSMP is a continuous simulation programming language oriented toward engineering and the physical sciences. A model is built using mathematical equations enhanced by a large number of special functions. The process of developing a CSMP model resembles modeling with an analog computer, and many of the functions are derived from operations performed by analog machines.

The CSMP statements presented in this chapter provide a basis for the development of an extensive collection of continuous simulation models. CSMP has many additional features that were not described because either they require special graphics facilities or their application demands considerable mathematical sophistication. These additional features enhance the modeling capability of CSMP particularly with respect to physical and engineering systems. More information on the CSMP language is available in the manuals [7.4–7.6].

EXERCISES

7.1 The orbit of a satellite around the earth can be described by the following system of equations:

$$vx = \frac{dx}{dt} \qquad ax = \frac{dvx}{dt} = \frac{-16x}{(x^2 + y^2)^{1.5}}$$

$$vy = \frac{dy}{dt} \qquad ay = \frac{dvy}{dt} = \frac{-16y}{(x^2 + y^2)^{1.5}}$$

Assume the following initial values:

$$x = 2, \quad vx = 0, \quad y = 0, \quad vy = 2\sqrt{3}$$

Simulate for 13 time units.
Plot the x and y values at intervals of 0.1.
Determine when the satellite completes one revolution.

7.2   Simulate a race among 3 cars according to the following specifications:
Car 1 starts 1000 feet ahead of the other two cars. Car 1 accelerates at 5 ft/s².
Car 2 has an initial acceleration of 12 ft/s², which drops to 4 ft/s² after 5 seconds.
Car 3 has an initial acceleration of 20 ft/s², which drops to 0 after 10 seconds.
Determine the velocity and distance traveled for each car. Plot the distance traveled
by each car.
Simulate for 1 minute.
Recall that the velocity is the integral of acceleration, and distance is the integral of
velocity.

7.3   Assume the existence of three populations, P_1, P_2, P_3. Each population initially
has N_k individuals, a birth rate of b_k, and a natural death rate of d_k, for $k = 1, 2,$
3. Interspecies fighting causes deaths at the following rates:

$$\text{For } P_1, \quad f_{1,2}P_1P_2 + f_{1,3}P_1P_3$$
$$\text{For } P_2, \quad f_{2,1}P_2P_1 + f_{2,3}P_2P_3$$
$$\text{For } P_3, \quad f_{3,1}P_3P_1 + f_{3,2}P_3P_2$$

Simulate the growth of these populations assuming

$$N_1 = 500 \quad N_2 = 1000 \quad N_3 = 1500$$
$$b_1 = 0.05 \quad b_2 = 0.04 \quad b_3 = 0.03$$
$$d_1 = 1 \times 10^{-5} \quad d_2 = 1.5 \times 10^{-5} \quad d_3 = 2 \times 10^{-5}$$
$$f_{1,2} = 1 \times 10^{-6} \quad f_{1,3} = 1.5 \times 10^{-6}$$
$$f_{2,1} = 1 \times 10^{-6} \quad f_{2,3} = 5 \times 10^{-7}$$
$$f_{3,1} = 2 \times 10^{-6} \quad f_{3,2} = 3 \times 10^{-7}$$

Simulate for 500 years; print and plot the number of individuals in each species at
50 uniform intervals.

7.4   Two identical projectiles with small parachutes are dropped from a plane. Assume
they fall with an acceleration of 13.5 ft/s² (gravity plus wind resistance).

a.   Projectile 1 is dropped with no initial velocity at a height of 2600 ft. Projectile
2 is dropped with an initial velocity of -10 ft/s at a height of 3100 ft. Simulate
until both projectiles hit the ground. The projectiles stop when they hit the
ground.

b.   Repeat the above simulation with initial velocities of -2.5 ft/s and -15 ft/s
for Projectile 1 and Projectile 2, respectively.

c.   Repeat the simulations of (a) and (b) with a height of 2800 ft for the first
projectile.

REFERENCES

[7.1] Acton, F. S., *Numerical Methods That Work*. New York: Harper & Row, 1970.

[7.2] Hildebrand, F. B., *Introduction to Numerical Analysis*. New York: McGraw-Hill,
1956.

[7.3] Hornbeck, R. W., *Numerical Methods*. New York: Quantum Publishers, 1975.

[7.4] IBM, Inc., *System/360 Continuous System Modeling Program Application Description Model*, 1972.

[7.5] IBM, Inc., *System/360 Continuous System Modeling Program User's Manual*, 1972.

[7.6] IBM, Inc., *Continuous System Modeling Program III and Graphic Feature General Information Model*, 1972.

8

Dynamo

8.1 INTRODUCTION

The structure and behavior of a tremendous variety of systems can be described best by continuous models. The production and marketing of products; the hiring, training, and performance of employees; the trading of investment properties; the effects of industrial development on water and air quality; and the life cycles of dependent species all fit into the category of continuous systems. In all of these systems and in many similar models, entities interact in a dynamic manner with the degree, or rate, of interaction changing with time.

A specialized approach to the modeling of continuous systems has been developed by Jay Forrester at MIT [8.1]. The technique, known as *System Dynamics,* focuses upon the relationship between the structure of a system and its performance. System Dynamics is oriented toward determining significant trends or behavioral characteristics of systems and not toward obtaining precise numerical results. Consequently, the Systems Dynamics method is intended primarily for the social and behavioral sciences in contrast to the orientation of CSMP toward engineering and the physical sciences.

Dynamo is the programming language that evolved from the System Dynamics method. The greater part of the chapter concentrates upon the features and applications of Dynamo. The next two sections emphasize the System Dynamics modeling method in order to provide a foundation for the Dynamo discussion.

8.2 SYSTEM DYNAMICS MODELS

A System Dynamics model is represented by a diagram in which entities flow from generation points, called *sources,* to termination points, known as *sinks.* The intermediate points in the graphs are *levels* at which entities may accumulate. The flow of entities between levels is defined by *rates.* The model also

298

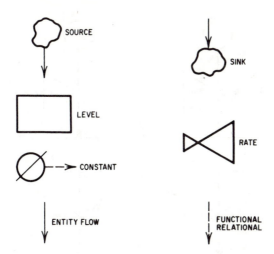

Figure 8.1   Elements of System Dynamics Diagrams

permits *constants*, which affect the rates. In a System Dynamics graph the solid lines indicate the entity flow paths and the dotted lines indicate a functional relationship. Figure 8.1 illustrates the interpretation of the shapes of the objects in a System Dynamics diagram.

EXAMPLE 8.1

Figure 8.2 is a System Dynamics graph of a very simple population model. The two populations are foxes and rodents. Each population has a birthrate and a death rate. In this case the birthrates are constants, but the death rates depend upon the number of creatures in the other population. The foxes die due to starvation; the rodents are killed by the foxes.

The graphical representation of a System Dynamics model provides a framework for the development of equations that describe the behavior of the system. Since System Dynamics is a continuous system modeling method, a system of simultaneous differential equations is formed from a System Dynamics graph.

The derivation of System Dynamics equations from a graph of the model is a straightforward process. The level equations follow a simple format, while the rate equations are formed by quantifying the relationships depicted in the diagram. The general format of the level equations is

LEVEL.NEW = LEVEL.OLD + TIME (INRATE − OUTRATE)   (8.1)

The value of a level is equal to its previous value plus the change since the last evaluation of the level equation. The change is given by the difference between the input rate and output rate multiplied by the time since the last evaluation.

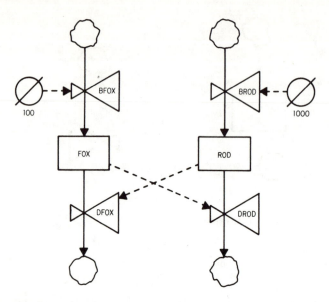

Figure 8.2   Sample System Dynamics Model

EXAMPLE 8.2

The system of equations shown below is derived from the fox-rodent model of Figure 8.2.

BFOX = 100
BROD = 1000
FOX = FOX + TIME (BFOX − DFOX)
ROD = ROD + TIME (BROD − DROD)
DROD = FOX * 60
DFOX = MAX (0, 60 * FOX − ROD)/60

The birthrate equations have constant values, whereas the level equations follow the format specified in Eq. (8.1). The death rate equations show the prey-predator relationship of the two species. Each fox kills 60 rodents per time interval, as shown in the DROD (rodent death) rate equation. Foxes starve if they cannot kill 60 rodents apiece, as indicated in the DFOX (fox death) rate equation. This example is an oversimplification of the workings of nature and will be expanded later. Its purpose is to illustrate the basic concepts of System Dynamics models.

8.3 FEEDBACK

A common physical phenomenon is that the output of a system has an influence upon its input at a later time. This phenomenon, known as feedback, is indicated by a loop in a System Dynamics diagram. The loop may be composed of entity flow paths, logical relationship paths, or both. Feedback occurs quite frequently in systems of even moderate complexity. Due to the possibility of feedback in System Dynamics models, a distinction is made between the current and past value of a level variable as indicated in Eq. (8.1).

EXAMPLE 8.3

The birthrates in Example 8.2 are assumed to be constant. It is more likely that there is some relationship between the number of animals in a species and the birthrate. Figure 8.3 illustrates this relationship for both the foxes and the rodents. The resulting equations are given below:

BFOX = FOX/BRCFOX
BROD = ROD/BRCROD

Feedback can be classified as either positive or negative, depending upon the relationship between the input and output of the system. If an increase in the output of the system results in an increase in the system input, then the feedback is *positive*. However, if increasing the output decreases the input, then *negative* feedback is observed. The relationship between population and birth rate in Example 8.3 illustrates *positive* feedback, since an increase in population results in an increase in the birth rate. Negative feedback occurs in a personnel system in which the hiring rate decreases as the number of employees rises.

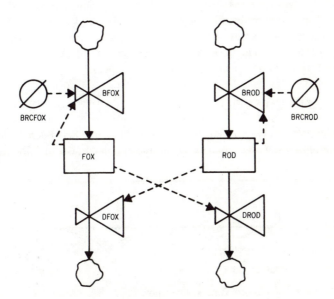

Figure 8.3 System Dynamics Model with Feedback

8.4 THE DYNAMO LANGUAGE

A programming language whose notation corresponds to the form of System Dynamics equations has been developed by Forrester and his associates at MIT to provide a vehicle for the implementation of System Dynamics models [8.2]. The language, known as DYNAMO, is a continuous simulation language with a notation directly related to the System Dynamics diagrams.

As indicated by Eq. (8.1), it is important in a System Dynamics model to identify both the previous and current values of level variables. Dynamo requires that suffixes be attached to all variables indicating whether they represent the current or the prior value. The interpretation of the allowable suffixes for level and rate variables is depicted in Figure 8.4. For example, FOX.K is the current value of the fox level, while FOX.J is the previous value.

A system variable, TIME, holds the value of the simulation time. TIME.K is the current time. TIME.J and TIME.L are related to TIME.K by the following equations:

TIME.J = TIME.K + DT
TIME.L = TIME.K + DT

DT is the time interval size and is specified by the user. The model equations are evaluated at uniform time intervals as indicated by the value of DT. As with the DELT variable in CSMP, both the numerical accuracy of the results and program execution time are inversely proportional to the value of DT. The selection of a value for DT is dependent upon the characteristics of the system being studied. However, if DT is too large, unsatisfactory numerical results may be produced. Dynamo has two types of statements: equation and control. All statements begin with an identifying type label followed by a single blank. The second blank marks the end of the statement, and the remaining characters are treated as a comment. The user must avoid embedding blanks in Dynamo statements, as difficult to detect program bugs will appear.

8.5 DYNAMO EQUATIONS

Dynamo supports six types of equations as listed in Table 8.1. Each equation in a Dynamo program must be labeled by the mnemonic shown in Table 8.1. The

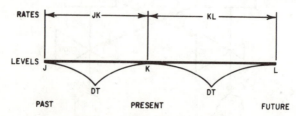

Figure 8.4   Representation of Time in Dynamo

Table 8.1   Dynamo Equation Types

Mnemonic	Equation Type
L	Level
R	Rate
C	Constant
N	Initial
A	Auxiliary
S	Supplementary

variable appearing on the left side of the equal sign has the same type as the equation. Level variables, rate variables, and constants have been discussed in the earlier sections of this chapter. The *N* equations serve to provide initial values for level, rate, or auxiliary variables. The functions of the auxiliary and supplementary variables are explained later in this chapter.

Dynamo enforces a set of conventions for the use of suffixes of the various variable types when they appear on the left or right side of an equation. Table 8.2 summarizes the proper use of variable suffixes. The Dynamo translator will verify all suffixes and attempt to correct any improper suffix utilization.

EXAMPLE 8.4

The System Dynamics equations for the fox-rodent model can easily be transformed into Dynamo statements. In order to make the model more

Table 8.2   Dynamo Suffix Conventions

| Equation Type | Suffix on Left | *Suffix on Right* | | | | | |
		L	*R*	*C*	*N*	*A*	*S*
L	K	J	JK	none	none	J	X
R	KL	K	JK	none	none	K	X
C	none	X	X	X	X	X	X
N	none	none	none	none	none	none	none
A	K	K	JK	none	none	K	X
S	K	K	JK	none	none	K	K

X ≡ not permitted on the right side of that equation type.

complete, values are assigned to the constants and the levels are initialized. An implicit time unit of one month is assumed for the model.

R   BFOX.KL=FOX.K/BRCFOX
R   BROD.KL=ROD.K/BRCROD
L   FOX.K=FOX.J+(DT)(BFOX.JK−DFOX.JK)
L   ROD.K=ROD.J+(DT)(BROD.JK−DROD.JK)
R   DFOX.KL=MAX(0,60*FOX.K−ROD.K)/60
R   DROD.KL=FOX.K*60
C   BRCFOX=4
C   BRCROD=.8
N   FOX=60
N   ROD=50000

The MAX function used in the DF equation is a system-supplied function. Dynamo also provides MIN and STEP functions. The STEP function in Dynamo operates differently than its counterpart in CSMP. STEP has two arguments, a value and a time threshold. The value of STEP is zero until the system time exceeds the time threshold. STEP then assumes the value of its first argument.

EXAMPLE 8.5

In Example 8.4, foxes died only from starvation. Let us introduce hunters into the model, who will kill foxes at the rate of four per month, provided at least four foxes are in existence. The hunters will not appear until the tenth year, 120th month, of the simulation. The fox death rate equation now becomes

R   DFOX.KL = MAX(0,60*FOX.K−ROD.K)/60+
    MIN(FOX.K, STEP(4,120))

As with CSMP, the Dynamo statements are translated into a system of simultaneous equations, which are evaluated iteratively. The Dynamo translator sorts the equations into the proper execution sequences. Thus the sequence of Dynamo statements in a program is irrelevant.

8.6 AUXILIARY VARIABLES

One of the key principles of software engineering is that a straightforward, understandable program is more beneficial to an organization than a program coded in a very clever, efficient, yet obscure manner [8.3–8.6]. Dynamo aids the programmer in the development of more understandable programs by permitting the introduction of intermediate variables that can be used to simplify complicated equations. Such variables are termed *auxiliaries*. As mentioned in Section 8.5, equations defining auxiliary variables are labeled with an A. Although, according to Table 8.2, auxiliary variables follow the same rules for suffixes as levels, they may represent either rates or levels in the model. Auxiliary variables are represented by circles in System Dynamics diagrams.

EXAMPLE 8.6

The fox death rate equation given in Example 8.5 can be simplified by the use of auxiliary variables, which indicate the starvation rate of the foxes and the number of foxes killed by hunters. Three statements now describe the fox death rate:

R   DFOX.KL=SFOX.K+HUNT.K
A   SFOX.K=MAX(0,(FOX.K*60−ROD.K)/60)
A   HUNT.K=MIN(FOX.K,STEP(4,120))

8.7 SUPPLEMENTARY VARIABLES

The modeler can define *supplementary* variables to obtain statistical information beyond the values of the level and rate variables. A supplementary variable is extraneous to the modeling of the system and has the sole function of appearing in printed or plotted output. Supplementary equations are evaluated only when output is to be produced, not at each DT interval. A supplementary variable may appear on the right side of supplementary equations only.

EXAMPLE 8.7

Let us expand the fox-rodent model to indicate explicitly young and adults in both species and also include the starvation of rodents as well as foxes. For each species there is a maturation rate, which indicates the time required for the young to grow into adults. The new model is pictured in Figure 8.5. Supplementary variables are used to compute the total number of animals, both young and adult, in each species.

The young foxes either mature, which requires eight months, or die of starvation. A young fox requires only ten rodents a month to survive. Each adult fox must consume 60 rodents a month to ward off starvation as in prior examples. The rodent young mature in three months, but die upon the deaths of their parents. Thus the death rate of young rodents is proportional to the death rate of adult rodents. Adult rodents are either devoured by the foxes or starve if their number increases beyond 100,000.

Using the diagram of Figure 8.5 and the numerical values provided in

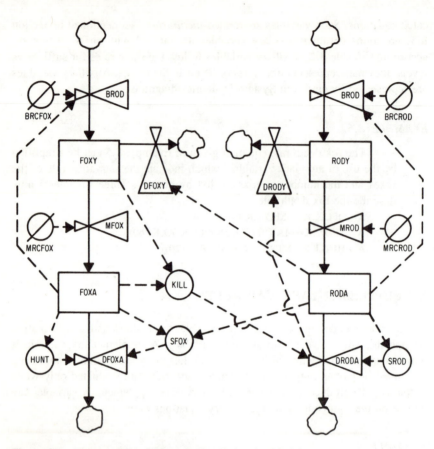

Figure 8.5 Expanded Fox-Rodent System Dynamics Model

the preceding paragraph, the following Dynamo statements can be formulated to describe the fox-rodent model:

R   BFOX.KL=FOXA.K/BRCFOX

L   FOXY.K=FOXY.J+(DT)(BFOX.JK-DFOXY.JK-MFOX.JK)

R   DFOXY.KL=MAX(0,(10*FOXY.K−RODA.K)/10)

R   MFOX.KL=FOXY.K/MRCFOX

L   FOXA.K=FOXA.J+(DT)(MFOX.JK−DFOXA.JK)

R   DFOXA.KL=MIN(FOXA.K,SFOX.K+HUNT.K)

A   SFOX.K=MAX(0,(FOXA.K*60−RODA.K)/60)

A   HUNT.K=MIN(FOXA.K,STEP(4,120))

S   FOXES.K=FOXY.K+FOXA.K

R   BROD.KL=RODA.K/BRCROD

L   RODY.K=RODY.J+(DT)(BROD.JK−DRODY.JK−MROD.JK)

R   DRODY.KL=MIN(RODY.K,DRODA.JK/4)
R   MROD.KL=RODY.K/MRCROD
L   RODA.K=RODA.J+(DT)(MROD.JK−DRODA.JK)
R   DRODA.KL=MIN(RODA.K,KILL.K+SROD.K)
A   SROD.K=MAX(0,RODA.K−100000)
A   KILL.K=60*FOXA.K+10*FOXY.K
S   RODENTS.K=RODY.K+RODA.K

N   FOXA=600
N   RODA=50000
N   FOXY=25
N   RODY=3000
C   MRCFOX=8
C   MRCROD=3
C   BRCFOX=4
C   BRCROD=.8

8.8 OUTPUT CONTROL STATEMENTS

Dynamo provides both printing and plotting options. The plot facility allows multivariable plots with user-controlled scaling. The PRINT and PLOT cards control the two types of output. The intervals for the output under both modes are indicated using the SPEC statement which is described in the next section.

The PRINT statement lists the variables to be printed in the sequence they are to appear on the page. The user has the option of controlling the scale factors. Dynamo prints only five significant digits. A scale factor is printed at the head of the column listing the values of the variable. For each individual variable, Dynamo will determine the scale factor. Consequently, the scale factors on some variables may be different. A maximum of 14 variables may appear on a single page.

The format of PRINT is
      PRINT *variable1*{,*variable2* . . .}

EXAMPLE 8.8

      All levels and rates in the model are printed by the statements below.
      PRINT BFOX,FOXY,MFOX,DFOXY,FOXA,DFOXA,FOXES
      PRINT BROD,RODY,MROD,DRODY,RODA,DRODA,RODENTS
      The values for all variables are printed upon the same page regardless of the number of PRINT statements utilized.

Each PLOT statement produces one graph. The user supplies the names of the variables to be plotted and a character to represent each variable. In addition, the user has the option of specifying the scale factors for the variable. If no scale factors are provided, Dynamo automatically scales the variables. Up to ten variables are permitted on a graph.

The format of the PLOT statement with automatic scaling is

PLOT *variable1* = *char1*{,*variable2* = *char2*...}

When scaling is done by the programmer, the following format applies:

PLOT *variable1* = *char1*(*up-limit,low-limit*){,*variable2* = ...}

EXAMPLE 8.9

The values of the four level variables for the fox-rodent model are plotted on the same graph by using the following statement:

PLOT FOXY=*(0,1000),FOXA=/(0,1000),RODY=$,RODA=+

The values of the fox population variables are explicitly scaled to 1000 while the rodent variables are scaled by the system. The determination of scale factors is often a trial-and-error procedure. Several attempts may be required to obtain a satisfactory graph.

8.9 EXECUTION CONTROL STATEMENTS

The SPEC statement in Dynamo is identical in function to the CSMP TIMER statement since it serves to assign values to system variables that control the length of the simulation, the printing and plotting intervals, and the interval between successive evaluations of the simultaneous equations defining the model. The names of the system variables are:

LENGTH—time of simulation

PRTPER—print interval

PLTPER—plot interval

DT   —interval between J and K

All four variables must be specified in a SPEC statement. If no printing or plotting is desired, the appropriate variable is assigned a value of 0. The order of variables in a SPEC statement is not important.

EXAMPLE 8.10

The SPEC statement shown below will execute the fox-rodent model for 200 months with DT set to 0.5, and print and plot intervals of 4 months.

SPEC DT=0.5,LENGTH=200,PRTPER=4,PLTPER=4

Other control statements in Dynamo include continuation, identification, RUN, and NOTE. The continuation of an equation is indicated by an X in the first position of the line or card. The equation continues following a single blank.

Each program may be given a title that is specified in the identification statement, which consists of an ∗ TITLE followed by a string of up to 40 characters that is printed on the program listing. The RUN statement allows repetitive executions of the model with different constant values. Each RUN statement may have an eight-character identifier attached that is used to label the output for that execution. One or more constant statements may appear between successive RUN statements. Each program requires at least one RUN statement. NOTE provides a facility for comment statements. Comments also may be appended to individual statements following the second blank.

EXAMPLE 8.11

Identification, NOTE, and RUN statements can be added to complete the fox-rodent model. The birthrate constants are modified following the RUN statements to determine their effect on the populations. The identification statement is

∗ TITLE FOX-RODENT POPULATION MODEL

The following NOTE statements would precede the rodent equations:

NOTE
NOTE RODENT SECTION
NOTE

In order to change the birthrate constants and reexecute the model, the following statements are placed at the end of the program:

RUN HIGH
C BRCFOX=6   FOX BIRTH RATE FACTOR (LOW VALUE)
C BRCROD=.95   RODENT BIRTH RATE FACTOR (LOW VALUE)
RUN LOW

The last two constant statements illustrate the attachment of comments to executable statements.

8.10 EXECUTION OF DYNAMO PROGRAMS

The listing and output of the Dynamo program that has evolved throughout the course of this chapter are provided here. The change in the birthrate factors had a substantial effect upon the populations. Using the high birthrates, the rodent population stabilized by the eighth month. Due to the introduction of the hunters in the tenth year, the fox population underwent very minor perturbations throughout the simulation, but exhibited little change beyond the thirteenth year. The system behaves in a radically different manner when the birthrates are lowered. Both populations plunge toward extinction. However, when the fox population disappears, the rodents successfully repopulate without their predator. By the termination of the simulation, the rodent population has grown to the point that some animals are perishing due to starvation.

```
TITLE    FCX - RODENT MODEL      9/05/78
* TITLE    FOX - RODENT MODEL
NOTE
NOTE      FCX SECTION
NOTE
R BFOX.KL=FOXA.K/BRCFOX                      FCX BIRTH RATE
L FOXY.K=FOXY.J+(DT)(BFOX.JK-DFOXY.JK-MFOX.JK)  YOUNG FOX POP.
R DFCXY.KL=MAX(0,(10*FOXY.K-RODA.K)/10)      YOUNG FOX DEATH RATE
R MFOX.KL=FCXY.K/MRCFOX                      FOX MATURATION RATE
L FOXA.K=FOXA.J+(DT)(MFOX.JK-DFOXA.JK)       ADULT FCX POPULATION
R DFCXA.KL=SFOX.K+HUNT.K                     ADULT FOX DEATH RATE
A SFOX.K=MAX(0,(FOXA.K*60-RODA.K)/60)        ADULT FOXES STARVING
A HUNT.K=MIN(FOXA.K,STEP(4,120))             FOXES KILLED BY HUNTERS
S FOXES.K=FCXY.K+FOXA.K                      TOTAL FOX POPULATION
NOTE
NOTE      RODENT SECTION
NOTE
R BRCD.KL=RCDA.K/BRCROD                      RODENT BIRTH RATE
L RODY.K=RODY.J+(DT)(BROD.JK-DRODY.JK-MROD.JK)  YOUNG RODENT POPULATION
R DRODY.KL=MIN(RODY.K,DRODA.JK/4)            YOUNG RCDENT DEATH RATE
R MROD.KL=RCDY.K/MRCROD                      RODENT MATURATION RATE
L RODA.K=RODA.J+(DT)(MROD.JK-DRODA.JK)       ADULT RODENT POPULATION
R DRODA.KL=MIN(RODA.K,KILL.K+SROD.K)         ADULT RCDENT DEATH RATE
A KILL.K=60*FOXA.K+10*FOXY.K                 RODENTS KILLED BY FOXES
A SRCD.K=MAX(0,RCDA.K-100000)                ADULT RODENTS STRAVING
S RODENTS.K=RODY.K+RODA.K                    TOTAL RODENT POPULATION
NOTE
NOTE      CCNTROL SECTION
NOTE
SPEC DT=C.5,LENGTH=200,PRTPER=4,PLTPER=4
PRINT BFOX,FOXY,DFOXY,MFOX,FOXA,DFOXA,FOXES
PRINT BFCD,RODY,CRCOY,MRCC,RODA,DROCA,RCDENTS
PLOT FOXY=*(0,1000),FOXA=/(0,1000),RODY=&,RCDA=+
NOTE
NOTE      INITIAL VALUES
NOTE
N FOXY=25
N FOXA=600
N RCDY=3000
N RODA=50000
NOTE
NOTE      CONSTANTS
NOTE
C MRCFOX=8                                   FOX MATUR. CONSTANT
C MRCROC=3                                   RODENT MATUR. CONSTANT
NOTE
NOTE      HIGH VALUES OF BIRTH RATE FACTCRS
NOTE
C BRCFOX=4                                   FOX BIRTH RATE FACTOR
C BRCRCC=.8                                  RODENT BIRTH RATE FACTOR
NOTE
RUN HIGH
```

TITLE FCX - RODENT MODEL   9/05/78   HIGH

TIME	BFOX	FOXY	DFOXY	MFOX	FOXA	DFOXA	FOXES	PROD	RODY	DRODY	MROD	RODA	DRODA	RODENTS
E+00	E+00	E+00	E+00	E+00	E+00	E+00	E+00	E+03	E+03	E+00	E+03	E+03	E+03	E+03
.0	150.00	25.00	0.	3.125	600.00	.000	625.0	62.500	3.000	3000.	1.000	50.000	36.250	53.000
4.	77.40	370.65	0.	46.331	309.62	50.808	680.3	19.411	46.510	3890.3	15.503	15.529	15.529	62.039
8.	78.67	471.06	0.	58.882	314.66	56.194	785.7	19.385	46.524	3877.0	15.508	15.508	15.508	62.032
12.	80.98	538.69	0.	67.336	323.93	65.461	862.6	19.385	46.524	3877.0	15.508	15.508	15.508	62.032
16.	82.59	585.36	0.	73.170	330.34	76.302	915.7	19.385	46.524	3877.0	15.508	15.508	15.508	62.032
20.	83.69	617.56	0.	77.195	334.77	79.356	952.3	19.385	46.524	3877.0	15.508	15.508	15.508	62.032
24.	84.46	639.78	0.	79.972	337.82	81.463	977.6	19.385	46.524	3877.0	15.508	15.508	15.508	62.032
28.	84.98	655.11	0.	81.889	339.93	82.918	995.0	19.385	46.524	3877.0	15.508	15.508	15.508	62.032
32.	85.35	665.69	0.	83.211	341.39	83.921	1007.1	19.385	46.524	3877.0	15.508	15.508	15.508	62.032
36.	85.60	672.99	0.	84.124	342.39	84.614	1015.4	19.385	46.524	3877.0	15.508	15.508	15.508	62.032
40.	85.77	678.03	0.	84.754	343.08	85.092	1021.1	19.385	46.524	3877.0	15.508	15.508	15.508	62.032
44.	85.89	681.51	0.	85.188	343.56	85.421	1025.1	19.385	46.524	3877.0	15.508	15.508	15.508	62.032
48.	85.97	683.90	0.	85.488	343.89	85.649	1027.8	19.385	46.524	3877.0	15.508	15.508	15.508	62.032
52.	86.03	685.56	0.	85.695	344.12	85.806	1029.7	19.385	46.524	3877.0	15.508	15.508	15.508	62.032
56.	86.07	686.70	0.	85.838	344.27	85.914	1031.0	19.385	46.524	3877.0	15.508	15.508	15.508	62.032
60.	86.10	687.49	0.	85.936	344.38	85.989	1031.9	19.385	46.524	3877.0	15.508	15.508	15.508	62.032
64.	86.11	688.03	0.	86.004	344.46	86.040	1032.5	19.385	46.524	3877.0	15.508	15.508	15.508	62.032
68.	86.13	688.41	0.	86.051	344.51	86.076	1032.9	19.385	46.524	3877.0	15.508	15.508	15.508	62.032
72.	86.14	688.67	0.	86.083	344.54	86.100	1033.2	19.385	46.524	3877.0	15.508	15.508	15.508	62.032
76.	86.14	688.85	0.	86.106	344.57	86.117	1033.4	19.385	46.524	3877.0	15.508	15.508	15.508	62.032
80.	86.15	688.97	0.	86.121	344.58	86.129	1033.6	19.385	46.524	3877.0	15.508	15.508	15.508	62.032
84.	86.15	689.05	0.	86.132	344.60	86.137	1033.7	19.385	46.524	3877.0	15.508	15.508	15.508	62.032
88.	86.15	689.11	0.	86.139	344.60	86.143	1033.7	19.385	46.524	3877.0	15.508	15.508	15.508	62.032
92.	86.15	689.15	0.	86.144	344.61	86.147	1033.8	19.385	46.524	3877.0	15.508	15.508	15.508	62.032
96.	86.15	689.15	0.	86.148	344.61	86.149	1033.8	19.385	46.524	3877.0	15.508	15.508	15.508	62.032
100.	86.15	689.18	0.	86.150	344.62	86.150	1033.8	19.385	46.524	3877.0	15.508	15.508	15.508	62.032
104.	86.15	689.20	0.	86.152	344.62	86.151	1033.8	19.385	46.524	3877.0	15.508	15.508	15.508	62.032
108.	86.15	689.21	0.	86.153	344.62	86.152	1033.8	19.385	46.524	3877.0	15.508	15.508	15.508	62.032
112.	86.16	689.22	0.	86.154	344.62	86.153	1033.9	19.385	46.524	3877.0	15.508	15.508	15.508	62.032
116.	86.16	689.23	0.	86.154	344.62	86.154	1033.9	19.385	46.524	3877.0	15.508	15.508	15.508	62.032
120.	86.16	689.23	0.	86.155	344.62	86.154	1033.9	19.385	46.524	3877.0	15.508	15.508	15.508	62.032
124.	85.01	686.64	0.	85.830	340.41	85.941	1027.0	19.385	46.524	3877.0	15.508	15.508	15.508	62.032
128.	85.01	684.14	0.	85.518	340.05	85.586	1024.2	19.385	46.524	3877.0	15.508	15.508	15.508	62.032
132.	84.95	682.42	0.	85.302	339.82	85.350	1022.2	19.385	46.524	3877.0	15.508	15.508	15.508	62.032
136.	84.91	681.23	0.	85.153	339.65	85.186	1020.9	19.385	46.524	3877.0	15.508	15.508	15.508	62.032
140.	84.89	680.41	0.	85.051	339.54	85.073	1019.9	19.385	46.524	3877.0	15.508	15.508	15.508	62.032
144.	84.87	679.84	0.	84.980	339.46	84.995	1019.3	19.385	46.524	3877.0	15.508	15.508	15.508	62.032
148.	84.85	679.45	0.	84.931	339.41	84.941	1018.5	19.385	46.524	3877.0	15.508	15.508	15.508	62.032
152.	84.84	679.18	0.	84.897	339.37	84.904	1018.3	19.385	46.524	3877.0	15.508	15.508	15.508	62.032
156.	84.84	678.99	0.	84.874	339.35	84.879	1018.1	19.385	46.524	3877.0	15.508	15.508	15.508	62.032
160.	84.83	678.86	0.	84.858	339.32	84.861	1018.0	19.385	46.524	3877.0	15.508	15.508	15.508	62.032
164.	84.83	678.77	0.	84.847	339.31	84.849	1018.0	19.385	46.524	3877.0	15.508	15.508	15.508	62.032
168.	84.83	678.71	0.	84.839	339.30	84.841	1017.9	19.385	46.524	3877.0	15.508	15.508	15.508	62.032
172.	84.82	678.67	0.	84.834	339.30	84.835	1017.9	19.385	46.524	3877.0	15.508	15.508	15.508	62.032
176.	84.82	678.64	0.	84.830	339.30	84.831	1017.9	19.385	46.524	3877.0	15.508	15.508	15.508	62.032
180.	84.82	678.62	0.	84.828	339.30	84.828	1017.9	19.385	46.524	3877.0	15.508	15.508	15.508	62.032
184.	84.82	678.61	0.	84.826	339.29	84.826	1017.9	19.385	46.524	3877.0	15.508	15.508	15.508	62.032
188.	84.82	678.60	0.	84.825	339.29	84.825	1017.9	19.385	46.524	3877.0	15.508	15.508	15.508	62.032
192.	84.82	678.59	0.	84.824	339.29	84.824	1017.9	19.385	46.524	3877.0	15.508	15.508	15.508	62.032
196.	84.82	678.59	0.	84.823	339.29	84.823	1017.9	19.385	46.524	3877.0	15.508	15.508	15.508	62.032
200.	84.82	678.58	0.	84.823	339.29	84.823	1017.9	19.385	46.524	3877.0	15.508	15.508	15.508	62.032

PAGE 3   TITLE   FOX - RODENT MODEL   9/05/78   HIGH

FOXY=*,FOXA=/,RODY=&,RODA=+

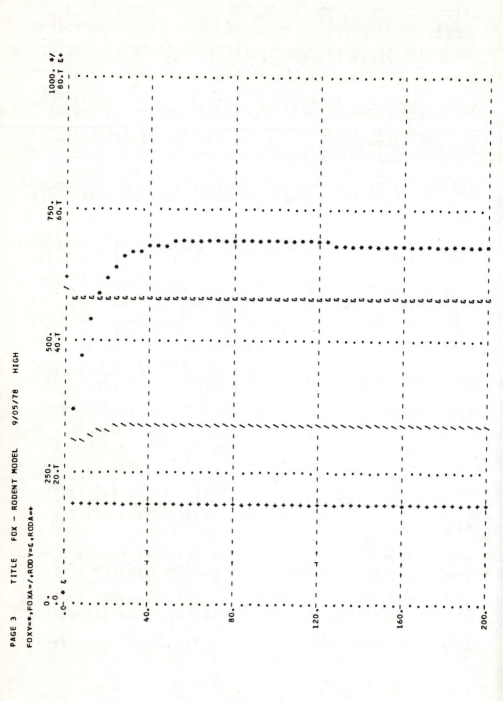

```
GE 4      TITLE   FOX - RODENT MODEL    9/05/78
          NOTE
          NOTE      LOW VALUES OF BIRTH RATE FACTORS
          NOTE
          C BRCFOX=6                           FOX BIRTH RATE FACTOR
          C BRCRCC=.95                         RODENT BIRTH RATE FACTOR
          RUN LOW

          BRCFOX  BRCROD
RESENT    6.000   .9500
GINAL     4.000   .8000
```

8.11 CONCLUSION

The System Dynamics approach to continuous simulation is a methodology aimed at the study of performance characteristics of systems. A graphic System Dynamics model depicts interrelations and dependencies among system components and indicates the flow of entities through the system. System Dynamics models are realized as programs through the use of the Dynamo language. Equations derived from a System Dynamics model are directly implementable in Dynamo.

The set of Dynamo language constructs presented in this chapter contains all the major features of the language. Certain built-in functions have not been discussed, but information on their usage is available in the language manual [8.2]. Additional details on the application of Dynamo and its internal workings can be obtained from the references.

EXERCISES

8.1 The System Dynamics diagram in Figure 8.6 describes a simple inventory control system. Develop a Dynamo program from the diagram using the following parameters:

(SR) SALES-RATE is initially 4 and increases to 6 after 4 time units.

(OR) ORDER-RATE is the rate of sales plus the product of the ordering constant, K, and the difference of the planned inventory, PI, and the retailer's current inventory, CI.

(RDR) RETAILER-DELIVERY-RATE is equal to the value of the retailer's backlog, RB, divided by the Retailer Time Delay, RTD.

(DDR) DISTRIBUTOR-DELIVERY-RATE is equal to the value of the distributor's backlog, DB, divided by the Distributor Time Delay, DTD.

All levels behave as shown in the diagram.
The inventories cannot be negative.
Initial values and constants:

TIME	BFOX	FCXY	DFCXY	MFCX	FOXA	CFOXA	FOXES	BROD	RODY	DRODY	MRCD	RODA	DRODA	RODENTS
E+00	E+00	E+00	E+00	E+00	E+00	E+00	E+00	E+03	E+03	E+03	E+03	E+03	E+03	E+03
.0	100.00	25.00	0.	3.125	600.00	.000	625.00	52.63	33.0	3.01	11.01	50.00	36.25	53.0
4.	40.71	238.66	0.	29.833	244.27	49.743	482.93	12.29	26.6	2.41	8.88	11.67	11.67	44.7
8.	32.89	255.71	0.	32.464	197.36	41.019	457.07	9.87	26.6	2.90	7.16	9.38	9.38	36.0
12.	27.51	252.57	0.	31.571	165.07	39.044	417.64	7.96	21.5	1.94	5.77	7.56	7.56	29.0
16.	22.84	232.05	0.	29.006	137.02	35.433	369.06	6.42	17.3	1.57	4.65	6.10	6.10	23.4
20.	18.84	205.78	0.	25.723	113.06	31.169	318.84	5.17	14.0	1.26	3.75	4.91	4.91	18.9
24.	15.48	178.21	0.	22.277	92.85	26.841	271.06	4.17	11.2	1.02	3.02	3.96	3.96	15.2
28.	12.66	151.78	0.	18.972	75.98	22.767	227.75	3.36	9.1	.82	2.44	3.19	3.19	12.3
32.	10.33	127.69	0.	15.962	61.99	19.096	189.68	2.71	7.3	.66	1.96	2.57	2.57	9.9
36.	8.41	106.45	0.	13.306	50.46	15.883	156.91	2.18	5.9	.53	1.58	2.07	2.07	8.0
40.	6.83	88.13	0.	11.016	41.00	13.126	129.12	1.76	4.7	.43	1.28	1.67	1.67	6.4
44.	5.54	72.56	0.	9.071	33.26	10.793	105.82	1.42	3.8	.35	1.03	1.35	1.35	5.2
48.	4.49	59.50	0.	7.437	26.95	8.840	86.45	1.14	3.1	.28	.83	1.09	1.09	4.2
52.	3.64	48.62	0.	6.078	21.82	7.218	70.44	.92	2.5	.22	.67	.88	.88	3.4
56.	2.94	39.63	0.	4.954	17.65	5.879	57.28	.74	2.0	.18	.54	.71	.71	2.7
60.	2.38	32.23	0.	4.029	14.26	4.779	46.50	.60	1.6	.15	.43	.57	.57	2.2
64.	1.92	26.17	0.	3.271	11.52	3.878	37.70	.48	1.3	.12	.35	.46	.46	1.8
68.	1.55	21.22	0.	2.653	9.31	3.144	30.53	.39	1.1	.09	.28	.37	.37	1.4
72.	1.25	17.19	0.	2.148	7.51	2.545	24.70	.31	.8	.08	.23	.30	.30	1.1
76.	1.01	13.91	0.	1.739	6.06	2.059	19.97	.25	.7	.06	.18	.24	.24	.9
80.	.82	11.25	0.	1.406	4.89	1.665	16.14	.20	.6	.05	.15	.19	.19	.7
84.	.66	9.09	0.	1.136	3.95	1.345	13.04	.16	.5	.04	.12	.16	.16	.6
88.	.53	7.34	0.	.918	3.18	1.087	10.53	.13	.4	.03	.10	.13	.13	.5
92.	.43	5.93	0.	.741	2.57	.877	8.50	.11	.4	.03	.08	.10	.10	.4
96.	.35	4.79	0.	.598	2.07	.708	6.86	.09	.3	.02	.06	.08	.08	.3
100.	.28	3.86	0.	.483	1.67	.571	5.53	.07	.2	.02	.05	.07	.07	.3
104.	.22	3.12	0.	.390	1.35	.461	4.46	.06	.2	.01	.04	.05	.05	.2
108.	.18	2.51	0.	.314	1.09	.372	3.60	.05	.1	.01	.03	.04	.04	.2
112.	.15	2.03	0.	.253	.88	.300	2.90	.04	.1	.01	.03	.03	.03	.1
116.	.12	1.64	0.	.204	.71	.242	2.34	.03	.1	.01	.02	.03	.03	.1
120.	.09	1.32	0.	.165	.57	.189	1.89	.02	.1	.01	.02	.02	.02	.1
124.	.02	.90	0.	.113	.13	.126	1.03	.02	.1	.00	.02	.02	.02	.1
128.	.01	.59	0.	.074	.08	.083	.68	.03	.1	.00	.02	.03	.02	.1
132.	.01	.39	0.	.049	.05	.054	.45	.13	.2	.00	.06	.13	.02	.3
136.	.01	.26	0.	.032	.04	.036	.29	.64	.8	.00	.28	.61	.01	1.4
140.	.00	.17	0.	.021	.02	.024	.19	3.24	4.1	.00	1.38	3.07	.01	7.2
144.	.00	.11	0.	.014	.02	.016	.13	16.33	20.9	.00	6.96	15.51	.00	36.4
148.	.00	.07	0.	.009	.01	.010	.08	82.43	105.4	.00	35.13	78.30	.00	183.7
152.	.00	.05	0.	.006	.01	.007	.06	210.65	369.6	22.06	123.18	200.11	100.11	569.7
156.	.00	.03	0.	.004	.00	.004	.04	299.10	608.1	43.65	202.71	284.14	184.14	892.3
160.	.00	.02	0.	.003	.00	.002	.02	370.37	800.5	61.04	266.82	351.85	251.85	1152.3
164.	.00	.01	0.	.002	.00	.001	.02	427.32	955.5	75.06	318.50	406.43	306.43	1361.9
168.	.00	.01	0.	.001	.00	.001	.01	474.14	1080.5	86.36	360.15	450.43	350.43	1530.9
172.	.00	.01	0.	.001	.00	.001	.01	511.47	1181.2	95.47	393.73	485.89	385.89	1667.1
176.	.00	.00	0.	.000	.00	.000	.00	541.56	1262.4	102.81	420.80	514.48	414.48	1776.9
180.	.00	.00	0.	.000	.00	.000	.00	565.82	1330.9	108.73	442.62	537.53	437.53	1865.4
184.	.00	.00	0.	.000	.00	.000	.00	585.37	1380.6	113.50	460.21	556.10	456.10	1936.7
188.	.00	.00	0.	.000	.00	.000	.00	601.13	1423.2	117.34	474.39	571.08	471.08	1994.2
192.	.00	.00	0.	.000	.00	.000	.00	613.84	1457.5	120.44	485.82	583.15	483.15	2040.6
196.	.00	.00	0.	.000	.00	.000	.00	624.08	1485.1	122.94	495.03	592.88	492.88	2078.0
200.	.00	.00	0.	.000	.00	.000	.00	632.34	1507.4	124.96	502.46	600.72	500.72	2108.1

PAGE 6   TITLE   FCX - RODENT MODEL   9/05/78   LOW

FOXY=*,FOXA=/,ROCY=Ɛ,ROCA=+

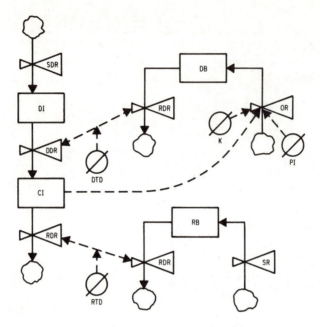

Figure 8.6 System Dynamics Model for Inventory Control

PI = 20, CI = 20, DB (Distributor's Backlog) = 16, RB (Retailer's Backlog) = 12, DI (Distributor's Inventory) = 100, SDR (Supplier Delivery Rate) = 4, RTD (Retailer Time Delay) = 3, DTD (Distributor Time Delay) = 2.

Control information:

Simulation length—50 time units.

Time interval—0.1.

Print and plot all levels.

8.2 Draw a System Dynamics diagram and write a Dynamo program to model the relationships among three hostile populations based upon the information given below.

Population 1 destroys members of both Population 2 and Population 3. Its natural birth and death rates are fixed percentages of the number of members of Population 1. Members of Population 1 are destroyed by members of Population 2.

Population 2 destroys members of Population 1. Its natural birthrate is a constant, and members of Population 2 do not die naturally. Both Population 1 and Population 3 destroy members of Population 2.

Population 3 destroys members of Population 2. Its natural birthrate is dependent upon the number of members in all three populations. The natural death rate is a fixed percentage of the number of members of Population 1. Members of Population 3 are destroyed by members of Population 1.

Parameters:

Population 1 birthrate—10% of Pop. 1.

Population 1 natural death rate—8% of Pop. 1.

Population 1 destruction rate by Population 2—5% of Pop. 2.

Population 2 births—50 per time period.

Population 2 destruction rate by Population 1—7% of Pop. 1.

Population 2 destruction rate by Population 3—4% of Pop. 3.

Population 3 birthrate—6% of Pop. 1, 9% of Pop. 2, 35% of Pop. 3.

Population 3 natural death rate—18% of Pop. 1.

Population 3 destruction rate by Population 1—14% of Pop. 1.

Initial values:

Population 1—500.

Population 2—600.

Population 3—400.

Time of simulation—100 time units.

Print all levels and rates, and plot the populations.

8.3 Draw a System Dynamics diagram and develop a Dynamo program for the simple personnel system described below.

There are two classes of employees: labor and management.

At any given time, the number of managers should be at least 15% of the labor force.

Laborers terminate employment at the rate of TL per month.

Managers terminate employment at the rate of TM per month.

It is desired to maintain the labor force at an optimal level, OLF.

In any given month, only one-half of the desired number of laborers can be hired.

If new managers are required, they are hired from outside or promoted from within with equal probability.

Initial values:

Labor force—1000.

Managers—100.

OLF—2000.

Vary the values of TL and TM as shown below to determine their effect upon the model.

a. TL = 7% of labor force.

TM = 20% of managers.

b. TL = 15% of labor force.

TM = 30% of managers.

c. TL = 1% of labor force.

TM = 96% of managers.

8.4 Figure 8.7 is a high-level (not System Dynamics) diagram of a durable goods flow model. Using the information provided below, construct a System Dynamics diagram and then a Dynamo program for the durable goods model.

General Information

1. Use one day as the time interval.

2. There is a one-day delay for processing orders into demands for goods.

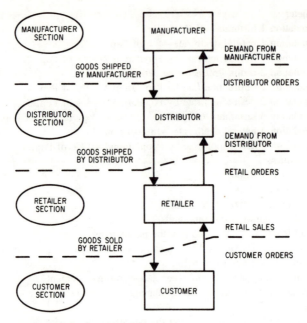

Figure 8.7 High-Level Durable Goods Model

Customer Section
1. Orders start at 6 a day, increase to 9 a day after four days, and drop to 5 a day after 11 days.

Retail Section (use Figure 8.6 as a guide)
1. Retail sales is customer order rate delayed by one day.
2. A backlog of orders is created by retail sales and depleted by retailer delivery rate.
3. Inventory is increased by the distributor delivery rate and decreased by the retail delivery rate. Inventory cannot be negative.
4. The retail ordering rate is the sum of the retail sales and the deviation in the inventory level.
5. The deviation in the inventory level is the product of the ordering constant and the difference between desired and actual inventory level.
6. The retail delivery rate is the backlog delayed by one day.

Distributor Section
1. Same as retail section except that distributor ordering is retail demand delayed by one day.

Manufacturer Section
Manufacturer requires two days to produce the goods upon recognizing a demand.

Initialization
1. Set ordering constant to 0.5.
2. Set all levels to 40.
3. Set all rates to 8.

4. The desired inventory is 50 for the first 10 days and increases by 2 each day thereafter.

Length of simulation—20 days.

Print all levels, and plot information for retail, distributor, and manufacturer sections on separate graphs.

8.5 Develop a Systems Dynamics diagram and then construct a Dynamo program to model the relationship between salesperson hiring and company business from the following information.

The number of salespeople changes by the salesperson hiring rate (which may be negative).

The salesperson hiring rate is the difference between the desired and present sales force divided by a sales adjustment constant.

The desired sales force level is the ratio of the current budget to salesman salary.

The budget is the product of the unit price times the delivery rate.

The delivery rate is the backlog divided by a two day delay factor.

The backlog level is a function of the ordering rate and the delivery rate.

The ordering rate is the product of the number of sales people and the efficiency coefficient.

Efficiency coefficient is 400 initially and declines to 100 after 3 years.

Initial values:

Salespeople = 10, Unit price = 12, Salesperson salary = 2000, Sales adjustment constant = 20, Backlog = 8000.

Length of simulation—5 years.

a. Plot orders booked, efficiency constant, backlog, and number of salespeople.

b. Rerun simulation with salesperson salaries of 1800 and 2200.

REFERENCES

[8.1] Forrester, J. W., *Industrial Dynamics*. Cambridge, Mass.: MIT Press, 1961.

[8.2] Pugh, A., III, *DYNAMO II User's Manual*. Cambridge, Mass.: MIT Press, 1973.

[8.3] Aron, J. D., *The Program Development Process*. Reading, Mass.: Addison-Wesley, 1974.

[8.4] McGowan, C. L. and Kelly, J. R., *Top-Down Structured Programming*. New York: Petrocelli-Charter, 1975.

[8.5] Van Tassel, D., *Program Style, Design, Efficiency, Debugging, and Testing*. Englewood Cliffs, N.J.: Prentice-Hall, 1974.

[8.6] Warnier, J. D., *Logical Construction of Programs*. New York: Van Nostrand Reinhold, 1974.

9 The Value of Simulation

9.1 INTRODUCTION

The previous chapters have concentrated upon the planning, implementation, and analysis of simulation studies. In this chapter, we assume the ability to perform a simulation study and attempt to analyze the inherent value of such studies in various disciplines. In certain subject areas, there exist intrinsic limitations on the closeness of the simulation model to the actual system. To a large extent, the precision of a simulation model depends upon the precision of the information describing the system being modeled. Many ideas in this chapter are derived from a paper presented by Walter Karplus in 1976 [9.1].

9.2 DEDUCTIVE AND INDUCTIVE INFORMATION

Information concerning a system can be classified as either deductive or inductive depending upon the exactness with which it describes the parameters of the system. Deductive information is factual knowledge or insight about the system and its internal operation. For example, those parameters that are represented by mathematical formulas or physical laws are deductive information. Included on the inductive side are parameters that are measured experimentally, estimated statistically, or, in the worst case, arrived at by intuition.

A system whose structure and behavior are represented wholly by deductive information has only one model that correctly describes its behavior. If the task of developing a model for a purely deductive system were assigned to several analysts, it is likely that the resultant models would differ in internal form. However, the models would produce the same results under all inputs if constructed correctly. For example, a model of an electronic circuit can be constructed completely from deductive knowledge since a precise set of equations that describes the circuit can be formed.

Inductive information is derived from experimental observations of system behavior. In the purely inductive case, sets of input and output parameters are

320

formed by observation, and the internal structure is hypothesized from the parameter sets. Many assumptions may be necessary and limitations imposed in order to derive a functional inductive model. The process of deriving a model based upon inductive information can lead to the formation of a variety of different models. Although statistical methods can be applied to ensure that the behavior of the model is close to the experimental observations, the modeler cannot claim, as in the deductive case, that the simulation model is a precise representation of the system.

The banking models of Chapters 3 and 4 are examples of inductive simulation models. Regardless of the confidence level attained in fitting the input and output parameters to experimental data, we could never claim that one of the simulation models exactly describes the business of a bank. Although the models in this text are tutorial in nature and not intended for real-world application, the information regarding the performance of the duties of a bank teller is intrinsically inductive and thus precludes the creation of an exact model of teller activity. A system with as much stochastic activity as the behavior of the bank teller cannot be described by a unique model. No practical amount of effort or sophistication in terms of data collection or model synthesis and verification can produce a bank teller model, which must be based upon inductive information, that is as precise a descriptor of the actual system as is a completely deductive model such as that of an electronic circuit. By reflecting upon the complexity of the behavior of bank tellers and customers as opposed to the complexity of an electronic circuit, the infeasibility of a precise banking model becomes apparent.

9.3 DEGREES OF DEDUCTIVITY

The nature of the system being modeled imposes a limit upon the degree of deductivity of its information and thus on the precision of the model. The designer of the simulation experiment should recognize the limitations imposed by the lack of deductivity in the interpretation of the results. Decisions made based upon inductive models should be tempered by other factors.

Karplus [9.1] has classified many disciplines in which the use of simulation models is prevalent according to the amount of inherent deductivity. The classification technique is based upon the engineering view of a system model as a collection of interconnected functional submodules, or "boxes." It is common phraseology to describe a submodule whose input and output are observable but whose internal structure is unknown as a "black box." The presence of a black box in a system model implies that only inductive information is available on the particular submodule. Conversely, a submodule that can be described completely by deductive information can be represented by a "white box," which permits a view of the internal structure of the submodule.

A discipline can be characterized by the shade of the boxes that comprise typical models. Figure 9.1 [9.1] presents a spectrum of model deductivity rang-

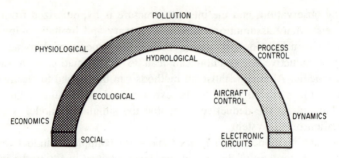

Figure 9.1 Spectrum of Model Deductivity

ing from white through various shades of gray to black. A correspondence can be derived between the whiteness (or deductivity) of the simulation models and the "hardness" of the science.

Figure 9.1 provides a guide to the degree of deductivity, and hence precision, possible in various disciplines. The applicability of basic laws of nature decreases with the darkness associated with the discipline in Figure 9.1. Electronic circuitry was mentioned earlier as an example of a system totally describable by mathematical equations, and thus appears on the white end of the spectrum. The system control models are slightly higher on the grayness scale since they are based upon mechanical laws with some randomness present due to external conditions. In the life sciences, the basic equations governing the behavior of systems involve more randomness than in the engineering areas. Environmental systems reside on the dark side of the spectrum since although the basic laws of nature are understood, measurements are not as precise as in the other disciplines and the system environment is beyond control. At the extreme dark, or inductive, end of the modeling spectrum are the economic, social, and political sciences, in which firm laws for the behavior of systems do not exist because of the inherent randomness of the systems.

Observation of Figure 9.1 indicates that the degree of deductivity of simulation models is inversely proportional to the impact of human behavior in the system under study. Knowledge on human systems is highly inductive and imprecise when compared to the knowledge of physical systems.

9.4 APPLICATION OF SIMULATION MODELS

As described in the previous section, there is a vast range of precision possible in simulation models for different disciplines. The precision possible within a given science dictates the application of simulation models in that area. In the hard sciences a simulation model can serve as a valid design tool or performance predictor. However, in the socioeconomic areas the predominance of inductive knowledge in the model limits the application of simulation studies to obtaining

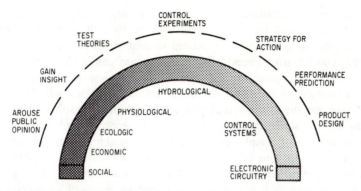

Figure 9.2 Spectrum of Model Application

insight into the system and influencing public opinion. Figure 9.2 [9.1] relates function of the model to the amount of deductive knowledge available on the system.

Figure 9.2 indicates that the degree of deductivity in a model determines the confidence with which its results can be accepted. The inherent randomness of certain systems prevents the establishment of a precise model and consequently should reduce the degree of acceptance of the results by the user. A properly validated simulation model can be accepted as an accurate representation of a system in engineering or the hard sciences. Such models are useful in the design of products and the prediction of their behavior. However, in the softer sciences, system models cannot be accepted without some degree of caution.

9.5 CONCLUSION

In this chapter the disciplines in which simulation models are applied frequently are classified according to the maximum amount of precision possible in the models. The degree of precision is related roughly to the "hardness" of the science. Highly accurate simulation models can be constructed in engineering and the physical sciences. However, models of social or economic systems are inherently less precise because of the inherent randomness of human behavior.

This classification scheme for model precision can serve as a guide for both the developer of a model and the interpreter of the simulation results in understanding the inherent limitations of a model. When interpreting simulation results, one must keep in mind that in the large majority of situations the model cannot be a completely faithful representation of the real system. This is especially true when the model projects the behavior of a new system or the performance of an existing system in a future environment. In those situations the prejudices of the experiment designer can influence very strongly the conclusion.

The above discussion is not intended to suggest that simulation is an unreliable design and decision-making tool. In fact, the opposite is true. A carefully planned and properly validated simulation study provides invaluable knowledge on the structure and function of a system. Simulation models are used successfully in the engineering and scientific disciplines to develop products such as aircraft and automobiles, to re-create the behavior of planes in flight or ships at sea for training purposes, to predict the effect of failures in space and computer systems and determine the optimal method of correcting such failures, and to study the structure of complex biological and chemical processes. Unfortunately, the great success of simulation in the hard sciences cannot be directly carried over into the behavioral, economic, and social sciences in view of the influence of the truly unpredictable human actions. Therefore, results of a simulation study involving human behavior must be treated cautiously. In all situations, the assumptions of a simulation study must be understood and a satisfactory validation technique performed before accepting the results of the simulation.

EXERCISES

9.1 Using the spectrum given in Figure 9.2, classify the system models listed below according to their degree deductivity or inductivity.
  a. The rocket model of Chapter 7.
  b. The prey-predator model of Chapter 8.
  c. The doctor's office model of Exercise 3.3.
  d. Xaviera's establishment (Exercise 3.5).
  e. The elevator model of Exercise 3.6.
  f. The parking lot model of Exercise 3.7.
  g. The computer system model of Exercise 3.8.
  h. The student registration model of Exercise 4.1.
  i. The supermarket checkout model of Exercise 4.3.
  j. The manufacturing process of Exercise 4.5.
  k. The satellite model of Exercise 7.1.
  l. The car race of Exercise 7.2.
  m. The projectile model of Exercise 7.4.
  n. The inventory control model of Exercise 8.1.
  o. The personnel model of Exercise 8.3.
  p. The sales model of Exercise 8.5.
9.2 Explain the circumstances under which you would invest $1,000,000 based upon information obtained by a simulation study.

REFERENCE

[9.1] Karplus, W. J., "The Spectrum of Mathematical Modeling and Systems Simulation" in *Simulation of Systems* (L. Dekker, ed.). Amsterdam: North-Holland, August 1976, pp. 5–13.

Index

Abstraction, 1
Activities, 1
  endogenous, 2
  exogenous, 2
Activity Scaning Approach, 20
Analog computers, 275
Analysis, 9
Antithetic sampling, 263
Attributes, 1

Bayes Theorem, 214
Black box, 321

Chao, Lincoln, 217
Chi-Square Statistic, 233
  table, 235
Chi-Square Test, 233, 254
  degrees of freedom, 234, 254
  intervals, 255, 256
  significance level, 234
Continuous simulation, 274
Correlation, 216
  coefficient, 220
Covariance, 219
CSMP, 274
  built-in functions, 278
  comments, 286
  CONSTANT, 283
  continuation, 286
  control statements, 277
    execution control, 286
    output control, 285
    termination control, 284
  data statements, 277, 282

DELT, 284
DYNAMIC, 280, 281
END, 281, 286
ENDJOB, 286
FINISH, 284
FINTIM, 284
INITIAL, 280, 281
INTGRL, 277, 278
LIMIT, 278, 279
organization, 276
OUTDEL, 284
PARAMETER, 283
PRDEL, 284
PRINT, 285
PRTPLT, 285
STEP, 278, 279
STOP, 286
structural statements, 277, 280
  ordering, 281
TERMINAL, 280, 281
TIMER, 284

Data collection, 260
Data modeling, 4
Deductive information, 320
  degrees of, 321
  spectrum of, 322
Design aid, 8
Differential equations, 274
Discrete simulation, 18
DYNAMO, 298, 303
  DT, 308
  equations, 303
    auxiliary, 303, 304

DYNAMO (*continued*)
   constant, 303
     initial, 303
     level, 303
     rate, 303
     supplementary, 303, 305
   execution control statements, 308
   LENGTH, 308
   MAX, 304
   MIN, 304
   NOTE, 308
   output control statements, 307
   PLOT, 308
   PLTPER, 308
   PRINT, 307
   PRTPER, 308
   representation of time, 302
   RUN, 308
   SPEC, 308
   STEP, 304
   suffix conventions, 303
   TITLE, 309

Entities, 1
   in GPSS, 35
Event, 11
Event distributions, 14
   continuous, 17, 230
   discrete, 16, 227
Event scheduling, 17
   dynamic, 18
   prescheduling, 17
Event Scheduling Approach, 19, 147
Experimental design, 9
Experimental parameters, 250
Exponential distribution, 237, 252, 255, 256

Feedback, 300
Final conditions, 261, 262
Fishman, George, 221, 237
Forrester, Jay, 298, 302

Goodness of fit, 254
GPSS, 35
   ADVANCE, 38
   assembly listing, 39
   ASSIGN, 88
   CLEAR, 42
   control statements, 42
   cross-reference list, 39
   debugging, 123

decisions, 70
DEPART, 52
END, 42
ENTER, 46
facilities, 38
   preemption, 111
FUNCTION, 60
GATE, 75
GENERATE, 36
identifiers, 36
indirect addressing, 96
interpretation of output, 39
JOB, 42
LEAVE, 46
LOGIC, 71
LOOP, 101
MARK, 122
parameters, 84
PREEMPT, 116
PRINT, 130, 135
PRIORITY, 80
QUEUE, 52
queues, 52
random numbers, 59
RELEASE, 38
representation of time, 37
RESET, 43
RMULT, 59
SAVEVALUE, 109
SEIZE, 38
SIMULATE, 42
standard numerical attributes, 53
START, 42
STORAGE, 44
storages, 43
   management, 47, 92
TABLE, 121
TABULATE, 122
TERMINATE, 37
TEST, 76
TRACE, 130
TRANSFER, 70
UNTRACE, 130
VARIABLE, 56

Hybrid computers, 276

Initial conditions, 261, 262
Inductive information, 321

Karplus, Walter, 7, 320, 321
Knuth, Donald, 24

Linear interpolation, 17, 232

Maximum likelihood estimation, 251
Mean, 211
Modeling, 9
Modularity, 6, 260

Normal distribution, 243
Numerical errors, 261

Output analysis, 161

Parameter estimation, 251
    improper, 261
Performance evaluation, 7
Poisson distribution, 237
Probability functions, 207
    conditional, 212
    cumulative, 209
    density function, 209
        mean, 211
    discrete, 211
    distribution function, 210
    joint, 213
Process Interaction Approach, 18, 35
Programming, 9
    errors, 260
Project planning, 8

Queuing disciplines, 22
Queuing models, 20
    multiqueue, multiserver, 24
    single-server, 21
Queuing statistics, 28
    bias in, 31

Random numbers, 224
    generation of, 226, 257
    pseudo, 224
    seeds, 224, 257
Relevance, 4
Representation of time, 11
    next event increment, 14
    uniform increment, 12
Roth, Paul, 7

Sample size, 262
Scheduling, 9
SIMSCRIPT, 146
    ACCUMULATE, 165
    ALWAYS, 158
    CALL, 197

conditional operators, 157
CREATE, 153
CREATE EVERY, 166
DEFINE,
    constant, 150
    function, 198
    random variable, 187
    set, 154
    variable, 150
DESTROY, 153
DO, 168
ELSE, 158
EVENT NOTICES, 147
events, 147
EVERY, 148, 153, 154
EXCEPT WHEN, 177
EXTERNAL EVENTS, 189
FILE, 155
FIND, 177
FOR, 168
GIVEN, 197
GO TO, 156
HERE, 156
identifiers, 151
IF, 156
IF NONE, 177
input/output, 159
JUMP, 156
LET, 151
LIST, 160
LOOP, 168
main route, 146
MAY BELONG TO, 154
OWNS, 154
PERMANENT ENTITIES, 166
preamble, 146
PRINT, 160
PRIORITY ORDER, 149
random distribution functions, 150
RANDOM LINEAR VARIABLE, 181
RANDOM STEP VARIABLE, 181
READ, 159, 187
REMOVE, 155
representation of time, 150
RETURN, 148, 197
ROUTINE, 197, 198
SCHEDULE, 148
sets, 153
subprogramms, 193
TALLY, 164
TEMPORARY ENTITIES, 152
TIME. V, 150

THE SYSTEM OWNS, 154
UNLESS, 177
WHEN, 177
WITH, 177
YIELDING, 197
Simulation experiment, 250
Simulation studies, 1, 7
  errors in, 257
  steps of, 8
Simultaneous equations, 274
Solomon, Susan, 143, 202
Standard deviation, 218
Statement of purpose, 9
Statistical independence, 214
  and correlation, 222
Stochastic variables, 207, 257
Structural investigation, 8
Structural modeling, 3
System, 1
  closed, 2
  continuous, 3, 274
  deterministic, 2
  discrete, 3, 11
  open, 2
  stochastic, 2
System diagramming, 4
System Dynamics, 298
  constants, 299
  diagrams, 299
  levels, 298
  rates, 298
  sinks, 298
  sources, 298
System model synthesis, 3

System modeling, 3
  invalid models, 260
  principles, 4
System models
  application of, 322
  spectrum of, 323
System parameters, 250, 257
  poor selection of, 260
System simulation, 6
System state, 1
  steady, 1
  transient, 1

t-ratio, 270
t-statistic, 268
t-test, 268
  confidence intervals, 268
  difference between means, 270
  standard error of difference, 270
  table, 269

Uncorrelated variables, 220
Understandability, 4
Uniform distribution, 212, 216

Validation, 9. 261, 267
Value of simulation, 320
Variance, 216
  reduction, 263
  of sample, 217
Verification, 6

White box, 321